RESULTS OF SPIRITUAL RESEARCH

RESULTS OF SPIRITUAL RESEARCH

Fourteen public lectures given in the Architektenhaus, Berlin, between 31 October 1912 and 10 April 1913

TRANSLATED AND INTRODUCED BY SIMON BLAXLAND-DE LANGE

RUDOLF STEINER

RUDOLF STEINER PRESS

CW 62

Rudolf Steiner Press
Hillside House, The Square
Forest Row, RH18 5ES

www.rudolfsteinerpress.com

Published by Rudolf Steiner Press 2022

Originally published in German under the title *Ergebnisse der Geistesforschung* (volume 62 in the *Rudolf Steiner Gesamtausgabe* or Collected Works) by Rudolf Steiner Verlag, Dornach. Based on shorthand notes that were not reviewed or revised by the speaker. This authorized translation is based on the second German edition (1988), edited by Ernst Weidmann and Johann Waeger

Published by permission of the Rudolf Steiner Nachlassverwaltung, Dornach

A catalogue record for this book is available from the British Library

ISBN 978 1 85584 599 2

Cover by Morgan Creative
Typeset by Symbiosys Technologies, Vishakapatnam, India
Printed and bound by 4Edge Ltd., Essex

CONTENTS

LECTURE 11

BERLIN, 13 FEBRUARY 1913

Leonardo's Spiritual Greatness at the Turning-Point leading to the Modern Age

The *Last Supper* in Milan. Leonardo's path of life. His drawing talent. His studies of facial characteristics for the most diverse soul-experiences.. Leonardo at the court of Ludovico il Moro in Milan. His technical inventions and plans. The equestrian statue of Francesco Sforza. Leonardo's many years of struggle to complete the *Last Supper*. His *Treatise on Painting*. The particular relationships of light and shade in the countenance of Christ and of Judas in the *Last Supper*. The mystery of the personality of Leonardo. The twofold significance of the development of natural science. The art of the Renaissance and the art of Greece. The statue of Marcus Aurelius in Rome. The loss of the feeling of connectedness with the spirit in the age of Leonardo. Leonardo as a tragic figure at the turning-point to a new age. His soul in supersensible existence.

LECTURE 12

BERLIN, 6 MARCH 1913

Errors of Spiritual Research

Healthy organs of perception and a full development and clarity of consciousness as a precondition for right observation. A sound faculty of judgement and a moral mood of the soul as a point of departure for spiritual-scientific schooling. The visions of the spirit-researcher are initially only the illusory mental pictures of his own being. Hence the spirit-researcher must also have the capacity to extinguish the spiritual phenomena that he is able to evoke. This is only possible by mastering the obstinacy of self-love. The spirit-pupil should not be frightened of fear. The 'Guardian of the Threshold'. The fear of the spiritual world as the reason for materialism, which can lead to phenomenalism and spiritism. In the spiritual world error arises through what is dead being taken as something living. Maurice Maeterlinck's book *Death* is phenomenalism and spectre-research rather than spiritual research. The other extreme of the possibilities for error is ecstasy. The so-called mystical 'God within' is often nothing other than an ego branded with God's name. Truthfulness as the outward sign of the true spirit-researcher. The communications of the spirit-researcher can also be understood by a person's faculty of thinking. The path of spiritual research between phenomenalism and ecstasy.

Publisher's Note

The lectures in this volume belong to the part of Rudolf Steiner's work as a lecturer where he was addressing the general public. 'Berlin was the starting-point for this public lecturing activity. What in other towns and cities was considered in individual lectures could here be expressed in a series of inter-connecting lectures whose themes were entwined with one another. Because of this they acquired the character of a carefully grounded methodical introduction to spiritual science and could reckon with a regularly returning audience to whom what mattered was to enter ever more deeply into the areas of knowledge that were newly opening up to them, whereas to those approaching for the first time the foundations for understanding what was being presented were reiterated in ever renewed ways.' (Marie Steiner)

Introduction

THE lectures presented here were given in the broader context of an annual series of public lecture-cycles that Rudolf Steiner gave during every winter term in the Arkitektenhaus (the House of the Architects) in Berlin between 1903 and 1918. These are published in the Collected Works as a distinct and continuous series (GA 52–67). As indicated in the (German) Publisher's Note, the endeavour to share the fruits of his spiritual-scientific research with the general public therefore remained of consistent importance for Rudolf Steiner over these years. However, with the exception of two of these cycles, these public lectures have in the majority of cases not been translated; and those that have mostly exist in the form of single lectures, thus making it difficult to discern the context within which they were given.

The period during which the lectures in the present volume were given is notable for the fact that it coincided with a series of events from October 1912 onwards leading to the separation of the 'German Section' from the Theosophical Society and the founding of an independent Anthroposophical Society, initially informally on 28 December 1912 in Berlin and, more formally, at the foundation meeting in the same city on 2–3 February 1913. Significantly, Rudolf Steiner gave a remarkable lecture in the course of this latter event entitled 'The Being Anthroposophia' (3 February 1913), indicating that 'what we receive through anthroposophy is our *very own being.* This once floated towards us in the form of a celestial goddess with whom we were able to enter into relationship. This divine being lived on as Sophia and Philosophia and now we can once again bring her out of ourselves and place her before us as the fruit of true anthroposophical self-knowledge.'

Rudolf Steiner's underlying intention throughout this cycle of lectures is to work consistently at the frontier between natural science and spiritual science. The tone throughout is one of dialogue, rational and open-minded discussion and conversation. Where, he begins, might a specialist in natural science want to take issue with certain things asserted by spiritual science? And where, on the other hand, are there issues which natural science is unable to illuminate (such as the mysteries of sleep and death) and which require the wider perspective that spiritual science is able to bring to bear? How, in other words, can there be a real, genuine collaboration between a natural science that is, at least to a certain extent, free from dogmatism and a spiritual science that does not fall prey to dilettantism or narrow-minded prejudice? This open-minded debate is throughout illustrated by examining passages from the work of scientists, philosophers and historians, some of these being contemporary writers, while others are chosen to exemplify a frequently expressed theme, namely, that just as there was a need at the time of the Scientific Revolution to have the imaginative boldness to break through the spatial barrier of the seemingly fixed blue firmament, so is there now an urgent need to achieve something similar with respect to the temporal 'barriers' of birth and death. These themes are deepened and extended in lectures devoted to carefully chosen historical figures, Jacob Boehme, the painters Raphael and Leonardo da Vinci, and the art and literary historian Herman Grimm; and a lecture on 'Fairy-Tale Literature in the Light of Spiritual Research' develops some indications sprinkled through these lectures about historical figures into a quest of illumination about humanity's deeper past. Nor was Rudolf Steiner's public audience denied lectures on the path leading to higher knowledge itself, with one lecture being devoted to 'The Paths of Supersensible Knowledge', while a pair of lectures later on in the cycle focussed on 'Errors of Spiritual Research' and 'Morality in the Light of Spiritual Research', thus touching upon much of the substance contained in the book *Knowledge of the Higher Worlds*.

The concluding, fourteenth lecture begins with a summary of the intention of these lectures:

> This winter's lecture cycle has sought to characterize from a variety of points of view the spiritual stream that has as its aim that of leading the human soul through a process of self-exploration to that knowledge which it must yearn for in connection with the most important riddles of life and existence. The attempt has been made to show that a study of present or future-oriented spiritual and intellectual streams makes it clearly apparent that the spiritual science referred to is the right instrument to guide the human soul in the context of the present and the immediate future time. For this reason it has been a kind of undertone of these winter lectures consistently to emphasize the achievements and results of the intellectual life and aspirations of the nineteenth century; for if one considers the way that the intellectual life and aspirations of the nineteenth century have taken hold of humanity and have brought about the great triumph of material existence, it can truly be said that it would necessarily seem to be a hopeless undertaking if this spiritual science under discussion here were to reject or set itself in opposition to the justified requirements of natural science or, indeed, the intellectual and spiritual achievements of the nineteenth century.

And towards the end of this same lecture, we find these sentiments confirmed in the following words:

> If one believes that there must necessarily be a break between what natural science is and has made possible and spiritual science, one would be mistaken about this spiritual science. If, however, one sees how natural science had to become entirely what it has indeed become so that the human soul finds the path to the spiritual in the new way that it must find it, one will recognize it as that which must necessarily be placed within evolution as something that has within it the seeds for that period that will follow ours in the same way that our present period follows on from the previous one. Then the apparent conflicts between the natural-scientific and the spiritual-scientific world-pictures will be reconciled.

Finally, there is a further theme that Rudolf Steiner introduces into these lectures. In one of the most beautiful, heartfelt lectures that he ever gave, that on Jacob Boehme on 9 January 1913, he brought an understanding, as mediated by this extraordinary individual who lived in the early part of the modern era, of the mystery of evil which can be grasped by anyone whatever his particular preconceptions may be.

Simon Blaxland-de Lange
February 2022

Lecture 1

BERLIN, 31 OCTOBER 1912

HOW IS SPIRITUAL SCIENCE REFUTED?

As in previous winters, it has been made possible for me to give a number of lectures about spiritual science here at this place in the course of the winter season. It will be apparent from the programme that the initial purpose of these lectures is to encompass what spiritual science has to say from its standpoint about the question of life; that the transition will then be made to shedding light on some important cultural phenomena and issues and on outstanding figures such as Raphael and Leonardo da Vinci; and that finally something will be said regarding the relationship of spiritual science to a number of matters concerning the intellectual life of our present times. These lectures will be inaugurated today in a quite distinctive way. The intention is to present at the outset not what can be said by way of consolidating and strengthening this spiritual research but, on the contrary, what possible objections of a more significant nature can be brought to bear against it.

It lies in the nature of things that, because of circumstances peculiar to our present times and because of several other factors, this spiritual research attracts much hostility. But nothing would be more inappropriate to this spiritual research than if it were to succumb to fanaticism and, so to speak, only wanted to see what can be adduced on its behalf from the standpoint of its representatives. Fanaticism must—and we shall see the reasons why this is said—lie far removed from this spiritual research. Therefore it must, more than is perhaps necessary in any other case, give thought to understanding the objections of its opponents and, indeed, it must tolerate them up to a certain point, and it must come to understand that a whole number of thoroughly worthy present-day seekers after truth are not able to ally themselves with it. It has been my custom—those who have attended previous lectures will know this, and this custom will be continued in subsequent ones—at the same time to consider possible objections to any statements that I may make. I shall today anticipate some of the more significant and weighty objections; for objections against what can be said from the standpoint of spiritual research indeed emerge not merely from opponents, but in any conscientiously undertaken spiritual research a person who has engaged in such an endeavour himself feels that at every step he is presented with these possible objections. Moreover, because the truths of spiritual research must be attained and struggled for within the soul, there is a sense in which one has also developed a counterweight to such objections as may have occurred to one; and there are distinct advantages in being clear in advance about anything that may be open to objection.

I do not consider it to be my task to enter here into those objections or alleged criticisms that can, so to speak, be found on the street or are the product of sheer fantasy but, rather, to take account of the objections which anyone in our time who is sincerely seeking truth can himself make out of the spiritual foundations of our present age and even to a certain extent must make. I shall also not concern myself with much that is often referred to today as spiritual research or theosophy; for it has to be admitted from the outset that what appears today as 'theosophy' is not really something to celebrate. However, what has been and will be presented here shall indeed be taken into account in the objections that I shall consider today. But if we are wanting to involve ourselves in such objections, much of what has been said in the course of the previous cycles and will come to expression in the coming lectures will need to be drawn upon at least in outline. We shall therefore briefly call to mind what is meant here by spiritual research as regards its content and its sources.

To begin with, spiritual science can in general be characterized by saying that it is based upon the standpoint that it must reach beyond everything that a person may perceive through his senses, and is able to discover by means of a science that is founded primarily upon the senses and on a reasoning power that draws its conclusions from the senses, to the spiritual causes of what can be apprehended by the senses and investigated by the intellect, so that everywhere behind these sense-perceptible phenomena it does not only acknowledge but endeavours to prove the existence of a spiritual world in which there reside the causes of everything that the senses can perceive and the intellect can study.

This spiritual science can be distinguished from many other spiritual disciplines of both past and present through the fact that it does not merely seek to assert in a general, hypothetical way that there is a spiritual world beyond the senses and the ordinary faculties of understanding but proceeds on the basis that man is capable of developing his cognitive powers and soul-forces in such a way that they can gain insight into a spiritual world, which they could not achieve without this development. Hence not only the possibility of a spiritual world but the knowledgeability of such a world is the distinctive quality of this spiritual research or anthroposophy, if that is what we wish to call it. That with the particular nature of the soul-forces and cognitive powers that people ordinarily possess—if we may put it thus—it would not be possible to penetrate into the spiritual world is something that can be acknowledged from the start. But to claim that these cognitive powers cannot be developed in such a way that once they had been raised to this higher standpoint they would be just as capable of perceiving the spiritual world as eyes are in perceiving the world of the senses, is disputed by spiritual science. With this we have already arrived at the sources of this spiritual research.

These sources become available to the soul when through inner work, through inner development—and I have often spoken here about the methods of this inner development—it raises itself to a higher vantage-point as regards its perception. Then in apposition to the sense-world that surrounds us, spiritual science makes manifest another, spiritual world from whence the true causes of all sensory phenomena originate.

By investigating the spiritual world we come to regard man as a far more complicated being than he is for ordinary sensory or narrowly intellectual perception. We come to see man as a four-membered being. That which one calls the physical body is regarded by spiritual research only as part of the whole of man's being. The ordinary life of the senses can observe this physical body, the reasoning faculties can understand it. This sensory body is the object of ordinary science. For a large part of our modern experience, the physical body is the totality of man's being. For spiritual-scientific research it is only one part out of four members of this human nature.

In addition to this physical body, spiritual research distinguishes the so-called etheric body or life-body, which is incorporated in the physical body. But it does not speak of this etheric body or life-body as though it were accessible only to the intellect but in such a way that the developed soul-forces are capable of beholding it, just as a developed eye can perceive the colours blue or red, whereas a colour-blind eye is unable to perceive these colours. And it then speaks of the necessary conclusion that occurs, namely that the physical body naturally disintegrates with death through the forces that are specific to it, because the forces that belong to the physical body bring about its decomposition, its disintegration and are only held together because during the time of life between birth and death the etheric body or life-body, which fights continuously against the disintegration of the physical body, is incorporated in it. Only when the separation from the etheric body occurs with the moment of death does the physical body proceed in accordance with its own forces, which then—because they work in their particular fashion—bring about its decomposition. Man has his physical body in common with the whole mineral, lifeless world. He has his etheric body in association with all living things, with the whole of the plant world.

However, spiritual science does not stop there. It recognizes a third member of human nature which is as independent as the physical body. We do not need to stumble over particular terms; they will be explained and have already been partially explained. It is the astral body that is distinguished as the third member. This is the real bearer of passions, desires, impulses, emotions, hence of everything that we call our soul-body, which unfolds its activity in our inner being. And in spiritual research we again distinguish from this astral body the actual bearer of the ego. Whereas man has the astral body in common with everything that can develop emotions and passions and an inner life of ideas, as exists for example in the animal world, he has the fourth member of his being—the bearer of the ego as the crown of his personal nature—in his own right. For spiritual research man's being consists initially of the physical body, the etheric body, the astral body and the bearer of the ego.

It further transpires for anyone who is able to gain insight into the spiritual world that a large part of the life's circumstances to which we are subjected is distinguished from ordinary life, namely the time that we spend asleep. Sleep is distinguished for the spirit-researcher from waking life in that when someone is asleep the bearer of his ego and his astral body are separated from his etheric body and physical body. The two latter members remain in bed as a plant-like form, while the bearer of the ego together with the astral body, its emotions, impulses, capacities for forming ideas and so forth withdraw from the physical and etheric bodies during sleep and then develop a life of their own in a self-subsisting spiritual world. For a normal person today, however, ordinary life is impossible when the ego and astral body are thus in a withdrawn state during sleep, because they have no organs with which to perceive their surroundings, they do not have eyes and ears as does the physical body. Thus it is impossible that the astral body and ego perceive the world in which they find themselves.

The higher development of the soul consists precisely in that the astral body and ego become capable of developing organs in order to perceive their environment, and that a state can thereby arise for the spirit-researcher in which he perceives the spiritual world. Thus in addition to the waking state and the state of sleep he also has a waking state of sleep—if we may refer to it in this way—which is that condition whereby the spirit-researcher can perceive the spiritual world to which man owes his true origin. Thus spiritual science tries to explain from spiritual facts the transition that a person makes every twenty-four hours between waking and sleeping.

A further aspect for spiritual science is that it approaches the great riddle of death and life, that is in other words the question that so stirs the human heart: the question of man's immortality. Spiritual science comes to the realization that man's true spiritual being is not merely a result of his physical organization but an independent entity and essence belonging to a spiritual world which builds up the physical body, which exists before birth, indeed before conception, and from the first moment that a human individual enters into existence as a germinal cell works as an up-building force upon his organism. This is, in other words, the soul-spiritual essence, the truly active and up-building force that brings to a person an organizing principle for his entire life, that bears only the fruits of his life's experiences through the gate of death and makes with death the transition to a spiritual world in order then to have further experiences, and which then organizes a new physical body for a further life in order to undergo a new life and to repeat the cycle.

Spiritual science speaks, in other words, of repeated earth-lives, it speaks of repeated earthly lives in such a way that we look back from our present embodiment within sensory existence to other incarnations in the past, but also look into the future to subsequent incarnations of our essential being. Thus we divide the entirety of human life into a life between birth and death and another life, which for the senses and the ordinary reasoning powers takes its course purely spiritually between death and the next birth. But spiritual science conceives of this not in an eternally recurring way but such that it recognizes these repeated earthly lives to be only intermediate states, whereas the entirety of human life goes back to a primordial spiritual source which preceded all life, the whole of planetary existence; so that earthly lives had their beginning in a condition where man emerged from a purely spiritual existence, and that once the necessary conditions have been fulfilled he will enter again into purely spiritual states which will include the fruits of everything that he has undergone through a succession of earthly lives.

This is to be sure only an outline which will be filled out in the coming lectures with distinctive colours but which is able to show the kind of results that spiritual-scientific research can obtain. If we place this whole tableau before our minds, we must indeed say that such a picture will, to a large number of those who reckon to be able to think today, not merely be incomprehensible and incapable of proof but even something that can call forth irony, scorn and derision. Already when there is any reference to spiritual science, anyone who wants to relate everything that is of importance to him today to the sure foundation of science must say to himself: What is the significance to such research of not only all the various achievements of science but also its methods, of what significance to spiritual science are the seriousness, the worthiness, the exactitude and also the great efforts that science has made in recent centuries and decades in order to arrive at an objective certainty? Spiritual research does not of course want to work against science (this has frequently been emphasized) but to be fully in harmony with it. It must therefore be conscious of the objections that science has against it, not only with respect to its content but also bearing in mind especially the seriousness and achievements of science in recent centuries.

It would be true to say that, according to spiritual science, these sources of spiritual research lie in a certain development of the soul, in that the soul engages in certain inner processes of ideation, feeling and will which one may call meditation, so that it has as a result inner experiences that are naturally limited purely to one's own soul and that no one can verify other than the person who experiences them, and then something of this unverifiable nature is presented as a scientific statement regarding the spiritual worlds. What, science can say, then remains of what is the most wonderful achievement of this science, that through all the research of recent centuries only that which can be verified everywhere and at any time by every human being objectively has validity? Outward experiments, outward observations have the distinctive quality that anyone can directly relate to them. This is not so with what is sought and struggled for in one's inner being. If one looks at people who have an inner experience of such things, does not the whole uncertain nature of the contradictory things they say in all their great variety show how little the experiences that a mystically intensified consciousness is able to bestow accord with one another? Surely we must harmonize the research that various individuals are undertaking in the clinic, in the laboratory or somewhere similar! The response will be that this could not be done any differently; so that what someone experiences subjectively shows itself to be unscientific through the fact that it cannot be verified by another person, since this other person cannot look into the soul of the spirit-researcher concerned.

Do not these experiences of the soul have, one might say, a total similarity with everything that is very evidently experienced in the soul as a result of illness, over-exertion and ecstasy? If the spirit-researcher protests that he has absolutely no intention of allowing any arbitrary vision that appears before his soul to count as the result of his research and that he proceeds in accordance with specific methods, someone can nevertheless still object, and this objection appears thoroughly justified: Yes, is it not so that whenever people experience visions, hallucinations and so forth and have the kind of soul-state that makes this possible, they develop a much greater belief in their fixed ideas, in their hallucinations and visions, than in what their senses persuade them to think? If one looks at a dreamer who is rigid and unbending in his beliefs, one will have cause to be concerned about what the spirit-researcher wants to draw forth from the depths of his soul as something that is not an illusion, that has objective existence in the spiritual world. Someone might say that it is possible for it to have objective existence in the spiritual world, but against the validity of such a soul-experiment it must be said that the dreamer has just as much confidence in his illusory ideas as the spirit-researcher in the results of his research, which he owes to what comes forth from the depths of his soul.

Only someone who has not followed the development of the objective research of what may be said to be the soundly based science of the last few centuries and decades can pass over such an objection with a smile. It is weightier than one ordinarily thinks for those who approach their spiritual-scientific results from a one-sided direction. It must be said, for example with regard to what is said in my book *Knowledge of the Higher Worlds*, where particular instructions are given for the individual soul, that when the soul is completely involved with such an experience it has no means of keeping itself in check. All this testifies to the fact that one must take very seriously such an objection, which to a superficial spirit-researcher may even appear trivial. There is so much that can be said about the nature of what could be described as erroneous ideas which could also be used against spiritual science, in that people say: Everything that you present as methods for developing the soul may be nothing other than a refined capacity for having illusions and hallucinations.

Then spiritual science appears particularly out of place with respect to serious, verifiable science when it refers to specific, isolated results. A conscientious seeker after truth of the present who is familiar with developments of recent years might say: Do you not know anything about everything that happened before? You speak of an etheric body or life-body that is supposed to have an existence independent from the physical body. Do you know nothing about what used to be called a life-force[1] that lurked in people's minds until the nineteenth century, and that the belief in this life-force has finally been disposed of through devoted scientific efforts? And are you ignorant of the following fact: It used to be said in earlier centuries that a chemical process occurred in lifeless nature between separate chemical substances. But when, so it was claimed, this same connection between substances enters the human organism the so-called life-force takes hold of it; then the process that takes place among the individual substances would not be what we learn in chemistry and physics but these various substances work upon one another under the influence of the life-force. It was a great step forward that this life-force has been swept overboard, that people sought to say that this life-force is of no help whatsoever, and that one's endeavour must be that what one can investigate in the lifeless world must be pursued further in the living organism, that one would need merely to take into account the more complex way in which substances interact there rather than resort to the dubious expedient of the life-force.

The life-force was indeed disposed of as such a 'dubious expedient of science', in that it was shown how the efficacy of certain substances that would formerly be conceived of only under the influence of the life-force is also brought about in the laboratory. And because that is not yet the end of the matter, science had to set itself the high ideal of considering also that combination of substances as exists in the cell of the plant, and had to avoid resorting to the dubious expedient of a life-force when it came to investigating how substances and forces are active in the organism.

So long as people were not in a position to give rise to combinations of substances in the laboratory, it was justified to say that they came about only if the individual substances were influenced by the life-force. But since it has become possible—especially through Liebig[2] and Wöhler[3], after which there has no longer been a belief in the life-force—to think of certain substances without the life-force, it must since then be said that also the more complicated constructions and interactions in the human organism do not any longer require the help of a special life-force. Thus in the course of the nineteenth century science embraced the high ideal that most researchers adhered to—even if there were also 'neo-vitalists'—the ideal that became a reality: to recognize such connections between substances as they interact in the living organism and without calling upon the help of a nebulous, mystical life-force which, as all serious scientific research of the nineteenth century has always maintained, serves absolutely no purpose, because it contributes nothing whatsoever to the objective knowledge of nature.

Anyone who acknowledges these facts and above all takes into account the seriousness and intrinsic worthiness that underlie these developments in science may well protest: Is it really so that a number of people have appeared as so-called spirit-researchers who are again reviving the old life-force in the form of their etheric body or life-body? Is it not a sign of scientific dilettantism? They—these people who know nothing of the ideal of science—may 'have their beliefs'; but the scientific researcher himself cannot be taken in by what can well appear to be a mere revival of the idea of the life-force. Thus spiritual science, one can say, works in a dilettantish way by failing to take account of everything that belongs to the most beautiful ideals of modern science, and it merely makes use of the circumstance that science has not yet managed to manufacture in the laboratory certain substances that are to be found in the living organism in order to be able to maintain that a special etheric body or life-body is necessary for the engendering of life. One might add that as science develops further it will eradicate this etheric body or life-body from man's being. So long as science has not yet succeeded in the course of its triumphant progress in showing that there is no such thing as an etheric body and that the combination of the substances of the living organism can also be engendered in a test tube, the theosophists or spiritual researchers can make a song and dance about the etheric body, which is nothing but a resuscitation of the old life-force! This is the sort of reproach that might be levelled against dilettantism when it arises.

If, now, spiritual science says regarding sleep-life that the emotions, impulses and desires that people have and are associated with what is specifically designated as the astral body, and that when a person is overcome by sleep it leaves the physical and etheric bodies and leads an independent existence, the criticism can be made that it is very easy to speak of an inner soul-life if one simplifies everything by referring to this inner soul-life without all the difficulties and riddles of which science is aware by saying: This is the astral body, and all that takes place internally has a connection with it.

Again, one can address the advances that science has made and say: What are the great advances that have been made especially in recent decades in order to explain purely scientifically a phenomenon such as sleep-life or dream-life? It would take a long time if I were to present to you all the efforts of science—which are to be thoroughly regarded with seriousness and respect—to explain sleep-life and the life of dreams. It would take a particularly long time because in recent times a considerable amount of research has come to light which could well be discussed.

It will suffice to consider one aspect, which can show how difficult it becomes for a serious truth-seeker at the present time to profess allegiance to what can initially appear as a mere assertion: the ego and the astral body of man withdraw from the physical body and etheric body when one goes to sleep.

If we gather together a number of different hypotheses and conjectures about sleep-life and arrive at an overall explanation of it, we arrive at something of this kind: It is said that in order to give a thorough explanation all that is needed is to look without prejudice at the phenomena of the human and animal organism. It becomes apparent that waking life consists in that the phenomena of the surrounding world make an impression upon the sense-organs, that they stimulate the brain. They exert such stimuli throughout the day. How do they work upon man's brain and nervous system? They do so in such a way that they destroy the substance of which the nervous system consists. What is going on the whole day, according to modern natural science, is that the outward colours, sounds and so on are penetrating our soul, that is, the life of our brain. By this means dissimilation processes are brought about, that is to say, processes of destruction. Certain products are deposited.

So long as these processes are taking place, man is not in a position to bring about the opposite process, that of the rebuilding of his organism. Thus every time after we wake up, our inner life of soul is to a certain extent destroyed, so that by the time we have become tired we have arrived at the point where we have destroyed our organism and it can no longer develop an inner soul-life; it comes to a halt. One needs only to acknowledge the wearing out of the organic substance, that the organic substance is for a certain time no longer capable of maintaining these inner processes. Outward stimuli no longer have any effect, and the consequence is that the inner organism now begins to develop its nutritional processes, the opposite of the dissimilation (or catabolic) processes, the processes of assimilation, that it now restores the destroyed organic substance and thereby causes nocturnal sleep. Once the organic substance is restored, the inner soul-life is also restored; and so waking life can cause fresh stimuli to arise until again tiredness ensues. Thus one is dealing with what we may call a self-regulation—or self-renewal[4]—of the organism.

It may be added that a conscientious seeker after truth who is familiar with the results of modern science will be bound to say: If waking life and sleep life in their rhythmic alternation can be well explained by the self-regulation or self-renewal of the organism, it is not only superfluous but directly harmful if you restrict the progress of such a human science by saying that it is not a matter of self-regulation or self-renewal but, because man has an existence that is independent from it, something goes forth from the organism.

Since it can be explained solely through the organism that the alternation between sleep and waking comes about, it is unnecessary and harmful to accept that consciousness is anything special and withdraws from the organism in order during the night to engage in life of a particular kind. It will also be pointed out that spiritual science is characterized by extreme dilettantism, in which only such people believe who do not themselves know the path of science to explain the organism purely on its own terms.

When the independence of intellectual life is spoken of, when it is said—and it seems a plausible thing to say—that intellectual life is independent, that through our senses we know of the human organism as a physical entity and can investigate it through scientific methods as we would any other physical process, whereas there is still such a thing as intellectual or mental life, this is something that has often been emphasized—for example, by Du Bois-Reymond[5] and also by others who would not readily profess materialism. One can, for instance, consider a conception of the brain: if one were to think of the human brain as so expanded—Leibniz has remarked on this[6]—that one could walk through it, one would only see material processes within it. Intellectual life does, however, have something distinctive about it, and this testifies to the fact that one is dealing here with an intellectual life that is separate from the processes of physical life. Whether this is justified can, however, be shown from what Benedikt[7] says: The fact of consciousness is in actual fact of no other order than that of the working of the force of gravity in connection with matter. For we see, for example, the physical matter of a cosmic body. According to physical science, physical matter exerts a gravitational pull, and then there is something that is attracted, for example by the Sun. People formerly spoke of a supersensible aspect to such influences between the Sun and the Earth or Moon. But this is merely equivalent to there being a piece of soft iron and an electrical or magnetic force outside it. And if we envisage the brain and its interplay of ideas, passions, emotions and so forth, this is similar to the fact that gravity and other forces exert their influence around the material Earth. Why, then, should there be an influence of a different nature if processes are influencing the brain that manifest themselves as does the force of gravity around the material Earth? The Earth in its connection with gravity and with whatever else invisibly influences it is no different from what influences the brain in the form of emotions, ideas and other processes. How does one have a right, it might well be asked, to speak of an independence of mental life if one does not allow oneself to speak of the force of gravity being exercised also when there is no body for it to attract? And one can say furthermore: Just as one has no right to speak of a cosmic body exerting a gravitational force in a situation where there is a free cosmic space, so one is not entitled to speak of a distinctive soul-quality that is not bound through a brain to material existence.

It should be clear to every serious seeker after truth that one should not be allowed to disregard such things through an unscientific fanaticism.

If weighty objections can be raised against the spiritual-scientific understanding of sleep and waking life, and against the independence of consciousness in general, how can someone who takes the scientific methods of the present seriously find a way of agreeing with what is said by spiritual science about repeated earthly lives, about the existence of a core of human nature that transcends death, that has experiences in the time between death and a new birth and then reappears in a new forthcoming physical earthly life! Here an objection is made not only by those who are reliant on scientific facts but also by those who want themselves to be in many respects spiritual scientists: by psychologists, by the present-day investigators of the soul. The question is raised: What is the necessary sign that the human essence continues in existence? The soul-researcher of the present can find this quite simply in that human consciousness has a memory of the states that it underwent during life. Continuation, continuity of consciousness is what psychologists currently take into consideration. They cannot become involved in what does not figure in the consciousness of the human personality, and they will always have to refer to the fact that a person does indeed have a memory of particular circumstances in his life between birth and death but can find no comparable evidence of the continuing existence of the human essence that may have issued from previous earthly lives.

Many serious-minded present-day seekers after truth will also have understandable objections with respect to many other things that have been said in the course of these series of lectures. Thus they may say: You can indeed adduce that certain things in human life seemingly cannot be explained from the events of a single life, that it is reasonable to suppose that a person brings certain dispositions such as talents with him through birth and that one can accept that the soul may have existed before entering physical life. But all this remains only a daring hypothesis. For modern research of the soul, everything of this kind continues to be unsatisfactory in so far as this research pursues a path that seemingly aims quite conscientiously towards an ideal.

One can characterize what is going on here in the following way: Anyone who considers human life without prejudice—with all the passions that engulf it, its shades of feeling, its inclination towards ideas of whatever kind—will, if he has at least a certain relationship to the standpoint of spiritual science, say: We have as a result of our education achieved many things; but not everything can be explained by this, for we bring through the portal of birth something that derives from previous stages of earthly existence. However, the serious-minded scientist may counter: Have we not made a beginning by investigating the early part of childhood, that part of early childhood of which we later have no recollection?

A modern naturalist or philosopher will then perhaps say: The spirit-researcher is wanting to suggest that a gifted genius, for example Feuerbach[8], brought certain powers with him from his previous life and was thereby enabled to work artistically. But the following discovery has now been made: such an artist paints with a quite distinctive mood of colour, prefers a particular facial expression and has other features that lead in a particular direction. If one looks further, one finds that in his early childhood he saw, for example, a bust in his room and that the particular way that the light always fell on it impressed itself on the soul of the child. This emerges again later, and it comes to be seen—so it is said—that such impressions are deeply influential and significant. It is possible to explain a great deal in this way. Spiritual science wants to lead everything back to past earthly lives, whereas through careful observation and investigation of early childhood one can perhaps explain everything.

One can then make reference to modern science, which shows through the fundamental law of biogenetics how in a pre-birth condition man also reflects the animal forms which it is supposed that the human race has passed through, so that it is therefore justified to show this. In this connection one can say: Where has spiritual science referred to something similar, whereby in a single individual life something is repeated that the human individual has undergone in former earthly lives? One would have to be able to ask this if, as a worthy truth-seeker of the present, one is to believe that in this connection a comparable seriousness and honouring of the facts is manifested in spiritual science to what is maintained on the ground of natural science. Thus what has happened—and there is a certain justice in saying this—is that if people have acquired a little scientific knowledge about human life, about the life of animals and about the planetary life that is accessible to us through astronomy, they can give free rein to their imagination, draw conclusions and think about all sorts of other worlds that give a strong impression of reality. It is indeed so that, in the case of someone who has no scientific knowledge an oppositional element will soon manifest itself, in that he will project all manner of ideas that do not harmonize with the fruits of scientific research. But anyone familiar with natural science will make it apparent that his ideas merge very nicely with what natural science indicates. Then he will not be contradicted. But if anyone speaks in defence of spiritual science, people may ask whether something of this kind has not been unjustifiably projected through such assertions. Who can vouch for the standpoint that only what is researched by each person should have validity? Thus one needs to get involved, for the simple reason that one sees how in the nineteenth century something emerged that also has validity in spiritual science.

We have indeed experienced that in the nineteenth century certain things have been asserted in German and French intellectual circles which spiritual science maintains. In 1854 a book by Reynaud[9] entitled *Terre et Ciel* appeared, and one by Figuier[10] about what happens with someone after death. There were numerous opponents with a scientific background who said: Yes, what is better—that you come up with ideas about a multiplicity of human earthly lives, about a life after death, on the foundation of natural science, or is it better to accept some other equally thought-through hypothesis about such matters?

If such objections are made and if they are not made in a frivolous way but wholly on the basis of an earnest quest for truth, one must say: These are not objections that arise purely from a spirit of opposition but ones that the human soul must itself make, and all the more so when one sees on the other hand how little conscientiousness is exhibited by those wanting to pursue spiritual science when 'proofs' are adduced that human life is something purely individual and when it is said that no explanation can be found outside individual life for phenomena such as human conscience and a sense of responsibility, when there is no wish to acknowledge certain predispositions and tendencies from former earthly lives. Many people say: When I take responsibility for something, I must myself have acquired the predisposition for this. Since I have not acquired it in this life, it must have been in a former life.

It is also said that human conscience is a phenomenon that proves that an inner voice dwells within us which we cannot derive from our present life and must therefore have come from a previous one. Furthermore, one sees the various children of the same parents, they exhibit quite different spiritual and intellectual qualities. But if everything is supposed to be passed on to the children from the parents by way of heredity, how can one explain such differences as appear even in twins? One should therefore conclude—so people say—that the children of the same parents have different individualities which are not inherited but must have been brought from a previous earthly life to the present one.

The conscientious truth-explorer will object: Have you not taken into account that a person's individuality, as he stands before us, arises from a mixture of the fatherly and motherly element and the mixture must therefore be different with the individual children? Even in the case of twins, would the individualities not have to be different because of these different mixtures if one is explaining them purely from heredity?

Such an objection is not far-fetched but is one that arises directly from the matter at hand. If one takes everything into account, one finds it absolutely understandable that those who always demand a science that can be 'verified' do not accept spiritual science, because it cannot be verified; and if one considers that such opponents are making a significant point, one grasps what they are saying. It can be said of them that, in addition to the critical spirit of our time, something different is living in them. This critical spirit is definitely present, and if spiritual science says something it immediately provokes opponents who are not only irritated logically but also morally outraged that such theories are expressed. Such opponents are called forth, and criticism is something that we see springing up everywhere. And because with its ideas spiritual science introduces a somewhat shocking element into the fabric of our time, such criticism is perfectly understandable.

But alongside a critical spirit there also exists in our time a certain gullibility, the tendency to be swept along behind anyone, provided that there is something in what he asserts that is derived from spiritual science. The longing to receive things into which one also has insight is just as little in evidence as the critical spirit and gullibility are strongly present. Thus we see that through gullibility, through a credulous public audience that accepts everything on authority, that accepts all manner of things from spiritual science, encouragement is given to precisely what true, serious spiritual research is accused of, namely charlatanism. It is an invitation to charlatanism when people accept things in a credulous way. And it is a great temptation for someone if every conceivable thing that he says is believed, if he is relieved of the difficulty of properly justifying these things before the forum of science, before the forum of the Time-spirit. Even in our time, what is spoken of here is far too widespread. We see how gullibility, how the crassest superstition is rampant. Thus there are probably no two other things in the world that are so closely related than are spiritual science and charlatanism. If one cannot distinguish the two paths, if one accepts everything purely on a blind belief in authority, just as by its very nature much must be taken on authority (as is often the case at present), one invites what is rightly criticized by those who are serious in their pursuit of truth: charlatanism, which is so closely linked with spiritual science. One can find it understandable if someone who is not in a position to distinguish a charlatan from a spirit-researcher objects that it is all charlatanism.

There is no speedier transition than to the moral and religious domain. We can characterize the objections that occur in this realm more quickly, because they are easier to understand.

One can indeed see that what must necessarily be the most intimate concern of the human soul, what a person believes in, what he subjectively considers to be true, is blown up into a would-be science! And one can register the following objection to the spiritual scientist: If you present this as your belief, we shall leave you in peace. But if you were to make what you present as a teaching from the higher worlds applicable to other people, this is contrary to the nature and character of how a person's inner being relates to the spiritual worlds, to the religious life as a whole. If one also seeks to demonstrate the fruits in this connection, one can say: Look at those in spiritual-scientific circles who have, for example, come to be convinced of the idea of repeated earthly lives; one can see in them how their whole moral conception of the world has been led by a spiritual-scientific outlook into the crassest egotism. And then it becomes possible to contrast what arises out of spiritual science with the materialism of the nineteenth century by saying: there have been many people who have with their spirit risen above purely material processes and have come to say: I see my higher morality not in laying claim after my death to a spiritual world where I can be received and continue to live, and if I do something of a moral nature I do it without hope of a spiritual world but because I see it as my duty, because I gladly sacrifice what I see as my own personal benefit.

There have been many for whom the morality of immortality is purely egotistical. This morality appeared to them to be far less good than that which lets everything that is done pass over into the general life of the cosmos. In contrast to this is the morality of those who say it would be meaningless if what they do were not to be balanced out in ensuing earthly lives. This karmic law, the opponents of spiritual science can say, favours only human egotism; in complete contrast to those who acknowledge that they will have many lives in the future. So what do I now need to become a decent human being? I have many lives before me, and although I may continue to be stupid at present, I can still become clever and skilled in subsequent lives. Thus it might be said that repeated earthly lives invite one to lead a comfortable and effortless life. According to this view, the idea of repeated earthly lives makes it apparent that the egotism that seeks to preserve one's ego is very far removed from selfless morality.

An objection to be considered is one that Friedrich Schlegel made against the way that the Indians interpreted the idea of repeated earthly lives[11]: the view of the life of the human essence that rushes from incarnation to incarnation leads to man being estranged from active, direct engagement in reality and losing interest in everything that he should be developing. A certain unworldly specialness can easily be observed in those who involve themselves with spiritual science. A certain spiritual egotism, a certain unworldly teaching is thereby cultivated. Indeed, it comes to manifestation when such people say: When I have been studying spiritual science for a certain time I lose interest in what was previously dear to me. This is something that often happens, and it shows that there is something to be said for the counter-suggestion that people should work in the world to which they have been assigned! It is a point to be taken seriously, that spiritual science should not alienate people from the immediate realities of life or make them into oddities who wander all over the place.

And now for the religious life! What is the fairest blossom, the most magnificent flowering of this religious life? It lies in the devotion, the selfless devotion of the human individuality that transcends human existence. The truly religious mood is engendered by the soul's willingness to lose or dedicate itself to a deity beyond human comprehension. Now spiritual science comes and explains to man that a divine spark is within him which comes to expression only in a small way in one earthly life; but as it is developed and achieves an ever greater degree of perfection, the God in man becomes ever stronger and stronger. This is to endow the self with godliness instead of a selfless devotion to a transcendent deity.

Yes, one can object with a certain entitlement if—from a serious religious standpoint—one takes the view that, through becoming immersed in one's own divine nature as it comes to realization through a series of incarnations, the true religious mood can be destroyed, just as life can also be destroyed in love. If a person does not feel himself to be motivated by a sense of loving devotion but if he thinks that in a later earthly life everything will be balanced out, he loves only the impending compensation. And the religious person can say: The religious life is, in the world-view of spiritual science, founded upon the egotistical view that man has no God outside himself but only within himself. And the objection is justified: What arrogance, pride and self-adulation can come to be established within the human soul!

Those who make such objections do not need to embellish them further. But one can see how faithful adherents of spiritual science can come to such an arrogance and repeatedly fall prey to self-adulation. It is therefore the case that we in the West find such a repugnance towards the existence of a human essence before birth. One should not take lightly an objection that a serious truth-seeker may make against the idea of repeated earthly lives in contrast to that of relationships based on inheritance.

One objection that I shall read—and I shall not speak about it, since this would detract from its force—is that of Jacob Frohschammer[12], who may be regarded as one of those people who have a great problem with accepting the idea of a pre-existence of the soul:

> ...It is not possible to regard the human soul as the being of God or as part of God's being, not so much because of a Thomistic concern about the oneness of God, since souls could reside in Him as fleeting elements without inflicting injury upon His oneness, but rather because of the personal consciousness and testimony of the human soul itself, which can regard neither itself nor the world as the direct expression of divine perfection or as the realization of the idea of God. As deriving from God, it can serve merely as a product or work of divine imagination; for the human soul must, like the world itself, in this case indeed come from divine power and influence (since nothing can come into being out of pure nothingness), but this power and

> influence of God must, as a model for all creation, also work formatively in its realization and continuing existence; thus as a formative power (not only of a formal, but also a real kind), therefore as imagination, i.e. as a sustaining power or potential that continues to work and be creative immanently in the world, hence as a world-imagination, as has already been discussed. As for the doctrine of the pre-existence of souls (souls that are regarded either as eternal or as created in time, but at the beginning and collectively at the same time), which, as has been observed, has again been put forward and is considered to be pertinent to a solution for all manner of psychological problems, this is connected with the teaching of the transmigration and incarceration of souls in earthly bodies. According to this view, therefore, there takes place through the procreation of the parents neither a direct divine creation of souls nor a creative engendering of new human natures in body and soul by the parents but a kind of new connection of the soul with the body, thus a kind of becoming flesh or an immersing of the soul in the body—at least to a partial extent so that it is partly embraced by and bound up with the body and partly extends above it and maintains a certain independence as a spirit but nevertheless cannot detach itself from it, until death breaks the connection and brings liberation and release for the soul (at least from this connection). The spirit of a human being would then in its relation to the body be like the poor souls in purgatory as they are usually portrayed on votive tablets by bungling artists as bodies that are half immersed in glowing flames but with the upper part (as souls) protruding and gesticulating! Just think what a position and significance would be ascribed in this view to the opposite sexes, the generic nature of mankind, marriage and the relationship of parents to their children! The contrast between the sexes would become a mere incarceration, marriage an institution for fulfilling this wonderful task, parents would be the mere vehicle for taking hold of and imprisoning children's souls, with children themselves being indebted to the parents for this miserable, wearisome imprisonment, while having nothing further to do with them! Everything that is linked to this state of affairs is based on a miserable deception!

If one is a fanatical spirit-researcher such a litany may elicit a smile, but fanaticism should be far removed from spiritual science. Its task is to understand and really tolerate what the soul has to cope with. For this reason this introductory lecture was conceived not as a 'foundation' but as a 'refutation' of spiritual-scientific research. But what will be presented in the next lecture ('On What Foundation is Spiritual Science Based?') will be able to stand all the more firmly if we can ourselves make the objections that can justifiably be made. As one may well imagine, I do not really want to refute spiritual science!

I have been able to present here only a small number of objections. Broad outlines of many others could be given. To some extent this can be done over the coming weeks, and the refutations of these will then follow directly. But one can see from everything that is being presented how through the receiving of spiritual-scientific research one is being inwardly summoned to a battlefield, as it is not merely a question of speaking about things such as repeated earthly lives, man's passage through a spiritual world and so on but all sorts of counter-arguments also emerge from the dark depths of the soul. It is good if someone who quietly concerns himself with spiritual research is also familiar with these counter-arguments. He will then be able to apply the right tolerance to opponents. It can never be the way of the spirit-researcher simply to concern himself with spiritual science or to be blind to or laugh at objections made by opponents. That this is not a good way to proceed can be seen from a particular instance in the nineteenth century, which I should like to recount.

In the year 1869 there appeared the *Philosophy of the Unconscious* by Eduard von Hartmann.[13] Even though one might not agree with it, one can say that it represented a good attempt to reach beyond sense-perception. Thus Eduard von Hartmann felt obliged to take issue with much that had been disseminated at that time as an ideal of science, especially with what derived from the growing fascination with Darwinism. Thus we find much in the *Philosophy of the Unconscious* with respect to Darwinism that continues to have relevance. But where those who from the standpoint of Darwinism could not approve of this book agreed with one another was that they rejected Eduard von Hartmann as someone who had not familiarized himself with what followed from modern science. A great flood of dissenting opinions appeared. These dissenting opinions did, of course, include some of sheer stupidity; but some were the work of real experts in the field, such as Ernst Haeckel, the zoologist Oskar

Schmidt and others. Among these dissenting statements and articles was one entitled *The Unconscious from the Standpoint of Physiology and the Theory of Evolution*[14] by an author who did not give his name. In the essay in question, compelling reasons were given why many things in the *Philosophy of the Unconscious* were not maintainable and why its author had shown that in the field of natural science he was no more than a dilettante. Many people were utterly astounded at the degree of insight that this anonymous person revealed in this essay, and Oskar Schmidt,[15] who was at the time at Jena University, thought it was the best thing that could be said from the standpoint of natural science against the *Philosophy of the Unconscious.* Many people said: He is speaking for us, for he is one of ours; and Ernst Haeckel said that he himself could write nothing better against the *Philosophy of the Unconscious.*

Thus it was no wonder that the first edition of this essay *The Unconscious from the Standpoint of Physiology and the Theory of Evolution* was soon out of print. A second edition appeared, and now the author revealed his name: it was Eduard von Hartmann! This silenced many of the voices who had previously said: He is speaking for us, he is one of ours. But the remarkable thing had happened that a person had shown that he knew everything that his most serious opponents could say against him. This does indeed prove that no credence should be given to the idea that something can be said against a view of the world that the person who advocates it would not himself have been able to express.

For spiritual science this is indeed a matter of considerable importance. Now I have not been able to say everything today that I might have said. But spiritual science must know what objections it is open to, and it can only be wished that many of those who believe they have found deep scientific reasons with which to refute spiritual science might sometimes be able to consider how much better the one who is the butt of the objections knows the matter at hand than the person who is doing the objecting. So is it with a conscientious spirit-researcher. He can, of course, not bore his audience by always also presenting counter-arguments. But if something is said on behalf of spiritual science and if many opponents come forward with their views, they should first ask themselves whether what they are bringing could not have been better said by the person speaking on behalf of spiritual science.

The task of the next lecture will be to pose the question: What is the right relationship of the soul to the counter-arguments that it may itself engender from the depths of its being? Should it indeed be so that, since so many objections can be made against spiritual science, people have to regard it in the way that Goethe—in a somewhat exaggerated way—lets his Faust say: 'Could I but banish magic from my path'?[16] Are the counter-arguments of spiritual science equivalent in nature to Faust's counter-arguments against magic? Are they of such a nature that a philosopher such as Geoffroy de Saint-Hilaire[17] is right when he says: With regard to observation of the world only the following is worthy of consideration. We see that man is in many respects weak. Why should we not admit this weakness, and why should it not be a strength to come to terms with one's weakness? People are only too ready to confess their weakness with respect to wind and weather, to volcanic eruptions and events of the elemental world! They have no problem with admitting that they are weak with regard to what nature imposes upon them, when they sow their seeds in the earth and the unfavourability of the weather does not allow them to ripen and causes all their industry to result in famine! If people often have to take their weaknesses to heart, why should they not say out of sheer honesty: The spirit can in many respects go beyond itself, but it is too weak and limited and cannot accomplish anything beyond what nature imposes upon them; so they cannot recognize anything beyond what lives in us by virtue of our nature—we must resign ourselves to it!

If the reasons that have now been cited were so weighty that the next lecture could not be given, there would be no possibility other than such an attitude of resignation, which not only Geoffroy de Saint-Hilaire but many others feel out of a sincere, truth-loving attitude of soul and believe they must represent outwardly, that man cannot gain access to a spiritual world. Because the counter-arguments do not spring from a spirit of opposition but from the nature of things itself, the debate about the nature and value of the counter-arguments of spiritual science is not merely a theoretical fact but something that must emerge from the battlefield of the soul, where conflicting opinions constitute a battle that is more or less justified and where one can recognize only through hard struggles which of the reasons advocated there can be victorious. If one openly and without prejudice weighs up the inner battle of the soul and can say what speaks for and against a recognition of the spiritual world, one will not be a fanatical representative of this or that abstract or arbitrarily conceived principle but someone who recognizes the principle that a quiet conviction rests on the basis of those foundations that only achieve validity after—and not before—they have eliminated their counter-arguments within one's own soul.

If the seeker after truth searches for his conviction in this way, he may say to himself that he may confidently approach the development of spiritual life in the future; for it is true what the serious truth-seeker has said: What is untrue—and however often it may be put forward—will be rejected by humanity's evolving aspiration for truth. But what is true and had to struggle for its existence against dissenting arguments, as we always see with regard to events and processes in world history, finds its path in human evolution in the quite particular way that one can stand before this development of truth over the centuries and millennia and can say: However many obscuring impressions—that is, prejudices and opposition—may rise up, the truth always finds cracks and crevices whereby it can assert itself for the blessing, advancement and benefit of mankind.

Lecture 2

BERLIN, 7 NOVEMBER 1912

ON WHAT FOUNDATION IS SPIRITUAL SCIENCE BASED?

IN what I said a week ago I allowed myself to cite a number of objections to or refutations of spiritual research or anthroposophy. It would be a misunderstanding if anyone were to assume that today's lecture will be devoted to refuting these objections; for it should be said at the outset that I do not intend to engage in a dialectical game of arguments and counter-arguments. The spiritual research of which I shall be speaking here (and of which I have always spoken) should be regarded as being in full harmony with science and modern culture. Hence the retorts that I mentioned a week ago were also not put forward in order that one might resolve them without further ado but, rather, in the sense that they appear with a certain justification in the soul that truly takes into account the advances of our present-day intellectual culture alongside the achievements of our spiritual science. They were put forward not as unjustified responses but as objections which, within their limits, are fully justified; and the feeling should thereby be awakened of the seriousness with which spiritual science should work and of the awareness that it can take full responsibility for itself from its own sources, despite the fact that this spiritual research understands all too well—quite especially in connection with these objections—that it is thrown back solely on its own resources as regards what is mainly a threefold hostility with which it is faced.

One aspect of this hostility arises from contemporary science or at any rate from that form of it that often believes that the foundations on which it is based cannot be contradicted. The second aspect arises from many forms of religious conviction, and the third derives from ordinary waking consciousness, which in many respects instinctively rejects what spiritual science, spiritual research, has to say.

It could easily seem as though the following question is clearly justified: How does spiritual science prove its assertions in the face of the objections that have been made? How does it prove what it has to say? In the course of these winter lectures we will be hearing much about actual results of research concerning a supersensible world. In these two initial lectures I need to be allowed to speak in a way that many people may perhaps find abstract—although it is not intended to be—and also difficult to understand or uninteresting; for even if some people cannot follow everything that I am saying in the first two lectures, they may nevertheless come to feel that the intention is to acquire a really good foundation for this spiritual research. Thus a number of questions will be addressed today which those who are more interested in receiving accounts of aspects of the supersensible world may find uninteresting. One question that may be raised is whether what are ordinarily regarded as proofs can be applied in a generally accepted sense to the establishing of a world-conception. Can one consider proofs to be something that—should they indeed exist—contain the compulsion that every single person should be convinced by them?

Everyone who seriously acknowledges a particular conception of the world usually believes that he could prove it, and he will present his proofs for this world-conception with full confidence if he wants to be taken seriously. In contrast to this widespread belief I should like to cite the view of an energetic and active German philosopher, namely Johann Gottlieb Fichte, who says: The nature of one's philosophy depends on the kind of person one is.[18]

If one wants to arrive at the essence of what Fichte is saying here and ask what he really means, one would say: It is not simply a question of proofs but of what proofs one considers to be authoritative, what proofs have weight in order that a person may, in accordance with his soul-development, gain insight into something or other. Thus we are guided by a philosopher such as Fichte towards our inner nature when it is a question of evaluating proofs.

The requirement is, therefore, that a person has through his inner development acquired the capacity to be able to perceive the compelling quality of proofs. Expressed in plain terms, one could say: What ultimately is the use of any amount of proofs to someone who cannot believe in them? And there is much that we can discern about the nature of these so-called proofs from the methods deployed by many world-conceptions that would appear to be based wholly on the firm foundation of scientific facts.

When I say something in the way that I want to express it now, I always have to prefix it by saying: I believe that there is no one who can have more respect and recognition of the advances in natural science in our time than the genuine spirit-researcher. And today I particularly want to say in advance that all the objections that were made a week ago were meant in such a way that they were justified to the extent that any direct refutation on the part of the spirit-researcher of what was said last week would be unjustified; for the spirit-researcher does not deny what scientific research maintains and rightly does so—he fully acknowledges it. This fact must also be taken into consideration.

Spiritual research is constantly opposed by natural science; on the other hand, spiritual research does not itself in any way oppose natural science, if one is in a position to appreciate the true state of affairs. But there are many scientific facts that are made use of today by streams associated with certain world-views and seemingly placed in a certain light such that one can be in full agreement with the facts but not with the way that these world-conceptions sometimes want to prove something on the basis of these facts. The facts that arise from natural science are for the most part only confirmed by spiritual research, and it may be said that the time will come when that which finds its justification through Darwinism and through the modern theory of evolution will find its true valuation through spiritual research.

It can also be especially clear through spiritual research that the human soul, if it is to be active in the outer physical world, must for certain mental operations make use of particular parts or portions of the brain, just as for other tasks one uses one's hands. Just as the hand is needed for certain things that people do, so are certain parts of the brain allotted as instruments for soul experience. Spiritual science is well able to have an overview of the right meaning and significance of this assigning of resources, and it has absolutely no quarrel with what natural science advocates in this respect. On the other hand, the so-called proofs that are put forward are for anyone who understands such things often not very convincing—as, for example, when with respect to the true facts that certain parts of the brain belong to the life of the soul it is said that the soul-activity concerned is eliminated through the illness of these portions of the brain, and one is therefore unable to perceive that the soul manages to carry out certain functions as, for example, speech in such a way that the speech-centre is eliminated.

For someone who understands matters of cogency, such proofs have met with the problem of the famous, albeit non-existent Professor Schlaucherl* who, as perhaps some of you will know, wanted to carry out a proof of how a frog senses things. To this end he placed a frog on the experimental table and knocked on the table, and behold: the frog jumped away, meaning that it had heard the knock. Now he ripped off its legs and knocked again on the table. This time the frog did not jump anywhere, because its legs had been broken off. But because it could no longer jump away, Professor Schlaucherl concludes that the frog hears with its legs; for if it has no legs, there is no evidence that it can hear.

If one cites such a scenario, one must of course crave indulgence. But it is logically and methodically in complete harmony with what is frequently adduced today for purposes of proof with regard to facts that spiritual science would not by any means consider to be dubious and which are even true. However, the proofs that are put forward are never really able to convince anyone who is able to judge what actually holds water.

This is how it is with much that was presented in the previous lecture as to how there is this weighty objection that can be made in the

* The word means something like 'someone who has been put through the mill'. An English equivalent might be 'Professor Fiddlesticks'. —Translator

scientific sense by serious and respected natural scientists of the present, when it is said: In the past people conceived of a life-force, and they tried to explain all processes in the living body by means of this life-force. But the nineteenth century has shown that there is no need for this idea of a life-force and that, purely on the basis of the ordinary forces residing in certain substances, one can show in the laboratory how certain composite substances that were previously thought to be able to come into existence in the living organism only through the life-force can be produced in the laboratory without it; so that the ideal of science must therefore consist in presupposing that it will eventually be possible to manufacture also more complicated substances of the living world in this way. Now along come the spirit-researchers and maintain that there is in the living organism a special life-body or etheric body, which is necessary for living things to exist. But this is none other than a revival of the old life-force. This could therefore only derive from dilettantes who are in their comfortable way looking for an explanation in an area where, because of their ignorance, they are not taking account of the advances of true science.

I should first like to explain through a kind of historical testimony how this whole inference has its effect on a soul who, while inclined in this direction by the—may it be said—justified advances of science does not so readily accept its conclusions. I intend to demonstrate this initially by means of a historical example. People think that the notion of an etheric body or life-body has been disposed of when it is said: It must be an ideal of science to compose living substance from its separate constituent parts in the laboratory; hence one can no longer believe that life came into being through something supersensible, but one must regard it as an influence in purely material substance when one works in the laboratory and puts composite substances together from simpler ones.

There was a time when people truly believed more than a serious modern scientist would dare to today that one could in a laboratory make not only a single living substance but also living beings of the lowliest kind, even a little human being, the familiar homunculus.[19] When people firmly believed that one could give rise to the homunculus in the laboratory, they did not by any means adopt this belief out of the idea that the supersensible aspect of living phenomena was created out of the world; the fact was that they believed precisely in the supersensible aspect of living phenomena. This is a historical objection against the assertion that there is an incompatibility for human thinking between believing in the supersensible origin of life and at the same time representing the view—shared with modern naturalists—that living things can be produced in the laboratory. The two things are perfectly compatible, and in order to see that this is so one does perhaps need to introduce an essentially trivial train of thought which is therefore no less significant for someone who not only does not allow himself to be hypnotized or be open to suggestion by a natural-scientific world-view but who is able to enter into the full dimensions of man's life of soul.

Let us suppose that we have before us certain substances. We amalgamate them. We see—hypothetically—that something living arises out of them. Are we justified in drawing the conclusion that from what we saw of the individual substances before us the life of the resultant phenomenon has come into being? No, we are not! And we are no longer so justified from the moment that we admit that the flies that have gathered after a certain time did not develop from the residues of food lying in the room. When we see a room full of flies, we can say that these flies are there because the room was a mess and bits of food were lying about. These bits of food were the condition, but they did not make the flies. However, flies are always present when the conditions are right, and when this is so life will appear. But no one should maintain that it has arisen from them, but merely that they have been the cause that life has appeared.

A supersensible process should also be assumed when such a sequence of events happens in the laboratory. Hence from the side of spiritual research it would be completely fallacious if it were to make a point of wanting in a more or less ironical or witty way to rise above what natural science strives towards as its ideal. It fully goes along with this ideal and is in full agreement with it. But this does not render any less relevant what spiritual science contributes to a real-complete understanding of things.

Let us take as another example the objection made against spiritual science in so far as it explains the phenomena of sleeping and waking by saying that there is in man a supersensible aspect, which rises from the physical body and etheric body when a person goes to sleep, enters into a particular spiritual world and dives down into them again when he wakes up. We have mentioned the weighty objection which is thoroughly compelling, that natural science tries to explain the phenomenon of sleep by putting forward a kind a self-regulation of the organism, by showing that the stimuli that are exerted by the impressions of daily life to a certain extent destroy, use up organic substance, so that a point is reached where this organic substance, the life substance, must be restored. While it is being restored a dullness extends over the consciousness, and once this restoration is complete the outward stimuli can function again. Thus we would have to do with a self-regulation of the organism and could say: What is the need for a special kind of spiritual research that engages in a description of what is alleged to go forth from a person during sleep—if the phenomenon of sleep can be explained from the human body itself?

The weight that can be attached to this scientific interpretation—which is absolutely true within certain limits—can be seen through the following examination. Even though what I am putting forward is only presented in the form of an outline, it harmonizes—albeit not in all its details—with the whole spirit of modern scientific research.

So what happens when the organism is lying before us in sleep, also in accordance with a scientific perspective? According to such a view we must say: The organic substances that have been used up through the impressions of the senses and through other outward impressions are, as it were, repaired. There therefore occurs an inner process, a process that is wholly conditioned by the nature and being of the human body, the human organism, and we can of course explain what thus occurs inwardly only from what lies within the laws of the human body, within the laws of the organism. However, these laws of the organism can never, either in the present or the future, give us anything different (anyone who has real insight into these matters has to acknowledge this)—as, for example, what the lungs give us for the breathing process. Anyone who investigates the human breathing process will be able fully to understand it from the laws of the functioning of the lungs. But what will not be understood from this is the nature and influence of oxygen. This needs to be investigated outside the lungs, for oxygen enters into the lungs from outside; and anyone who thinks he can come to know the nature of oxygen by studying the lungs would be gravely mistaken.

The process enacted by the lungs, everything that takes place within the organism, can be studied from the inner aspect of the lungs themselves. In order to understand breathing as a whole, it is necessary that we go beyond the activity of the lungs and understand the nature of oxygen itself—and we shall gain nothing by way of knowledge of the nature of oxygen from the process of lung activity. We shall gain equally little by investigating what happens in the organism during sleep if we want to know about everything that occurs in waking consciousness from morning until evening, with all the impulses, passions, emotions, ideals and so on that buffet us to and fro. Just as little as the activity of the lungs is one and the same thing as the nature of oxygen and as sure we can be that oxygen has to enter the lungs from outside, we also know with certainty that everything that is encompassed within the phenomena of consciousness must unite with, must enter into from without, what we can study and observe inwardly during sleep as inner bodily processes.

Such a train of thought is not so easy to grasp immediately. However, if you follow it through you find it is no mere analogy, it is more than that: it is a kind of educational means enabling one to gain a right overview of the elements of the life-situation that has been characterized. And anyone who really clarifies in his mind the relationship of the oxygen that is outside and enters the lungs to what happens in the lungs learns to recognize through such a concept, through such an idea, how he needs to think about what goes on during sleep outside the physical body and what must be added to the processes that occur in the physical body during sleep if consciousness is to be experienced, just as oxygen must be added to the inner organic processes of the lungs if there is to be any real vitality in the breathing process.

What one may refer to as the 'founding principles of spiritual science' is by no means as simple as people often think. Because there is nothing simple about such things it may often seem as though they have been formulated as a result of some light-weight refutations from the world. It is actually a case of recognizing arguments and counter-arguments in connection with Fichte's adage as to what kind of person one is, that is, what kind of soul-constitution one has, in order to see things in their true light. How often one hears people say: Oh, here come these spirit-researchers or anthroposophists, saying that man, whom one can clearly perceive to be a single entity and on whose behalf we have struggled to perceive as such, is divided into various members or parts, into a physical body, an etheric body or life-body, an astral body and an ego. Yes, they divide everything up in this sort of way. But it is not a matter of simply making divisions but of engaging in methods of research in accordance with the justified demands of a thinking that really penetrates into the nature of things. If someone has some water, he will not disagree with the chemist when he says: As long as you let this 'water' remain as it is, you will never arrive at its chemical components; for this you must separate it into hydrogen and oxygen.

So long as one remains on such solid ground, one will probably not hear the objection: You are committing a sin against monism, for water is a monad. You should not divide it into hydrogen and oxygen, otherwise you become a wholly superstitious dualist. One is not so likely to hear such an objection in an area of such tangibility, because here it is perfectly obvious that such a division needs to be made. What, then, is the main characteristic of a justification of making such a division if one is not merely considering water but if one is surveying the whole realm of existence that comes into question here? The essential point here is that oxygen can not only be in water but, as the chemist would agree, also in other substances with which it is able to unite, and that hydrogen can likewise unite with other substances, so that one can therefore divide water and the separate parts can take up quite different connections and have in these connections their particular destinies.

If spiritual science was only concerned with distinguishing the components that make up a human being, thus the etheric body and the physical body, not to mention the other parts, one could say: You are making a division. But if you pursue spiritual research (and it is not possible to consider everything today), the situation is exactly similar to, for example, chemistry. We do not divide man into a physical body and an etheric body because it suits us to separate out the respective phenomena in this way but because we do indeed need to show: just as hydrogen and oxygen, when they are separated from their water-nature, have their different destiny in a variety of substances, so does the physical body in death undergo its particular destiny, as the etheric body and also the astral body form different connections. Just as the chemist pursues the path of water, if he is not content to leave it in the form of a monad but conceives it as a duality of hydrogen and oxygen, so does the spirit-researcher follow the path of the physical body, the etheric or life-body, the astral body and the ego into the most varied areas of life. This gives him the justification to speak of a real division. An objection that he would thereby be infringing against monism would be of a similar significance to the idea that dividing water into hydrogen and oxygen is infringing against it.

It is therefore a matter of understanding, through real insights into the situation, the value, the justification of objections and also the limits of the objections. It can be seen from any true, serious spiritual science, if one really enters into it, that it does not skim lightly over the objections but that it tries to find precisely through them the concepts for its results, that it really considers the arguments and counter-arguments. If we again refer today to Fichte's assertion that the philosophy that one has is shaped by the kind of person one is, we could also say what was said a week ago: Everything comes back to an inner subjective quality, the strength of one's convictions is not sought in what is presented outwardly but in the way that one has been able to relate to the phenomena of the world. We then come to a consideration of what was referred to in the first lecture: to the sources of spiritual-scientific knowledge. It was said that these sources arise through a development of the human soul. We shall speak later about how this development unfolds, what paths the soul has to follow in order that it actually ascends to knowledge and perceptions of the supersensible world. Today I shall simply say that the soul has to undergo inner processes such as meditation and concentration on the inner life. What is brought about by such processes?

If someone really wants to become a spirit-researcher and wants, so to speak, to make his soul an apparatus for spiritual research, he must endeavour to create for himself a similar state to what is otherwise experienced in sleep, that is, he must through intense concentration of the will be in a position to induce a state that otherwise arises only through tiredness in the form of sleep. He must be able to exclude all outer sense-impressions, to suppress all brain-bound thinking, and nevertheless he must avoid that condition that otherwise manifests itself in sleep: the complete emptiness of consciousness. He avoids this by giving himself up to quite definite imaginations—we shall characterize these later on—which are suitable for concentrating, for drawing together his soul-forces, so that they become stronger than they would be otherwise. Whereas they are normally, as it were, 'thin' and, hence—when they leave the physical body during sleep—are unable to know anything of themselves or of the world because their inner perceptive power is too weak, they are strengthened and condensed through such meditations and concentrations. The person does not extricate himself from ordinary thinking in such a way that he has no knowledge of himself, as is the case with ordinary sleep, but rather that he is able to remain conscious and experience through the particular nature of this state: Now I am hearing nothing through my ears, I am no longer seeing with my eyes or thinking with my brain-bound thinking, but I am now experiencing myself in the purely spiritual domain and experience a reality there.

A normal and justified objection to such a description of spiritual research that is expressed is as follows: One can through such a soul-development come, for example, to inner imaginative worlds which one regards as an expression of a supersensible world. Through the way in which these imaginative forms arise, one can also have the opinion that they point to something real. But one surely knows—so it may be said—that someone who has hallucinations, illusory ideas and visions also believes very strongly in these hallucinations and whatever else, and it is therefore completely impossible truly to make a distinction between hallucinations, illusory ideas and so forth and what appears to a spirit-researcher. Why should one not also regard what the spirit-researcher arrives at in this way as a mere hallucination? Quite apart from the fact that one can say that what is experienced inwardly in this way is purely subjective and cannot be verified at any time by someone else, as is, for example, the case with a physical experiment.

However, it should be indicated that it does not lie in the nature of all truths that they can be found or even only confirmed through outer events. One can say that, for anyone who wishes to think, the ideas of mathematics could be highly convincing; and they are arrived at inwardly. In order to indicate this we need no more complicated idea than that three times three is nine. For such an insight, all that is needed is an inner imagination of the soul; and it is nothing other than a way of making this visible if someone, for example, illustrates that three times three is nine by means of three groups of three peas. It depends on the soul's inner development if someone has the knowledge that three times three is nine, and he does not even need to confirm this through an outer process. He knows what he has experienced, he knows it without any outward verification. There is therefore an inner soul-exercise for which external verification is no more than a way of making something visible and is confined to this, and through which one sees that this inner process is true.

The difference between falsehood and truth in the supersensible world is experienced in a quite similar way, though on a higher level. The spirit-researcher must want to pass through all the things that can lead him to knowledge: where do hallucinations, visions and illusions cease, and where does supersensible reality begin? Where the one ends and the other begins can only be seen in a manner similar to how mathematical truths can be discerned. But it can indeed be seen. Anyone who is a real spirit-researcher and knows nature, which truly leads to spiritual research, will not in any case entertain the world with his visions; and if you find someone who entertains people about the supersensible world by speaking about his visions, you can presuppose that he is far from being a true spirit-researcher. After all, the true spirit-researcher knows that all imaginary, visionary life that is acknowledged by people in the outer world merely represents a projection of one's own soul into one's own space; and his science has its foundation not in this space, not in what people actually mean when they speak as ignoramuses about the imaginations of the spirit-researcher, but in that which lies behind this rhetoric, once he has followed through the whole process of how the life of the soul is made objective and how the wall that is erected as a reflection of our inner soul-processes has been broken through.

It is particularly important for the spirit-researcher that he has recognized the nature of hallucinations, visions and illusions in their connection with the inner life of the soul and can say to himself for a sufficiently long time: What happens is something objectively definitive, but which can be grasped purely as an inner soul-process. And it does not belong so much to the requirements of a real spiritual-scientific schooling to bring the soul through certain exercises to the point where it has experiences that are free from the body; it is, rather, more important that the soul acquires a right judgement about these experiences outside the physical body, in the purely spiritual domain.

From a certain point onwards the soul knows through what it is experiencing that it is no longer experiencing subjective processes but that it has stripped away its subjectivity and is entering into an objective space which is objective for everyone, just as mathematics is objective—in spite of the fact that the burden of proof is a purely inward matter. The mistake that people who believe in their illusions make consists in that they are not able to maintain their power of resistance to the world of illusions for long enough, that belief enters in too early in what they are experiencing, that they do not for a sufficiently long time say to themselves about their experiences: This appears initially to be only a reflection of myself, and only when I have stripped away everything of a subjective nature from myself—as I have to do in the case of mathematics—will I enter into the sphere of objective reality.

Thus the objection that with spiritual-scientific experiences one is dealing with something of a subjective nature falls away. One has just as little to do with anything subjective as in the case of mathematical truths. When spiritual science is communicated, there is actually no question of providing proofs. If this question arises, one needs above all to understand the nature of proof. If it had never happened that someone had seen a whale, no one would be able to prove that whales exist. From all the knowledge that he has, he would never be able to prove the existence of a whale; for a whale is a fact, and facts cannot be proved but can only be experienced. A logical point of quite some significance is being made here, but one must first be convinced about its importance.

From this same standpoint, it is not the concern of spiritual-scientific communications to provide proofs of the existence of the supersensible world or, for example, of the immortality of the soul, but something altogether different. Those who have been involved for a sufficiently long time in the genuine pursuit of spiritual research will come to be convinced of this. It is not a question of a logical spiritistic tendency but of learning to know, and communicating, supersensible facts. If the spirit-researcher has, through the soul-development previously described, come to be able to survey the life of the soul between death and a new birth, what he then does is to communicate the facts that he has to present as regards the life of the soul in the time between death and a new birth, communicate what he experiences in the supersensible world. It is a matter of communicating experiences, or facts, that he passes through or traverses in his soul.

One can also say what results with the help of these communications. When it is shown how the soul continues to be a self-contained entity when the parts of the body disintegrate, how the soul then undergoes certain processes, how it experiences something in a purely supersensible world and gathers the forces for a new life in order to enter again into physical existence, when this is stated in all its details, it is indeed being shown how the soul lives when it passes through the portal of death. Then facts are being referred to. This is a matter of referring to facts, of communicating facts rather than an abstract proof.

Now one might say: Such learning about these facts only has significance for someone who can perceive the spiritual world, someone who has a developed soul. Oh, such an objection appears to be highly convincing, and it should definitely not be thrust aside. But anyone who knows the real life of the soul will also acquire a completely different relationship to this objection to what many people think. So we need to raise the question: Are we inwardly convinced in ordinary life when someone gives us abstract proofs of something? Let us take an example—shall we say, the picture of the *Sistine Madonna*. Someone who has no idea of what lies in such a picture comes before this image. Another person is beside him and begins to try to convince him of what is in the picture; while the one who listens understands absolutely nothing of what he is saying. He can spend a long time 'proving' that there is something special in this picture; the person listening is unable to believe his proofs. For what really matters is not that one produces proofs but, rather, that the listener has the possibility of believing in these proofs. Someone else stands in front of the picture; a second person comes up and speaks to him, and the listener now has the possibility of perceiving something that is being expressed through the picture. Then through what he has recognized, the other awakens within him what enables him to believe that it lies in the picture. This other person may not perhaps have been speaking in such a way as to prove something. He merely describes what is actively present within him, describes only that which speaks within him; and once the listener has grasped in his soul what the other is speaking about and then himself looks at the picture, he then sees something else in the picture, with the result that he knows: it is indeed there in the picture. What matters is not an abstract cogency of proof but that someone comes towards us who knows what lives in the picture, and that we are really able to be receptive to what is in the picture if we have the will to gain an insight into what is there.

This is how it is when someone confronts the world and phenomena relating to humanity, and the spirit-researcher approaches him. Were the spirit-researcher to try to come with abstract proofs, the person who is not in a position directly to experience what the spirit-researcher says in his own soul cannot possibly be convinced by a proof. But the spirit-researcher does it just as the one interpreting the picture of which I have been speaking. He explains what has arisen in his soul, which he has first made an instrument for the spiritual truths that stand in the background of spiritual and human life. He gives the facts that he has experienced. And if the other person is in a position to be able to receive these concepts and facts into his whole life, he now sees the world in such a way that, through what the spirit-researcher has to say, this becomes the content of his own soul.

Of course, it cannot always happen like that. If the spirit-researcher—the one who has spiritual experiences—comes to the listener with quite obscure assertions which for him may well be truths that he has experienced, if he tells him—and he may have experienced much in the spiritual world—about all the beings that are there and what they do, the listener—who may be hearing it for the first time—is not in the least obliged to believe what he hears. He will not, and cannot, believe it. Why is he unable to believe it? Because the gulf between what he experiences in his soul and what such a spiritual seer has experienced in his soul is too great.

It would be equally unjustified if someone believed he could say that in thirty years a new world saviour or a new messiah will come and be expected, and who will impart great truths of a quite particular kind. This person could only make such an assertion to another person who had not been prepared for it if he had no respect for the human soul and for the achievements of human culture. But there is a way of doing this quite differently, by taking up what every unprejudiced person can follow up to a certain point. Thus it must again be stated that the objection that spiritual research is valid only for someone who, because of his developed soul, is able to enter the spiritual world is unjustified. This is not correct. One can undertake research into the spiritual world only if one makes one's soul into an instrument for perceiving it. But one is, so to speak, obliged to clothe what one experiences there in such concepts as can, in accordance with the cultural circumstances of the time, be understandable for every human individual who approaches them without prejudice and does not resist them through, for example, a presumed or false erudition. Hence it is, far rather, a question of *how* the facts of clairvoyant consciousness are communicated to an age than *that* such facts are communicated.

One can, for example, experience when someone confesses to have read only *one* book and then believes himself entitled to make a judgement and to be able to say: These spirit-researchers always begin to use the word 'esoteric' when concepts elude them. But it could also be the case that with the person concerned who says something of this kind, the word esoteric always has the consequence that his concepts become empty of meaning, so that the word 'esoteric' has a numbing effect upon his thoughts. Thus if someone puts up a resistance in this way and does not call upon what is within his soul in order to enable the results of spiritual research to work upon himself, then—as we saw last week—it is completely natural that the most fundamental objections against spiritual research will be put forward. But if the soul devotes itself in an unprejudiced way to what spiritual research gives, the healthy human understanding—healthy, unprejudiced thinking—is sufficient in order to share in the experience not of what fades from view in the unschooled soul but of what can be understood by it. For how does every human soul relate to the spirit-researcher, who has a judgement about certain specific facts of the supersensible world because he has ventured into it? Each soul relates to the soul of the spirit-researcher as a germinal essence of life to life that is fully developed; and in the same way that in a germinal essence, for example in an egg, the complete living being is already contained, so in every soul is there present what only the spirit-researcher can ever say to this soul. Just as in the undeveloped germinal essence it can also be shown how the individual comes forth from it, so can the individual soul which receives the results of spiritual research that have been shared with it gain insight in a germinal way, but with a complete power of conviction, into the spiritual worlds.

Hence there is never any foundation for accusing someone who relies not merely upon his intellectual power of logical ingenuity but upon the full power of his soul that he must be a gullible person if he lets himself be drawn into what the spirit-researcher has to say. The intellect alone will not be able to accept it. Thus it is actually possible to test spiritual science (as opposed to accepting it on authority); this has always been so and it will always continue to be possible.

It should be pointed out that I didn't call today's lecture 'On What Foundation can Spiritual Science be Proved?' but 'On What Foundation is Spiritual Science Based?', that is: Where does it come from, and how can the human soul acquire a relationship to it? This relation will for many people be really difficult to find, for the reason that many objections against this spiritual science seem to carry weight. How should it not have weight—and here I again come to a point where I have to speak abstractly and more uninterestingly—when someone says: The spirit-researcher maintains that in his supersensible consciousness he can follow the soul to the time beyond birth or conception, how it lives between death and the next birth and how it then makes its way into the present life. Now one can indeed show—it might now be objected—how certain qualities that the soul develops during life are fashioned in childhood or before birth in the body of the mother! Perhaps for many people there is nothing among the objections against spiritual research that has such weight as just this objection. Those who have often heard such lectures will know how I also make such objections myself, as for example in the Bach family there have been so many musicians of varying degrees of talent, so that one might with a certain justification make the point that a person receives that which makes him a musician purely through the physical line of inheritance. Thus one can make the point that it is through heredity or through acquisition during life that what a person later manifests as his particular qualities and as his individuality comes to belong to him. Oh, such an objection, if one lives with it and abandons oneself to its suggestive power, is very significant; and every spirit-researcher will understand that there are people who are unable to free themselves from it and who are very strongly influenced by the force of what is put forward in this regard.

But there is something else that belongs to this matter of being impressed by the cogency of arguments, namely the awareness that there can be causes, correctly identified causes, which nevertheless do not cause anything, which are not actually the reason that something arises. I am saying something that is apparently very paradoxical, and for someone who allows the weight of spiritual-scientific facts to work upon his soul it is unnecessary to be drawn into this. But the point at issue here is that, in responsiveness to the age in which we are now living, we develop an awareness of what can show us from a philosophical standpoint that there can be causes which nevertheless do not cause anything.

Why does a hen have feathers, a beak or this or that property of its body when it comes into being? Someone can surely say: It has inherited these from the parental hen, and the causes for the particular form of the beak and so forth are the inherited characteristics that we find in that hen from which the feature in question derives. But one needs to see that something else of significance is involved when the qualities of having feathers, of having a particular beak and so on which are possessed by the mother hen also appear in the daughter hen: something may be a correctly identified cause, but it is necessary that one particular germinal essence among others arises if the causes can become 'causes'. What matters is not that one refers back from what follows to particular causes but that one shows to what extent the causes also have been able to become causes.

Here we are standing at a point where spiritual science out of its own facts can acquire a relationship with, for example, Darwinism. No one who is not a presumptuous but a serious spirit-researcher will quarrel with the facts and serious observations of Darwin and Darwinians. He will even agree when Darwin asks:[20] Why does the kitten snuggle up to someone when he comes close to it? The researcher indicates that it has already been snuggling up to its mother on the bed, and one sees from this that the later event is connected with the earlier one. One can refer to the causes as to how a person has this or that quality which he has perhaps received through the mother before he was born. One can make such statements; but one has not said anything about the extent to which the causes have now become causal elements. Everything that can be said by a world-conception that is seemingly firmly based on the ground of natural science, which can be explained through inherited characteristics and so forth, is indeed readily accepted by spiritual research; and anyone of this persuasion who raises objections is usually living under the presupposition that what they say is not acknowledged. They are acknowledged, but the other party does not realize that causes have first to become causal elements, so that what is at issue is therefore something at a much deeper level than he realizes. This is generally the case today, that people always only judge what spiritual science endeavours to draw forth from the depths of existence on the superficial level that they are themselves able to survey the world. If this were not always happening, articles like the one that appeared last Sunday in the *Berliner Tageblatt*,[21] which by its own admission is based only on a single book, would not have to be written. I should, by the way, like to ask what one would say to someone who had made a conclusive judgement on, for example, chemistry based only on a single book? But this is what our contemporaries do. One might say that spiritual research has weighty reasons to feel substantiated in the present time.

For those who have been listening for some while to these lectures, I should probably say that much has been said here from a philosophical background. Whoever recognizes this may perhaps come to the judgement that many philosophers must have supplied proofs for the immortality of the human soul. I must myself admit that I have never felt really comfortable with what has been put forward from the philosophical standpoint as regards proofs for the immortality of the soul or for a supersensible world; for what philosophers mostly have in mind are only the concepts of things. Thus with respect to the human ego philosophers themselves merely have the concept of the ego. However, it should be just as clear that nothing real can be deduced from the concept of the ego as it is clear that a painter who has barely painted at all cannot paint a picture. One should be equally clear about the fact that the image of the ego says nothing for the ego itself. Anyone who becomes involved with spiritual science will see that a conviction of the reality of the ego is acquired through something entirely different, namely through the whole path of the ego's continuing existence after death.

Thus what innocently trusting philosophers adduce along these lines cannot lead one to feel at ease. But from what those who as opponents make such powerful denouncements put forward, anyone who looks at things more deeply acquires a really good proof for the nature of the ego; for there are philosophers who say that they could understand the ego as nothing more than a summation of all possible physiological etc. activities. One then sees that these researchers say all manner of things, but what they say has no possible relationship to an ego. They are in this respect along the same lines—although in an opposite sense—as those who want to explain the phenomena of life through the life-force; for just as the life-force is superfluous to requirements, so not only is nothing explained by the explanations that are put forward for the life of the soul but they are equally superfluous when it comes to a true investigation of the soul. It then becomes apparent that such would-be interpreters actually leave the soul in peace and do not come anywhere near it, so that therefore the soul remains intact and proves to be something that outward explanations are unable to approach. Only if in the consciousness of the time the feeling arises that one cannot judge spiritual science superficially but only through an intensified study of it will all purely external judgements about spiritual science cease to be able to carry any weight.

As it is with scientific objections, so also with the objections that were put forward in the first lecture in a moral or religious respect against spiritual research. When, for example, it is said that it is infinitely more worthy if someone does something good out of pure selflessness (with the view of being annihilated in death), out of the insight and the will that the good that is done passes over into the general whole, than if he does it in view of a compensating balance in ensuing earthly lives, such a judgement has absolute validity and should not be quarrelled with. It is true when it is said that a person does something good purely out of egotism if he believes that through karma he will as a kind of reward be the recipient of something beneficial in a new earthly life, or if he refrains from an evil action because it could manifest itself as a kind of punishment in the new life. It is certain that one can view such an assertion as grounded in egotism and that one can therefore say with full entitlement: What spiritual research is alleged to say about man would therefore promote an egotistical quality among human beings.

Schopenhauer once rightly said—you know that I do not by any means always agree with him—that 'it is easy to preach morality but difficult to implement it'.[22] What does it mean to implement morality? It means to bring about a state of soul through which a person can accomplish a moral action. Anyone who has experience of people knows that it is not only easy to preach morality but also largely futile; for people are very good at knowing all about moral principles—and very bad at acting on them. If it were merely a question of listening to moral preaching, there would be far more moral people than is actually the case.

Someone might say for instance: Let us take a parental couple who make every effort to encourage their children to become decent and capable people. For, so say the parents, if we make them into decent and capable people they will be able to be a support for us in old age, and we will be able to derive all sorts of benefits from them. If the parents bring their children up with this in mind, it is a highly selfish point of view to have. But let us suppose that the children do become respectable citizens, so that they are decent and capable people when they have grown up. Then the parents have, to be sure, done something egotistical but they have not themselves been preaching morality but have established it; and it could turn out that, if they make their children into capable people and the children then later manifest something quite different than they would have imagined, they may arrive at quite another ethical attitude. This would also be a case of the parents establishing a moral attitude rather than preaching about it.

Let us suppose that someone may not have had the opportunity to think in terms of a compensatory balance for wicked deeds in his next life. But by performing actions under the influence of such a perspective of karma, he gradually develops a moral view of the world. It will be established out of human nature. To be sure, someone who is still at a lower moral level will act out of an egotistical view of karma; but a person who has arrived at a higher standpoint and therefore has a higher attitude towards karma will be capable of fulfilling selfless moral demands.

Thus what matters is that one does not refer abstractly to something by giving expression to an egotistical notion of karma but that one shows how it leads a person towards a higher development. This could be further explained by showing how spiritual research is directed towards the true reality of human nature. If someone were to raise the other objection that many people might say to themselves: I have future earthly lives before me, so I need to become a decent person only in later lives; now I still have time, now I can still be a disreputable person—this would be an objection that can also be countered theoretically. But in order to approach it in the right way, one needs to be aware of the practical implications. One must know that someone who is of the view that he does not yet need to be a decent person but will become so only in his next life has through such an intention exerted an influence upon his next life. If he does not decide to become a decent person, he will not have the necessary basis for his next life either. He therefore now acquires the capacity in order that he may subsequently become a decent person; he takes steps to gather together the forces for this. Thus little by little it might become possible again to speak about the justified moral objections.

The religious objection can also be taken into account. People say that spiritual research needs to explain that in every soul there is a spark of the divine and that a human being increasingly develops this divine spark from life to life. A spark of divinity therefore comes to dwell within the human breast.

I tried to show how one may relate to this matter and how one may present it in its true perspective in the first scene of my Mystery Play *The Soul's Probation* (1911).[23] It is true that through such an interpretation what may be called the religious principle—the feeling of dependence on the divine world outside which man stands, the childlike looking up to this divinity external to himself—is lost. But one should also acknowledge that which can be said from the other standpoint, that a person can fully see that the divine world has implanted a spark within him which he must experience and must bring to full development; that he can indeed come to see that he bears within him a divine spark, and if he leaves it undeveloped it will wither away! This sense of connection with the divine together with the necessity of having to develop this spark is an impulse of an infinitely much greater strength than any other religious impulse.

Anyone who involves himself with spiritual science will see that there is never any question of antagonism towards any religious confession. People think that because religious faiths and denominations are so eager to oppose spiritual science, spiritual science will also oppose them. But a similar situation prevails here as with the previously characterized scientific objections: spiritual science is not hostile to the intentions of any religious faith, for its concern is with the relation of the human soul to the supersensible worlds, while religion has to do with the relation to the individual soul.

Anyone who is really able to see this will understand how it is absolutely possible for someone to engage in spiritual research despite being involved in a religious faith of his own choosing. However, as spiritual science becomes established through becoming accepted by the world, it will be able to give man what one may call a deepened conception of the life of the soul, both of the soul-life of the individual and of the interaction between individual souls. Anyone who is able to convince himself only to a small extent that all outward human interaction can only be an outward picture of how souls relate to one another will have an insight into the immeasurability of what results for the soul if it comes to understand how the individual soul relates to other souls, how the individual soul can relate to another soul when it has rightly grasped the nature of the destiny of one soul with respect to another in the life between death and the next birth, what the destiny of an individual soul is, what it means to be separated from another soul, what it means to acquire a new relationship to the departed soul if the soul that has remained here is able to know something of the supersensible world. New light will be shed on all human knowledge and all other areas of human life when that which can be derived for each individual soul from the depths of the supersensible world can become incarnate in human souls. The recognition, perceiving and understanding of spiritual truths is not merely a matter of thinking about reality but of becoming livingly part of it.

This has not only been recognized in recent times by spiritual science but has actually been recognized wherever people have spoken out of a real knowledge of the spiritual world. I say what I have to say regarding the place of spiritual research with respect to those who reject it without really knowing much about it not on my own behalf but on behalf of Johann Gottlieb Fichte. If there is much of a serious—perhaps for many, wounding—nature in what he says, one should bear in mind that it comes from a man who, with full enthusiasm for spiritual research, wished to proclaim his anger towards all those who, without really wanting to acquire an insight into spiritual research, reject it and think they have to attack it. Fichte makes the following stern pronouncement:[24]

> All they can do is to pour their enmity upon that conviction which they find so shameful of a higher aspect in man and all those phenomena that would seek to confirm that conviction; they must do everything they possibly can to keep these phenomena away from them and to suppress them; they battle for their life, for the finest and most intimate root of their life, for the possibility of continuing to endure. All the fanaticism and all the rage associated with it has, from the beginning of the world to this day, derived from the principle: if the opponents are right, I am a miserable wretch of a human being. If this fanaticism can attain to fire and sword, it attacks the hated enemy with fire and sword; if these are not accessible there remains (this is still also applicable to our present time) the tongue which, if it does not kill the enemy, is nevertheless capable of powerfully laming its activity and outward influence. One of the most used and favoured tricks with this tongue is this, that they confer a generally hated name upon the thing that they specifically hate in order thereby to decry it and surround it with suspicion. The lasting power of these tricks and appellations is inexhaustible and is constantly augmented, and it would be futile to aim for any kind of completion. I shall call to mind here just one of the most usually hated names: that whereby people say that this teaching is mysticism.
>
> Observe first and foremost in intention the form of that accusation that, in the event that an unprejudiced person would reply: Well then, let us accept that it is mysticism and mysticism is an erroneous and dangerous doctrine, so let him say his piece and we shall listen to him; if he is mistaken and dangerous this will have every opportunity to become obvious—those people would, in accordance with the categorical decision that they believe that they have dismissed us with, have to answer: there's nothing further to listen to; for a long time, probably from well before you were born, mysticism has been decreed

> as heresy by the unanimous resolutions of all our reviewing councils and subjected to excommunication.

This is what Johann Gottlieb Fichte says. Fichte expresses himself in a way that can also have validity today about the relationship of spiritual research, let us say to those who want to trust only their senses and want to have the world arranged in accordance with what their senses impart to them. Fichte compares such people (although this comparison is perhaps not wholly justified), those who would trust only their senses and do not want to admit that there is a more adequate knowledge of truth, with the deaf and dumb and those who are born blind, who have also not wanted to acknowledge sounds and colours if those who can see speak to them about such phenomena. Now someone who is blind and deaf cannot be compared with those who do not want to accept what can be given through clairvoyant research, because every soul is capable of finding a relation to supersensible truths. But Fichte says:[25]

> That one also cares for the deaf and dumb and those who are blind from birth and has thought out a way of educating them is worthy of gratitude—that is, from the deaf and dumb and the blind. But if one were to apply this manner of instruction to education in general, also for those who are born healthy, on the grounds that there could also be some among them who were deaf and dumb and born blind, and one were certain that one had seen to everyone's needs; if the person who can hear were to speak just as laboriously without any respect for his hearing and to learn to recognize the words on people's lips like someone who is deaf and dumb, and the person who can see were to read letters through touch without any respect for his vision, this would earn very little thanks from the healthy; although of course this would immediately be resolved as soon as the arrangements for the lessons open to everyone were made contingent on properly seeing to the needs of the deaf and dumb and those born blind.

If one were wishing to make an objection to what Fichte is saying, one might perhaps remark that it would not even work with those who are born blind and the deaf and dumb. But if it were a matter of those who trust only in the senses and their reasoning power to come to think of how the world might be fashioned, they would not view this as those who can see perceive it. They would curse and swear and reject all spiritual interpretation of the world other than their own, while regarding what they say about the world as beyond reproach. They would laugh scornfully if it were put to them that only someone who knows about such a matter should speak about it, and that those who know nothing about it should keep silent. The main motivation for all who deny the validity of spiritual research is simply that they know nothing of it. Logically it would be a basic requirement that only someone who knows about something should be entitled to speak about it; but such motivating factors leading to people rejecting something of which they are ignorant are used in our time to reject a spiritual-scientific conception of the world.

However, anyone who is able to experience in his soul what was said in the first lecture and does not need to await the objections that he may experience in himself and is capable of identifying in his spiritual life will always find a path towards making a beginning with spiritual research, so that what I have expressed in the first scene of *The Soul's Probation* may become a guiding principle. Through this it may be possible for the knowledge that can be imparted from the supersensible worlds for all that we may hope for in life, for our strength in what we do in life, for our sense of certainty in life and for everything that we need for a worthwhile human existence, to be brought together in the whole fabric of our consciousness. Everything that can be said, what one can say by way of uplifting the soul, of enlivening it and imbuing it with feeling, can be summarized in the words: You are not alone with your thinking, feeling and will. As you live with your body in the substances that are spread out in the entire universe, so are you living with your thinking, feeling and will in something that is disseminated in the entire cosmos, in the widths of space. This means that the words that I have brought to expression at the point previously indicated in my Mystery Play can become a conviction:

In your thinking cosmic thoughts are living,
In your feeling cosmic forces are weaving,

In your willing cosmic beings are working.
Lose yourself in cosmic thoughts,
Experience yourself through cosmic forces,
Create yourself from beings of will.
End not in cosmic distances
Through dreaming play of thought—
Begin in widths of spirit,
And end in the depths of your own soul:
You will find aims of Gods
Knowing yourself in you.[26]

Lecture 3

BERLIN, 14 NOVEMBER 1912

THE TASKS OF SPIRITUAL RESEARCH FOR BOTH PRESENT AND FUTURE

Spiritual science, as it is meant here in these lectures, does not wish to be something that springs from the arbitrary whim of this or that person and is accordingly based on the subjective idea of an individual or several people but, rather, a spiritual conception of the world that involves itself with a certain necessity in the needs and demands of our time, in so far as this time is a recognizable product of the evolutionary history of mankind. Only if a world-conception is in a sense demanded by its time can it lay claim with a certain justification to those confident words that were spoken in the first lecture of this winter series. Only on such terms can it be said on its behalf: However much hostility may be directed against it from one direction or other, if it contains something of the nature of truth it can rely on the fact that truth, however hard people try to bury it will always find cracks and crevices through which it becomes more widespread in the cultural life of mankind.

We shall now try not with vague generalizations but with concrete facts to indicate how in the course of the last few centuries, and especially in recent times right up to the present, the seeking human soul has been steadily developing towards what the spiritual science that is being advocated here wants to be for the questing human soul.

Anyone who feels inwardly compelled today to seek explanations of life's riddles in order to imbue his life with strength and certainty surely cannot fail to pose questions concerning what natural science—which, far from being unappreciated by spiritual science is fully recognized by it—has come to promulgate. Countless people today do, after all, believe that it will depend on a further development of scientific questions, on scientific research, whether it will—by bringing together these scientific facts and laws—also become possible to arrive at a world-view which gives man insight into what lies behind the phenomena that he can perceive with his senses, that he can comprehend with his intellect and with which he feels connected in his existence—phenomena that he endeavours to recognize in order that he can acquire a real understanding of the destiny of his soul and of its work in the world as a whole.

In the light of such a longing and such a hope, it should be said that in the course of human evolution the relation of the soul to what outward science is able to represent has completely changed, as exemplified in the fact that the relationship that we can have to science with respect to questions of the soul is able to show us that our time should be characterized not simply as a 'time of transition' (to use a trivial and frequently employed term) but one that as regards spiritual research is eminently a new beginning. We need only to recall the example of a great personality who, like many others of his kind, has contributed to bringing spiritual culture forward, namely Kepler, who is the actual great fashioner of the Copernican world-conception,[27] whence many questions of our modern conception of the world are nevertheless raised.

Even though not everyone has a devotion to spiritual science, surely there is no one who would not be able to say that through such achievements as those of Kepler's mankind has succeeded in experiencing the movements of the heavenly bodies with the pure objectivity of science and its laws. And how—someone might say—can, additionally, the belief exist that these movements of the heavenly bodies are in some way ruled by spiritual beings to whom spiritual science seeks to refer, by spiritual beings who stand behind the material world and its laws, since everything can, after all, be explained in a mechanical way! What is the need for spiritual forces of whatever kind standing behind these physical laws?

Such a claim appears highly persuasive, and one can indicate that it was precisely the release from long-established prejudices of the old spiritual world-conceptions that people such as Kepler achieved through the explanations that they gave of the movements of the heavenly bodies in space from purely physical laws. But if we study Kepler himself objectively in his particular soul-qualities and without historical prejudice, we find, remarkably, that everything that guided Kepler's gaze to the celestial spaces and gave him his real inner impulses to discover his great, mighty laws emanated from the awareness of being embedded with his soul in spiritual archetypes of existence, in the influence of spiritual beings who fill the heavenly spaces and exert their influence through time. It was clear to him that what he ascribed to the planetary movements as 'laws' could be instilled within him only through the laws being the thoughts of divine-spiritual beings. If we investigate what these impulses that Kepler had were based on, we would have to say that they had their origin in that the whole course of human evolution has always maintained the connection of the human soul with the soul-spiritual domain; and in Kepler's time the existence of such a domain was still naturally accepted as part of traditional, general belief as a means of inspiring and giving wings to the soul and engendering wakeful thoughts within it.

But who could deny that this quality that stood so clearly in the background of Kepler's creative work has in the course of recent centuries gradually faded from view through what has arisen from it, so that today the human soul can very easily believe that Kepler's laws and everything that has come into existence in this way could be used as proof against the acceptance of a divine-spiritual world. If we survey the period from Kepler through the centuries to our own time, we see how that which is still born from the consciousness of man's connection with the divine-spiritual realm increasingly itself obliterates this consciousness, and how a time is approaching—empowered and enhanced by the achievements of natural science, by the emergence of significant knowledge from the scientific sphere—when the human soul will, because of the abundance of this scientific material and of what has been discerned on a material level, gradually become incapable of ascending to the spiritual domain. One could say: The way that our intellectual development has unfolded in recent centuries can be characterized such that the increase in what it has brought forth is great and worthy of admiration, but that the possibility of the human soul being able to gain an insight into a spiritual world on the basis of these achievements has, precisely through the abundance and the nature of these achievements, been well-nigh destroyed.

We can come to see this if, for instance, we consider the way that Goethe, with his manner of researching into the processes of nature, was positioned in the whole ideological framework of his time. It is interesting how, for example, Herman Grimm,[28] this brilliant and at the same time profound student of Goethe's work, feels himself to be obliged to characterize Goethe's place in the scientific developments of his time. Herman Grimm asks: How did people in the centuries before the time of Goethe think about man's relationship to nature?

Anyone who knows these centuries will admit that Herman Grimm is right: they differed from the later view that man stood on the Earth and people believed themselves authorized, in connection with the nature of animals, plants and so on, to view man as something like a conclusion of the whole of the rest of earthly and, indeed, world creation; that people believed themselves to be entitled to say: The meaning residing in the whole of evolution is that one can, if one looks upon stone, plant and animal, recognize how an inner being has gradually evolved, already having man in view, in order to put everything else at the disposal of man and his own purpose. How far there was still an intention to subscribe to the Mosaic story of Creation is not the point. But this conviction was indeed present: to see in all kingdoms of the world something like an impulse that already includes man and makes everything else merely the preparation whereby man, who has been spiritually there from the beginning, is made the pinnacle of the whole of Creation.

What was it that gradually developed from this? Firstly—as Herman Grimm also says—astronomy began. The Earth became an insignificant cosmic body in the universe and man's position on the Earth was such that, without any previous antecedents in the other kingdoms, he had arisen as a necessity of nature, so that he was not justified in associating his significance with the whole origin of the created world. Geology assumes that vast periods of time have elapsed before man appeared on the Earth which, in a scientific sense, would by no means show any evidence that the purpose of all this was to prepare for a future appearance of humanity. In a certain sense one may call Goethe a radical natural scientist. I have frequently mentioned here that through his own scientific discoveries his endeavour was to separate out from opinions about the outward structure of man's being what could distinguish him from the other organisms of the Earth, and one may call Goethe an evolutionist before Darwin and the other proponents of the theory of evolution in our time. But Herman Grimm correctly points out how Goethe did not allow himself to accept that, behind where Darwinism sees nothing more than material processes, he could perceive a spiritual world that spiritually evolves in all material processes, so that man comes to find his place there.

We have a remarkable saying of Goethe's[29] that makes us so clearly aware that, although he was so thoroughly scientific in orientation, he was at pains to place man at the summit and crown of spiritual existence. He says: What in the end are all the millions of stars in the world for if a human eye is not eventually able to perceive them, and then observe them and receive them into his being? And not without justice. If we peruse all these scientific facts and laws, there is much that can substantiate the right to pose the question: Where in this outer world can we find something other than man that could become for us the grounds for the supposition that the spirit holds sway in all living and lifeless things? Where, if we consider man himself scientifically once it has been ascertained that the life of the soul is bound up with the processes of the brain, do we find an indication regarding thinking of soul-existence outside the confines of birth and death?

One needs today only to turn to one of the more significant and renowned philosophers, for example the world-famous Wundt,[30] and one will everywhere find—when such philosophers base their work on natural-scientific research—that certain conclusions, certain results are drawn from scientific facts and that the philosophers always—so far as I can see—arrive at a conception of the spiritual, but that in the moment when it would be a matter of taking hold of the spiritual domain they are compelled to grind to a halt. Why is this? For the simple reason that the whole manner of thinking that has developed with the support of scientific research and accords precisely with scientific facts yields no possibility of finding the path within these habits of thinking, within this whole manner of research, from matter and its laws to real spiritual happenings and their essential nature, because at every point the thread of thought breaks off. Why did it not break off with Goethe? Because Goethe was still imbued with impulses that had come as primal elements in the evolution of mankind, because there still lived in him something of what has remained from the historical past, from ancient spiritual perceptions (which we shall come to later), and because his soul was in a certain sense not as yet devoid of what had come towards the soul in a direct spiritual path in the course of the centuries when its outward perspective was coloured by the things of the material world.

But our time evolved rapidly, and hence through its rapid development in those who structured their habits of thought in accordance with natural-scientific research there is hardly anything left of what was still present in Goethe. We have therefore experienced that Darwin[31] has displayed the inter-relationships of living beings more fully and searchingly than Goethe, but nevertheless in the whole significance and manner of his research he was unable to go beyond a certain point. Whereas in the whole nature and significance of his research Goethe saw the spirit behind outward phenomena, the Darwinians—not Darwin himself!—were obliged to conceive of that which did not prevent Goethe from coming to the spirit as an obstacle to approaching the spiritual domain in some way.

Thus we can understand that those who see their real hopes for an outlook on the world [as lying] in modern science are inevitably largely disappointed. To be sure, something of what existed amongst mankind is not so easily lost. We can experience in the most recent times that even serious researchers who wish only for science are by no means of the opinion that this science must present only outward facts but could very well serve as a means of substantiating the ongoing course of a world-wisdom that lives in material things. It is interesting that a historian from the school of Ranke, Lord Acton,[32] was able to say as a history teacher to his listeners in the course of an important university address in Cambridge in 1895: I hope that the whole way that historical facts are described will reveal the working of a divine world-wisdom. Yes, Lord Acton even spoke in those days of the influence of the 'Risen One' in history.

Thus we see that, from the times when the existence of a spiritual world was accepted as a matter of course, there extends into our time a continuing thread of research, a living echo of the whole scientific thinking of such a set of convictions, that in this sense of being carried by what emanates from former times the soul continues to feel itself to be imbued by the world of spirit. But it is equally true that anyone who forms a strong link today with the thought-forms of natural science and, for example, takes up the idea that the various soul-functions have their corresponding expressions in processes of the brain or other parts of the nervous system, that such a person may, by working through a series of facts, easily say to himself: Yes, for what man is enabled to think, feel and experience in the material world there are always factors that the researcher can identify; but as for what might lie before and after it for the soul, natural science tells me nothing.

How widespread is the error that, because natural science is unable to reach beyond its observation of facts and their laws to the spiritual domain, it must therefore also reject all notions of this domain! And yet it is again characteristic of the whole situation of the modern world-conception that those who base their ideas on the standpoint that we can arrive at a conception of the world only by bringing together scientific facts and laws are forever warning about jumping to conclusions, about forming hypotheses on the basis of a few facts, in order to draw conclusions as to how the life of the soul is linked to this or that, how the world situation is and so on.

Such a warning emerged only recently at a significant place. At this year's gathering of naturalists, the leading naturalist Wettstein gave a talk about biology,[33] about the science of life in the way that it can be utilized for the [prevailing] world-view, and from the relevant facts he warned about drawing general conclusions as regards this view of the world. But many people nevertheless believe that one should therefore wait for answers to the riddles relating to the life of the soul until science has finished researching the facts. This kind of idea—and to be specific it would have to be voiced by someone wanting to gain insight into the mysteries of the soul and the spirit in order to come to conclusions about them who was wholly immersed in the world of scientific facts—reminds one of a beautiful saying of Goethe: 'In order to understand that the sky is everywhere blue, one does not need to travel round the world'.[34]

I should like to show in concrete terms how the path of the human soul to its mysteries in the spiritual domain is in a certain sense independent from everything that the various laws of natural science, the various laws of learned people, are able to give to the human soul. In order to substantiate this, I should like to refer to the following fact: In the nineteenth century there was a notable philosopher in Munich called Moritz Carrière. He was one of those who tried to understand the world and its phenomena out of a richness not only of thoughts but of real scientific erudition. Through his great work about cultural development,[35] Carrière has indeed shown how he brought together one fact after another of what was taught in olden times in order to understand the passage of the spirit through world evolution. From all such processes Carrière formed a world-view that I am all the more glad to mention because it wholly preceded the development of a true spiritual science, a world-view that out of itself came to an insight of the soul's connection with a spiritual world that is extended through space and time in such a way that there is a connection between that which resides physically in the human body and the substances and forces that are spread out in space and exert their influence in time.

One day Moritz Carrière was shown the manuscript of a simple man, someone who was not in the least learned, who had none of the richness of the erudition through which Moritz Carrière had come to a perception of the connection that has just been described of the soul with the world of spirit. This simple man was called Zeuner,[36] and he was born in 1813. As the result of a life which there is no time to describe here, it came about that Zeuner had to spend many, many months alone; he let himself be carried away by the revolutionary movement, and this led to his imprisonment. But despite his lack of learning, he was a highly sensitive soul. In the manuscript that he showed Moritz Carrière in the 1870s, he relates how in his solitary cell he pondered and pondered, filled only—as befitted the spirit of his time and of those who had surrounded him—with materialistic opinions, but how his soul had become desolate in solitude, how it had suffered from the hunger of having something in which it was unable to believe. Then he goes on to explain how from his cell he heard some remarkable singing that rang forth outside which reminded him of experiences of his early childhood and brought him into connection with other experiences, how this again released a spark of joy in his soul, and how this impulse that was thereby given to his soul—an impulse of inner freshness and activity—released thoughts in this simple, unsophisticated soul that Zeuner now wrote down. And this was the manuscript that he later sent to Moritz Carrière. When one reads it (Moritz Carrière later has it printed), one must say that Carrière was right: Zeuner, by abandoning himself to the soul that in solitude poured forth imperiously from his breast, found something that in the same way represents the soul's connection with the world-spirit, as Carrière was able to portray it after he had a life of erudition and science behind him.

One does not need to travel round the Earth to understand that the sky is blue everywhere. The path to the spiritual domain has quite specifically to be found in a way other than by merely summarizing scientific laws or by drawing conclusions from scientific research. But the debate with natural science has to be a very different one. No world-view can exist today and no world-view may exist—because the needs of the human soul would brush it aside—that would be in contradiction with natural science. Hence it had to be so sharply emphasized in the first two lectures what can be said on the part of natural science against spiritual research and how spiritual science has to relate to this. And it cannot be emphasized often enough that one should feel mistaken with respect to any spiritual-scientific knowledge if one now uses it to oppose a justified result of natural science. But if one again considers this natural science and if one has a sense and a heart for the necessary authority that must flow from it, one will all the more have to indicate what can confuse the soul, what must necessarily confuse it because of the abundance of what is there if it wants to tread the path to the spirit. This, too, I should like to substantiate by means of examples.

I shall draw attention to two researchers who both stand on the ground of the history of evolution, on the ground of natural science. Both researchers conceived of the emergence of separate living organisms from one another as the Darwinians also did, but they excluded man. They were clear that one does not have to apply the laws applicable to the animal world to man, but that just as one must derive his bodily nature from the physical realm, so should one derive his soul-spiritual nature from a soul-spiritual context. They were both completely clear about this. They were just as good at researching nature as they were in their understanding of spiritual matters, but their habits of thinking were dominated by those of natural science. They thought as one thinks as a true natural scientist. How did the one, Mivart,[37] and how did the other, Wallace,[38] a contemporary of Darwin, think about the actual processes of evolution?

Wallace said to himself that man could not so simply be included in the animal kingdom: already for the reason that there is in the outward structure of the brain a considerable difference between man and the most highly evolved apes (even if the comparison is with a primitive person), and because the brain of an ape is—by contrast to the brain of a primitive—far too imperfect for man to have evolved from the ape purely in the direct course of evolution.

The other researcher, Mivart, found that the level of civilization of a primitive person does not differ outwardly from the developmental level of a highly evolved ape. But if one considers the intellectual activities of the primitive and, in contrast, those of the highly evolved ape, one would have to presuppose that—although the brains of both have so much similarity to one another—man does not belong to the animal kingdom. If one again considers the brains, one sees very clearly that man's brain has not evolved from the brain of an ape through adaptation to outward tasks but through civilization it develops all possibilities in such a way that it only appears that everything had been brought about in order that it could become a tool of civilization.

Thus because the brain of an ape and the human brain so strongly differ from one another, one of the naturalists, Wallace, believes that he must accept that there is no relationship between man and the animal kingdom. And for Wallace it was precisely the similarity of the intellectual qualities that was proof for what he was saying. For Mivart, his contemporary, the exact opposite was the case; he was of the view that, if one compares the intellectual qualities of the primitive with the highly evolved ape, there is so great a difference that—on account of this difference—it would be impossible to accept a fundamental relationship between the primitive and the ape.

We therefore see two naturalists, both accustomed to thinking in accordance with natural science, who for opposite reasons pronounce their opinion: the one, because the qualities of the primitive and the highly evolved ape are so similar, the other because they are so different. If, then, two researchers who are both inclined to derive man from a spiritual origin can become so confused by the abundance of facts available as regards their grounds for proof, how is anyone who is even more biased in his prejudices in favour of purely materialistic thinking to be not rendered still more incapable of arriving from the sheer abundance of available facts and laws at a spiritual awareness!

Natural science merely leads us from fact to fact. When we have spiritual science, we can from this spiritual science actually understand natural science and place it in its true light. However, the laws of spiritual science can never be derived from natural science. Thus it will inevitably happen increasingly that the human soul will be drained of spiritual nourishment if it depends on 'scientifically' valuing only what comes from natural science. Natural science will itself achieve its greatness and significance by knowing its own limits.

However, anyone who even to a small extent casts an eye upon human soul-life will soon find that the soul needs answers to the question of the spirit for its strength and confidence and for what it has to do in life. Whereas in former times—we have substantiated this when we spoke of Kepler and Goethe, and we could find other examples—such answers were available to the human soul in the way people experienced the world, this is not the case today; and a new task arises today that we have been able, and will continue, to characterize: the task of spiritual science. Precisely that which has disappeared through the greatness of natural science must again be found independently through spiritual science, in that the paths are shown on which the human soul can attain its spiritual home. Anyone who rightly understands the age in which we are living will, once the background to the present situation has been thus described, grasp the extent of the need and longing that manifests itself increasingly to comprehend the world also out of the spirit and to establish an independent spiritual science alongside natural science.

When we enter into specific issues such as the law of repeated earthly lives that is probably rejected by many spiritual believers today, we see it gradually coming to find its place in modern culture, for example in Lessing's treatise on *The Education of the Human Race*.[39] Again and again we see, even though there is little awareness of this today, how in the nineteenth century inwardly consistent researchers of the soul have been led towards the law of repeated earthly lives, which is alone appropriate as a means of understanding the human soul.

The more that natural science celebrates its great triumphs on the ground of matter, the more does the longing blossom for the spirit to pursue its own paths. I should like to show by means of a further specific example how the course of modern cultural life is such that as though out of itself it leads to what spiritual science wants to be in our time. I want to draw your attention to a thinker and researcher concerning whom I shall be speaking further in the course of these winter lectures, and who is interesting with respect to a yearning for spiritual science, namely Herman Grimm,[40] the art historian. A person with extensive and comprehensive knowledge, he manifests himself to us as one of those in modern times who strongly feel the urge to go beyond a purely natural-scientific view of, in particular, human life but who are held back by the impulses and forces of the age from taking the final step of embracing spiritual science.

Whoever carefully peruses Herman Grimm's writings will see that he seeks a world-principle, though not a dead world-principle but a creative law which the practical historian can adhere to and which must be something different from so-called historical ideas. Ideas are just as little able to create something as—with reference to the image from the last lecture—a painter who has been painted can paint a picture. Ideas are something dead. Only something living can achieve anything. Herman Grimm looked for the living in history, for what is able to work creatively from one age to another, for what in the primal age of humanity created the form of the human soul from impersonal foundations and then magically brought forth its individual achievements from age to age, from one popular culture to another. And what did he think that he had, as such, found? Creative imagination.

There was also a German philosopher, Frohschammer,[41] who viewed imagination in this way not only in historical processes but also as a creative force in nature. Herman Grimm did not—as he wanted to—manage to show how imagination is actually a kind of divine force that lives in the will and brings forth deeds in human history, just as the individual human being calls forth from himself the deeds that his soul accomplishes. What he did was to enunciate in the light of this view that behind historical development there lies the creative imagination, that everything has come about from the creative imagination. But what is the imagination to him? Do we not see in the urge of a researcher to be able to understand the facts a drawing towards something spiritual which, however, is no spirit? For the creative imagination remains a mere abstraction, which is indeed more living than historical ideas but for someone who thinks realistically is nevertheless only an abstraction.

One might say that a researcher such as Herman Grimm is pushing hard at the gate of spiritual science. He cannot remain with outer material facts and external happenings; he sees behind all outer events that which imagination creates, and he objectivises it in what happens in the world. But no one can recognize anything real, a truly creative force, in the imagination. It remains an abstraction; and only if one penetrates to what is no longer an abstraction, to what is spiritual, which is as real as anything sense-perceptible, only if one penetrates to the spiritual facts, which are not ideas that have been written about but are intrinsically real, can one understand how that which is around us is really happening in the world. Thus we see in such a deep thinker how the longing of our time draws him to the spiritual domain, and how the grounds of hindrance that have arisen through the age are so mighty that human beings are unable to come through the gateway to the world of spirit. Do we not see how this spiritual science has tasks for present and future that correspond to the longing, the urgency, the demands of the age?

Let us look at the forces hindering modern souls more precisely! In the longing for the spiritual domain we can recognize so clearly how human beings can—if they have a clear insight into the circumstances of the age—do none other than wish for the spirit and its laws, but how they are as yet unable to reach the world of spirit and are now, as it were, awaiting it. Wherever one looks, one observes the urge towards that which one does not yet know. But one can see very clearly in the nature of the urge that a time will come that is no longer so far away when people will understand that spiritual science is the solution to the longing, to the urge that they have.

Not so long ago it was possible to see in the bookshops on every station a book that was indeed not written by a man who would easily give way to effusiveness of any kind. This book was not the work of an introspective loner, of someone who is unaware of the intellectual and spiritual needs of the age. If spiritual science is wanting to demonstrate its legitimacy, it should not rely on those enthusiasts who, in their sectarian way, want to understand what can help humanity further; but it should indeed make reference to what is expressed in the book in question, *A Critical View of the Age* by Walther Rathenau,[42] which was written by someone who is directly involved in industrial and commercial life and knows how our times really function.

Not that I would want to agree with everything in the book. On every page there is something that I can take issue with, but what does Walther Rathenau say? He presents exactly what I have sought to establish at a somewhat deeper level out of the spirit of what has unfolded in the last century. According to Rathenau, through the advances of natural science a general mechanization of life has come about. Whereas man formerly tried to interpret what presented itself to his senses out of the spirit, he now explains it from a mechanistic standpoint. But the relationship of one person to another has also been mechanized. 'Mechanization' is what has come about through the great advances and the significant achievements of the age. And one can sense—and Walther Rathenau indeed feels this—how the soul becomes barren amidst this intellectual and social mechanicalness, how it gradually becomes empty in the context of such aims, how one can indeed take nourishment from it but, because of this mechanistic quality, cannot assuage its hunger.

What many of the best modern authorities have said is also expressed here: If one stands up for what the soul craves spiritually, one will be able to see that, even if the soul is content with something of an illusory nature, the hunger will become all the more manifest. So we see how a person who is thoroughly in tune with the age writes:

> The age seeks not its meaning and its God, it seeks its soul, which has grown dark in the mingling of blood, in the whirl of mechanistic thinking and desires.
>
> It seeks its soul and will find it; of course, against the will of mechanization. It has been of little account to this epoch to develop the soul-nature in man; it has set out to make the world profitable and, hence, rational, to shift back the threshold of wonder and to conceal what lies beyond. Nevertheless we are as ever before surrounded by mystery; it manifests itself beneath every smooth surface of thought, and from every daily experience it needs but a single step to arrive at the centre of the world. Mechanization has been unable to rob the individual of the three emanations of the soul: love for created things, for nature and for the Godhead; for the life of the collective whole they have been dispersed to the point of insignificance. Human love has sunk down to cold pity and to a duty of care and nevertheless signifies the moral summit of the whole epoch; love of nature became a sentimental pleasure for Sundays; love of God, overshadowed by the ruling operation of mythological, dogmatic rituals, was enlisted in the service of this or that interest and therefore became suspect not merely to ignoble natures. There is probably no single way in which people can render themselves unable to find their souls (if only by having delight in flying). But humanity will not fail to

> keep to the beaten track. No prophets or founders of religions will come, for no individual voice will be heard by this deaf age: otherwise it could still listen to Christ and Paul. No esoteric communities will take over the leadership, for an occult teacher will be misunderstood by the first pupil, never mind the second. No unified art will bring its soul to the world, for art is a mirror and a plaything of the soul, not its originator.
>
> What is greatest and most significant about all this is something very simple. Nothing will happen unless, under the pressure and urgency of mechanization, of lack of freedom, of fruitless battle, humanity will sweep aside the hindrances that impede the growth of its soul. This will happen not through thinking and brooding but through free understanding and experiencing. What many people speak about today and some understand is something that in future many and in the end all will understand: that no power on Earth can stand up against the soul.

In so far as such words express longings, and in so far as our time demands the spirit, one can be wholly in agreement with them. It should only be added: There is a clear sense here that the writer knows what the age needs, but there is a total lack of awareness of what can satisfy this urge and these needs. Also in evidence is a clear judgement that the justified individualism of our time is no longer suitable for receiving an individual religious founder or prophet, or for establishing occult schools on some kind of sectarian basis which seeks to call itself 'esoteric'.

True spiritual science will want neither the one nor the other. True spiritual science knows how the truly esoteric has legitimacy if it does not wish to become exoteric but remains within itself; for it is not a question of what seeks to establish itself as something esoteric but, rather, of what wants to find its place in our time such that it can be accepted by a sound manner of thinking. To this extent the authority of a prophet of whatever kind will not be able to satisfy the age in which we are living, but only a truth that is wholly independent of a human individual and his subjective individuality and to which the human soul can dedicate itself if it so wills. To the extent that this is so, what is here intended with spiritual science tallies precisely with the words of this practical person Walther Rathenau.

But why is it so difficult for people in our time to approach spiritual science? Why is there something like an unscalable wall between the urgency of the age and true spiritual science?

This is another way of showing where the actual hindrances lie. What, for example, would someone say about a natural science that wants to be a 'science' and wants to engage with the needs of the time if the person wishing in this sense to be a natural scientist were always only to answer every question regarding the connection of the physical human body with scientific facts by saying: Whatever aspect of the organization of man's physical body you may want to consider, it corresponds to what you also find outside in nature. Can anyone conceive of a serious natural science that only always answers any question that one may ask: This is nature! Nature is behind the movements of the stars, nature is behind chemical reactions, nature, nature, nature. A mere word! Can one possibly imagine that a person who behaved in this way would be regarded as someone who really knew anything about nature?

Again one can say: The impulses of the human soul to enter the spiritual world have recently become so weak that the urge that manifests itself so actively in our time comes to expression in what in spiritual science would bear a considerable similarity to the situation in natural science if people were always only to cry: Nature, nature, nature! Some important voices are raised who energetically declare that the natural-scientific research of our time must direct man to affairs of the soul. But in demanding this direction of attention towards the soul they do not go beyond emphasizing: 'Man has a soul, there is a soul', and so on; 'Soul, soul, soul—spirit, spirit, spirit', they say, just as the somewhat unsatisfactory natural scientist would say: Nature, nature, nature!

So we see—and the facts that are being stated here are by no means insignificant—how a significant individual of our time gives a lecture at a festive celebration at Harvard University in America about how a general world-conception that leads to the spiritual domain must be born out of natural science: Dr Eliot,[43] a man who stands firmly on the ground of natural science and who is thoroughly knowledgeable about present-day scientific research. I should like to cite a passage from a lecture that has been given at a place of such eminence. Dr Eliot said:

> Men have always attributed to man a spirit distinct from his body, though immanent in it. No one of us is willing to identify himself with his body; but on the contrary everyone now believes, and all men have believed, that there is in man an animating, ruling, characteristic essence, or spirit, which is himself. ...This is something just as real as the body, and more characteristic. ...This spirit, or soul, is the most effective part of every human being, and is recognised as such, and always has been.

Dr Eliot says nothing further, other than referring to the 'soul' in an analogous way to how someone would always only refer to 'Nature, nature, nature'. We have in our time not yet reached the point where the thought-habits with respect to the spirit would sink into the same mould as with nature. In natural science we distinguish oxygen and hydrogen in water, and we do not say: Oxygen and hydrogen belong to 'nature'. This is how we enter into the specific details of nature. Spiritual science similarly has to come to what lives in the soul by way of forces and activities, not only to relate to a 'general spirituality' but to a spiritual world, to a specific realm of the spirit that is distinguished in detail like the individual facts of natural science.

Only when spiritual science comes to contemplate the various facts of the human soul in the way that natural science studies the various facts of the natural world will it be able to give the human soul what it demands. The purpose of the next lecture will be to give an indication of this process. But the main thing is to discuss how in our time there is the urge towards something regarding whose nature and significance people continue to lack clarity, and how the task that awaits spiritual science in our time is to bring a knowledge of the world of spirit, just as natural science brings a knowledge of the facts of nature. And just as natural science considers its task to be that of tracing a substance that is also to be found in the human body as it has evolved out in the world in order to understand the whole context, so will spiritual science consider its task to be that of relating a particular function of the human soul to the spiritual forces and spiritual creative principles out in the universe.

From this it will also recognize how that which lives in the human soul relates to the whole universe, to space and time. Only through this can it arrive at answers to the riddles of immortality and man's destiny between death and a new birth. Abstract references to 'spirit' and 'soul' cannot in general lead to something fruitful. They will always only lead to doubt with respect to the true answers, for example regarding the question of immortality. Only when one sees that there is a connection with something altogether different that is not subject to the transitory course of time will these questions find an answer from spiritual science.

If one bears this in mind, one may indeed say: The tasks of spiritual science for the present and future are similar in nature to the tasks placed before natural science at the dawn of the scientific developments of the modern age. Just as at the time of Copernicus, Galileo, Kepler and so on the old traditions were superseded and the human mind itself was directed towards natural-scientific facts, with the result that a pursuit of this path until our own time has led to a certain abundance of scientific achievements, so must it be the most serious task of our time to establish a spiritual science with a degree of thoroughness and to indicate the paths that the soul has to follow in order to gain access to specific spiritual beings and spiritual facts.

Natural science has not had an easy time of it. It has also had to struggle against obstacles, as we are again experiencing in the case of spiritual science. I have often referred to these obstacles. Thus, for example, Galileo sought to explain to people in his time how throughout the Middle Ages it was believed that the nerves of a human being proceed from the heart, and he wanted to show how the nerves have their source in the brain.[44] Then a friend said to him: This contradicts everything that Aristotle has taught. In spite of the fact that this is not what Aristotle meant, it was believed that the nerves of a human being originate from the heart. Throughout the Middle Ages people did not look at nature itself but simply maintained old traditions and prejudices. So when Galileo demonstrated to a friend by means of a corpse that he should convince himself that nerves issue from the brain, the friend replied: If I look at it for myself, it seems as though the nerves derive from the brain, but this contradicts Aristotle; and when I come in conflict with Aristotle, I believe Aristotle and not nature.

This demonstrates how strong people's prejudices can be. And when later, wholly in accordance with Galileo, Francesco Redi[45] delivered a crushing blow to the prejudice that was still dominant at his time that living beings could develop from something non-living, that lower animals, worms and the like arise from river sludge, when he expressed the principle: 'Something living can only arise from the living' and that it is simply a matter of inaccurate observation if one believes that worms could emerge from river sludge where there is no germinal seed present, he escaped Giordano Bruno's fate only by the skin of his teeth.

Now when today the spiritual-scientific researcher says: If you believe that in a developing child everything that it manifests in a soul sense is conditioned solely through inheritance from its parents and ancestors, your observation is inexact; it derives, far rather, from a spiritual seed that passed through a previous earthly life, was on the Earth and then underwent a life in the spiritual world—when in this way spiritual science refers to a spiritual seed, as Francesco Redi pointed towards a material seed, you are again encountering the prejudices of the age. If today people are no longer burnt at the stake, there are now other means whereby such assertions can be made harmless or at least ridiculous. The way in which the age treats its people does of course change from one epoch to another, but the nature of prejudices remains the same. Similarly, the age in which we are now living is the time for researching spiritual needs, just as the age of the dawn of natural-scientific development was the time for exploring natural-scientific needs. And if natural science has through its fruits brought to mankind a raising of the level of outward culture, the fruits of spiritual culture will be of a completely different nature. They will above all be fruits for the life of the soul.

How does many a person today suffer because of the prejudices of natural science! Thus a human individual may—if he believes in the conclusions of natural science and denies the spirit—quite likely say to himself: I possess individuality of a certain kind; I look at my blood relationships and must recognize that I am the result of the way that I have inherited them. Then a sense of depression, a lack of energy and an inability to battle against destiny afflicts many a soul; for if it is so that a person is merely the result of inheritance, it would then be impossible to keep the baneful influences of inheritance in check, just as it is impossible to prevent from striking someone. But if spiritual science does not remain a mere theory but becomes a power within the soul, so that a soul-essence lives within us for which what we have been given through the line of inheritance is merely an outward garment and which must seek ever deeper and deeper forces within itself, there grows the courage, the hope, the energy wherewith to master and improve that which manifests itself in outward bodily existence as weakness through spiritual forces. Then there is no longer a moment in human life when with respect to the spiritual forces within man one can lack the confidence to overcome outward impediments.

So it is on many levels. Thus merely to believe in the matter in which the life of the soul is said to be entwined is enough to suppress our happiness, our energy, whereas spiritual science, if it becomes a living inner power of the soul, can give us confidence to withstand the mechanization of life. This is another task of spiritual science, that it will create the possibilities in all areas for relating to life in a sure and healthy way. Dr Eliot also in his way promises a science that is sound and healthy. As he is also someone who knows the urge of the soul towards the spirit, while having the attitude of the student of nature who would always speak of 'Nature, nature, nature', he says: Such a new science will not speak of death and sorrow as does the old science, but of life and joy.

I gladly share his view that the soul eagerly awaits a world-conception that is oriented towards 'life and joy', that wants to turn away from and not be overwhelmed by 'death and sorrow', with which old world-conceptions that have specifically confronted man with the riddle of death are mainly preoccupied. I gladly believe that people want to reject death and sorrow. But death and sorrow will come regardless. Human beings are not at liberty to resist to this extent and say that they want to get rid of death and sorrow and want to have life and joy. But death and sorrow will come anyway, and one must be prepared to deal with them; and yet one can only do so if one knows the living spirit that even takes life beyond where outer nature has placed death and sorrow, and which also knows the creative principle in grief, suffering and sorrow. Moreover, we shall see that spiritual science, as it is meant here, is able to view that force of evil which hinders evolution and is at variance with life as something that nevertheless advances world-development and serves life.

One might say: What the truth of spiritual research—where it arises not from the arbitrary whim of an individual but from what a person can recognize today if he rightly comprehends the world that surrounds him through paths of the soul leading to a spiritual knowledge—can signify in the context of world evolution can become apparent by comparing how the spiritual-scientific researcher relates to the natural-scientific researcher at the dawn of the modern age. Let us turn our attention to Giordano Bruno, in whom the world-conception of Copernicus comes most succinctly to expression! How does he stand within his time? He takes up the laws of Copernicus, directs his attention towards the widths of space.[46] Previously there was a world-conception that was wholly reliant upon outward sense-perception. When one hears today that everything is uncertain that has not been investigated by customary science, one could object that this was how science itself was viewed at the time of Copernicus and Giordano Bruno! So long as people relied on what their eyes conveyed to them as regards the starry heavens, they did not have the right view of the outer world-configuration; and it was only when they went beyond outer sense-experience and began to focus on thoughts that through inner energy they found what is today recognized as true.

Only when Copernicus and Giordano Bruno arrived at the point of overcoming the deception of sensory appearance were they able to indicate how mistaken people had hitherto been to believe that the Earth is a fixed point in space around which orbit the Moon, the Sun and the planets, then the sphere of the fixed stars and behind it the so-called eighth sphere, which is the boundary of everything. If you direct your eyes into the celestial spaces, there is no 'eighth sphere', which you put there yourself; but there is the blue firmament, and the widths of space are filled with worlds like ours, and we gaze into a sea of infinity, if we are able to overcome the boundary that we ourselves have set! The overcoming of limits of space was the greatness of the world-view of Copernicus and Giordano Bruno, in that it was recognized: because man's gaze did not extend any further, people believed in an eighth sphere, whereas in truth the widths of space are unlimited.

Mankind stands with respect to spiritual science on exactly the same ground. Just as Giordano Bruno showed that the blue vault of heaven is there only because man's gaze is unable to reach beyond it, so does spiritual science show that human life between birth and death is limited only because the perspective of an ordinary person cannot go beyond this. Just as little as the firmament is a boundary for the contemplation of the world of space, so are birth and death no less a limit for the contemplation of human existence, a limit that we establish because the perception of an ordinary person extends only so far. As through natural science the natural boundary of the world was swept away and cosmic space was opened up, so are the limits of birth and death swept away for man by spiritual science, in that it teaches the eye of the spirit to direct its attention to the life of the soul in eternal duration, in the same way that natural science has in the dawn of modern times directed its gaze into eternity, or, to be more precise, into the infinitude of space. Exactly the same, today as then, though in a different realm.

Just as it is true that natural science, which turned towards outward human life and towards an outward knowledge of it, has yielded infinite advantages and achievements, so is it also true that the perceptive quality of the human soul that extends beyond birth and death and beyond the purely temporal will bring infinite value as regards what the soul needs for its life. For spiritual-scientific research will, if it is rightly carried out, be transmitted to the human soul and will there become life, will engender strength and confidence, will place us in the whole social context and bring to the soul that for which those souls who are beginning to understand even to a small degree are so greatly longing.

It is absolutely true not only in theory but in life and in strength of will that spiritual science will achieve what I have tried to summarize in some words with which I would like to conclude my presentation today—which was intended to show the nature of the spirit, significance and purpose of spiritual science, and what it is to mean for the human soul. We can express the significance and purpose of spiritual science somewhat as follows:

> All that lives in widths of space
> Speaks to the sense of man,
> Transforms itself in course of time.
> The human soul, as knower, enters,
> Unconfined by spatial widths
> And undeterred by bonds of time,
> Into the realm of spirit-land.

Lecture 4

BERLIN, 21 NOVEMBER 1912

THE PATHS OF SUPERSENSIBLE KNOWLEDGE

ALREADY in the introductory lectures to this year's winter cycle I have frequently made reference to the sources of the supersensible knowledge of man which, together with its relationship to the world, is the thematic basis of this whole cycle of lectures. I have indicated that these sources of supersensible knowledge reside in the human soul, in every human soul, as slumbering forces and faculties which can be brought forth in intimate inner experience through appropriate means, so that a human individual can become capable of gaining insight into the spiritual worlds. The development of these faculties will be characterized this evening in broad outline. Further explanations of what I shall present today will be given in the further lectures.

If the object is to present an initial understanding of how the supersensible forces of cognition slumbering in the soul can be called forth, one can always draw attention to a phenomenon or fact that is enacted in the case of every person in the course of twenty-four hours: the alternation between sleep and waking. People usually take little notice of these riddles of life that are a familiar part of everyday life, and the infrequency of this attention and the oppressive feelings that can result readily call forth the longing to resolve such riddles. Some of these more troubling riddles of life will be addressed in the next lecture. Today, however, I shall begin with a riddle that as a matter of fact only eludes attention for its enigmatic quality because the phenomenon in question is so familiar, namely the alternation between sleep and waking consciousness.

In order to maintain ourselves in life we must with every day pass from the state of consciousness to that of unconsciousness. What has actually occurred—we need only to indicate it in layman's language—when someone passes into the unconscious state of sleep? The receptive capacity of the senses ceases, thinking—which is linked to the activity of the brain, in so far as it is engaged in the outer world—ceases. We feel all the activities and all the acts of consciousness that fill our daily lives sinking into the oblivion of sleep. It would be a logical impossibility for anyone judging without prejudice to think that all our conceptions, our feelings, sensations, emotions and passions—indeed, all that we have by way of ideals and ideas—that surge within us from morning to evening in a conscious state pass every time we go to sleep into 'nothingness' as far as our being is concerned—and the following morning again come into being. Only a logical bias can deny that a person's soul-spiritual essence is also present while he is in the unconscious state of sleep.

If today we hypothetically presuppose—the following lectures will justify this presupposition—that while someone is in sleeping consciousness the soul-spiritual core of his being has withdrawn from his physical body and from the forces that enliven it and is living in a spiritual world, it is not improbable that this is the reason why this person whose soul-spiritual essence has withdrawn from his body is unable to perceive his surroundings in the way that he perceives them when in the physical world he avails himself of his eyes, his other sensory tools and the instrument of his brain. It is, I say, not an improbable supposition to think that a person's soul-spiritual forces have the initial purpose of making it possible for there to be a world around him in the ordinary life of the senses and the brain, and that when—as in sleep—he does not have the possibility of perceiving through these instruments, they are too meagre, too weak, actually to behold, feel and think what they might then be able to perceive.

Such a supposition could be proved to be correct only if it was actually possible to draw forth the forces that are supposedly weak from their hidden recesses, that is, if one were in the position to give substance to or concentrate the soul-forces that are in ordinary life 'thin', so that instead of what a person experiences in sleep when he ceases to make use of his senses and his brain a condition could arise that is similar to sleep while nevertheless being in a certain sense completely opposite to it. This condition would have to be similar to sleep in that a person would not forcibly, as in going to sleep, but voluntarily bring about a process of withdrawal from the senses or from the brain through his inner forces, through his will; so that he could make it possible for himself to be fully awake but not to see his surroundings with his eyes or to perceive anything with his other senses and to bring both eyes and the other senses to a state of complete silence. In other words, that he is able likewise to suppress ordinary thinking, that thinking which engages in everyday life through ideas concerning the outward physical world of the senses; while in being able voluntarily to suppress what otherwise enables him to perceive, he would additionally have to be capable of not entering in his soul-spiritual essence into the unconsciousness of sleep but of concentrating forces which are otherwise weak or rarefied, so that he can rightly be active without his body, outside his body.

The question arises whether what has just been expressed can in some way be achieved. This can of course be answered only through what the person concerned brings about on his own account, namely through the fact that he enters into the position of applying to his soul the means whereby what has been characterized occurs. By applying such means to the soul one comes to supersensible knowledge. The path to supersensible knowledge is not one that leads there by outward means, that requires all manner of machinations existing purely in the outer world, but it is an intimate inner path; and everything that must be undertaken for it occurs in the depths of the life of the soul itself.

Now if we are wanting to ascend to the worlds that have the potential to explain to us the outer world in which we live, if, therefore, we want to ascend to the supersensible worlds, there are three stages through which we must pass. A fuller description of these three stages can be found in the book *Knowledge of the Higher Worlds: How is it Achieved?* They can be indicated here only in broad outline. In characterizing these stages I beg you not to become fixed on particular words—partly because the words are habitually used today to mean something quite different, and because these words do not resound well in the thought-habits of the present because they are used for all sorts of things of which one has a vague or imprecise knowledge and also for certain things that one rightly rejects. Thus at times a particular kind of feeling is called forth when one hears these words, and it is easy to see that for the things that are to be spoken about here it has to be as it is, for our language is there for the outer world. Hence the words for what is to be characterized are derived from the outer world and cannot ever be precisely suitable for what lies outside the outer world of the senses for which language has been created.

The first stage of higher, supersensible knowledge is what is referred to as Imagination, imaginative knowledge; and I would ask you not to make the mistake to which I have just alluded of understanding by this quality of Imagination for today's purposes only what I shall immediately characterize. The second stage of supersensible knowledge is Inspiration, and the third stage is what—if one uses the word as we shall later characterize it and not as it is often imprecisely used—one can call Intuition. To these three stages of supersensible knowledge the outward sensory and intellectual knowledge that we employ in ordinary life and also in acquiring knowledge of the outer world is related as a kind of preliminary stage, so that one can in all, if one adds the supersensible stages of knowledge, speak of four stages of human knowledge.

Now there are many ways—and many ways must also be used—of raising oneself from the ordinary knowledge imparted through the senses and intellect to the first stage of supersensible knowledge, Imagination; and, because there would not be time for a detailed description, I want to emphasize specifically how the soul can achieve this with one of the means—others can be found in *Knowledge of the Higher Worlds*—of awakening the supersensible faculties of knowledge slumbering within it. One of the means is what is referred to as meditation.

If we pose ourselves the question as to what meditation is in a spiritual-scientific sense, we would have to say: Meditation is devoting oneself to a mental picture, a thought-sensation or a will-content in so intensive a way and in such a manner as does not happen in ordinary life but as is suited for concentrating or condensing forces that are otherwise present in a rarefied form in our soul-life.

Although the alternative path is also possible, it is good not to use for such soul-knowledge ideas or mental pictures that one would otherwise encounter in ordinary life or in the pursuit of ordinary knowledge. These mental pictures can also be used, but they are not as good. The mental pictures that are of the greatest use for meditation are of a symbolic nature. I should like to develop one such symbolic mental picture here which will already be familiar to some listeners from other contexts.

It may at first appear grotesque and paradoxical that it would be asked of anyone to let what will now be spoken of to take effect within his soul, but we shall characterize afterwards why it may happen. Let us suppose that someone imagines that he has two glasses before him; an empty glass and one partially filled with water. He now visualizes himself pouring the water from the glass containing water into the empty one and imagines that in pouring the water from the one glass into the other the glass that had water in it does not, as happens in the outer world, become emptier and emptier but ever more full. This is indeed a paradoxical idea, but this idea has a symbolic quality, and it should live as such in the consciousness of the spirit-researcher. It is a way of symbolically characterizing for our soul the nature and essence of human love. With human love and with everything that has to do with the idea of love, it can be said with certainty that the source of love is so infinitely deep and of such infinite richness that if we see ourselves in comparison with the reality of love in the world we must on every occasion modestly admit that this riddle of love is in its true essence surely unfathomable for every soul. And the more we have this feeling of unfathomability, the better it is for the content and intensity of our life. But we can know and emphasize one quality of true love with all clarity; and this is the quality that is portrayed to us symbolically through the image of which we have just spoken.

A person who behaves lovingly towards another person by enacting deeds of love never becomes poorer or emptier through what he does out of love, but he becomes ever fuller and fuller, ever richer and richer in his soul-life. This quality of love is clearly exhibited before us if we imagine the picture of the two glasses and of pouring water from one into the other.

We do something similar when we apply this to another area of cognition and thereby arrive at important conclusions for the outer world of the senses. Let us suppose that we have before us a circular plate-like form consisting of an unknown substance. If we have an initial look at this circular form we can say that the nature and composition of this substance are unknown to us. However, there is one thing that we can do if we want to come to know something about this disc: we can draw a circle. Then we have extracted something from this disc, namely that it is circular, and what we have extracted from it is definitely true, however little we may know otherwise about the object. This is what we are doing when we think mathematically (and the whole of mathematics is in this sense symbolic in nature), that we emphasize something symbolically. This process of forming images that can be perceived with the senses and then apprehended by the soul is, as regards experiences of a soul and spiritual nature, the preparation for imaginative knowledge.

Were someone to say that the spirit-researcher sets out to allow images and symbols to live in his soul that do not correspond to any truth and that he thereby embarks from the premiss of thinking untruths and letting them live in his soul, one would have to answer—of course, the true spirit-researcher is aware that what he allows in this way to live in his soul as symbols does not correspond to any outward reality. If he were for a single moment to mistake the symbol for a reality of some sort, he would not be someone who was on the way to supersensible knowledge but, rather, on the way to illusion. The purpose of these symbols is not to depict outward realities but to live in our soul, so that we connect and combine them with our soul-life and concentrate upon them.

Once we are in a position to think about such a symbol so strongly that we employ the whole power of our soul to allow only this symbol to live in our soul and put all other outer impressions and other thoughts aside, so that we bring nothing but this image to the focal point of our consciousness, such an image is for this very reason better than a direct impression of an outer reality, because such an impression always draws our soul-forces back to the outer reality and, as it were, takes us out of ourselves. But if—with the full awareness that we have something that is a pure fabrication—we have formed for ourselves a pictorial mental image to which we now devote ourselves, this is something that contains reality only in so far as it is derived from it. Whatever images we may form, we have taken them from outer reality. These images have been imagined in colours, forms and so forth, they are derived from outer reality but they are not related to it; for in outer reality it does not happen that a glass becomes fuller when one empties it of its contents.

Such an exercise has the consequence that the soul has to concentrate its forces in a completely different way than if it is helped by what it has otherwise experienced. If the person who wants to follow the path into the supersensible worlds has the patience and endurance repeatedly to practise such concentrations of his soul-life, he will be able to have a quite definite inner experience. Having such an experience is the first step towards imaginative knowledge. He will have the experience that he has by this means inwardly changed his soul-life, and that after some time he can become aware how from his soul itself—without his having brought this about—symbols or images appear, and in such a way that they come before him with all the appearance of reality, as is otherwise the case only when we have had perceptions of the outside world and have formed ideas or mental pictures about them.

Whereas in ordinary life mental pictures rise up from the soul as mirror-images of outer reality, through the exercises in question ideas arise from the depths of soul-life that are, of course, initially only images. But the elevation of soul-life consists in that the soul feels itself inwardly strong and that it can enter into a state that is similar and yet of an opposite nature to that of sleep. In sleep we withdraw from all outer perceptions and also from the thinking that is bound to the brain, but we fall into a state of unconsciousness. In imaginative cognition we likewise take leave of all outer perceptions and of all brain-bound thinking, for we suppress all of this. But nevertheless the soul does not become empty, does not become bereft of consciousness, but images rise up from its depths, images that become ever richer and richer, ever more all-encompassing, and that appear like a new world before the soul. This is the world of which indications have been given in these lectures, that can by someone lacking expertise in such matters easily be mistaken—also in its true worth—for the world of pathological illusions, hallucinations, delusions and the like. But only someone who does not know reality on this level but judges only in accordance with soul pathology can make such a misjudgement; for there is a great difference between ideas that are even in the smallest degree pathological and those that have been arrived at in the true sense through methodical soul-development.

Anyone who has learnt even only a little about what is referred to as pathological soul-manifestations such as hallucinations, illusions or delusions knows one thing: that those people who have succumbed to such notions believe so firmly in their reality that the belief that they evince for experiences of the outer world of the senses cannot compete with it. This is what is characteristic of delusions and illusions: that those who have fallen prey to them also develop an overwhelming belief in them. Nothing is more difficult than to talk a person who has illusions out of them—and they do not even need to be on the level of hallucinations but may be no more than ordinary delusions, paradoxical ideas. When, for example, a person begins in a pathological way to develop within himself the idea that he is being persecuted by another person, it is extraordinarily difficult to coax this idea away from him through mere persuasion, and what happens is that such a person builds up the most astonishing logical thought-structures in order to prove how right he is to perpetuate such delusions. A person can be possessed by what comes over him, and he firmly believes in the objective reality of such ideas.

If you review only to a small extent what is said in the book *Knowledge of the Higher Worlds*, you will see that while a person is in the process of letting such images and ideas work upon his soul, everything is at the same time done by a right spiritual schooling to ensure that, in the same measure that this world of images blossoms in the soul, any sense of being imprisoned by these images, any belief in them as an objective reality, is driven from the soul, so that at no moment is the spirit-pupil ever able to arrive at the idea that what is thus arising for him by way of imaginations is an objective reality.

All spiritual schooling is aberrant if it does not at the same time evoke in the soul the clarity that miraculous creations such as new worlds that manifest themselves from time to time have, in the way that they present themselves, no objective reality. Its sole purpose is inwardly to enliven the soul in order to make it richer in itself and, to use a paradoxical expression, inwardly more real, filled to a greater extent by what is truly real. And this is the best, indeed the only right achievement of the pupil, that he knows that the imaginations that appear are none other than a mirror-image of one's own being.

When the spirit-pupil develops the possibility of overcoming all belief in the reality, in the objectivity of these imaginations of his in the moment that he receives them, the spiritual schooling has found its right course. For many people it is generally difficult to add the one to the other, since by engaging in exercises such as these they have, as it were, been gifted with a new world, with a world of at times magnificent ideas and mental pictures. Thus it is for many such people an extraordinary source of satisfaction and comfort, something that fills them with a sense of congeniality. And anyone who sought to impart to them even to the least degree the belief that this has no objective reality but is merely a reflection of their own being, and that their own being is only being expressed more fully than before, would be viewed by them as an enemy, as someone who is ruining their finest inner aspirations. But it must be understood that such imaginations in the way that they initially appear are not suitable for giving true knowledge of the higher worlds but only provide a bridge for the soul; for a quite different task now begins for the soul, that task which gradually leads from Imagination to Inspiration. There now begins a kind of battle between the soul and that which appears in this way as its imaginations. In order to characterize the nature of this battle, I need to employ a picture from ordinary life.

In ordinary life we constantly have the experience that we do not have a full awareness of our inner life. Just think how it would be if you had everything that you had ever imagined in your consciousness! You would be able to recall ideas that you have had several decades ago. These reside in the depths of your soul, and at any opportunity they are summoned forth. This means that in ordinary life one has the possibility to forget, and to bring forth from the soul what has been forgotten. Thus one has the possibility of drawing forth from one's consciousness what it experiences in terms of ideas, and to separate this from one's conscious life so that it abides within one's soul independently of one's conscious life. The content of one's consciousness can therefore become submerged, so that it ceases to be part of one's conscious life.

Although a somewhat different situation pertains in this realm, something similar has to be achieved as regards all our imaginations when we become spirit-researchers. We must be able voluntarily to obliterate from our soul every imagination that appears, to extinguish it and bring it into a state where it is cast forth from our consciousness as a forgotten idea that we can later recall again. This is necessary. In the whole area of our imaginations we have to achieve mastery over every single imagination, we have to be able to make every single one independent from us.

Any conscientious spirit-researcher who wants to carry out spiritual research that he then wants to share with the wider world again and again sees to it that he thrusts down, makes unconscious, obliterates, what thus appears before his soul as a picture. Then it returns again, though now not only voluntarily but through something entirely different: through an inner power of which we become conscious only in this moment when we stand at the appropriate level. And not all imaginations come to the surface of consciousness, but we have the clear awareness that there are imaginations that remain submerged and are not brought to the level of conscious knowledge, or if they reappear they show themselves to be of such a nature that we reject them.

Imaginations change when they are recalled by us; they are then also something entirely different. They come through to us in the same way as perceptions of the things of the physical world present themselves. For the same reasons why we are—if we are of sound mind—able to distinguish outwardly something that we have dreamt, something that does not exist, from something real, we can similarly recognize the true reality, the spiritual essence, of what reappears as an imagination.

When such things have been discussed it has been asked: By what means can someone be convinced whether the imaginations that he has cast forth from his subjectivity, and has given over to the realm of objectivity in order that they may be given back again, represent realities or unrealities? After all, we know that there are suggestive forces and fantasies that are so strong that they overwhelm a person, so that he experiences as a reality something that is not actually there. This has been exemplified by someone who is so sensitive that, without drinking lemonade, he has the taste of lemonade in his mouth by the mere idea of doing so; this is an example of an instance where something manifests itself that does not really exist. One might therefore attribute certain imaginations concerning reincarnation to a similar deception.

An objection of this nature can always be made. It can also be maintained in the realm of dialectics through a mere play with words, though not where reality is concerned; for anyone who develops his soul in the manner described arrives at the same possibility of distinguishing between truth and falsehood, just as one distinguishes between truth and falsehood in the outer world, where one also only has the soundness of one's mind, one's common sense, as a basis for distinguishing truth from falsehood. Anyone who, for example, recalls Schopenhauer's proposition that the world with which I am surrounded is my idea or mental picture can form for himself an idea of what is meant.

I do not underrate the philosophy of Schopenhauer, otherwise I would not myself have edited it and written an introduction to it.[47] But great minds often make the simplest errors; for the proposition 'The world is my mental picture'[48] can be refuted if one draws attention to the very trivial fact that if someone forms for himself the idea of a piece of steel heated to 900 degrees and thinks of his fingers as he does so, he does not burn himself. He will never burn himself by having such an idea, however much he may be filled with it; but if he has an actual piece of steel he will burn himself. Thus he can distinguish the reality of an idea not through concepts and philosophies but through experience; and there is no other way of doing so. And there is also no way of making distinctions on the supersensible level other than by acquiring through schooling the right relationship with supersensible reality.

Thus it is necessary for our consciousness that we know that the way that imaginations manifest themselves initially can be attributed to our soul itself; and they are therefore merely a reflection of our own being. A person can have the most wonderful imaginations, but he would do well to interpret them by saying to himself: What do these images that appear before my soul tell me about my hidden feelings, my hidden suffering, my beliefs and superstitions? When he sees in the images nothing other than the reflection of himself, he has acquired the right state of consciousness to follow the paths into the supersensible world. He must then be prepared by the strong forces residing in his soul to be a fighter against himself. He must tear out by the roots what he has often sought most strongly to believe in, what he most loves and what for many people could already signify a state of bliss, and be able to let it be immersed in a sphere of forgotten ideas. When he has then so selflessly wrenched from himself what his soul has achieved and has surrendered it to the world, it then comes back to him again as Inspiration. He is then at the point of being able to live with those beings—the actual beings and facts of the supersensible world—to whom such ideas belong.

At first such imaginations appear thoroughly familiar to us, because we are able to investigate how the way they are formed is due to the fact that they are a reflection of our soul. One can always prove from the world of imaginations that their character is a reflection of ourselves and of our state of soul. But when they reappear, the situation is completely different. The images that return are not the same but different in character, something new that we have not previously encountered and which presents itself no less as a reality than do outer realities show themselves to us. Nevertheless, one has a totally different feeling towards them.

We stand with regard to the things of the outer world in such a way that we have an external relationship to them. A table that we contemplate is outside us. Where the facts and things of the higher worlds that we encounter are concerned, we have—if we have prepared ourselves for this in the manner described—at the same time, as an inner experience, the awareness that we have been able to gain access to them only by having given something to them that we have first brought forth in ourselves from the depths of our soul. Indeed, just as an object is lying before me and I want to take hold of it, and I must stretch out my hand and become aware of its reality, so by means of what I achieve only through the method described do I have to separate what has come towards me in the form of an imagination from my own egoity, submerge it in oblivion, in order then to reach out with my own being to a world that I can take hold of.

People register their objections to many things, also with respect to what I have just said. But however much one may look around and with however much goodwill one may familiarize oneself with these adversarial comments, one thing always becomes apparent: the people who repudiate what has now been said have not as yet understood it. This is shown by the way in which they speak about it. And it does not occur to anyone who has understood it to want to refute it. Thus one very frequently encounters this supposed objection that one hears: But surely, these supersensible imaginations that you have and which you consider to be impressions of beings who inspire you are not to be distinguished from perfectly ordinary illusions or delusions! On the contrary, they differ quite massively from these in that a real spirit-researcher has a consciousness that is different from them, a consciousness which enables him to maintain his healthy human understanding with respect to these things and equally to the things of the outer world. Hence superstitious or credulous individuals, those who are habitually referred to as dreamers, are the least suited to be real spirit-researchers.

Anyone who readily accepts a truth will quite definitely not be able to undertake proper research in the spiritual world. Fantasy and belief are the greatest enemies of true spiritual research, despite the fact that fantasy in art and belief in reality can be the most wonderful gifts to spiritual research. For what can be researched in the spiritual domain can be transformed into something imaginative and into a work of art. Similarly when it is said that what spirit-researchers impart is something that speaks only to belief, the following principle applies: the spirit-researcher believes what he knows. He would, however, also be a fool if he did not believe what he knows; but he believes nothing other than what he knows.

What is actually being said is that we have to draw forth from the soul what we have acquired, that we must extend organs that have, as it were, become spiritual and, through them, receive back the spiritual reality. When we increasingly come to live into such a soul-life, we also grow more and more together with the beings and things of the spiritual world. It then comes about that what occurs in our consciousness is that we do not associate with these beings as one human being associates with another through outer organs but through what speaks directly from being to being, what is, as it were, perceived directly by the beings, in that our soul is in immediate proximity to the being whom it perceives, so that it is, so to speak, not outside this being but within it. Then Initiation ensues, which is actually the conclusion of supersensible knowledge, of that supersensible knowledge that leads not into a vague, nebulous spiritual life but into one that is penetrated with being and filled with reality. There is no other way of really coming into proximity with the spirit and its existence than, as it were, to merge with it, as has now been described. But everything with which we do not fully unite ourselves can never serve as a proof for the spirit, for there is no other proof than finding the point of coincidence between one's own experience and the experience of the spirit. Anyone who wants to gain knowledge of a spiritual being must bring his soul to the point where he is able to let his own experience come together with the experience of this spiritual being.

The whole course of spiritual experience as it has been described can make it understandable—it would serve no purpose to obscure the actual realities and one must, rather, express them openly—that a person can most easily already through imaginative knowledge come to a knowledge of what I might call 'pure' spirits, whose existence is purely spiritual and who are not enshrouded with any mantle other than of a soul-spiritual nature. Spiritual beings who do not enter into incarnation, who do not manifest themselves in outer influences of nature, can be recognized already at the stage of Imagination, if we do not yet have the capacity to reach through to Inspiration. Thus it happens in such a way that the imaginations that we have submerged in forgetfulness return to us in a transmuted form, and we recognize them as images of spiritual beings who are as spiritual as our soul-spiritual nature as conceived without a body.

On the other hand, one has to rise to Inspiration if one wants to come to know beings who are, for example, connected with the elements of nature, with what radiates within nature, with the warmth relationships in nature and so forth, in short, creative powers and beings who express themselves in outer existence and can be recognized there only in their outer manifestations. This is possible only through Inspiration. To this end what we have in our soul must be drawn forth more intensively so that it reaches down further than is the case with beings who have a purely spiritual existence. And the strongest forces of seership must be used if one wants to come to know those creative forces which outer intellectual consciousness identifies only as materialistic nature-forces, which are, however, in truth creative beings.

If we want to recognize these creative beings who lie hidden behind all outer existence, we must be able to draw our inner soul-life forth from ourselves as strongly as is the case when we have ascended to Intuition. This means that it is one of the most difficult challenges to come to know about the previous incarnation of a particular individual, for in the case of someone whom we encounter in the world of the senses we are also dealing with what manifests itself in the effects of nature, in bodily influences.

Behind these bodily influences these lies something of the nature of creative powers. But for the spiritual seer this is hidden behind the externalities of the body just as the spiritual beings who are present in lightning and thunder and behind all nature are concealed behind such phenomena; and the one is hardly easier to find than the other. Thus it is a frequent experience that people who come to Intuition relate all kinds of illusions about earlier incarnations. It is therefore good if one sets as little store as possible by this. The true spirit-researcher knows that this is something of the greatest difficulty which even for a developed soul is possible only at fleeting moments.

What has been said so far relates to the investigation of the supersensible world, of what lives and weaves within it. Anyone who prepares his soul in the manner described thereby makes his soul into an instrument for gaining insight into the supersensible worlds. However, for the spirit-researcher who wants to communicate spiritual knowledge of the world, it is only then that the most significant task arises; for this beholding of the spiritual worlds is generally something that people who do not have the appropriate knowledge of it misunderstand and fail to appreciate. And this, too, forms part of a right appraisal of the paths of supersensible knowledge—that people are able to form a judgement as to what real spiritual knowledge is and what is either a load of nonsense, charlatanism or self-deception.

It has to be said again and again: In order to engage in researching the spiritual world, in order to search for supersensible facts and beings, it is necessary for the soul to educate itself for this. But if a spirit-researcher who has gained access in the right way to the supersensible worlds has appropriately clothed his observations in concepts which are familiar to anyone of sound mind and are in accordance with a right feeling for truth, what the spirit-researcher describes can also be understood in the right way by anyone who does not labour under a misapprehension. A suitably prepared soul is needed for researching supersensible facts and beings but never for understanding them. This is in a sense the mystery of the description of spiritual things, that once they have been investigated through supersensible forces of cognition they can be described in such a way that they can be understood by anyone.

One thing that clearly needs to be said is that the human soul needs the results of spiritual research in order to understand those things of which we shall be speaking in the next lecture about 'vital questions and the riddle of death'. The human soul thirsts for ideas and concepts regarding what goes beyond death, for ideas and concepts that can really encompass the nature of the soul. And anyone who wanted to reject the idea of understanding the nature of the soul would probably be able to suppress for a while the soul's longing to solve the riddles of the world. But it will become all the more apparent that in refusing the soul spiritual nourishment we are unable to suppress the hunger that presents itself and can drive the soul not only to despair but to ill-health. Both for his well-being and his self-confidence in life a person needs the results of spiritual research, and all that is needed for the soul to become acquainted in the right way with the results of spiritual research is a good measure of common sense. A natural sense of truth is sufficient in order to understand what the spirit-researcher communicates. For as long as it has not been researched, nothing can be said about it; but if it has been researched and rightly formulated, it can be understood.

How very true this is can be shown by the fact that the spirit-researcher receives absolutely nothing for his soul-happiness, for everything that he needs in general for his soul, from his 'visions'. He has a new world. But this new world is of absolutely no use to him so long as he has not brought it to the point where it has come to shed light on the soul-life that we lead on a daily basis and which yearns for solutions to life's riddles. What the spirit-researcher can have from his research he has fully in common with the others to whom it is related and who understand it with a natural sense of truth and a healthy human understanding. But as regards what the soul needs for life, the spirit-researcher has nothing through his research but solely through what comes about through the research and can be communicated to everyone. Moreover, the spirit-researcher can only mean something to humanity as a whole if he is in a position to embody the results of his research in concepts and ideas in such a way that they can be grasped out of the ideas of the respective age, provided that they are sufficiently free of prejudices and preconceptions. There is, to be sure, a widespread lack of such open-mindedness at present, because people believe that other ideas, for example those of natural science, contradict these results of spiritual science. However, if one enters with greater precision into the results of spiritual-scientific research, one will everywhere see that it is not the case.

But there is something else that stands between the spirit-researcher and his public; for the very fact that he is able to perceive the spiritual world means that what he beholds is widely unrecognized. People fall prey to the gravest errors with respect to the spirit-researcher as such precisely when they want to approach spiritual research or have a longing for it. To put it in a nutshell, I shall point out that the greatest error amongst well-meaning people is that, because the spirit-researcher has prepared his soul to gain insight into the spiritual world, they look upon him as a kind of 'higher animal', that he has something that places him ahead of other people. But through such a view someone who cherishes the wish to come to supersensible knowledge succeeds only in placing barriers in his path. Out of a certain goodwill it comes to be thought that the spirit-researcher, because he can see into the spiritual world, is therefore a step above other people and is of greater worth than they are, that it is a particularly worthy aspiration for the human soul and its true significance to be able to gain insight into the spiritual world. That this aspiration manifests itself in our time in the widest circles has its origin in a circumstance that can be characterized in the following way.

In former times we also find communications from spiritual research that have been made to human beings. For the most part, however, only the results were communicated. There was not the kind of discussion of the methods as is, for example, possible today or as can be disseminated in a published book such as *Knowledge of the Higher Worlds* or my book *An Outline of Occult Science*. For certain reasons the methods were spoken about only before a few individuals in whose particular qualities one had complete confidence. This was appropriate for former times because people in general had the right feeling and also the sense for truth to let the results work upon their souls and also let their souls benefit from them, but not sufficiently to overcome the difficulties in order that the soul can enter the spiritual world.

Today souls live differently. Today there is the possibility of a completely different thinking. Let us simply compare how people are able to think quite differently today, not only through the continued progress of natural science but the way in which people learn to think quite differently through the advances in education, than was formerly the case. Because of this people today have been enabled to judge things better; and this means that things can be communicated. But this is only in its initial stages. Hence it is inevitable that mistakes will be made.

One such error arises when one sees the spirit-researcher as something special. However, simply because a person has heightened his level of knowledge in the manner described, it does not mean that he is superior to those who are unable to have such knowledge. Just as a chemist is no different from other people because he knows about chemistry, so is the spirit-researcher also no different from the rest of humanity. The worth of a person is not determined by such things but it is defined within certain narrower limits through intellectuality, through the power of sound thinking. A person who can think is of greater value than another person whose thinking is of poor quality. And in a wider sense a person's worth is determined by his morality, through the fact that he fulfils moral acts and has a moral soul-condition. He gains an advantage not through a particular soul-development but solely through intellectual and moral qualities.

For this reason the bad habit of considering that the spirit-researcher who can behold the spiritual world has a particular authority, is someone special, simply because he can do this—a habit that is such a barrier to the path of supersensible knowledge—must be completely eradicated from those who want to approach such knowledge. This habit calls forth a belief in authority and a quality of blind discipleship, which are already bad enough in other areas but which are worst of all in the realm of spiritual-scientific research; for with regard to the matter of spiritual research, experience attests to the following.

Anyone who has acquired healthy, sound and logical thinking within ordinary life, as do other people who stand within ordinary life, carries this logical, healthy thinking also into the supersensible worlds and is therefore able to judge what is real, what is right and true and is, as a result, able to convey right judgements to his fellow human beings from what he has come to know. It is not by beholding the supersensible worlds that one formulates right judgements but by entering into the situation with a right understanding, with good logic. A fool who is able to perceive a great deal in the spiritual world, who beholds vast amounts of all manner of spiritual things because his soul has some sort of proclivity for this, will also speak a lot of pure nonsense as to how it is in the spiritual world. Whether one comes to the truth depends on how one is able to judge. Thus someone with a sound mind—even if he cannot perceive the spiritual world—is at any time able to judge whether that which someone who claims however ardently to have 'seen' in the spiritual world is nonsense or whether it makes proper sense. If someone shows that he is unable to think properly, that he cannot connect things in the right way, then instead of listening to the spirit-researcher he would do better to pay proper attention to this problem; for then he will always know whether something is coming from an intelligent or a foolish source.

Even more significant in this respect is one's moral state. Anyone who approaches the spiritual world with passions and unpleasant feelings and emotions, especially if combined with vanity and inordinate ambition, will see what is presented to him in a distorted and untrue fashion. He will perceive the worst parts of the spiritual domain, and these will appear to him in such a way that they do not impart truth to him but bind him to illusions. His moral state has a decisive influence over what, as a spiritual seer, he is able to behold in the spiritual world. Thus spiritual seership in itself is by no means a reason to set up someone as some kind of authority. It is far more important that we pay attention to the way in which spiritual research is prepared, and we must know that we wreak the greatest havoc if we do not watch attentively with our healthy powers of reason and see only what has to be objectively evaluated.

This is the path for forming judgements about spiritual knowledge on the part of those who long for such knowledge for the benefit and happiness of their souls. When someone relates in this way to the spirit-researcher, this relationship of the world to the spirit-researcher is no different from the relationship of the world to other sciences and disciplines. Just as not everyone can go to the observatory or to the laboratory, relatively few people have real insight into the spiritual world (although a certain depth of insight is always possible today). However, it is not necessary for everyone to have such insight, for the fruits of spiritual knowledge can be understood by an unprejudiced mind when they are communicated. This can become the right relationship of the spirit-researcher to his audience, and this is also the right way for human interaction to proceed.

The more one endeavours not to regard the spirit-researcher as an authority but to rely on one's sound common sense to examine everything, and the more one measures everything that the spirit-researcher says by how one views it if one compares it with life, if—in other words—one uses one's sound common sense, the more firmly one stands on solid ground. We should make it very clear that spiritual science, to the extent that the world needs it, is accessible today to every human being because of the fact that it can be comprehended, even though not everyone can perceive the spiritual worlds. We are today already at the point where no soul is any longer denied the possibility of following the path into the spiritual world. It is a demand of our age that human beings are increasingly convinced that the path into the supersensible worlds is one that can be explored. This is the right course, in contrast to that which leads a person to a blind belief in authority; and only what is right has value for the happiness and benefit of the soul.

These are some indications about the paths to supersensible knowledge, to that knowledge which truly leads us into a spiritual world that lies behind our sensory world, and which also enables us to comprehend this spiritual world. The spirit-researcher himself only has something from the spiritual world for his own being and personal circumstances if he is not only able to perceive it but can also understand what he has perceived; for to perceive everything without enabling it to be understood is of no value. But if it has been understood and, moreover, with the sound common sense or healthy human reason as has been characterized and a natural feeling for truth, then it is engraved in our soul, becomes intimately connected with it; and our soul immediately feels what resides within it, just as when the soul comes before a picture it immediately feels what is in the picture, even if it has not itself painted it. Just as in order to receive something from a picture it is not necessary that one must be a painter, it is equally unnecessary for the purpose of gaining insight, or at least sufficient insight, into knowledge that is highly necessary for the soul—for example, of immortality or passing through repeated earthly lives—that one can oneself form this knowledge in visionary perception (although it would be good if more and more people were able to do so). But the time demands that ever more people will do this, because the need to gain access to the supersensible world will come to be ever more pressing if not overwhelming. Souls will increasingly be compelled also in a certain sense to become seers, to grow together with the spiritual world.

This makes possible—whether in the form of an understanding of oneself or of another person—the possession of the supersensible truths, the supersensible knowledge, that our soul knows, just as we know through outer science how all the outer substances that are in our body are present in the whole universe, so that we are, as it were, embedded in the likeness that is spread out in the entire universe (investigations that have been made possible only through spectral analysis), how man has been fashioned out of the universe. Thus he also learns through spiritually based research that in everything that weaves and surges in his consciousness or in his subconscious he is connected with a world of spiritual beings who are indeed more real than the substances with which the body is connected.

Thus a person gradually feels the fruits of spiritual research in his restfulness of soul, and feels also the strength to work and be active in the spiritual whole, in the divinely and spiritually imbued universe. But this enables him to know for the first time what he is and what knowledge is necessary for him that he lives calmly and actively, thinking, feeling and willing in the spirit-imbued universe and feels and knows himself to be connected with it. And this constitutes what the soul cannot do without, what it seeks, if it does not have it for a certain length of time. This requires the soul, if it is not to become desolate and, through desolation, not to become incapable, to work together on behalf of humanity, lest it does not only enter into a state of desolation as regards divine powers but also into decadence. The awareness of this affinity with the supersensible worlds lies at the foundation of what was instinctively living in Goethe when he said:

> Were the eye not Sun-imbued,
> It could Sun's glory ne'er perceive;
> Were God's own power not in us laid,
> How could we God's delights receive?[49]

The eye is indeed Sun-imbued! The same power that is in the Sun is in the eye. In this way, like can—as the old philosophers said—be recognized by like.[50] There is a divine power within man, the whole world is impregnated with divinity; and because of this the inner divinity can comprehend the divinity without. But Goethe recognized that the opposite is also true.

Although he makes the whole world into a manifestation of the will, Schopenhauer is unable to see that not only is what is within us necessary for knowledge of the world around us but, on the other hand, the outer is also necessary for the inner world. Schopenhauer would say that the Sun is there only because we have an eye.[51] Through this reasoning the strange philosophy has arisen which regards the world as without sound, without warmth and so on and all this is enabled to begin only when the human organs make their presence felt in the world. But Goethe rightly knew that not only do we see things because we have eyes and hear sounds because we have ears but that an eye can come into being only because the Sun is there. From his previous eyeless state man became a being who can see through the fact that light filled space; and from the organism that as yet had no eye brought the eye forth. The power of the Sun created the eye through the light that it radiated. Thus it is not a matter of our bearing the divine within us and of simply projecting into the world the divine that we have first created within us, as is, for example, indicated by Feuerbach,[52] but we must know that we would not have this 'sense of God' within us if the divine-spiritual powers did not fill the world and had not created an organ for the spirit within us, just as the outer Sun has created the outer eye.

So we can say: The consciousness that soul and world belong together that gives strength and power to the soul and enables it to rest and be active in the spiritual universe is composed of two things, two things of which we can characterize one with Goethe's beautiful words:

> Were the world not Sun-imbued,
> It could Sun's glory ne'er perceive;
> Were God's own power not in us laid,
> How could we God's delights receive?

But it is wholly in accordance with what Goethe says if, by complementing this one-sided truth with another that makes it into a complete truth, we add another verse which could be worded thus:

> Were the world not Sun-endowed,
> How could eyes from beings bloom?
> Were existence not God's revelation,
> How could men come to fulfil God's Word?

Lecture 5

BERLIN, 5 DECEMBER 1912

RESULTS OF SPIRITUAL RESEARCH FOR VITAL QUESTIONS AND THE RIDDLE OF DEATH

THE greatest riddles of life that are of general human significance do not arise as a result of any particular scientific research but confront us in the daily course of life. And the greatest poser of questions is life itself with its constant flow of questions that not only arouse our curiosity and our thirst for knowledge but can signify happiness and sorrow, satisfaction or despair to our soul. Spiritual science as it is presented here in these lectures is primarily concerned with resolving these questions posed by life itself in so far as it falls within the scope of human knowledge, with gaining insight into the mysteries of existence. Even though this spiritual science appears as something new and unfamiliar as compared with the ordinary science of today, this can be understood by anyone who merely casts an eye at those branches of ordinary science that concern themselves with questions of the soul, with questions of spiritual life. What people today call psychology or soul-science can in what it presents to a large extent be investigated, and one will find that the great questions of existence, the great riddles of life, are dealt with very inadequately in science as we ordinarily know it.

One of the greater soul-researchers of the present, Franz Brentano, has remarked in his *Psychology*[53] on how one finds questions answered—or how at any rate people attempt to answer them—in ordinary psychological research, how one idea follows another, how one feeling awakens another in the soul, how those soul-forces may perhaps develop within our consciousness to which we give the name of memory, all this—says Franz Brentano—could not possibly be a substitute for what psychological research formerly sought to establish as in a certain sense a solution to the mystery associated with the notion of the immortality of man's being. Similarly today, one will search in vain in ordinary treatises about psychology for answers to questions such as the immortality of the soul, and also to other questions. Indeed, such questions are not even raised in the context of ordinary research.

One very basic way of approaching the most everyday great riddles of life is to raise the question: How is a person supposed to cope with himself and with the world when his experience of himself is such that at every age he becomes different, that as he grows older new tasks are placed before him in his life between birth and death? How should a person answer the great riddle of existence that presents itself to him every day and which, as anyone can observe, is intimately connected with a person's entire being: the great riddle as to the source and significance of the fact that everything that from morning until evening floods our lives in waking consciousness by way of ideas, impulses, desires, passions, emotions and so forth is submerged when we go to sleep into a vague and indeterminate darkness when we begin the new day? Sleep and waking, which are so intimately connected with the riddle of human existence, are phenomena regarding which science must confess, and must continue to confess, that it has hardly anything to say by way of an answer to these riddles. And then there is the riddle of death that was mentioned previously, that riddle regarding which a significant researcher of recent times already referred to here has nothing further to say other than what results from the observation of the outward nature of the body. At the very beginning of his *Principles of Physiology*,[54] Huxley cites the words of the melancholic Prince of Denmark:

> Imperious Caesar, dead and turn'd to clay,
> Might stop a hole to keep the wind away.
> O, that that earth which kept the world in awe
> Should patch a wall t'expel the winter's flaw![55]

And he goes on to explain what he wants to say by showing that the separate material parts of which man is composed are, when he crosses the threshold of death, so to speak gradually scattered to the four corners of the Earth and turn into other material substances which are all around us, and how if we would seek what has become of a human being we would have to look for the material atoms where they are to be found after a certain time in the cosmic expanses.

That what has become of the atoms of the great Caesar is certainly not the question that actually concerns the human soul is something of which ordinary science is blissfully unaware. For the real question is this: Where are the soul-forces that were active within Caesar? What has happened to them? How are they working further in the world? That this is the great question is something that ordinary science can no longer even feel. And then there is that question which is included in the significant word 'destiny', the destiny-question that pursues us at every step in life and which presents us with the riddle that manifests itself to us everywhere. We see a human individual enter into existence, born in a state of misery and need, so that we can predict at his cradle that the lot that he has been granted will not be favourable; or we see him enter life with seemingly little in the way of attributes, so that we can again foresee that he will be of small advantage to himself or to others. In the case of another person we see that he enters life amidst good fortune and abundance, surrounded by caring hands from his cradle, endowed with attributes which show from the outset that he could both for himself and his fellow human beings become a useful part of the world order. How much of everything that we associate with happiness and sorrow and which comes towards us on a daily, even an hourly basis is included in this question of destiny! One could say that the great questions of existence only begin from where science stops. And anyone who tries to familiarize himself with a world-conception that is predicated by purely scientific foundations will say to himself: What has been presented to me in terms of a summary—however well-expressed—of scientific truths shows to me only the beginning of the questions that I must raise regarding the great riddles of existence; I find little by way of answers there.

With respect to all this one must, however, emphasize that the present-day cultural environment offers scarcely any possibility for entering into questions that are of vital importance for the human soul, for the simple reason that as a result of facts and phenomena that have featured over the course of recent centuries—and which will be addressed in the coming lectures—the habits of thought, the conceptions underlying human thinking, have been directed more towards the outward material realm and only really feel at ease when they can associate something with the judgement and research that derives from the world of appearances, or which is accessible to brain-bound thinking. For the most part these habits of thought have been deprived of the possibility of acquiring insight into the human soul, of perceiving those events that are enacted specifically within the soul as opposed to the body.

It is probably already apparent from the lectures given this winter that the answering of these questions does not have so much to do with whether a person is, through following the paths into supersensible life as have been indicated in the last lecture, able to gain insight into those realms where answers can be given to the questions referred to. It has been emphasized on several occasions that certain things have to be researched on this path, but that the unprejudiced human understanding, one's unprejudiced judgement, is thoroughly capable of seeing what supersensible research is able to give. If this is so, it will also be understandable that the path of supersensible knowledge described in the previous lecture always gives the possibility of rightly comprehending what is in any case present in life, what life offers in every situation, and of receiving through a right perception answers to the great riddles of existence.

The spiritual aspect of man's being is present everywhere, it is always there; and in order that it may impart to us knowledge of its immortality it is not so much necessary for there to be a direct insight into the supersensible world as, rather, a right view—such as can be evoked and explained—of what is actually going on within our life of soul. In evaluating what is referred to here as spiritual science, attention should mainly be directed towards the way in which life is considered, the way in which the phenomena of soul-life are presented through the particular quality of thinking brought about by spiritual science. Anyone who wishes to examine this precisely will find that spiritual science considers the phenomena of soul-life in connection with the outer life of material existence in such a way that the great riddle of existence referred to is approached out of a direct observation of life.

It has already been indicated several times that spiritual science today is in a similar situation to natural science at the time of the dawn of the modern cultural period, when for example Francesco Redi[56] expressed the great truth that is accepted as normal and is universally acknowledged: Something living can only arise from the living. With this a powerful prejudice was combated, an assumption that was at the time not only confined to the general public but dominated science as a whole (and this time lies only a few centuries in the past), in that some three centuries ago—when Francesco Redi was writing—people believed that lower animals, such as fish, earthworms and the like, can arise from river sludge simply through the fusion of outward material substances. Francesco Redi showed that this was an inexact observation. He showed that no living existence can arise without a germinal essence deriving from a comparable living source being incorporated in the unorganized material substance, and formulated the proposition: Something living can only arise from the living. Within the limits in which this proposition is being spoken of here, it is acknowledged by everyone from Haeckel to Du Bois-Reymond. This was not so at the time of Francesco Redi. He first had to show how only an inexact observation could give rise to the belief that non-living matter could form itself into something living.

Spiritual science is today in the same position with regard to the spirit as Francesco Redi was with regard to the living. Through the way that it is able to observe soul-phenomena, spiritual science shows today that it amounts to an inexact observation if one believes that what comes into existence by way of a person's inner soul-life could derive, for example, from inheritance, from the parents or grandparents and so on, or could derive from what a person's soul receives into itself through outer experience, through an experience of the surrounding world. Spiritual science is obliged to show that the belief that could be so, rests just as much on an imprecise observation as the belief that a living form could develop out of non-living substance. Just as non-organic matter can only be composed from a living seed, so everything that the human soul forms for itself from inherited characteristics and qualities, everything that it receives from the outer world through the senses and through the intellect, can only be linked together with what lives and weaves within us as a living soul-nature if there is a living spiritual seed, a germinal spirit-essence that embraces both the inherited characteristics and everything that is taken in from the surrounding outer world.

Spiritual science takes this germinal spiritual or soul-essence into consideration, and with this it is at variance with a very widespread prejudice of present times. If one speaks today of the special character of the human soul, if one speaks of everything that a human being represents, one will—and this is what has occurred as a result of the most conscientious research that needs to be recognized in its own way—refer to this or that which has been 'inherited' from ancestors. People will always try, as it were, to link what lives within the human soul and what a person develops with one or another cause that lies within the line of inheritance, which they will allow to be influenced only by what streams in from without as a means of fashioning the whole nature of the human soul.

A certain harmony between natural science and spiritual science will come about in this realm if one gives consideration to a question that spiritual science must constantly have in mind when there is any discussion of the essential nature of the human soul and of inherited characteristics, a question that is connected to the continuing existence of the whole human race or species. Within the line of descent, within what is passed on through the generations from grandfather and father to the son and so on, we see characteristics being inherited from generation to generation. But one thing comes towards us as a question if we consider this succession of human existence in the course of the generations: That at a certain time man, as it were, attains manhood, sexual maturity, he is capable of bringing forth his own kind and therefore has the capacities which must exist in order that he may do so.

As regards human evolution, therefore, what happens until sexual maturity is that until this point man develops all the capacities which make it possible for him to bring forth a being of his own kind.

But after sexual maturity man continues to evolve. New forms, new content of the soul also appear after sexual maturity; and it is impossible to bring what the soul undergoes in its evolution after sexual maturity into connection with the whole evolution of the human race in the same way as that which a person passes through until sexual maturity as regards the human species. A sharp distinction must be made in man's whole relation to the world with respect to his evolution until sexual maturity and with respect to the time afterwards. This is a question which, as we shall shortly see, can be properly considered only by spiritual science.

Another highly significant question emerges with this which shows how what can be characterized with the term 'heredity' should be understood, in contrast to what takes place wholly in the human soul and belongs to human evolution. We can come to an understanding of what appears in a person and clearly manifests itself as a product of heredity within the human race by means of a radical instance, where something is inherited under all circumstances simply by virtue of his being a human being who is descended from a being of a similar nature, a being of his own kind. Such a case is, for example, the change of teeth in approximately the seventh year of life. This is something that lies within the forces that the person has inherited and which manifest themselves under all circumstances, even if we separate the individual concerned from the human community and deposit him on a solitary island where he would grow up in an uncivilized manner.

So is it with all qualities that have their origin purely in the line of inheritance. But if we take something that is as intimately connected with the human soul as language, we immediately find that the concepts of inheritance are of no avail. Where it is justified to speak of inheritance, the inherited features appear as in the case of the change of teeth; whereas if we take someone to a solitary island and let him grow up without human contact so that he does not hear the sound of a human voice, he will not develop language. This means that there is something here that shows us that there is something in the human soul that is not linked to heredity in the same way as the forces that we have primarily to regard as being inherited.

Thus we could cite much that would show us how little one can rely on the forces of inheritance for an explanation of the totality of man's being. But when it comes to the study of the spiritual world through spiritual science people make one error after another—errors that must simply be regarded as errors in logic—when they embark on making their judgements with a whole set of preconceptions. Thus, for example, they think that spiritual science wants to reject everything that natural science has to say, whereas it actually has the highest respect for the achievements of natural science.

Thus this is thought, for example, when spiritual science asserts that what we call the essence of the human soul derives not from the parents, grandparents and so on but can be traced back as a soul-spiritual kernel to a previous human life far distant in time, so that spiritual science says that a human being does not have only one but many earthly lives. When we make our way into earthly life through birth, a soul-essence or kernel enters into existence which has received certain qualities, certain forces in earlier earthly lives. By virtue of the fact that it has received these forces in previous earthly lives and has, as it were, concentrated them within itself, it enters in a certain way into a new body, a new physical environment. Just as the living seed is incorporated in physical life into its inorganic surroundings and from there takes up inorganic forces and substances, so does this human soul-essence coming from previous earthly lives approach the inherited characteristics, concentrates and links them together, takes what the outer world can give and thus forms and shapes the new life which we then lead through the time from birth until death. The present life is again such a drawing together partly of the inherited characteristics and partly of what the outer world offers us. And when we pass through the gate of death this soul-essence is at its most concentrated. Then in the time between death and a new birth it passes through a purely spiritual existence and, when it has in this state achieved the necessary maturity, enters through a new birth or conception into a new earthly life.

That any aspect of conscientious and well researched scientific results should be at variance with or even only affected by such insights of spiritual science is an unfortunate but nevertheless widely held prejudice. As has already been stated, spiritual science fully understands when a scientist comes along and shows how through the mingling of the paternal and maternal seed a particular individualization of the child's germinal essence takes place in each individual case, and how different the individualities of the various children can be as a result of the mingling of the paternal and maternal elements. Spiritual science fundamentally does not involve itself with the trivial assertion that it would be a proof for the existence of a distinct human individuality that in one and the same family the children are different both individually and from one another, for this individualizing element can be understood from the different ways that the paternal and maternal elements intermingle. If, moreover, the ordinary scientist comes and draws attention to how what a person manifests in life could be an indication of a particular organic constitution or of a particular formation of the brain or some such thing, spiritual science is in full agreement with this; and it is a sign of dilettantism in spiritual science not to go along with it. But if what natural science has with full justification to say in this realm is intended as an objection to what spiritual science indicates, that in spite of all that natural-scientific research would propound the soul-essence of a human being first approaches the inherited characteristics in order to form a life, one is making a logical mistake which can be characterized in approximately the following way.

Let us suppose that someone sees another person before him who is breathing healthily, and he says: That this person is alive and is now standing before me as a living being is due to the air and the lungs that are manifest here. Who would deny that this is completely true! Just as little as this can be denied by any kind of spiritual science, it can similarly not be disputed when the natural scientist comes and takes into consideration the material conditions from the line of inheritance in order to explain the individual form of the soul-life. This is just as true as if the ordinary scientist were to say: This person I see before me is living at this moment because he has the air outside him and a set of lungs inside him.

Is, therefore, someone who researches the natural world entitled to refute spiritual science when it says: In spite of everything that has been said here, what has taken place in your soul is determined, is soul-spiritually determined in a purely spiritual way, by what the soul has experienced in former lives; in spite of everything the whole of a person's destiny is determined by the fact that he has himself prepared this destiny in previous lives? No, the natural scientist should not feel entitled to dismiss the spirit-researcher when he makes such an assertion. The natural scientist who says that the person who is standing before me is living at this moment because of the air outside him and the lungs within him should no more be dismissing what the spirit-researcher says than he is entitled to disregard someone who says: No, it is not because of this that he lives but he is alive at this moment through something quite different; this person wanted to hang himself, and he would quite definitely have departed this life through his suicidal attempt at that time if I had not come. I intervened, and because of this he is alive now.

So from this we see how the objective truth that the person concerned is alive only because of the air and the lungs does not conflict with the fact that he is alive at this moment only because the other person intervened! This latter incontrovertible truth is no less at variance with the knowledge of the natural scientist that a person lives because of the existence of air and lungs than what natural science has to say contradicts what spiritual science asserts, namely that the ultimate, spiritual foundations for human existence lie in repeated earthly lives.

Thus it is a matter of looking appropriately at the right thing, and we can well exemplify this by considering speech. Every spirit-researcher who looks into the depths of things and understands natural science can understand that one can easily be tempted to say that a person is able to speak because he has a speech-centre in his brain. There is quite certainly some truth in this. But it is equally true to say that this speech-centre of the brain was only formed into a living speech-organ through the existence of the world of language. Language has created the speech-centre. Similarly, all the formations of the brain and of man's entire organism have been created through soul-spiritual factors. It is they that have imprinted something of a spiritual nature upon the undefined human material substances. Thus we need to search for the truly creative aspect of man's soul-essence or soul-kernel in the soul-spiritual domain. We should regard the soul-spiritual element not as a result of the brain but, in contrast, the brain with its refined formation as a result of soul-spiritual influences.

When we consider human life, it manifests itself to us at every point such that we feel that what has just been said is reinforced by looking at life in a balanced and healthy way. Let us for instance again consider what we may call human evolution as it unfolds in terms of the species, what therefore also develops within a person when, so to speak, the forces working within heredity are fully developed, when he has developed the sexual maturity to bear within himself the forces that are able to bring forth a being of his own likeness. In contrast, the soul-forces that constitute human evolution manifest themselves quite differently if we compare them to those forces that are present throughout human life as those that are, for example, developed in maintaining the species, in reproduction. Within what lies in the reproductive forces we see how, as it were, everything develops from within outwards, how through the forces that are active in this realm a person brings forth beings of his own likeness, that is, how what is within him is externalized. The forces that belong to inner human evolution take the precisely opposite path. One has but to be able to regard the spiritual domain in general as something real. One will then from the outset be able to accept the considerations that will now be presented as justified.

How do we live our life if we take the inward soul-aspect into consideration? We live it in a totally opposite sense from the way that we live our life as a member of the human race: as regards the species all development takes place outwardly, in the individual life all development is inwardly oriented. It occurs in such a way that we take that which comes towards us from without into ourselves and develop it further, and do not thrust it out as with reproduction but that we concentrate what we experience in this way with ever greater intensity within ourselves, as it were, all the more intensively divest it of its character as something from the outside world and make it the content of our own ego.

Anyone who considers human life without preconceptions will find how it would, for example, be impossible for one's soul-life ever in a single moment to have in its recollections everything that the soul is capable of remembering from what it has experienced. Let us imagine that one of the people sitting here were in this moment to have all the concepts, ideas, feelings, emotions and so forth that have ever lived in his soul. This would be completely impossible. But has what we have previously experienced, what we have inwardly received, become lost because at this moment we are unable to recall it? It is not lost. If we compare our soul-life in successive moments of time, we shall find that what we have apparently forgotten but has developed within us and has made us a different person is quite possibly more important than what we remember.

In the course of our development we do indeed always become a different person, we feel ourselves imbued with an ever-changing content. If we observe ourselves as we are now and compare ourselves with what we were some ten years ago, we will not deny that we are a different person and that what has brought this about are the assimilated experiences that have streamed into us, have been apprehended by us and have taken the opposite path from the forces that serve reproduction. It is as though with our intuitive vision, with our reflections upon our memories, we destroy what we experience but thereby take it into our ego. Our ego becomes continually different. Hence we can say that an exact observation of life shows us how this ego changes throughout life and how it is the assimilated experiences that have brought about this change. We feel how the ego becomes inwardly fuller, ever richer and more imbued with forces than it was when we embarked upon our youthful lives. At the foundation of this is a very significant phenomenon of life to which insufficient attention is normally paid.

Goethe, whose knowledge of life was profound and who viewed life above all else in the way that it presented itself to him in his own personality, expressed the thought: In old age we become mystics.[57] What did he mean by this? What does Goethe mean by 'becoming a mystic'? We must distance this thought from any suggestion of unclear, vague ideas. Goethe meant that as a person becomes more and more mature he has increasingly less of what the world offers him outwardly and that the forces of experience well up from the reserves within his own soul, wherein he has let them be submerged. 'A person becomes a mystic' means that his soul has become ever more full, it has come to contain more and more forces in its inner regions.

If we look more carefully at what it is that our soul-essence has brought together within us, at how it has assimilated what it has experienced and what it has made out of it, we will be able to bring those who have independently of their age become mystics a little further on the track of what is actually going on within the human soul. Let us consult the mystics! What do mystics mostly speak about? They speak of a 'second self', of a 'higher man' within a person, of how in this human ego that develops within us from our youth onwards a second ego or self can unfold which many mystics interpret as being 'divine'. But the point is not to emphasize this but rather, as they have felt, that as a person grows up something akin to a second human being matures that he takes hold of, that concentrates itself within him. We see the exact opposite with reproduction, whereby a second human being is born alongside the first and is thrust away from it; whereas what becomes the 'second self' is not something that a person thrusts away from himself but develops inwardly to a point of ever greater concentration.

Thus we can actually say that as a person lives his life he develops within his individuality something that works in the opposite direction to reproduction. He does not give birth to anything out of himself; he concentrates something within himself, he does not let something go forth from himself but imbues himself with something that the mystic can well relate to as a 'second man' who, as it were, develops within the skin of the first and attains an ever greater degree of soul-spiritual definition. This is in the case of different people either more or less obvious; but the significance of such a course of human development is that the germinal process that we undergo is of an opposite nature, where we do not unfold but, on the contrary, concentrate something within us. If we call the direction associated with reproduction one of evolution, of unwinding or unfolding, we can call that which the ego undergoes an involution, an in-winding, an inner forming of experiences. And it is natural that the inner vigour which the developed ego bears within itself as a second ego or self is the greatest when we are at the end of our physical life, thus when we pass through the portal of death.

If we examine this and submit to greater scrutiny what has in this way come into being as a second self, we would have to say that people are not always inclined to look at this more closely. They become taken up with their lives, and they do not pay sufficient attention to the second being that is being developed. But if they devote enough attention to it they will find that this second being has quite particular qualities, above all a very significant urge to have an independent and free relationship to what we are able to receive in later life. In life as it proceeds we will be living in a particular linguistic environment. However, what we have developed inwardly aspires towards a certain liberation from what only one particular linguistic environment can give, and to nurture a view of life that is free and independent from any specific linguistic environment. We want to grow beyond what one particular linguistic environment can give, and we thereby grow beyond that in which we had grown up when we were young. In our younger years, for example, we have to develop a certain formation of the ear. From what we develop within our ego we notice that it is something that always wants to be freer and freer from our outward bodily nature. We are forming a new human essence that is independent of what has been fashioned from the outward physicality of our early life.

This is what spiritual science would guide the soul towards: that from the human ego a second ego or self is developed in the course of life, whose nature consists in that it feels itself all the fuller and all the more intense to the extent that it can feel itself independent of what has grown up from its early days. And if we consider this second ego that has been formed within our ego more carefully, we will see that it is endowed with such forces that we can characterize its whole nature by saying: This ego bears within itself the forces to form a new, a different human being from the one through which it has itself been fashioned.

It is not an analogy but merely a clarification if we say that the ego that we have within us can be compared with the seed of a plant that has been formed from the root through the stem and the green leaves to the blossom. It is then most fully endowed with life and provides the foundation for a new plant. The whole being of the plant has come together in the seed, and when the seed is ripe the stem, green leaves and blossom die off. It is thus that a soul-spiritual essence matures with us. Just as the seed of the plant continues to grow when the leaves fade and the outer physical form of the plant approaches death, so does the soul-spiritual essence within man mature as the outward aspect gradually dies when the organs gradually lose their vigour and approach their demise. With this we have a right soul-observation of the distinctive fact that comes to expression in that the inner strength of a new ego is at its greatest when we pass through the portal of death. Thus we bear this system of forces, these force-relationships, through the portal of death into a world that can have nothing to do with the world within our body.

Even if we do not want to pursue any further (the following lectures will show this) how the spirit-researcher can also show us what happens with this soul-spiritual essence developed within the ego in a purely spiritual world which a human being experiences in a life that lies between death and a new birth, we can nevertheless say: In the same way that the natural scientist proceeds when he wants to understand plants, we can likewise proceed if we want to understand human nature. The natural scientist directs his attention to the seed of the plant and sees how the seed can enable the life of a new plant to flourish. Thus he seeks to understand the new plant from the basis of the seed, how the seed that remains appears again in a new plant. Similarly, the spirit-researcher can observe man, how he enters life through birth or conception. We see how to begin with man manifests outwardly only that his organs are fashioned in a certain way. There then appears that soul-life that we have characterized by saying that the time when it appears also marks the moment until which he is later able to remember. Then he will say to himself: Before this time I was quite obviously already there, but I am only able to remember back to a certain time. This is that point in time when a person becomes capable of feeling himself as an ego; but there can be no doubt that he is already present as a being of soul and spirit. Why, spiritual science may ask, does the possibility of being able to remember back appear only from a certain time? Were the inner forces that bring this about not previously present? It would be a completely illogical thought to conceive of the soul-spiritual dimension of man's being as beginning only at the time back to which a person can subsequently remember. The sleep of every day can teach us how the soul-spiritual forces live in us before retrospective memory awakens.

People today have all sorts of strange ideas about sleep. The right way of looking at it has already been partly addressed in the lectures about waking and sleeping.[58] Thus people today have the idea that sleep could only be brought about by something such as tiredness. I beg the listeners to the earlier lectures to be aware that spiritual science wishes to be precise in what it says. If someone were to say that spiritual science has itself declared that sleep derives from tiredness, this is not quite correct, for it was said that sleep is needed to take tiredness away. In spiritual science it is always of importance to understand things very precisely, because there also has to be the endeavour to describe things with a similar precision.

Can tiredness be the cause of sleep? Anyone who maintains this will be contradicted by life itself. Anyone who maintains that a person has to sleep only because he is tired will find himself contradicted if he engages in self-observation, or if he considers how often a pensioner who is not at all tired goes to sleep in the afternoon in his chair, despite not being in the least tired. And he will especially be refuted if he takes into consideration when sleep mostly happens—not when people are most tired but in childhood. There needs to be accurate observation of what actually happens.

Spiritual science shows that both during the ordinary state of sleep and also during the more subdued state of consciousness of a child the forces that are used for consciously experiencing the world are sent into the organism and are active there. The same forces that we use from waking up until going to sleep in order to form ideas, sensations and so on work on us during sleep, but in such a way that the bodily forces that have been used up are replaced, are again restored. So they regenerate us, they repair what has been used up and is worn out, they form and work restoratively. Whereas in waking life they break up and disfigure the form—and this is indeed what we do during waking life—sleep enables the form to be restored, that is, it works directly on the human physical structure. Because during sleep we are frequently using our forces of consciousness for building up certain forces that have fallen into disrepair, these forces withdraw from us and we sink into a state of unconsciousness. Because at the beginning of life, before the moment arrives until which we are later able to remember back, we in early childhood use the same forces that live in us and fill our consciousness for the more refined process of forming the organization of the brain, they withdraw from the conscious ego. The ego is present during early childhood, and it is a strange situation today if the way that the ego first appears is regarded as a determining factor in the study of human nature. Again, a significant error of logic!

You can read whole volumes today where it is stated: We see how self-consciousness emerges, how it becomes established in a human being. One cannot think of anything more misleading than this, and in any other area one would strictly reject such a declaration, just as it would for example be rejected in the case of someone whose knowledge of a clock was confined solely to his awareness of how it is made. In no realm is this so. Similarly with regard to self-consciousness, if one would examine how ideas are engendered one could show the extent of the errors that are made in this respect. This can be done only by someone who concerns himself with such things from the point of view of spiritual science. Otherwise people do not notice this. Ego-consciousness, self-consciousness is of such a nature that the gradual knowledge of the ego, of how it develops, has nothing to do with the reality of the ego itself. On the contrary, because the ego, the essence of human nature, evolves continually from the time when it is not yet conscious in the child until the time when it is experienced consciously, we cannot say that it is not there! It is there, it fashions the human being in his more refined aspects. Indeed, moreover: it fashions the human being in his connection with the whole of human life—something that we notice only if we study human life in a more or less selfless way.

In the manner in which a person ordinarily observes life, he can say with respect to his destiny: I meet with one or another aspect of it. I have a liking for the one, but not for the other; I regard one as good fortune, the other as misfortune, the one as something that expedites my progress in life, the other as something that impedes it. However, this is only a superficial observation, for it could be possible for someone to be convinced that in every moment of his life he is nothing other than his concentrated destiny. That I am speaking to you now, what does it mean? It means that it is my concentrated destiny. My life experiences are being expressed to you, and I am nothing other than my life experiences, my destiny; and were I to take something away from my destiny, I would have to cut out part of myself. A human being is what he has made of himself, what his destiny is, what he is in a given moment. We cannot separate our ego from ourselves, from our destiny, or regard the ego as something different as regards its content from destiny.

But in that we are as a child placed in a particular life's circumstance we see how we are not only determined by our attributes, by our ego—even if we are not as yet aware of this, since our ego works through our blood circulation, and since it will also subsequently develop quite definite attributes and so on—but we also see that we have been placed in a particular national context, that we are children of particular parents and have grown up in a particular climate and have to live together with certain people. In this way we see that for our whole life we are determined by destiny. If we examine what we are consciously able to pursue and identify as our destiny, it is natural that we must identify this as the destiny associated with our ego, just as we have through our circumstances been placed in a life that is either arduous and burdensome or surrounded by caring hands. It is not only our later destiny that is connected with what we have ourselves done but also the strokes of destiny that come to us from the unconscious and whose origins we are unable to follow with our consciousness.

Thus we are led to the soul-spiritual essence that contains within it all the forces that fashioned the brain, formed the blood system and so on and thereby defined us. But we are also defined as regards our destiny by the same ego that has been placed in a particular life-circumstance. In the realm of nature observation this is admitted by every individual when he says, for example: When I observe an Alpine plant, I know that the whole of Alpine nature belongs to it, and therefore the Alpine plant cannot grow on the plain. What everyone admits in the realm of nature observation needs only to be applied to the soul-spiritual essence. One will then see that the soul-spiritual essence, which pervades its bodily nature, seeks out this bodily nature and enters into it, while on the other hand it also seeks out its destiny.

If this destiny is felt to be harsh and it is then said to the person: You have created this situation for yourself, you have brought this upon yourself through your soul-spiritual essence—if one ascribes the full responsibility for the harshly experienced destiny to the person concerned, this feeling is nevertheless based on a short-sighted observation. A deeper principle would judge differently, and we can gain an understanding of how it would do so if we draw a comparison from life by way of an example. Let us imagine a young man who, having a prosperous father, has been living at his father's expense and has not needed to worry about anything. Then the father for some reason loses his means of livelihood and the son can no longer live in the way he did before. He will perhaps say: What a bitter blow I have suffered! How unfortunate I am! But if he has learnt something, if he has been buffeted by life and has become a capable person, will he when he has reached the age of fifty say something of that kind? No, he will now perhaps say: That turn of destiny was something of a blessing for my personal life, for I would otherwise have become a good-for-nothing; this misfortune of my father has contributed to my happiness.

What can be said from the standpoint of eighteen years is not especially far-sighted; at fifty we can see further. The deeper life-principle within us seeks out misfortune, it seeks out hardship and misery, because it is only through the overcoming of hindrances amidst hardship and misery that we have developed further and thus become something that we would not have become otherwise. Viewed from a higher vantage-point, and once we have admitted that there is in a person a deeper essential nature that goes from life to life and makes it necessary for us to regard life from a higher vantage-point, much immediately becomes understandable to us.

If we are able to see a person in such a way that as he approaches old age he develops within himself a system of forces that prepares the way for a new human being who is well-nigh independent from what he has outwardly developed from his previous life or from the circumstances of his present life, and if we see how he carries an inner tension of forces through the portal of death, then we can say: This human individual cannot now return into existence immediately after death. Why not? What would happen if he did so? He would find the outward environment still similar to that from which he has just departed and from which he wanted to become free by developing his inner soul-essence. Just as the inner soul-essence does not have a direct relationship to itself such that it wants to revert to being merely 'itself', so is a person unable to incarnate again immediately after death, for he would be growing into himself. This means, however, that the inner soul-essence can reincarnate only after a certain time. During this time he lives in a purely spiritual atmosphere, not in the physical world. What has developed as a spiritual essence, has developed in such a way as one sees the seed of a plant developing within the stem, leaves and blossom, lives in a spiritual world, and it will feel itself drawn to embody outwardly what it has developed when other circumstances have emerged; that is, when the Earth has changed such that the person concerned is growing into different circumstances, thus enabling him to develop further.

Thus between death and the next birth so much time will elapse that we will, for example, not be born into the same linguistic area and that other associated circumstances will also have changed. We know that outward earthly circumstances change over the course of centuries and millennia. We learn about what has taken place in the meantime outwardly in cultural terms through being informed about it, through education. Thus with our soul-spiritual essence we therefore take our leave from a particular time in history with the forces that we wanted to make free and wait until new circumstances have been brought about on the Earth; whereas we have to catch up on what we have not in the meantime been able to participate in through education. Thus education and instruction have to supplement the attributes and capacities that we bring as the fruit of previous lives.

In the relatively short time available I have only been able to indicate what one may call a way of observing the circumstances in which the human soul finds itself. I have sought to ensure that this study is on the one hand strictly scientific but that on the other hand something real is seen in these soul-spiritual experiences, and that it can be perceived how in a person as he lives amongst us there is already being developed what will appear in a next life as a seed that draws upon the forces of inheritance together with the forces of the outward environment in order to develop further.

Such a way of looking at the world as emanates from spiritual science can have an eminently sound influence not only upon theoretical life-questions but upon strength and certainty and upon the power of life itself. Anyone who for reasons of his own does not want to familiarize himself with spiritual science will not see that a sound and healthy outer life is conditional in many essential ways on a sound and healthy soul-life, that such a soul-life rays its forces into one's bodily nature; and that if the soul has become empty and desolate and is unable to draw forth from itself what fills its consciousness with a sense of satisfaction, then dissatisfaction, disconnectedness, a tendency of the soul-life to be engulfed in confusion, manifests itself in nervousness and other unhealthy symptoms right down into the physical organism. Someone who does not see this may nevertheless experience it. Life poses the greatest riddles, and in instances that have significance for everyone something occurs which one can only express by asking: From where else do certain illnesses afflicting a life that is discontent with itself derive than from the fact that the soul-life is unable to regain health, is bereft of inner substance and is therefore incapable of exerting its influence upon the bodily nature? But someone who finds the possibility of bringing the health-giving influence of a healthy soul-life to bear upon the physical body will also be able to say the following.

When a person in our time refers again and again to inherited qualities and with respect to one thing or another—for example, to a disposition towards a certain illness—claims that this has been inherited from his ancestors and there's nothing he can do about it, this idea is one that inevitably oppresses him in his deepest inner soul-life and signifies a depressive soul-condition which rapidly exercises an unfavourable influence upon the outward life of the body; and this is felt by the person concerned as a dispiriting influence that cannot be changed, because it lies wholly in the line of physical inheritance. However, someone who is from spiritual science able to gain the conviction that what is living in him is not solely a collection of inherited characteristics and forces but something that as a soul-spiritual essence goes from life to life can—if spiritual science is for him no mere theory but something that pervades his life—develop the awareness that alongside all the inherited characteristics and forces there lives within him his soul-spiritual essence from which he is able to draw the forces through which he can overcome these difficulties, even if the line of inheritance might bear a strong indication of decadence.

The awareness that one can gain from spiritual science does not only answer riddles of life of a theoretical nature but answers all questions that influence our entire feeling life as riddles to which we have to have an answer in order to live within our soul. If we know nothing of that soul-spiritual essence that hastens from life to life, we feel ourselves weighed down beneath the yoke of heredity which oppresses us and makes us weak. We only feel ourselves to be strong and actively alive and to be living as people with a soul and spirit if we keep an upright stance with respect to our soul-spiritual essence and are able to say to ourselves: The forces of our soul-spiritual essence are unconquerable, for it is they alone that bring together what we have been given through the line of inheritance; and through them we are able from the centre of our soul to bring what is seemingly doomed to decline to a true ascendancy. The solutions that spiritual science brings are inscribed into life itself; but spiritual science will only be able to bring its true fruits if it can be linked in this way with the whole orientation and inner conviction of the soul, and if we become strong and not only clever through spiritual science. But we also become more capable in our thinking, especially with regard to certain more delicate distinctions that life asks of us, and gain in strength and judgement for a more refined conception of life.

Just one example of this! When those who love to trace everything back to heredity investigate some significant individual with respect to his or her ancestral line, they will probably say that there are certain qualities that this person possesses which can be found in one ancestor, while other qualities can be traced back to another ancestor. And they may then say that this has all accumulated and been passed on and the inherited characteristics have come together in this individual's soul. They then coin the proposition: So you see that the genius stands at the end of a line of inheritance and has inherited from the ancestors.

When expressed in this way, the lines of the thought have, so to speak, become crossed. For who would have proved anything through this succession of ideas? Something would only have been proved if one were able to show that the genius stood at the beginning of a hereditary sequence, though not if he or she appears at the end of it. For if the genius appears at the end of a sequence of ancestors, if you will forgive my saying so this proves nothing more than if one were to speak of someone falling into the water and being wet once he has come out. This proves only that he has passed through a particular element and has taken something from it, since someone who has emerged from water is indeed wet. If one wanted to prove something through the line of inheritance, one would have to show that the genius stands at the beginning and not at the end of a line of inheritance. But people will leave this well alone, for the world speaks otherwise.

Spiritual science seeks everywhere to pose and answer questions in the right way. One will then see that spiritual science is not at variance with natural science, but also that an answer does not suffice. Probably the greatest wisdom for life will be drawn from spiritual science if the whole of human education can be placed in its light, if man advances in his development in such a way that this is translated into becoming conscious of the soul-spiritual essence.

The soul-spiritual essence will then develop with a person between birth and death in such a way that not only does that fullness of the soul that was spoken of earlier become a reality but that the soul also becomes conscious of the second self, that germinal essence that becomes ever more concentrated. The awareness of this will then pass over into a different form of life. The person concerned will indeed see how the time is coming when his hair loses its colour, his face becomes wrinkled and the forces that support the outer organs wane. But he will then look at what he has seen developing from when he was young, at what is for him the residue and inheritance of an earlier life, and will feel in the way one does with the seed of a plant, when the falling leaves signal the end of the plant's form but the seed grows ever stronger. Thus the person will feel himself to be the seed of a new life and will say to himself: What falls away from you must go through death, for you cannot remain within it; for there must be another vessel that you can indwell, you must build for yourself another body, for you have already prepared it within you. He will feel the life that he will live in the far future maturing within him.

That repeated lives are not without a beginning and an end, and how the question as to what extent these incarnations of man's essential being have a beginning and an end can be answered, will be considered at a later point.[59]

If a person regards life as a seed for a following life, he will also see how this life again develops a seed. He is then not clinging to a theory of immortality that he investigates philosophically, but he sees a succession of lives blossom and thrive and fills himself with the awareness of immortality, because he knows that from every life the seed for a new life must arise. It is in the constantly growing and hope-inspiring life-seed that the human individual finds answers to questions relating to the riddles of life and death. He does not only answer them theoretically but embraces, understands and experiences immortality in his living inner experience, and does not merely say that he has understood immortality but he embraces the soul in its essence as a being that cannot but be immortal, because from every life it develops a new life-seed; and the individual human being inwardly beholds the maturing of this new life-seed. Hence we may say: Spiritual science answers the question that arises from the riddles of life and death not only theoretically—it does not only give a theoretical certainty—but it can inwardly transform our life in such a way that with the grasping of immortality we summon forces together and feel what goes from life to life and, hence, through all lives.

So in this way theory is transformed into practice, the riddle of immortality into a grasping of immortality itself. This is the best fruit of spiritual science, when it is transformed from mere study into something that truly lives within us. And one may say: When spiritual science is understood by a person in this sense, then it is not merely something that makes an experience comprehensible to him but something that immerses itself into his own soul as a life-force and dwells within him.

Thus we may conclude our studies for today by saying that spiritual science teaches us by also livingly demonstrating for the human soul what casting an eye over the rest of the world teaches us—the great vision of the constantly changing nature of life, and at the same time also of the eternity that forever manifests itself to us in all its changing nature; it teaches us the eternity present in everything temporal. As though in brass tablets the great life-experience is inscribed in our soul that everything that lives in the universe lives only by creating within itself the seed for new life. And the soul only gives itself up to old age and death in order to mature immortally towards constantly renewed life!

Lecture 6

BERLIN, 12 DECEMBER 1912

NATURAL SCIENCE AND SPIRITUAL RESEARCH

Among the reproaches that are presently levelled against spiritual science and spiritual research, one of the most significant is that spiritual science or spiritual research is opposed to the assured results of natural science, which is after all—and rightly—the pride of our present intellectual life and, indeed, of the whole of our modern culture. If this reproach were to have any foundation and that spiritual science and spiritual research have the intention of placing themselves in opposition to these assured results of natural science, it would be reasonable to say that this would not bode well for spiritual research. Not only would this affect any possibility that it may have of gaining access to the minds and hearts of people today but also the very justification for its existence. Thus in addition to everything that has been said in the previous lectures about the relationship of spiritual research to natural science, this special episodic study about the relationship of spiritual research to natural science will be inserted today before considering on the next occasion a figure who is eminently accessible only to spiritual science, that of Jacob Boehme.

Spiritual research, as meant here in these studies, presents itself without doubt as something that in many respects distinguishes itself from the intellectual habits and endeavours of our time as something new, as something that asserts its independence from the ways of thinking of present intellectual life. And the question therefore arises: How is it that precisely at a time when an educated person who is interested in a broad range of intellectual questions places considerable hope in what natural science is able to give—how is it that at such a time this spiritual science wants to succeed in putting itself in the very midst of the triumphant march of natural-scientific thinking?

This question can most easily be answered if one briefly surveys the intellectual life of the last third or perhaps the second half of the nineteenth century. This is not only the time when natural-scientific research has achieved one conquest after another and risen to its most brilliant heights but also when the hopes that all conceivable information about the meaning of what one may call mental and intellectual life would surely emerge from natural science were to become ever greater and greater. Anyone who has with full consciousness accompanied intellectual life in the last third of the nineteenth century or, shall we say, has been in a position to let the great hopes of this nineteenth-century intellectual life to exert their influence upon him (for example, in the 1880s) could observe at that time how from all areas of scientific research the only questions that emerged were such as to place all human thinking directly on a new foundation that breaks all connection with the old.

Attention will be drawn here to one instance of this. In the 1860s and 1870s someone interested in intellectual matters could become familiar with what was at the time a more or less new area in science, namely the mechanistic theory of heat. Anyone involved at that time in scientific knowledge regarded something such as the mechanistic theory of heat as an immense achievement of the human mind. But perhaps the standpoint of such a person is of less interest to us than the standpoint of someone who was primarily concerned with the intellectual question of cognition. What did such a person see?

Such a person had perhaps been able to observe that among the many sense-impressions that besiege someone by way of his senses is the sensation of what one may call warmth or, shall we say, warmth and cold. Like colour, like light and like sound, warmth is likewise initially a sense-impression. A person feels through his senses how the world around him is in a certain state of warmth, and he initially perceives this warmth as an impression on his feeling-life. At this time that has just been spoken of, it was according to current research considered to be a proven fact that what people call warmth, in the way that—as they believe—it works in their feeling, is diffused in space, pervades bodies and affects beings, that what is thus objectively out there in nature is none other than the movement of the minutest bodily parts. Thus one could say: If you put your hand in lukewarm water and perceive a certain degree of warmth, this sensation of warmth is only apparent. What appears to you as a direct impression is only an apparent one, it is only an effect on your organism that is brought about by something. It is merely a miniature form of movement; you do not perceive the movement itself. The smallest parts of the water are in activity, but you do not perceive the activity or movement; largely because the movement is so rapid, you do not perceive it as such but it makes on you the impression of warmth. When at the time books appeared such as, for example, *Heat considered as a Mode of Motion*,[60] this was considered to be a great achievement of the time; and we then had younger people studying how the smallest molecular parts move in a liquid or gas, bump against the walls and against one another, and it became clear to them that the inner activity that is present stimulates the apparent sensation of what is referred to as warmth.

From this arose a certain habit of thought, a particular way of observing natural phenomena, and I myself still recall that when I was a little boy the head teacher of my school, enthused by this scientific achievement of his time, considered all natural forces as such, beginning from gravity and extending to warmth or heat and chemical and magnetic forces, merely as an illusory manifestation and saw the truth as residing in those movements, in those delicate states of movement within bodies. That head teacher—his name was Heinrich Schramm[61]—for example saw gravity, the tendency of objects to fall, purely in terms of a movement of the smallest parts of bodies. Within such an observation of nature, the only thing that could be said to be genuinely 'real' was the space that extends into infinity, the matter divided into the smallest parts that exists in this space and the movements of this matter! And the hope could probably arise that, just as one could, for example, explain heat, electricity, magnetism and light as the refined working of the smallest parts of matter, one would also eventually be able to explain the activity of thinking, soul-activity, as the refined working of that matter of which the body of a human being or animal is composed.

There then came to be several phases in the evolution of natural-scientific theories. Whereas in the 1880s one had to conceive of, for example, light and the whole world of colour—if one was a physicist—as a kind of appearance and had to study infinitely complicated, refined functions and movements within matter and the ether, in the course of the 1880s what occurred was that people began to have doubts about these refined functions and confined themselves more to considering the way that the phenomena and facts present themselves, to describing them through the means of calculation, and not so much to speculate about what is after all not perceptible but merely underlying everything—that is, about the more refined functions of matter and the ether. This was how things were in the realm of physics.

In this latter realm it was the case that people saw no real possibility of coming away from the habitual kind of thinking that resulted when they considered these refined workings of matter in relation to anything that might make it possible to comprehend the spirit in a direct way. Something in natural science was, so to speak, holding them back from giving consideration to the spirit, as has been asserted here in the previous lectures. Certain other factors also presented themselves. Anyone who was involved with the developments in natural science did not only have to deal with what has just been characterized but also with the outcome of everything that had, for example, resulted from the great discoveries of Schleiden and Schwann[62] in the first half of the nineteenth century, through which the smallest parts within the organisms of plants and animals—cells—were discovered. This did not amount to a demonstration of the reality of atoms and molecules, but organic forms were traced back to their smallest building blocks, to cells, the forms of which were accessible only to the microscope. There then came the further influence of everything associated with the name of Darwin, and also of the great deed of Ernst Haeckel, who in the course of the 1880s extended Darwin's theory to human beings.[63]

Thus one was presented with a form of scientific observation which at its simplest began in the plant and animal worlds and considered how the individual organs arose from imperfect to more perfected beings and ultimately to man in such a way that one could, as it were, detect through comparison the emergence of individual organs that were more complicated from simpler ones. An immense wealth of knowledge was collected. The breadth and width of this material was, indeed, so great that, for example, in the 1870s one of the most significant comparative anatomists of the present time, Carl Gegenbaur,[64] could say in his *Comparative Anatomy* (1878) that in recent decades an immense amount of knowledge has been assembled which shows how related living beings are as regards their organs, and that one would—Gegenbaur believed—have to await the possibility of raising this knowledge to the level of 'findings' or 'insights'; and he had great hopes that it would be possible for the Darwinist method to show what a comparison of the organs of the highest, living beings with those of less perfected beings would incontrovertibly demonstrate, and that there also exists what in a physical sense may be referred to as a descent of perfected living beings from less perfected ones. Thus one saw the chain link up in the evolution from less perfected living beings to more perfected ones and then to man, and one could say to oneself that through a kind of summation of those forces and activities that exist among the simplest living beings—and indeed, even through a summation of the forces and activities of lifeless nature—there finally arises the most complicated being that we know, the human bodily structure.

Enormous hopes were associated with this natural-scientific ideal. The situation at the time was that it was difficult for people to understand the difference between what constituted scientific facts and the thoughts and speculations arising out of these facts, for any thinking person could see that there was a difference between the facts and the theories. The difference that existed could be outlined as follows. When people embarked upon research so carefully and so subtly, as Darwin himself did especially in his early years,[65] they found an immense amount of material concerning mutual relationships, mutual points of comparison between individual living beings, from the less perfected animal and plant kingdoms up to man. But there was—they could say to themselves—a difference between what thus emerged as the fact of the similarity of the inner processes, and what could only be thought about: the hypothesis, the acceptance of the idea of the descent of perfected living beings from less perfected ones; for this descent could not be derived from the facts that had hitherto become known. Researchers were confronted by a whole range of living beings, of greater and lesser degrees of perfection; but descent as such remained for anyone who really had his head screwed on a mere hypothesis, if he wished to continue to stand firmly on the ground of natural science. But the material was impressive.

All that emerged of this nature from natural-scientific research entered deeply into people's souls, sometimes in a tumultuous way because of the magnitude of the insights that could thereby be gained. Much else also needs to be taken into account. For the purposes of today's lecture of orientation, there is much that needs to be investigated in greater detail. Thus reference must be made to the great discovery which for example Helmholtz had made in the area of the phenomenon of light[66] and the effects of light upon the organ of the human eye, and as Helmholtz had also made with respect to the phenomena of sound and tone and the effect of sound and tone on the human ear, on the human organ of hearing. As a result of this it became possible to gain insight into the process of seeing, which had hitherto remained mysterious, and also to understand what, for example, happens in the ear and what a complicated miraculous structure is to be found in the piano-like apparatus within the ear. In place of much that formerly seemed merely thought-out, there was now some precise knowledge of the structure of the human organs. It could be said that what was outwardly only movement and activity was as though transformed—as we have just seen, such a transformation had emerged quite significantly from the mechanistic theory of heat—by what had been revealed about miraculous qualities in the organs with respect to the perceptions living in human souls. And the inner life of the soul is ultimately fashioned from what our organs form from the influences of matter and space.

One can perhaps characterize the whole spiritual process that was being enacted within souls at that time by saying that souls were numbed by everything that had been discovered on a broader and a more detailed scale. There was a recognition that nothing had formerly been known about any of this. Many traditions that had existed regarding the human soul now seemed to be invalid whenever one began to study the influence of matter and its movements upon the human organism, that is, when one in the true sense of the word began to study natural science.

For the spiritual scientist what really mattered was not so much all the various details but rather that it had to be admitted that in order to enter into the wide perspectives that a world of the truly factual reveals, something needs to be taken into account that one does not associate with old ways of studying the life of the soul or the spirit. In many souls that experienced everything in the last third of the nineteenth century, the following feeling arose. Such souls could say to themselves: It is true that people in olden times have ventured to think much about the great questions, for example about the alternation between sleep and waking life, about the question of the immortality of the human soul, about the questions of death and life, about the origin of existence and so on. But if one compares the whole methodical way of thinking, the whole way in which spiritual research was conducted in those far-off times whence such traditions of soul-research may be evoked, if one compares this with the strict, scientific manner of modern scientific research, that which has come from those ancient times is simply no match for the strict, conscientious methods of modern scientific research. Even if the spirit-researcher is not directly touched by the results of natural science, even if he is perhaps not in the least enraptured by them, one thing worked powerfully also on him: the strictness of natural-scientific thinking, the conscientiousness, the enormous sense for truth that characterizes natural-scientific thinking.

With respect to such a fact, anyone who wanted to have anything to do with science, irrespective of whether this was with natural or spiritual science, had to develop the impulse that can be characterized in these terms: science in the true sense of the word, such as can set the tone for the intellectual and cultural life of the present day, can seek its salvation only in that strict thinking, in that truly conscientious research, that one can learn from natural science. Such an impulse is gradually transformed (and it also had to be transformed in the spiritual-scientific researcher) into a kind of scientific conscience. Such a researcher could say to himself: To be sure, as at all times so also in modern times the soul has the urge and the impulse to come to know its own nature and being and above all else the processes that extend beyond birth and death. But only that which presents itself to its time in accordance with the model of natural-scientific thinking can make an impression on someone who has a clear and unprejudiced outlook. Much could be seen appearing, as it were, on the spiritual market about all manner of soul questions. One saw much that was and is truly far-removed from a conscientious mode of thinking that is in tune with natural science. It is true that such things may through carelessness, through the laziness of contemporary thinking, sometimes make an impression here and there for a while; but such an impression cannot be of any duration, for even the laziest people will eventually ask: What can a conscientious thinking that is in tune with natural science say about what is alleged to have been researched about the spiritual world?

Thus the need arose also for soul-researchers to adapt their mode of research to the model of natural science. It could be said that the psychology, the soul-teaching of the aforementioned Franz Brentano,[67] which has been conceived to fill several volumes, is a kind of ideal picture of this which has not been completed. Of all these volumes only one has appeared, the first, in the spring of 1874. And although it was promised that the next volume was to appear in the autumn of the same year, it has not appeared to this day.

Brentano did not proceed in accordance with the model of those soul-researchers of whom it was said last time that they wholly exclude the great questions such as the nature of the alternation between sleep and waking life, the question of the immortality of the human soul and so on, but he wanted to deal with all these questions wholly in accordance with the model of strict natural-scientific methodology. He failed. And why did he fail? Franz Brentano was never able to make up his mind to follow the path that is shown to be the one necessary for the present by the very fact that such a spirit as Brentano failed after not wishing to do so. This path has been characterized in the preceding lectures and especially in the last of these. It was indicated of this path that it alone is suitable for leading us into the higher realms, into the higher regions of existence, into that which also extends beyond birth and death. Franz Brentano could not summon the resolve to follow this path. That one must follow it if one wants to arrive at an endpoint or goal is something that he has formally proved in the negative sense through the fact that his study of the soul, or psyche, has been confined to the first volume, which has nothing to do with all the great questions that have been mentioned, that he has not been able to arrive at the great questions as he would have wished to do.

I attempted to give you a picture of the intellectual and cultural life of the 1880s, which included anyone who at that time was looking for a path into the realms of spirit. If everything that has now been mentioned has made an impression, one will not so readily be able to relate to the initially sporadic testimonies of the growing interest in spiritual science that were appearing at that time. I shall merely draw attention to how not only in the midst of natural-scientific research itself but also of scientific education a book such as *Esoteric Buddhism* by A.P. Sinnett found its place.[68]

I shall not now address the leading question that 'Buddhism' here has nothing to do with the Buddha and what is known as the religion of Buddhism, but will simply state that with this book, which became known in German-speaking regions in the 1880s, an overview was given of world phenomena, of the great course of cosmic events and also of the questions that relate to the nature of man's being, and also to the relationships concerning a life that extends beyond birth and death. What was communicated in this book could initially appear astonishing. For anyone who directed his attention towards spiritual things could in certain respects express agreement as such with much of what Sinnett writes in his *Esoteric Buddhism.* There was little to disagree with as regards what one could and should think, even if one stood strictly on a natural-scientific foundation. But one thing was at variance with the scientific education of that time, one thing that meant that one could indeed accept this book as an interesting phenomenon of the age but that it was impossible to be fully in agreement with it: that in the whole manner of the book's presentation, in the way that things are brought together and traced back to their sources, nothing was justified in terms of strict natural-scientific education and truthfulness; and that someone with a scientific education, however much he might agree with particular conclusions and other information imparted by this book, necessarily felt himself repelled by the whole manner of its presentation.

It was a similar situation with many other books that appeared in this area. This was even the case with the book by an author who has a certain entitlement to fame, H.P. Blavatsky,[69] which appeared at the end of the 1880s and the beginning of the 1890s, *The Secret Doctrine*. Anyone who had anything to do with these things could say to himself: There is in this book a deep knowledge and insight about spiritual things, but the whole way that it is presented is so chaotic, so intermingled with scientific dilettantism that is especially demonstrated in the contesting of natural-scientific theories and hypotheses, that no one with a scientific education can respond to this book in a positive way.

Thus two things emerged from this. For someone who with his mind and heart affirmed the continuing existence of a spiritual world, there was on the one hand the mode of thinking of natural science, the whole scientific way of forming ideas. Through this he could cultivate his scientific conscientiousness, through this he could free himself from all dilettantism, if he seriously put his mind to it. Through this he could, however, also learn how strictly research is carried out about factual things, and how through such research about factual things one arrives at definite results that relate directly to life, that are fundamental not only for a theory but for the actualities of life. On the other hand such a person could say: Yes, but when one seeks to gain from natural science itself something towards a spiritual interpretation of the phenomena of life, indeed, when natural science attempts this through its own resources, little can be squeezed out of it by way of spiritual content, and all the less so as it ventures more strictly into the realm of factual realities.

This probably gave such a person who was confronted with this situation a reason to look back a little at the evolutionary history of mankind. From this he could learn that, even if one ignores spiritual-scientific research, something has been assembled in the various cultural documents of peoples and former epochs, something is extant in the form of outward documents that contains a very extensive core of knowledge which, if one studies it more closely, is not to be taken lightly; and the more one deepens one's knowledge of this assembled evidence, the more it offers by way of illumination about spiritual life, even if one cannot directly approach the way in which it manifests itself or even the manner in which it must inevitably be found when presented in this way.

For someone who works on a superficial level, something of the nature of what Ancient Egyptian or Chaldean wisdom contains can be nothing more than an accumulation of dreamy imaginings. But anyone who enters more deeply into it will not find mere fantasies but will actually see that a quality of enlightenment about the nature of the spirit and its influence is contained in these things in forms that from a modern perspective seem in many respects to be grotesque. And something similar to what can be discerned in Egyptian or Chaldean wisdom is also evident in Ancient Indian wisdom, in so far as this evidence has been preserved. Admittedly, one should not view something like Indian wisdom, with the impression of vast significance that it must inevitably make upon anyone, with the eye of a modern philosopher such as, for example, Deußen,[70] but one will need to place oneself without prejudice within the inwardly illuminating quality associated with certain spiritual relationships. But one thing may strike one: from the manner in which everything is portrayed it becomes apparent that a spiritual knowledge of the kind that manifests itself to us here is not gained in the same way or by the same methods as the ones we employ for our research today, which have enabled natural science to go from one triumph to another. But if one is sufficiently unprejudiced on the one hand to have a sure recognition of natural science and, on the other, to become drawn to the way in which a spiritual achievement and a spiritual legacy emanate from ancient times, one will be able to be open to the overwhelming nature of these light-filled insights into spiritual life and also to see how very different the methods must have been with which these spiritual-scientific insights have been won in ancient times.

It is indeed so that spiritual science itself shows us how, for example, what can rightly be called Ancient Indian wisdom, which reveals to us penetrating insights into the nature of things, is obtained in a very different way. We find that that wisdom is not gained through outward observation, not through that thinking which in our time we call natural-scientific thinking, but by means of an inner process of self-knowledge such as we were able to characterize also here for modern times. Yoga methods, methods of self-education of the soul were employed. These methods led the soul no longer merely to behold and perceive and understand as one perceives and understands in ordinary daily life but to feel higher cognitive forces germinating within it which are able to penetrate into the spiritual worlds that reveal themselves to us if we do but develop within ourselves the requisite organs. But for existence within physical life, everything that we have by way of soul activities is in a particular way bound up with the instrument of the physical body. And spiritual research now shows us how Ancient Indian research was connected specifically with the instrument of the physical body in a manner that differs from our modern research, as it has been and continues to be conducted in natural science. Natural science conducts its research today through the senses and through the intellect, which is bound up with the instrument of the brain. What did the yoga method bring to human beings? We can address this only briefly here, because our intention is to orientate ourselves only around the relationship between natural science and spiritual science.

The yoga method enabled a person to a certain extent to exclude the thinking instrument of the brain, even to exclude everything that is mediated by the rest of the higher nervous system. That part of the human nervous system which appears today in natural science as a subordinate part but which is connected in the most intimate sense with what goes on in the human organism, namely with what we associate with the solar plexus and the sympathetic nervous system, became in the yoga methods the instrument for a strictly inward form of perception. Just as our present natural-scientific research is bound up with the higher nervous system, those ancient methods of enlightenment were similarly connected with that nervous system which we today even consider to be in a certain sense of a lower order. But because this subordinate nervous system is linked to the forces of existence and to the life-forces and is intimately connected with that through which man is himself merged with divine-spiritual existence (because it is therefore associated with the sources of human existence), with the help of this instrument one recognized the in-streaming of the spiritual world into the human organism. Thus just as with the eye one beholds the worlds of light, so with the instrument of the sympathetic nervous system did people behold the worlds of spirit and perceived in them actual facts and beings.

Anyone who can understand how someone who has thus penetrated into his own depths by virtue of this instrument is capable of relating to the universe will also understand how that ancient oriental wisdom has come down to us. If we investigate ancient sources of wisdom, we find that they are consistently unveiled, brought to the surface of human thinking, through ancient methods of research, through yoga methods. Among different peoples we find the most diverse aspects of this wisdom, and if we do but devote our attention to them we enter ever more into the depths of this wisdom and come to recognize how human beings approached it in those times when they knew relatively little of modern physical astronomy, anatomy, physiology and so forth. People living amidst Ancient Indian wisdom had no knowledge of what it is like to live in a physical human body in the way that one does today; but they were able to engage with an activity of the organism by employing a deeper level of the nervous system. This was also the case with other peoples.

By, as it were, casting one's eye over everything that was influential in terms of such ancient wisdom until the sixth century BC, one can approach a time approximating to the age of Ancient Greece. There we find, in addition to much else, an outstanding thinker who has as often been misunderstood for the good as for the harm that he may have wrought, namely Aristotle, who was active only a few centuries before the founding of Christianity. He continues even today to strike one as a remarkable figure. If we peruse his work, we find in it for the first time in many areas something of what in our time one calls natural science. For in ancient wisdom there is no trace of natural science in the modern sense. Aristotle's contribution to natural science has been acknowledged in terms of the highest praise by people in the nineteenth century who wish to stand strictly on, and only on, the ground of natural science. Thus we therefore find in Aristotle the starting-point of what can be referred to today as natural-scientific research. We additionally find in him a developed teaching of the human soul.

I shall not enter into the details of his teaching about the soul but merely draw attention to how what Aristotle says in this regard is related to what shines forth from former times by way of illumination regarding the human soul and its connection with the great spiritual worlds. One only understands what Aristotle has written about the soul if one is clear that everything that he says is given as a legacy of the old, ancient thinking that was acquired in the manner that has been characterized. Aristotle is no longer familiar with the research methods of ancient times; they are more remote for him. But what he was able to say about the composition, about the divisibility of the human soul, about the difference between that aspect of the human soul that is related solely to the physical body and therefore also to death and that which participates eternally in a spiritual life after passing through death, what Aristotle is able to say about all this has as though come over from ancient times, it is something with whose content he is familiar, something that he has received such that he could say: It illuminates my understanding. But of the various [soul] members he has knowledge only, for example, of the vegetative soul, the spirit-soul and so on. How the individual members connect with the spiritual world he no longer has any knowledge. He is able to enumerate the various parts, describe and classify them intellectually and also make them comprehensible in an illuminating way; but he can no longer show how these parts of the human soul are connected with the spiritual world.

The approach pioneered by Aristotle was carried forward into later times. Natural science became increasingly developed. There was of course the low point in the Middle Ages and the new dawn of natural science at the beginning of modern times, but if one disregards this one can say that natural science developed to an ever greater degree.

What, then, is the basis of man's relation to natural science and to the objects of natural science? Let us imagine that a person was alone with his senses, that he was unable to open up, as it were, to link, his senses to the kingdoms of nature that are outspread around us. What would individual human life be like without this relationship to nature? Consider this quite simply. If we were unable to form a connection with nature, we could perhaps dispense with our eyes and thereby have some possibility of something like an inner manifestation of light. But compare the miserable inner life in the whole physical world that a person could have through himself alone if he was unable to have a connection with the kingdoms of nature. Compare it with the rich life that is revealed when a person opens his eyes and his other sense organs to the kingdoms of nature and its impressions. We are human beings in that we live not only in ourselves but open up our organs to the kingdoms of nature that are spread out around us, and in that we are in a state of interaction with these kingdoms. Were we only to know what the eye, what our other sense organs are able to engender, how poor in content would we be as human beings here in the physical world! This gives some way of comparing what gradually became of the inner life of the soul in the times when natural science emerged and went from triumph to triumph.

With regard to the life of the soul, what Aristotle had given was, as it were, taken further; and people concerned themselves only with the observation of soul-phenomena. However, this is as though one were to allow the senses to be active only within themselves—and to this day this is what the official science of the soul does. Even in our own time, all content of official soul-science is confined to what can be compared with the mere inner activity of our sense organs or our brain when the thoughts of the brain are not directed out into the widths of the world. But we have seen in the previous lectures that through the methods of spiritual science—and this was also the case with ancient forms of spiritual science—the soul is affiliated to spiritual domains that are just as real and inwardly coherent as the realms of nature by which we are surrounded in the physical world are affiliated to the sense organs.

These spiritual domains, these wholly real spiritual facts and beings, were for a certain time—which was to allow outward natural-scientific research to come to maturity—not accessible; and so the knowledge of the life of the soul became increasingly impoverished, because a spiritual perspective of the very real evidence for the spiritual world was lacking. The soul was at best investigated in relation to its inner life, as Franz Brentano still did in the 1870s, as you can see for yourself in his *Psychology*.[71] But the nature of his research is as if one were to investigate the eye only with respect to what it can be out of itself, and not with respect to what it is capable of when it is directed towards the facts of nature.

Now one may say that it was precisely through a more exact perception of the physical processes of man's being that attention was diverted from the spiritual worlds with which the soul is connected. The soul is on the one hand indeed connected with these spiritual worlds that receive it when it has crossed the threshold of death, or when it enters another world through sleep. But the soul is connected with the physical world through its organs, through the entire nervous system and through the entire circulation of the blood. Through the fact that natural science has become ever more significant in its methods, the attention of human beings was directed towards that connection of the soul that arises between the soul and physical circumstances. The results of natural science were in this respect so colossal that human beings completely found fulfilment in, for example, how the soul fully expresses itself in its associations with the circulation of the blood and so on. Every new triumph of natural science was in a certain way unfavourable to directing the soul's attention to the connection with the spiritual world.

It is also valid to look at it in this way. Anyone who wants to acquire familiarity with a clock will have a poor idea of its whole organism if he says: When I look at how the hands of the clock move forward, there is perhaps a little demon sitting there who is moving the hands in a clockwise direction. If a person who says something of this kind felt himself to be superior to someone who merely studies the mechanism of the clock, one would have a good laugh at him, for only someone who really studies the clock's mechanism learns about it. And someone else again learns about the intellectual or spiritual life of the clockmaker or of the one who invented the clock from the clock's mechanism. One can follow both paths: investigating the mechanical process of the workings of the clock and getting to know the sequence of human thoughts that led to the clock's invention. But it would be nonsensical if someone wanted to infer that demons of some sort were setting the whole mechanism of the clock in motion.

That aspect of research into human nature which would correspond to tracing the sophisticated mechanism of the clock back to the thoughts of the inventor has gradually been lost to humanity. For as regards the human soul it would correspond to tracing thoughts back to the beings of the spiritual world. Instead it went triumphantly in natural science from one fact to another, thus to what corresponds to the 'clock's mechanism'. And one can make an interesting observation: the knowledge that is still extant from ancient times is usually lost to humanity in those periods when knowledge relating to it can be investigated with precision by natural science. It is remarkable that at the end of the sixteenth and the beginning of the seventeenth century we see how the philosopher Cartesius [Descartes] still had a certain notion of how something spirit-like works within a human being from the heart to the head, to the human head.[72] Cartesius still speaks of certain life-spirits that are not of a physical nature but whose forces interact between the heart and the head. We then see how such knowledge increasingly disappears in the intellectual life of mankind.

If anyone asks why this is so, he can be answered as follows. We see that, simultaneously with this historical disappearance of the knowledge of spiritual processes relating to the heart, there emerges the knowledge of the physical organism of the heart and of the circulation of the blood. At the beginning of the seventeenth century we first see how the English physician Harvey[73] publishes his discovery of the circulation of the blood, and how Marcello Malpighi[74] in Bologna was the first to show as an anatomist through the blood circulation of the frog how elaborate the whole blood circulation is.

Thus attention was directed towards processes associated with the senses. Knowledge about spiritual facts was, as it were, driven out by a precise knowledge of the sensory process. Whereas it signified a triumph for natural science that Francesco Redi (born in 1624)[75] formulated the proposition—which stood in opposition to many assertions of a former age—that 'everything living derives from the living', we can nevertheless say that when humanity came to trace the organic element as such back to the seed or germinal substance, to the physically indeterminate aspect of the organic seed, it lost sight of how the spiritual aspect itself intervenes in evolution independently of the organic seed. The understanding for the spiritual seed or essence was lost to humanity. This happened by degrees. The more natural science advanced as a conquering force, the more lost did the awareness of the spiritual world become.

Such things are not chance occurrences, they are also not something that one should censure or criticize but they are necessary evolutionary processes of the whole history of humanity. This is how it has to be. It often happens that when one thing is in the ascendancy and arrives at a culmination, something else declines. What we today admire about natural science and, indeed, recognize as necessary presents itself to us—if we are aware of its true evolutionary purpose—in such a way that we say: Spiritual science does not have the least reason to take issue with natural science (if it keeps within its boundaries), it also has no reason to complain about the one-sidedness of natural science. For the great achievements of natural science to this day have come about not by mixing up scientific research with all manner of speculations but only by calmly keeping one's gaze directed towards physical processes related to the senses. Indeed, one can discover in the dawn of modern cultural life how it was only through the opposition to Aristotelianism, also to what was inherently justified about its content, that spirits such as Galileo or Giordano Bruno[76] arrived at their successes, in that they refused to include in their research anything other than what was accessible to their senses and was sufficiently informative.

In our time the spiritual-scientific researcher must relate to the natural-scientific researcher in such a way that he says: The more that natural-scientific research is itself kept free from all speculation and all philosophizing, the more that one directs one's attention solely to the facts and does not conjure up all sorts of intellectual or spiritual essences, the better it is for natural science. The spiritual-scientific researcher would wish to advocate that natural-scientific facts are kept free from any speculative discussion of a natural-scientific or spiritual-scientific nature. Thus one can today on the one hand be a spiritual-scientific researcher and on the other hand stand up for the authenticity and groundedness of natural-scientific research. And it is merely a false preconception if one believes that the spirit-researcher has to oppose natural science.

It is somewhat different when one has to deal with numerous theories thrust in the direction of spiritual science that some people would wish to derive from natural science. The natural-scientific researcher is then himself embarking on the path of spiritual science, and in the majority of cases he is only very little familiar with it. But one aspect of natural-scientific knowledge nevertheless holds good both for spiritual science and natural science: this is the conscientious method previously characterized, the conscientious sense for truth of which we have often spoken in these lectures and which we also characterized as sticking with the facts.

How do these facts arise? We have seen how they do: through certain forces becoming accessible in the human soul that from this soul give rise to the connection with the higher worlds in the same way that the senses give rise to the connection with the physical world. Just as the senses ascertain the facts of the physical world and should leave them as they are and not tarnish them with speculations, so is it also a case of not philosophizing or speculating about the results of clairvoyant observation but adhering also here strictly to the facts. Then one is indeed adhering strictly to the standpoint of spiritual science but in a similar way in its realm to how one relates to natural science on its own ground. This is the approach of spiritual science as it is represented here.

This is what a spiritual science that feels a responsibility towards the spiritual needs of our time should have as its unalloyed concern.

And in any natural-scientific research that is worthy of its name, this also immediately happens with respect to facts that are available to spiritual science when natural science has knowingly reached its limits.

Here again, some very strange results arise purely out of the facts themselves. I should just like to recall what arises if we consider the views of the great natural scientist Du Bois-Reymond as he has expressed them in his addresses. The most significant of these was perhaps the one about the 'Frontiers of a Knowledge of Nature',[77] which he gave at the 45th Assembly of German Scientists and Doctors in Leipzig on 14 August 1872. Here we find a passage—and I am still aware of the deep impression that this passage of his address made on me as a young man when it first appeared—where he says something along these lines: If we have a person before us in his waking life, natural science can say nothing about how feelings, ideas, wishes, passions or emotions arise out the activity of the minutest parts of his brain. 'What conceivable connection is there between particular movements of certain atoms in my brain, on the one hand, and, on the other, facts that are fundamental to my nature which are indefinable and cannot be explained away: "I feel pain, I feel pleasure; I taste sweetness, smell the fragrance of roses, hear the sound of an organ, see redness", and the resultant constant, but questioning, certainty that I must exist. It is utterly and lastingly incomprehensible that it should not be a matter of indifference to a number of carbon, hydrogen, nitrogen, oxygen etc. atoms how they lie and move, how they lay and moved, how they will lie and move.'

Du Bois-Reymond considered it to be impossible to understand the soul-life of someone in a waking state through natural science. He therefore said: If we have someone before us who is asleep, in whom the life of feelings, ideas, wishes, emotions and passions has been extinguished, we can understand this sleeping human being in a natural-scientific way; we then have something before us that we can call an inner organic activity. But as soon as life enters into this organism when the person wakes up, this changes. Then this life, this soul-content cannot be explained scientifically from what the natural scientist is able to understand. The sleeping person, thinks Du Bois-Reymond, is scientifically comprehensible, but not one who is awake.

This on the one side. Read on the other hand the latest treatises about the nature of sleep: you will everywhere find it agreed that natural science has nothing to say about the reasons for sleep, that it has nothing to say about people when they are asleep, which according to Du Bois-Reymond was something that can be ascertained. So we see on the one hand indications that natural science on its trail-blazing path is admitting its limits in that the soul-life of a waking human being is scientifically opaque; while on the other hand we have in our own time to confess that sleep has to this day no explanation. Why not? Because sleep belongs in those regions where the spirit rays into ordinary life; and we cannot explain sleep if we are unable to explain waking life.

In one of the first lectures of this winter cycle[78] I referred to how natural science can at best conceive of a mechanism that after a certain time automatically calls forth the urge to eliminate consciousness and sensory activity in order to take away tiredness. But as was previously said, if one confines oneself to the idea that sleep is brought about by a kind of independent process of the organism that proceeds on an automatic basis, one has no explanation of the elderly person who has not been working and yet has his afternoon nap, and we also have no explanation of a small child, who sleeps most of all. In contrast, I have drawn attention to the fact that sleep is explainable only if we presuppose that when a person is asleep only the physical body and the etheric body are lying in bed and that when he goes to sleep an essentially spiritual element, namely the astral body and ego, departs from his being. What is enabled to happen through a person's soul-nature being, as it were, outside the physical and etheric body during sleep? We shall speak more fully about these things. Today the following brief indications will be given.

When the soul-nature as such leaves the physical body and its enlivening companion, something is called forth that is of an opposite nature to the waking activity of the soul. In waking activity the soul is animated. No limb moves without the soul's knowledge. Mental images are to the very least degree called forth without the soul making use of the instrument of the brain. The soul must be active in the waking state. The opposite is the case in sleep. We can say that the soul enjoys its own bodily nature in sleep life. If we proceed in accordance with spiritual research, we do so in awareness of the difference between soul-activity and soul-enjoyment in the waking and sleeping states, and we comprehend the mutual relationship between soul-work and -activity and soul-enjoyment, the latter of which must flow into soul-activity if this is to be sustained in the appropriate way. Now the elderly person no longer puzzles us by taking his afternoon nap, even though he is not tired; and we know that if the soul enjoys its body it can carry this too far, and that one can sleep when one is not tired. We understand this if we know how in certain constitutions the pleasure of the bodily nature can be taken to excess.

All this one will understand if one knows how to explain sleep from a spiritual-scientific point of view. That is to say, there is an area where natural science believes that it has undisputed authority, and where spiritual science only has something to say to it in so far as the spirit pervades everything, including the processes of nature. But then there is an area where what natural science is able to research is no longer present, where there are indeed facts, but facts that can only be perceived if the process of perception is not of a sensory but of a supersensible nature. If spiritual science proceeds with the same conscientiousness and becomes accustomed to think in its realm as strictly as natural science does in its domain, it cannot come into a collision with natural science. With this, however, spiritual science stands on a ground which is in many respects at variance with what has gradually developed in the course of the cultural life of mankind.

Thus we see how those who can be seen as the predecessors of true spiritual research, Goethe for example, had to battle against that which arose that was contrary to a spiritual-scientific endeavour. We see this most clearly if we look at the way that Goethe defended himself against Kant. It was Kant who sought to establish that the knowledge that has developed in recent times is bound up with the instrument of the brain, must be limited to outer experience and is unable to penetrate into the foundations of the world with which our soul-spiritual life is connected. This is the source of Kant's strict demarcation between 'science' and what he calls 'faith'; and higher realms are for Kant accessible only to belief. Hence he puts in the place of knowledge about a world of eternity or of the divine-spiritual a belief that insists on the 'Categorical Imperative'. Thus he decrees that the position of knowledge within spiritual science is one of pure belief. But Goethe says in his fine essay on 'Contemplative Judgement'[79] with regard to Kant: If one can in the sense envisaged enter with one's feelings into a spiritual region in which the divine-spiritual originates and from which morality is derived, why should the human spirit—if it raises itself into this spiritual region—not also truly sustain the adventure of reason? For Kant called it a 'daring adventure of reason' if man wants to enter into realms in which—according to Kant—there can be no knowledge.[80]

The question that matters for Western thinking is: How does one make the transition from natural science to spiritual science? The point is not that one needs to combat natural science but that one fully acknowledges it, indeed, truly recognizes its successes, while nevertheless, wholly in accordance with the model of natural-scientific research, one extends human knowledge to those realms with which the soul is connected in its spiritual foundations as regards those impulses that endow it with life, even when it has left the physical body and is preparing to form a new bodily organism.

It will be the task of a true spiritual research increasingly to abandon in our time an unwarranted mockery of, or wish to take issue with, the justified claims of natural science. This will of course depend on spiritual science also only being recognized as justified if it is familiar with the current situation of natural-scientific research and if, therefore, it is not motivated by a spirit of dilettantism to infringe against what can rightly be demanded by a present-day scientific education. But just as the natural scientist cannot confine himself to studying the inner nature of the eye, the ear, the sense of warmth and so forth but explores how a person has to direct what the senses are able to experience inwardly towards the rich, solid surroundings of the physical world, so must the soul-nature be recognized in that through self-education—through a new kind of yoga schooling, as was described last time, but through a new kind that is significantly different from all the old kinds—the soul lives together with that with which it is connected in the spiritual domain; and this begins only where natural-scientific research reaches its limits.

This is the precise relationship between natural science and spiritual science, but it also indicates the possibility of an on-going peaceful coexistence of and mutual understanding between natural science and spiritual-scientific research. If what has already been said in the previous lectures in this respect is brought into connection with what I have been permitted to say today in brief about the relationship between natural-scientific and spiritual-scientific research, one will also be able to gain some understanding of the justified aspect of spiritual-scientific research and also of the possibility of spiritual research acquiring a place of equal importance in our modern age alongside natural science. And one will be able to hope that the justified objections, the justified reservations that still exist today on the part of modern scientists will gradually disappear, once they see that spiritual science, far from being a lot of confused nonsense or a random set of assertions and superstition, is well familiar with what a natural-scientific education of the present requires.

If such a thing happens, spiritual research will increasingly appear as justified before the natural-scientific conscience of the present; and people will gradually also be able to understand from what arises from the actual realities of cultural life that spiritual research is indeed both possible and justified, and that the objections to spiritual research actually belong to a realm regarding which one can say something similar to the way that Goethe once spoke about a different realm, namely about the need to raise oneself above all lack of understanding and all illogicality.

With a view to summarizing the relationship of the spirit-researcher to those who appear as enemies of spiritual-scientific research, I should like in conclusion to say a few words by way of comparison about something that Goethe once said about an entirely different matter. Goethe was thinking about an Ancient Greek teaching and explanation regarding movement[81] which, however, still had an influence upon modern philosophy, a teaching that asserts that when an object moves, one can observe it at every moment, and at every moment—even in the shortest period of time—it is at rest. It is at rest, even if only for a moment. Thus there can be no 'movement', for at every point of time a moving body is at rest, and therefore is without movement. This is Zeno's conclusion about movement, and this legacy from Ancient Greece has continued to haunt the modern age.

Goethe approached this objection to the idea of movement in a quite distinctive way, and he once expressed this beautifully:

> If hostile forces you espy,
> Stay calm, stay silent too;
> And if your movement they deny
> Surround them through and through.[82]

I cannot but recall this verse when, as in recent times, I am assailed with the assertion: What you call 'spirit' is the result of purely material activities, material processes and movements; spirit is derived from matter. Just as—in the sense of what has just been said—movement derives wholly from stillness and has nothing real about it, there is also nothing real about spirit that is not matter.

If, in the way in which we are trying to penetrate into the spiritual world in these studies, one tries to gain knowledge of the spiritual world and enters rightly into spirit's essential nature, one may perhaps be inclined to define what spiritual-scientific research has brought to light about the spirit in its relationship to the opponents and enemies of spiritual science by means of a small change of Goethe's words—and this may serve as a summary of what I have to say about the relationship between natural science and spiritual science—such that one characterizes the right view of the true spirit-researcher with respect to his enemies as follows:

> If something hostile does take place,
> Stay calm, but cheerful too!
> And if the spirit they're minded to efface,
> Brood not, and do not rue,
> And grant that ultimately they're right:
> It bodes ill for their spirit!

Lecture 7

BERLIN, 9 JANUARY 1913

JACOB BOEHME

At that point in modern cultural development when we see the dawning of the new world-conception, at that time when we have to record the great deeds of Kepler and of Galileo, and when Giordano Bruno in a certain sense outlines the great problem of the modern conception of the world, we encounter the solitary thinker who is the subject of today's lecture, the simple shoemaker of Görlitz, Jacob Boehme. He struggled with the highest problems of existence in a way that can deeply occupy our thinking and feeling to this day and will probably continue to occupy people's thinking and feeling for a long time to come.

This Jacob Boehme was a quite distinctive figure who strove and struggled in isolation, while the various streams in cultural life were otherwise uniting to form a great comprehensive tableau. In a certain sense one might say that the solitary struggle of Jacob Boehme is from a certain point of view almost as interesting as the totality of the various viewpoints that we encounter at that time. And then we see how, quite remarkably, what Jacob Boehme still found in his own century in his inner solitude achieved the greatest conceivable dissemination—bearing in mind that one is dealing here with a matter of deep spiritual significance. We see from what his opponents have said how far his influence extended once only a few decades had elapsed after his death. Jacob Boehme has again and again been the object of appreciative and admiring, or dismissive and ridiculing attention; and when we observe the extent of his following and the forces that opposed him, we have the impression that both the adherents and the opponents knew that they were dealing with something quite remarkable.

Such a phenomenon is particularly remarkable to those who want to understand every personality who appears in the cultural life of humanity on the basis of the immediate circumstances of his time and his surroundings. We see, for example, how the attempt is made to understand Goethe by bringing together all sorts of details—however insignificant—about his life in the belief that by assembling these details one will be able to arrive at something that can explain some aspect of his intellectual life. It is not really possible to gain much that can lead to an understanding of Jacob Boehme in this way, for the external influences are difficult to establish through outward means. It is even harder to understand how he developed out of the intellectual life of his time. Many people have therefore come to think that in the case of Jacob Boehme we are dealing with a kind of spiritual meteor. Everything that appears here, everything that this personality had to give, seems suddenly to have emerged and come to manifestation out of the depths of his very particular soul. Others have then tried to explain that many of the things that Jacob Boehme said and many of the ways that he expressed his ideas in words and phrases bear a similarity to the formulae of alchemists or other philosophical schools of thought that were still active at his time.

However, anyone who looks more closely at Jacob Boehme's whole mentality will find that such a procedure has hardly any more value than if in the case of a significant personality—who is after all obliged to use language as a means of expression—one were to examine his language; for when Jacob Boehme avails himself of alchemical formulae this is only the way in which he clothed his thoughts linguistically. But what makes so immense an impression on anyone who tries to understand him is an originality that one finds only in the very greatest minds. There are on the other hand certain aspects that are not entirely in tune with modern thinking but which, for someone who is capable of entering into such things, nevertheless shed light on how Jacob Boehme was able to raise himself to his lofty spiritual level. In order to form a connection with his life, in so far as it is relevant here, we need to mention a few biographical facts.

Jacob Boehme was the son of very poor parents and came from Alt-Seidenberg near Görlitz. He was born in 1575. In his early years he had to tend the cattle with the other village boys. He therefore grew up in complete poverty; and since in such an environment there are no particular means of education, we will find it understandable that Jacob Boehme could barely read as a boy of twelve or thirteen and was able to write only with difficulty. But he had another experience during his boyhood which a faithful biographer heard him relate from his own mouth.[83] This experience will first be recounted. As already noted, it is not one of those things that a modern consciousness would readily find intelligible.

Once when Jacob Boehme was looking after the cows with other boys from the village, he separated himself from the other boys, climbed a moderately high mountain near his home, the Landkrone, and in the broad light of day claimed to have seen something like a gateway into the mountain. He went inside and found there a vessel, a kind of vat, filled with pure gold. This made such an impression of awe on his soul that he ran away and retained only the memory of this extraordinary experience.

One can, to be sure, speak of a dream dreamt in a waking state; and one may grant those who are satisfied with such an explanation the right to uphold it. But what really matters is not whether one calls such an event a 'dream' or gives it another name but what it releases in the soul of the person who 'dreams' it, what kind of effect it has on the soul. From the way that Jacob Boehme subsequently related this event to his friend, we see that it had become deeply engraved on his mind, that it had liberated significant forces within his soul so that it had the highest psychological significance for him.

Let us, therefore, grant rationalists the right to interpret such an experience, which was in any event a significant happening in Jacob Boehme's soul, in the way that they also want to explain the event of Christ's appearance to Paul before Damascus. However, an explanation of this kind which resorts to such interpretations must also admit that a work of the significance as that of Paul, which is so intimately connected with Christianity, had its origin in a 'dream'.

When he had this experience, the boy Jacob Boehme felt something like a profound stirring of soul-forces not otherwise active in his soul. It was a case of an inner liberation of forces lying deeply within him. This testifies to the fact that we are dealing here with a person who could descend more deeply into his soul-life than many thousands of others.

Mention should also be made of an event of a very similar nature, of which it must again be said that it continued to live in Jacob Boehme's memory in such a way that the radiance and significance of this event pervaded his entire life, in so far as this life was of an inward nature.

In his fourteenth year Jacob Boehme was apprenticed to a shoemaker and often had, as it were, to be on watch in his master's shop; he was not allowed to sell anything. On one occasion—and again this story is related directly from the mouth of his faithful biographer, Abraham von Franckenberg—a person who immediately made a curious impression on Jacob Boehme came into the shop and wanted to buy shoes. Because, however, the boy was forbidden to sell shoes, he explained this to the stranger. The latter offered him a high price, and it then came about that the shoes were sold. But then the following sequence of events unfolded, which Jacob Boehme remembered for the rest of his life. When the stranger had left and a short while had elapsed, Jacob Boehme heard someone calling his name 'Jacob, Jacob!', and when he went out the stranger came up to him even more curiously than before. He had a sun-like, radiant quality in his eyes and spoke words to him that sounded most distinctive: 'Jacob, Jacob, you are still only little, but you will become someone entirely different who will provoke great astonishment in the world. Nevertheless, remain humble before your God and diligently read the Bible. You will have to endure much persecution, but be strong; for your God loves you and will be merciful to you.'

Jacob Boehme regarded such an event as far more significant than any other, outwardly biographical events. And his biographer goes on to relate how Jacob Boehme told him that in 1593 he felt for seven days as though withdrawn from his physical body and as though living in an entirely different world; he felt as though reborn in his soul.

Thus we are dealing here with what might be called a lastingly abnormal state of soul. But Jacob Boehme also experienced this 'rebirth' of his more or less as something that he understood as being able to take place within a human soul. He did not thereby become a dreamer or a false idealist, nor did he become arrogant, but continued to practise his craft as a shoemaker in all humility and, one might say, in all sobriety. Even what he experienced in 1593, the state of being transported to another world, remained to him a phenomenon of which he said to himself: 'You have had a glimpse of a joyous kingdom, a realm of spiritual reality, but that is a thing of the past.' And he carried on pursuing his craft in a completely matter-of-fact way.

In 1600 and 1610 this experience of rebirth was repeated. He then began to record what he had experienced in his states of exaltation, since he believed that this was required of him. Thus in 1612 he wrote his first work *Die Morgenröte im Aufgange* ('Dawn in the Ascendant'), later entitled *Aurora*. He said of it that he did not write it with his ordinary ego but that it was given to him word for word; that he was living within a being that—in contrast to his ordinary ego—was of an all-encompassing nature, extended throughout the world and immersed itself within it.

However, the revelations did not do him much good. When some people became aware of what he had to say and what he had written, the manuscript of *Aurora* was copied and circulated in a small way. The consequence was that Gregorius Richter, the deacon of Görlitz, where in the meantime Jacob Boehme had established himself as a shoemaker, inveighed against him from the pulpit and not only condemned his work but managed to have him summoned before the council of the town of Görlitz. I shall now merely repeat the words that his biographer has made known to us. He relates that the verdict of the council was that Jacob Boehme must be forbidden to write anything further; for only those who were academicians were permitted to write, and Jacob Boehme was not an academician but an idiot and should therefore refrain from writing!

Thus Jacob Boehme was branded as a idiot; and since he was on the whole a good-natured person who, because of the simplicity of his nature, could not wholly think that people would consign him to damnation entirely without reason, he did indeed decide not to write anything further in the immediate future. But the time then came when he could no longer do otherwise; and between 1620 and 1624, the year of his death, he quickly wrote a large number of books such as, for example, *Das Buch vom beschaulichen Leben* ('The Book of the Contemplative Life') and *De signatura rerum oder der Geburt und Beziehung aller Wesen* or *Erklärung über das erste Buch Mose* ('Signatura Rerum, or an Explanation of the Book of Genesis'). But the number of his works is considerable, and some readers may find them baffling. Many have said that Jacob Boehme is forever repeating himself. It cannot be denied that he does say certain things over and over again; but if someone concludes that it is possible to know everything about Jacob Boehme if one knows a few of his works (on the grounds that he is always repeating himself), it must—while acknowledging that such people are making a valid point—be said that whoever contents himself with having read *one* book by Jacob Boehme and has no appetite to read any of the others does not understand much about him. Whereas anyone who takes the trouble to read his other works will, in spite of all the repetitions, not rest until he has read every single one.

If we turn from such a characterization of Jacob Boehme's nature to trying to enter into his thought-life, into his spiritual nature, it must be said that a person of today who lives only in a modern cultural environment will find much that is incomprehensible not only in the content of his books but also in the whole manner of their presentation. Everything seems at first to be completely chaotic. To be sure, one gradually gets used to it; but then for many people there continues to be something that is a difficult nut to crack, namely that he comes up with strange definitions of words that are totally unintelligible to the modern mind. Thus in his explanation of the world he is always using words like 'salt', 'mercury' and 'sulphur'. And when he wants to discuss what 'sul' and 'phur' signify and then finds all sorts of profound things to say, these modern minds then feel obliged to say that one cannot make head or tail of this; for what does it mean to offer explanations about a universal principle by giving individual interpretations of the syllables of a word, such as 'sul' and 'phur'? That is quite alien to the modern mind.

If, nevertheless, one continues to study Jacob Boehme, one finds that he clothes what he wants to say in all kinds of alchemical formulae. However, only when one penetrates to what comes to living expression as Jacob Boehme's spirit in what he discovered does one find that something is living there that is completely different to what we know today as scientific thinking, as thinking based on world-conceptions of whatever kind.

What lives in Jacob Boehme's soul most closely resembles that which has been characterized in these lectures as the first stage leading to a higher spiritual life, as the stage of imaginative knowledge. We have emphasized the fact that someone who rises from ordinary life in the sense-world comes by way of a special development of his soul to the point where he perceives a new world of pictures, of imaginations. And it was emphasized—I would ask that you call to mind the way that this was described—that when a person has managed not only to form imaginations but that pictures, imaginative conceptions shoot up from the unknown depths of the soul-life and he experiences a new world, he must—if he would ascend to new insights—make the firm resolve wholly to suppress this first glimmering of an imaginative world in the soul and to wait until it appears for a second time from a far more deeply-lying world.

The whole state of soul, the whole inner mood to which Jacob Boehme gains access can best be compared with that which a person who attains supersensible knowledge experiences in his soul-life. That is not to say that there is anything of what modern spiritual science proclaims as its methods to be found in Jacob Boehme; but there is no justification for the belief that all this became manifest in him as though of its own accord. He himself once said that he had unremittingly striven for the spirit's—for God's—assistance, and that a radiant, imaginative world had resulted from this ceaseless effort. So we cannot say that his imaginative knowledge was purely of a naive nature; we should rather say that there was something naive about the way that he took hold of the means whereby a person is led to the heights of imaginative cognition. It can be assumed that such an imaginative power was his by nature. Thus he arrived at imaginative knowledge by exactly the same paths, only more quickly, more as a matter of course, than one can arrive through such methods as are described in the book *Knowledge of the Higher Worlds: How is it Achieved?*.

Thus Jacob Boehme stands before us as someone with imaginative faculties of knowledge. But this imaginative faculty struggles with a primal force of nature to the surface, as though carried by a strong inner will. Thus we see in him this strong inner will which is unable to find full expression in outward deeds (his humble occupation prevents this), surrounding his soul like a flood, so that his soul immerses itself in this flood. And from this will we see mighty pictures being engendered, through which he tries to solve the riddles of the world. With Jacob Boehme it is not so much the various results that matter but rather this mood and particular constitution of his soul. He feels that in his aspirations he is impelled towards something that has to do not with the ordinary cognizing human ego but is connected with the forces that link the subconscious regions—the very depths—of man's soul with the entire cosmos, thus with what weaves and lives out there in nature.

A person who has a serious yearning for knowledge indeed feels that in the process of cognition there is not only something rational but something that he achieves for himself through suffering and pain and through the overcoming of suffering and pain. And when he tries to gain insight into nature and existence with the means generally available today, he notices that through such means he actually becomes ever more distant from nature and existence. But when we uncover the forces in our soul that otherwise reside in the subconscious, we feel that they are connected with nature and existence in a quite different, more intimate sense. In order to explain this, I should like to make reference to the following.

It is a familiar and frequently reported fact that when an earthquake or some other elemental event is imminent certain animals flee from the place of the earthquake or at any rate become restless, so that they are like prophetic harbingers of what is to happen. One might say that the instinctive life of animals is more closely connected with what takes place out in nature than is the entirety of man's state of soul. But in the depths of the human soul there lives something that is not the same as the instinct of animals but is deeper than this animal instinct, and is also closely connected with the forces of nature; and in descending to the depths of his soul

Jacob Boehme felt himself to be intimately involved with the forces of nature. But one thing stands out particularly. It has been emphasized that only when what appears as imaginations and then lights up again as if of its own accord, only then does this *second* imaginative world have any value. Now it is highly instructive if we compare Jacob Boehme's path with this. In 1600 he experiences a rebirth, he feels himself transported to a spiritual world, to a kingdom of joy. He then continues to live in sober simplicity. For ten years what he has experienced is as though submerged. It then appears for a third time in 1610. Did not the path that we have described as the right one manifest itself in Jacob Boehme's soul as a natural phenomenon? It is this that draws Jacob Boehme so closely towards what we have ourselves conceived as being the natural path into the supersensible world. If we take this into account his experience will not seem as strange as it may appear to be at first sight.

It will of course have no value for the objective knowledge of the sceptic if one deliberates at length about the combination of the syllables 'sul' and 'phur' or about such other things. But I ask you to recall what was said on a previous occasion about human speech, when it was explained that in the course of human evolution speech actually precedes abstract, conceptual thinking, and that Jean Paul is absolutely right when he emphasizes that the child learns to think through speech rather than developing speech through thinking. Speech is, therefore, of a more primal, more elemental nature than thinking. When we see how the whole of nature arises again in our thoughts, we feel how thought is separated from the realities of nature by a cosmic abyss. But when a sound bears a greater similarity to the sounds of nature (and language was after all originally composed of such sounds), when the sounds of speech are wrested from the human soul, something of the whole rulership of the world is working into the depths of the soul; and then a kind of echo of nature struggles towards liberation in an entirely different way than if something from the realm of thoughts is released as an echo.

A soul of the present time no longer has any feeling for the affinity between speech and the sounds of nature. As modern souls, people struggle only gradually to feel that in all language there is something which directly resembles an echo of the impressions of the outer world. In a figure such as Jacob Boehme, who draws deeper forces from his soul with elemental power, it is only natural that he is in this respect carried back, as it were, also in feeling to that awareness regarding speech which was once characteristic of humanity and which the child still develops to a more or less unconscious degree.

If we now extend what has just been said to the somewhat puzzling discussions concerning the combining of syllables into words, we can understand that this is a way of feeling through the sounds of the impression that nature makes upon the human soul, of how nature wants to create a language through sound itself. Precisely because Jacob Boehme was closer to nature in his soul, he also lived more in speech than in thoughts, and his whole philosophy is more a matter of feeling, of sympathizing with what lives and weaves out in nature than some kind of abstract understanding of anything. If one really allows a thought of Jacob Boehme's to exert its influence, one could say that one feels as though the relationship of the thought to what he observes is similar to the relationship of the sensation of taste that one has to the nature with which one feels in contact.

This is how Jacob Boehme feels the contact with nature. He feels inwardly what weaves and works outside in nature. He shares in the life of nature, and in his characterizations of it he does indeed transmit what he experiences, so that in his words one feels that what he has perceived continues to resound. To him, therefore, the words are also something that he especially feels to be the essence of the 'how' in nature. So one does not need to ponder whether discussions regarding such matters as 'sul' and 'phur' mean anything particular for Jacob Boehme, but one should try to re-live how this soul makes its experience of the world into an experience of the soul and gives as its revelations what the soul is able to experience.

People do not understand Jacob Boehme when they have the idea that he perceived thunder and lightning, clouds and their transformations or the growth of grass as a modern human being does. The pathway to understanding him lies through the knowledge that with the flashing lightning, with the rumbling thunder, with the constantly changing clouds something is transformed for his soul-life, with the result that something takes place in his soul which represents the solution of the riddle that confronts him. Thus what happens in the world becomes for Jacob Boehme a riddle belonging to his own experience.

If we consider him in this way, we now understand how he was able to wrestle with a task that we also encounter elsewhere in his time and which has long occupied the minds of others, not least the greatest mind of more recent times. This same sixteenth century that saw the birth of Jacob Boehme was the source of the riddle of Faust, which places man's adversary, who draws man's striving nature down to a base, sensual or—as Jacob Boehme's age would have it—'devilish' realm, alongside the striving and struggling human individual. Goethe struggled constantly in a poetic context with the problem, which places 'evil' into the world-context. Does it not have to be asked again and again how it can happen that something irregular and inappropriate is inserted by hostile forces into the harmony of the universe, into the wise guidance of the world? This question regarding the origin of evil lies in the riddle of Faust. It actually lies already in the Book of Job, but it came to particular prominence in the sixteenth century.

How was this question able to manifest itself to Jacob Boehme? We need to take only a few words from *Dawn in the Ascendant* and we shall see at once that what is otherwise a world problem becomes for Jacob Boehme initially an inner soul problem. He says something along these lines: When a sensible and thoughtful person appears anywhere in the world, the devil immediately meddles with his soul and seeks to drag him down into vulgarity, banality and sensuality and to ensnare him in pride and conceit.

Here we see at once that for Jacob Boehme this is a soul problem, that he seeks the power of evil that interferes with good soul-forces in the soul itself. And the question arises for him: What does the soul have to do with soul-forces that aspire towards evil? Thus the problem of evil in the end becomes for Jacob Boehme an inner soul-question. But because for him 'soul' and 'world' correspond to one another, the soul at the same time expands into a world; and now what defines his particular impulse is that the question of evil develops into a quite different question, into the question of human—and indeed of spiritual—consciousness, of the whole nature of the life of consciousness.

It is difficult today with our current conceptions to gain insight into Jacob Boehme's soul-life and into the way that he related to world questions and their solutions; and one would not so easily be understood if one were to use Jacob Boehme's words, because they no longer have currency in our time. Thus I shall try—wholly in the spirit of Jacob Boehme but with somewhat different words—to approach what he wanted to say about the question of evil, which for him becomes a question that concerns the whole nature of spiritual consciousness as a whole.

Let us try to think how our consciousness works and what our consciousness would be like if we were not in a position to take hold of what we have experienced in our soul, in our consciousness, as thoughts imprinted in our memory. Let us try to think how different our consciousness would have to be if we did not have the capacity to draw forth from our memory what we experienced yesterday, the day before yesterday or several years ago. The whole content of consciousness rests on the fact that we are able to remember past experience; and our consciousness does not go beyond the point in time to which our recollection extends. It was then that we began to conceive of ourselves as an ego, to have the connecting thread of our consciousness enabling us to establish ourselves in our life of soul.

Upon what, therefore, does the whole nature of consciousness depend? Its basis is that we know that we are now experiencing something in consciousness. When we experience something, we are directly connected with this experience: in the moment when we experience something, we are none other than the experience that we are having. When someone imagines a red colour, he is in the moment when he visualizes this red colour united with the experience of it. When someone conceives of an ideal, he is in this moment at one with the ideal. Only afterwards is he distinguished from his experience, whereas previously he was at one with it. Thus our consciousness is something that we have first experienced and then stored up as an objective reality in our inner soul-life. Such a process of storing away makes our consciousness possible. We could not develop any consciousness if everything that we have experienced were immediately forgotten, removed from view.

Our actual consciousness is awakened only when we confront our experience as a kind of counterpart, by placing ourselves over and against it. We can observe this with the simplest phenomena of our consciousness. Jacob Boehme extends this experience, which every consciousness can have, in his clairvoyant perception of the whole world. He says: If a divine being in the world had only had the capacity to live in itself but not to confront its experience (as a counterpart), consciousness would never have become a reality even in a divine being. But for the divine being the counterpart is the world. Just as we place our conceptions over and against ourselves and become conscious of ourselves through the object, so is the world the counterpart for the divine consciousness. And the divine consciousness has set forth from itself everything that surrounds us in order to become aware of itself, just as we develop our consciousness only by representing our own experiences as a counterpart.

For Jacob Boehme this thought was not a theory but something that brought him satisfaction with regard to a question that was a matter of destiny for him, the great Faust question. He could now say to himself: If I carry myself back in thought to divine consciousness *prior* to the world, as it were, this divine consciousness could come to itself, become real consciousness, only by setting itself over and against the world, in order that it might become aware of itself through its counterpart. Thus everything that lives and weaves and is has arisen from the divine soul-nature, from a will of this divine soul-nature, which developed the desire, as will, to become aware of itself. And it now became clear to Jacob Boehme that in the moment when the onefold consciousness established the counterpart and wanted to become aware of itself, thus duplicated itself and—as it were—created the reflected image of itself, it created this mirror-image in a multiplicity of individual members, just as the individual human soul does not simply reside in single limbs but in limbs that have a certain independence, such as hands, feet and head and so on. One cannot approach Jacob Boehme by seeing him as a pantheist.

It is necessary to follow through this train of thought consistently, and thereby understand that he conceived of everything that appears before us as a counterpart of the Godhead.

The nature of man's being is also an aspect of the counterpart of the Godhead, which the Godhead has set forth from itself in order thereby to become aware of itself. Jacob Boehme expresses his viewpoint somewhat as follows:[84] Human beings look up, they see the stars, the masses of clouds, the mountains and the plants, and often seek to presuppose the existence of another, special region of the Godhead. But I tell you, you ignorant person, that you yourself form part of the counterpart of God; for how could you sense and become aware of something of the divinity in yourself if you had not flowed from this divine being? You derive from this divine being; it has placed you over and against itself and has as though given birth to you, and you will be buried in it. And how could you be raised from the dead if an alien Godhead stood over and against you? How could you call yourself a child of God if you were not one with the substance and being of God?

That Jacob Boehme does not have some ordinary kind of pantheism in mind is made clear when he says: The outer world is not God, it will never in all eternity be called God, but a being in which God reveals himself. If one says that God is everything, God is heaven and Earth and also the outer world, there is some truth in this; for everything has its origin from and in Him. But what can I do with such talk, which is no religion? One cannot call him a pantheist. Just as the question concerning the essential nature of the world is not some kind of abstract pursuit for him, neither is the answer that he gives to it; rather is it an experience for him. He felt the conditions of his own consciousness and extended these to divine consciousness, because it was clear to him that his capacity of consciousness is an echo of the actualities of the world.

And in the answer to the question of the soul and the divine nature of the soul he also finds an answer to the question concerning the origin of evil. This is something highly characteristic of Jacob Boehme, which has aroused the admiration of some deep thinkers. Thus, for example, Schelling was significantly moved when he became aware of the way in which Jacob Boehme approached the question of the significance of evil in the world; and other nineteenth century thinkers also admired the profundity of thought with which Jacob Boehme tackled this question.

It can be said of many people who have explored the question of the origin of evil that they have searched for its primal cause. What is characteristic of Jacob Boehme is that he goes beyond that absolute point that many people think that it is possible to go; for where is one to go if one does not want to stop at this primal cause? Jacob Boehme goes beyond the primal cause when he wants to solve the question of the significance of evil. He reaches to what he significantly calls not the primal cause or ground but the groundless; and here we indeed encounter in Jacob Boehme an experience of the human soul that one can admire to the highest degree if one has the requisite organ. To be sure, the ordinary soul which has its roots in the modern world-conception will quite possibly not possess this organ; but one can have this organ which feels admiration when, in the case of Jacob Boehme, the transition is made from the primal ground to the groundless. It is actually something like the 'egg of Columbus', something extremely simple. For in the moment when Jacob Boehme had solved the world riddle for himself in the way that we have described, when it was clear to him that there is a relationship between God and the world as there is between the soul and the limbs of the body, he was also able to say to himself (these are not his actual words, but in our endeavour to understand him more closely we want to characterize the essence of what he meant): When the world came into being as a counterpart of the Godhead, 'dividedness' appeared in the counterpart, differences between the limbs, as we might say. A dividedness of the individual bodily members with respect to the single soul came to manifestation. Is not every individual bodily member good in relation to the functions of the soul? Can we not say that the right hand is good, the left hand is good, everything is good, in so far as it serves the functions of the soul? But because of its relative independence, indeed precisely because of its inherent goodness, can the right hand not injure the left hand? Here we have, in contrast to what constitutes harmony, placed the independence of the bodily nature, that which needs to have no 'ground' or 'cause', we have placed this in the primal ground, which deed is the direct result of passing from the 'primal ground' to the 'groundless'.

Just as we do not need to seek the cause of darkness in light, so do we not need to seek the cause of evil in good. But since for Jacob Boehme the world is the counterpart of the Godhead, the possibility arises in this world of dividedness for individual limbs or members to work in opposition to one another, in that, because for the purpose of the world—in order that the world might achieve its goal—they must have their independence, they must also develop this independence. Thus for Jacob Boehme the root-cause of evil lies not in what people give by way of an explanation but in what arises as groundlessness, without there being any need to explain it. This arises of itself as a counterpart of the good; and now evil, what is inappropriate and harmful, becomes for Jacob Boehme itself a counterpart in the world to good, just as we become aware of ourselves through contact with an object.

We move along in space, we do not think of ourselves; but we begin to do so as soon as, for example, we bump our head on a window—we become aware of ourselves through the counterpart, through the object. Just as Jacob Boehme places consciousness over and against the counterpart, just as he experiences *himself* through the counterpart, the good, the appropriate, the advantageous and useful becomes aware of itself for him through the fact that it has to preserve itself from the harmful and inappropriate, it becomes aware of itself in that 'evil' became the counterpart of good, in a similar way to the objects that are experienced through collision with the outer world.

Thus Jacob Boehme sees in good the power which assimilates its counterpart, just as a person constantly assimilates in his memory what he has himself set forth from his consciousness. Thus we find a constant absorption of evil and, hence, an enriching of good with evil. And as darkness relates to light, in that light shines into the darkness and thereby becomes visible for the first time, the good only becomes an effective influence by working into evil and by relating to evil as does light to darkness. Just as light is differentiated through darkness into various colours and could not appear as light if it did not encounter darkness, so can good fulfil its function in the world only by experiencing itself through its counterpart, through evil.

This is how Jacob Boehme views the world—he sees good having influence by virtue of the fact that it finds itself confronted by evil, but that it takes evil into its own domain, as it were, absorbs it. Thus a pre-earthly event is visualized by Jacob Boehme in such a way that he says to himself:[85] The Godhead once placed other spiritual beings over and against itself. These were, like our present nature at a later stage, a counterpart of the Godhead. Thus these beings were already a counterpart of the Godhead, whereby the Godhead achieved consciousness of itself. But they related to the Godhead as limbs that turn against their own body. By this means, for Jacob Boehme, the being of Lucifer came into existence. What is Lucifer for him? He is the being who, once the counterpart had been created, made use of the dividedness, the manifoldness, in order to rebel against his creator as an independent counterpart. Thus in the forces of the world that are differentiated from and struggle against one another Jacob Boehme finds what has to be, what contributes to evolution as a whole by being absorbed in the evolutionary process. In the same way he also visualizes that all deeds of the opponent of the Gods are—in order that the deeds of the Godhead itself may come to fulfilment all the more strongly through the counterpart—absorbed by the Godhead, and that the self-fulfilment of the Godhead will become all the more glorious through the forces which the opponent develops.

Jacob Boehme pursues to the deepest level the thought that extends the experiencing of consciousness to the cosmic experience of the origin and primal state of evil. And he expresses it—and this is not something that he has given as a theoretical solution to the world riddle but what he has experienced—by means of a simple formula: No 'yes' without a 'no',[86] for the 'yes' must first experience itself through its counterpart, through the 'no'. 'No yes without a no' is the simple formula into which Jacob Boehme brought the whole problem of evil.

It is not a theoretical formula, but in this philosophy there lies something like a most primal, most elemental experience. For to know that there is no yes without a no, that evil is absorbed by good and contributes to the evolution of the world, may yet be nothing. But it is something else to be a struggling soul, a soul that experiences pain and suffering, temptations and seductions, and to say to oneself: All this must be, and in spite of this I can out of my living—and not theoretical—philosophical words furnish myself with the certainty and the consolation and the hope that the best in me will find the possibility of overcoming what is only the counterpart, the no, through the primordial impulse, through the yes. And no matter how much I become entangled in evil, and no matter how small the ray of light may be that extends over it, I can and may hope for liberation, so that the good in me and not the evil will be victorious.

When such a philosophy develops into a certainty of redemption, it is something that is indeed linked with the personality but at the same time has a universal human significance. If one allows this to work upon one's soul, one will gladly go from this struggling soul that ponders the cold abstractions of 'yes' and 'no' in order to acquire from this the warmest soul-content and the warmest soul-experiences, one will gladly progress from this soul that struggles for confidence in its world-conception to the solitary man in Görlitz, who had no opportunity to found a school; for he had to spend the time that people otherwise devote to intellectual matters to making shoes. He had to carve out the time needed for his many books. One is glad to go to this person whose books reveal how he struggled with language, because his outward education was so limited, but whose teachings nevertheless became widespread and gained notoriety after his death; to this man who sat on his cobbler's bench and had only a few friends with whom he shared his thoughts. It is true that he had friends to whom he wrote letters, but their number was only small. Thus one perceives him in his solitude and has the feeling that there is in this some kind of necessary connection. Just as one can only think of Giordano Bruno as journeying through the world, moving from one country to another, in order to impart something about the world by trumpeting it forth, just as one feels with him, who involves himself with a multiplicity of phenomena, that this journeying belonged to this world-conception, so does one feel in the other case that this solitary shoemaker experienced something that could, as it were, only be experienced in a solitary dialogue with the spirits of existence, in this solitary seership that we characterized at the outset.

If we feel in this way, we begin to have a clearer sense of what a person needs in order to bring his thoughts to bear on solving the riddles of the world: that the greatest things that can be experienced in the world are independent of place and time and that they are linked only with the human soul's meditative power, and that the soul can undertake the most extensive journeys into regions of the spirit, always and everywhere. Then these significant words that characterize Jacob Boehme's world-conception sound a chord within us and stir our thoughts:

> Those who time as eternity,
> And eternity as time decree,
> They indeed are freed
> From strife and hostile deed.[87]

This does not characterize his world-conception in a theoretical sense but it characterizes what his world-conception really came to be through the fact that he was so special a human being. For we have been able to emphasize that through his whole being he was more intimately connected with nature than most other people are, that he experienced the weaving and working of nature in the experiences of his own soul. This leads us to sense a certain necessity in the way that Jacob Boehme's friends characterized him. They portrayed him in a favourable light. For let us bear in mind that when there was in the East, in the Orient, a widely diffused and wonderfully detailed knowledge whose wisdom we admire when we become familiar with it, we still find on Central European soil the very simplest intellectual culture, we find that in all the souls of Central Europe there still lives something like an intimate connection of the forces in the depths of the soul with the forces of nature and nature-beings, and that the people threw twigs on the ground and from the 'runes' that they formed they saw and endeavoured to solve all kinds of riddles. These people were 'rune-decipherers'. And from everything that speaks from the souls of the people in the forests of Ancient Germania of what lives in nature, of what rustles through the trees or lives mysteriously in human souls themselves, we feel something of what was alive in Jacob Boehme's soul.

We then begin to understand something about Jacob Boehme which we would otherwise find very difficult to comprehend today. It is no arbitrary conjecture if we compare the picture of the decipherer of runes, who solves all sorts of riddles from the twigs which have been strewn on the ground and seeks to come to a knowledge of the revelations of the Godhead itself, with the way that, for example, Jacob Boehme depicts the syllables 'sul' and 'phur' in a rune-like way out of his relationship with a feeling for language and from this wants to solve world riddles. He then appears to us as a last living vestige from the forests of Germania, and we understand why his friends gave him the name 'Philosophus Teutonicus'.[88] This includes, however, his significance for the times to come.

We look upon the way that he struggled with the most stirring issue that can preoccupy the human soul, that in this struggle he arrived at peace and that his last words: 'Now I am going to paradise' were the seal of soul-consistency, or soul-practice. It is this that led him to peace in his soul. A breath of faith lives in all his books, and from this point of view Jacob Boehme can have significance for us and for all times. This 'Philosophus Teutonicus' will always set the tone for what he can really mean to the soul that familiarizes itself with him as regards the practical implications of a philosophy.

His opponents sometimes make a strange impression, beginning from 1684, when the first more forceful refutation of Jacob Boehme by Calov appeared,[89] until our time, when in the past century there has also been a critical appraisal of Jacob Boehme written by a Leipzig scholar, Dr Harles.[90] Harles wants to show, somewhat curiously, that Jacob Boehme merely raked up old alchemical writings, and then says that after often spending the day tormenting himself by presenting Jacob Boehme in this way, he was glad when in the evening, after thus toiling away with Jacob Boehme, he could approach Matthias Claudius in order to find recuperation and edification in his words; and he also wishes for his readers that they do not allow themselves to be captivated by the glittering and glistening formulations of Jacob Boehme but that they likewise take refuge in the simple and naive Matthias Claudius, whose gift to the soul is such that it does not need to seek its salvation in being elevated to the loftiest heights of spiritual life. It may be the case that this Dr Harles, the opponent of Jacob Boehme, had to take refuge in Matthias Claudius in order to escape from the glittering, high-flown formulations of Jacob Boehme, and that in Claudius he could find a peace that contrasted with his experience of studying Jacob Boehme. However, this gives a strange impression for someone who knows that Matthias Claudius himself, after he had achieved what Dr Harles appreciated in him, for his part took refuge in someone who was not only familiar with Jacob Boehme but even translated him—in Saint-Martin,[91] who was a faithful pupil of Jacob Boehme! So it is very good if one not only knows from whom Dr Harles, Jacob Boehme's opponent, sought edification but if one also knows from whom Matthias Claudius in turn sought *his* edification!

But the world-view of Jacob Boehme is one that has the capacity to lead beyond contradictions, if one does not simply stop there. The whole nature of the lectures that have been given here has shown that, where the world-conception that is being represented here is concerned, we should not be focused solely on a particular phenomenon but that we should be trying to understand what can be understood of the spiritual world directly out of our own time. There is no doubt that Jacob Boehme remains a significant personality, a star of the first magnitude in the spiritual firmament of mankind, and yet no one will be preoccupied solely with him. Thus the descriptions that have been given in our time through spiritual science are not presented from Jacob Boehme's standpoint but from that of our own time, and in the next lecture it will be shown what an entirely modern figure has to say. But Jacob Boehme becomes even more interesting when we call to mind his spirit-nature, standing upright in simplicity and solitude and taking flight with his soul into the highest region of clairvoyance, and when we find how this spirit-nature could spread peace over Jacob Boehme's soul such as can be felt by all who approach him with understanding or at least try to understand him. Hence intellectually-based characterizations will also not come close to Jacob Boehme, but only those that endeavour to sense what a person like Jacob Boehme felt what streamed forth from him in, for example, the four significant lines that have been cited. For the words with which I tried to characterize Jacob Boehme acquire their significance if those present feel that they were not said in order to give rise to a theory or a theoretical characterization of him, but so that as we directly contemplate this figure of Jacob Boehme something streams forth from him—and streams forth so much the more warmly and intensely the more we come to know him—which can summarize what has been said in words that epitomize his peace, his deep serenity:

> Those who time as eternity,
> And eternity as time decree,
> They indeed are freed
> From strife and hostile deed.

Lecture 8

BERLIN, 16 JANUARY 1913

THE WORLD-CONCEPTION OF A CULTURAL RESEARCHER OF THE PRESENT, HERMAN GRIMM, AND SPIRITUAL RESEARCH

It might easily seem as if what is represented here as spiritual research is quite isolated from present-day cultural life and has no connection with what otherwise occupies a dominant position in the intellectual life of modern times and in a certain sense sets the tone for it. However, this can appear to be so only to someone who understands this spiritual science or spiritual research in a limited, narrow-minded way and sees in it nothing more than a collection of teachings and theories. But someone who sees in it a spiritual stream that wants to receive into itself everything towards which the various trends in cultural life are leading it will become aware that from this spiritual stream the seeds for the future development of many aspects of modern cultural life can be derived, and that this way of contemplating life known as spiritual science can be applied to other schools of thought that have a greater or lesser affinity to it. I shall speak today about one such school of thought, which can be represented by a very notable figure in modern cultural life, namely the modern cultural researcher and art historian Herman Grimm.

Herman Grimm, who was born in 1828 and died in 1901, indeed appears on the one hand as a quite especially characteristic example of modern cultural life, while nevertheless being so individually distinctive, so particular a figure, that it is especially good to link today's studies with this personality. Herman Grimm appears to someone who has concerned himself with him as a kind of intermediary between that cultural life of more recent times which is associated with the name of Goethe and our own modern cultural life.

Herman Grimm is connected in a quite particular way with everything that can be linked with the name of Goethe through his marriage with that personality who was so closely related to the circle around Goethe, the sister of the Romantic poet Brentano. Thus Herman Grimm was related as a son-in-law to that Bettina Brentano who had published the remarkable correspondence of Goethe with a child, that Bettina Brentano from whom derives that unique memorial of Goethe where we see him sitting enthroned like an Olympiad, a musical instrument in his hand, enmeshing a child in the strings in whom Bettina Brentano portrayed herself. It was as a child that this personality deriving from the Frankfurt circle of La Roche appeared in her relationship to Goethe, and she was able to become absorbed in Goethe's spirit as was possible for only few people. And even if so many people find inexactitudes in the letters that Bettina Brentano made known, together with a colourful mixture of truth and fiction, one must nevertheless say that everything that we have in this remarkable book *Goethes Briefwechsel mit einem Kinde* has genuinely arisen from Goethe's cast of mind and gives us in a quite wonderful way an echo of it. Bettina Brentano's second marriage was with the poet Achim von Arnim, who was involved with the beautiful collection of folk literature *Des Knaben Wunderhorn.* Through his relationship with this circle—as said, Herman Grimm's wife, Gisela Grimm, was a daughter of Bettina Brentano or Bettina von Arnim—Herman Grimm had from a young age grown up amidst personalities who were really close to Goethe and who in all that he received in his education passed on to him something like a personal and directly elemental breath of Goethe's spirit. Thus Herman Grimm also felt from his early days that he belonged with all those who still stood close to Goethe, in spite of the fact that he was still a child when Goethe died. And Herman Grimm was not like someone who has studied Goethe and Goetheanism but he had received Goethe's being, the whole vitality of his magical power and the entirety of his living human nature directly, elementally and personally into his own being.

Thus Herman Grimm had an intimate part in the evolution of German life in the middle decades of the ninteenth century; he participated in it in such a way that he, as it were, established his own realm within this German life. One can call him a spirit who in the most individual way always directed his energies towards what he found stimulating, what was fruitful for the development of his own spiritual forces. By this means Herman Grimm carved out for himself from the full extent of cultural life what was suitable for him: a cultural sphere in which he felt at home. Within this cultural sphere in which he felt at home, Herman Grimm recognized himself to be a kind of spiritual representative of Goethe. To him Goethe's spirit appeared as a being with a continuing existence. And where he sought the streams of what in cultural life conformed to his own inclinations and allowed them to work upon him, this was always more or less the essence of Goethe's nature, which he not only sought to become aware of but became the measure of everything that he encountered in his intellectual and cultural endeavours.

The years that Herman Grimm lived through were decades that witnessed a struggle in German cultural life. These were decades when after Goethe's death the essence of his spirit withdrew to some extent, when people had to attend to many other things which, one might say, more concerned daily affairs than the influences that proceeded from Goethe. In that time when many other things had become somewhat quiet, Herman Grimm probably saw himself through his direct connection with the being of Goethe as a person whose task it was quietly but also livingly to cultivate the essence of Goethe's nature and to carry it over to a time that he surely hoped would come, a time when Goethe's star might once more shed its light more livingly in the European cultural firmament.

Thus the way that Herman Grimm regarded himself as a kind of spiritual representative of Goethe, of his spiritual sphere, was somewhat characteristic of how he quite naturally dealt with cultural life, of how he related to intellectual affairs. It belonged to him as it would to an intellectual prince. Even in his outward form and physiognomy, his gestures and his whole appearance, he had something of the quality of an intellectual prince. And one can say that even if one was, so to speak, unaccustomed to regard someone as having 'princely' qualities, Herman Grimm's whole manner compelled one to attribute to him the rank that has been characterized. Thus I still fondly recall meeting with Herman Grimm in Weimar, where he so often and so gladly came. He had invited me as his only guest to a midday meal. We spoke about many things that affected him. We also spoke—and it was a fulfilling experience for me that he wanted to have this conversation with me—about his extensive plans as regards his intellectual life. And when a certain time after lunch had passed, he said, with his distinctive humour but nevertheless in a wholly natural way, so that one could receive it from him as something purely as a matter of course: 'Now, my dear doctor, I want to dismiss you in good favour!' It was indeed something that at the time made upon me an impression of being the most natural thing in the world to say, because Herman Grimm's appearance was of such a kind that one attributed to him a certain princely quality

The whole of Herman Grimm's life's work bears something of this character. One cannot attentively read any of his larger or smaller writings without having the feeling that, amidst the wonderfully harmonious and yet so precisely constructed sentences that envelop one's soul, the personality of the author is constantly present behind them, looking at one and with an immensely personal interest is directly imparting to one what he has to say. This is responsible for the wonderful soul-quality that sounds through Herman Grimm's writings, so that they are in this most beautiful way invariably the expression of his soul-filled personality and also directly work in this way. Because of this, his whole style acquires the character of a certain justified, noble pathos. But this noble pathos is everywhere moderated by the personal element that one feels breaking forth from it. One accepts this style in spite of its elevated quality as something quite natural, and one constantly feels that the Goethean element is pervaded by the romantic nature of German cultural development. A certain sense of separation from everything that one can in the broadest sense call the everyday, the popular, a withdrawal into a single personality, a wholly individual being, a wholly individual manner of approach—this is what we sense in the style of Herman Grimm.

This tendency in Herman Grimm's spirit might perhaps have led to a certain one-sidedness if another stream had not worked within him in combination which connected him so fervently with everything of a popular nature and rooted him deeply in the spirit of popular culture. For Herman Grimm was himself the son of Wilhelm Grimm and the nephew of Jacob Grimm.[92] These are the two men who established German linguistic research in the ninteenth century, the men who collected those German fairy tales that have meanwhile become so deeply a part of German cultural life, those men who listened to what simple folk from the people related through legends and fairy tales; legends and fairy tales that had lived for hundreds of years in the minds of the simplest people and were almost forgotten before they were conveyed by a few individuals to modern times, when they were enabled to live again today through the agency of the Brothers Grimm.

If, therefore, Herman Grimm—despite the elevated style of everything he wrote—shows something of an affinity with everything of a popular nature, we must emphasize something further that harmoniously connects an intellectual tendency that might otherwise have developed in a one-sided way with another stream, so that everything in him appears to us as a kind of inner harmonious totality. If we allow Herman Grimm to make an impression on us, we do, after all, find a certain softness, a kind of eager receptiveness to all the cultural phenomena with which he was involved in the course of his life. A person needs a degree of isolation if he wants to immerse himself in the facts and phenomena of many centuries of intellectual history. But this softness additionally acquires its skeletal aspect, its hardness in Herman Grimm through something else that flowed into his upbringing: his father and his uncle belonged to those 'Göttinger Sieben',[93] who in 1837 lodged a protest against the abolition of the constitution of their state and were therefore dismissed from Göttingen University. Thus already as a boy Herman Grimm experienced a deed of a rare nature and experienced this deed with manifold consequences; for there were numerous consequences for both father and uncle that extended to their daily lives, in that they had lost not only their positions at that time but also bare essentials. And Herman Grimm frequently emphasized how he formed a connection with the impulses of history already as a nine-year-old boy, not through the 'book' but through a significant historical deed.

Thus Herman Grimm stands before us as a personality. He came to prominence as a kind of bearer of Goethe's spirit at the time when matters relating to Goethe in Germany had entered into a period of relative quietness and people had turned towards other things. But he experienced that this interest in Goethe was again restored, and that he himself could contribute much to the re-enlivening of this mood. At the beginning of the 1870s he was able to give his famous lectures on Goethe at Berlin University,[94] those lectures on Goethe that feature in his important book about him. And what a book this is! Anyone who acquires it as a young person and is able to relate to it in the right way can without doubt speak of it in later life as something significant. And just as it comes to expression in this book, so does Herman Grimm appear before us as one who has the capacity to relate to Goethe, as one who has entered fully into the various aspects of his soul-life. Thus he explores Goethe's works in succession, examining what passed through Goethe's own soul when he was engaged in the creation of these works.

So we can listen to the way that Herman Grimm considered such a personality as Goethe as he saw him. We find nothing resembling a search for pernickety biographical details or a pursuit of essentially insignificant aspects of his life. There is instead an immersion in everything in Goethe's life that was of significance and importance for his soul-development: the endeavour to trace the effect of what Goethe experienced, what was working and living in his soul, how it was transformed so that it acquired certain forms, so that it became a picture, a creation of his imagination; for Goethe himself, forgetting everything about the original life-experience, reached up to that new insight that had emerged from the experience in the creativity of imagination, in the creativity of imagination which now is itself an experience.

Thus with every consideration of a work by Goethe through Herman Grimm's study of him, Goethe rises a stage higher in his experiences, he rises directly into a sphere of pure spiritual perception. Through each one of Goethe's works, Herman Grimm shows how Goethe ascended from his life to spiritual experience and spiritual existence; and we are always glad to accompany him on this path that he follows because nowhere in Herman Grimm does something happen that can so easily occur with such a presentation: that a single soul-faculty, the intellect or the imagination, accompanies the observer, and one no longer feels oneself to be in contact with the life itself. No, Herman Grimm never goes further than—but always as far as—he as a personal individuality can himself go; and he is therefore able to encompass the whole work. Overall one feels that when Herman Grimm has led one to the point where the work in question had its origin in Goethe's experience, one has been transported to a purely spiritual life. Goethe becomes for one a being whose inner nature is purely spiritual, a sum of purely spiritual impulses. This breath of the world of spirit extends throughout everything that Herman Grimm presents in his book on Goethe.

What Herman Grimm directed towards Goethe became deeply rooted in his whole mental outlook. Probably a long time prior to this, when he embarked upon the studies that culminated in his lectures on Goethe, he conceived of a great idea of vast proportions, that of studying the cultural life of the West as a whole in the way that he came to study it on an individual basis with respect to Goethe. The idea came to him of tracing three thousand years of Western cultural life such that it everywhere becomes apparent how everyday events and facts existing in the physical world acquire their true worth by being transformed through human minds and sensibilities into what the human soul experiences when it ascends to the realm of what Herman Grimm called the 'creative imagination'. Thus Herman Grimm became a historical observer of a quite distinctive kind. For him, history was something entirely different than it was for all other observers of history.

History is usually studied in such a way that one assembles documents and other materials and then tries to present a picture of human evolution out of these materials. For Herman Grimm, materials of this kind—outward facts—were indeed highly important, but not the main thing. He frequently had the thought running through his mind: Could it not be that for a particular period of time precisely the most important documents, those that are decisive if one wants to study the impulses of the age, have disappeared without trace and have been lost, so that if one considers documents to give the most exact, the most faithful picture one will for the most part miss the truth? He was therefore convinced that someone who has the greatest faith in outward documents is least able to give a true picture of human evolution. In Herman Grimm's view, only a false picture of human evolution could emerge if one relies on outward documents.

But there is another whole facet of the cultural life of mankind: what has occurred outwardly, what has taken place in the form of outward facts, has come to a spiritual rebirth in particular individuals, it has found expression in those personalities who have transformed it artistically, who have given it cultural and spiritual worth. Thus, for example, Herman Grimm looked at the time of Ancient Greece. He said to himself: A number of documents exist about this Greek period. From these documents the understanding that can be gained for the world of Ancient Greece will be lacking in authenticity. But what the Greeks have experienced has been reborn in the works of Greek art, it has come to life again in particular Greek individuals. If one devotes one's attention to them, one opens oneself up to the influence of the world of Ancient Greece through the medium of the personality; and one will have a more faithful picture of this world than if one merely combines facts in an outward way. And so these facts in a sense disappeared for Herman Grimm. One might say that they evaporated from his world-picture, and what remained in his world-picture was a continuing stream of what he called the creations of popular imagination.

If, for example, he wanted to study Julius Caesar, he not only concerned himself with the historical documents but he believed that what Shakespeare made of Caesar had just as much significance for Caesar as what can be found in the historical documents. He viewed the times through human beings. Not only that the course of human evolution became to him something that one personality always passed on to another, but the whole course of human evolution itself became to him a spiritual process which he believed he had thoroughly dealt with in what he called the creative imagination. He wanted from this standpoint increasingly to acquire for himself a picture of the popular imagination creative in the Western cultures, he wanted to form a connection with the course of human evolution in the West such that he could say to himself: As the various streams of the Western cultures merge with one another, as they become detached from the oldest times to which he wanted to go back and extend to his own Goethean age, so do they appear as an ongoing stream of the weaving of popular imagination among the Western peoples.

On the strength of this impulse the focus of his attention was at an early stage directed towards that magnificent manifestation of Western cultural life which concerned him for a while and regarding which he wrote in the 1890s a book unparalleled in its beauty, his *Homer*,[95] his description of the *Iliad*. This book, which is always good to have around if one wants to study the early period of Ancient Greece from a modern spiritual standpoint, again shows us Herman Grimm—if we presuppose his general intellectual approach—from a quite particular aspect. His attention encompasses the Gods and the world of the Gods portrayed in Homer's *Iliad*, it takes in the battling Greek and Trojan heroes, and the question arises before his soul: How is it, then, with this interaction of a world of the Gods with the ordinary human world of battling Greeks and Trojans? This becomes a question for him. He is struck by the immense difference that exists in Homer's descriptions between a humanity that roams the Earth and those beings who are portrayed as immortal Gods. And Herman Grimm now tries to present the idea that the Gods as Homer portrays them represent an 'older' layer of beings inhabiting the Earth. Even though Herman Grimm in his more realistic way sees these beings as 'human beings', he is nevertheless looking back to a culture which has become detached from another culture to which the Trojan and Greek heroes belong. Herman Grimm discerns an older and a younger layer of humanity interacting in Homer's *Iliad*, and what remains of the living influences from a previously living layer of beings plays for Herman Grimm into Homer's portrayal of what is enacted between Greece and Troy.

In this way Herman Grimm altogether sees in the progress of human evolution a constant process of detachment of older, what we might call circles or cycles of culture from newer ones, and an interplay of the old into the new. Every new cultural cycle has a certain task, the task of bringing something new into the general evolution of mankind. The old continues in existence for a while, exerting its influence upon the new.

One could say that Herman Grimm's insight into what must also be presented today from the standpoint of modern spiritual science extended as far as was possible for anyone in the last third of the nineteenth century. He did not go back beyond the age of Ancient Greece. He was therefore unable to give what more recent spiritual research describes in reaching back to purely spiritual beings higher than human beings who existed before humanity. But he touched everywhere upon these results of more recent spiritual research, and as closely as anyone who has not himself come to embrace spiritual research can do so.

In spiritual research we try to represent the idea that, when we go back in human evolution, we do not come to the animal kingdom as the Darwinist theory—which is interpreted materialistically today—would have it but that we come back to spiritual, purely spiritual ancestors of human beings, and that behind that cycle of humanity where human souls live incarnated in the physical body we have another cycle of humanity in which human beings are not yet incarnated in the physical body. Herman Grimm, as it were, leaves unresolved the question as to the nature of the 'Gods' before human beings came to tread the Earth. But he recognizes the lawful succession of such cycles of humanity. This gives a significant point of contact with the descriptions of spiritual research. That he altogether recognizes such regular advances occurring over periods brings him, so to speak, especially close to us.

He sought to extend his cultural researches over three millennia. The first millennium for him is that of Greece. One could say that it sounds something like an undertone through Herman Grimm's research—if one hears from him how he characterizes these Greeks in this way—when he says: Yes, if one looks upon the Greeks, they appear to one—especially in the earliest period—as not so formed as present-day human beings. Even a person like Alcibiades still appears to one as a kind of fairy-tale prince. One is beholding something of a super-human nature. And yet from this spiritual world of the Greeks—whom Herman Grimm, as we have said, portrays as dissimilar to the later human world—everything that gave rise to impulses in the world of the Greeks also projects into the later world, so that it forms the most important element within our cultural life even to our modern times. And at the end of the first millennium that Herman Grimm considers, there comes before his soul the most important impulse that he recognizes in the evolution of mankind: the Christ impulse.[96]

When Herman Grimm speaks about the figure of Christ, he is in a certain sense reserved, as he is altogether reserved about many things. But the observations that he generally makes about Christ show us that he would just as little agree with those who, so to speak, would like to make Christ evaporate in a cloud of thoughts as with those who want to see in the personality of Christ Jesus only something of a generally human nature. He emphasizes that a twofold impulse proceeds from the figure of Christ, an impulse of colossal strength which then, also for Herman Grimm, continues to work through the whole of the rest of human evolution, and the other impulse of an immense gentleness. Herman Grimm finds that the whole second millennium of Western cultural development is shaped in such a way that the world of Ancient Greece is as though absorbed by the Christ impulse and with this combination of Christianity and Greek thought now enters into the human world, overpowers it and brings forth something quite special. This is his second millennium, the first Christian millennium. The impulses of Rome are not of primary importance for him, whereas those of Christianity are. Everything political, everything outwardly matter-of-fact disappears for Herman Grimm's perception, and he everywhere examines how the Christ impulse makes its presence felt, and how diversified is its form. Thus his conception of Christ is not narrow, not small, but wide. When the book about the *Life of Jesus* by Ernest Renan appeared,[97] Herman Grimm followed this up with a remarkable study in the journal that he published at that time *Künstler und Kunstwerk* ('Artists and Works of Art'). He tried to show how pictorial representations of the figure of Christ have changed over the centuries both in painting and sculpture and also in literature. Thus he tried to show the variability, the changeability of the Christ impulse; and he showed how people have always conceived of the Christ impulse in accordance with the way they thought about things. And he then sees in Ernest Renan someone who in the nineteenth century endeavoured to conceive of Christ from a certain narrow point of view.

Christianity—thinks Herman Grimm—needed a thousand years in order to transmit its impulses to the rivulets and streams of Western cultural life. Then came his third millennium, the second Christian millennium in which we now still are, that millennium at the beginning of which spirits such as Dante and Giotto were active and artists like Michelangelo, Leonardo da Vinci, Raphael and so on and which then led to the spiritual achievements of Shakespeare and Goethe. These cycles in the evolution of humanity were for Herman Grimm always defined wholly in accordance with spiritual laws. He perceived spiritual laws governing human evolution whose on-flowing stream he identified in the nature of creative imagination. In his lectures Herman Grimm ever and again sought to place the organizational principle of the stream of human evolution before his students, in order to be able to show how individual spiritual creativity has its place in the totality of the stream.

Thus Michelangelo, Raphael, Savonarola, Shakespeare and others, also Goethe, were to him a spiritual content that can be explained if one sees it against the background of that on-flowing stream of creative imagination, which for Herman Grimm became especially discernible in its source in Homer in the ninth or more likely the tenth century before the Christian era. For this reason Herman Grimm addresses one on such an unfathomable level because he often, when he evokes in one an interest in a work of art—for example, Raphael's *Marriage of Mary with Joseph*,[98] one of the Madonna pictures or other works, one of Leonardo da Vinci's pictures, or when he points out something that he has observed in Goethe—gives one the feeling that one is experiencing what is most directly individual about this work of art. If one now observes with him how the particular colour or gesture has been depicted in the work of art, and in this way believes oneself to be standing in isolation before the work of art, something like a tableau of the whole progress of humanity suddenly appears, a part of that on-flowing stream of creative imagination that extends over three millennia and includes within itself all the various individual elements.

Thus one is led by Herman Grimm into the intimate individual nature of the works of art concerned and then to the summit from where the whole stream can be observed. However, this was not something that Herman Grimm viewed in a theoretical way. It seemed to be something so natural for him to behold in this way the totality of the on-flowing spiritual stream of human evolution—as he explained to me, as I said, at the time when we shared a midday meal—because he really lived with his whole soul in this spiritual stream and he could by no means perceive a single phenomenon other than as a fragment of this mighty stream of the evolution of mankind.

That the whole of Western cultural evolution is a development of popular imagination was to him no general, abstract idea but was full of the most tangible content. He knew himself to be so connected with his soul with this content that radiates through millennia that everything that he wrote actually appears to one as the separate little sections and extracts of a work of vast proportions. Even if one reads no more than a review of one of his books, one has the impression that it has been extracted from a colossal work which presents the whole of human evolution as an imaginative creation. One feels oneself to be placed before a work of vast proportions, as if one had embarked on it and was reading just the first few lines of it, when one reads an article or essay or anything from a book by Herman Grimm. And one now understands how Herman Grimm himself could say, when towards the end of his life he wrote the Preface to his collection of fragments,[99] that to him it appeared that they contained a description of the whole of Western culture. One understands that the individual work that he has undertaken seemed to be one of several individual parts that he had taken from a finished work. Thus he never attributed more value to what he had published than to what he had written, and never more value to what he had written than to everything that lived in his thoughts.

When one indicates something of this kind, one would—without involving abstract formulations—want to have said something about that feeling that—as someone who has been and still is fond of Herman Grimm—one has about the fact that he was never able to arrive at the point of really carrying out what so beautifully, so hugely and so magnificently stood before his spirit, that even his writings on Homer, on Raphael, Michelangelo[100] and on Goethe appeared to us as fragments from this unwritten, all-encompassing work. It is with a certain melancholy feeling that one can read those lines of the Introduction already mentioned to his *Fragments*, where he states that he was constantly revising what he had to say to his students year after year about the evolution of European cultural life and that it might perhaps be permissible to turn the last form that these lectures had received into a book which would in a certain sense represent the progress of European cultural development—but that unfortunately there would probably not be another of these revisions. One reads these lines today all the more wistfully, since this revision indeed did not come about; and we have to see Herman Grimm dying in the knowledge of what lived in his soul, and have had to see that what lived in his soul for the culture of the present had to go with him to the grave.

This gives us some idea of the viewpoint from which everything of Herman Grimm's was written. If spiritual research wants to be that which can be attained through the expanding of one's range of vision, one must say that anyone who truly enters into Herman Grimm's mind and manner of expression has the most perfect guidance from modern cultural life for gradually entering into the whole mode of perception that belongs to spiritual research. But even if the breadth of Herman Grimm's range of vision is disregarded and one seeks to gain insight into his soul, into how he sought to approach phenomena, how his feelings and thoughts led him to everything that he has written in his extensive studies of Homer, Raphael, Michelangelo and Goethe, and if one takes into consideration what he has presented in his other writings, one finds that he can to a significant degree be distinguished from other spirits, and that he has something that belongs to that deepening of the soul that was spoken of here when the path was described that the soul has to take in order to enter the spiritual worlds themselves.

We have already emphasized that the intensity of the soul-forces must become stronger for the spiritual path, that if deeper soul-forces are to be drawn forth which otherwise slumber the soul must employ more inner strength, more inner courage and boldness, must identify itself more with its own being, with the forces of thinking, feeling and will. Herman Grimm wrote a constant flow of essays to this end, essays that, it is true, took a different course, essays through which he became able to describe works of art in so intimate and personal a way, as he described those of Raphael or Michelangelo, but was on the way to gaining deeper insight into the spiritual world. For it is not that which one calls 'objective' today that lies at the foundation of Herman Grimm's historical research but, rather, an affinity with the phenomena of the cultural life that he is depicting. Thus he immerses himself in the respective cultural themes in complete self-forgetfulness, and yet in a strange way possessed of self-consciousness.

This is especially apparent when he first leads his own soul to focus on a particular cultural figure, for example on Raphael, and then raises this single cultural phenomenon to the collective stream of human cultural life. His feelings then become bold, mighty ideas, and what many others did not dare to express in such nuances of feeling and in such nuances of ideas is achieved by Herman Grimm, who thereby becomes an interpreter of the spirit who so impresses us with the boldness of his interpretations that we are sometimes truly reminded of those who wrote the Gospels. It is only that they wrote with more of a mystic quality, and Herman Grimm with more modern spiritual observation. And just as they reach up to the horizon of the whole of humanity, so does Herman Grimm with his 'Raphael' reach up to the horizon of humanity as a whole.

It is wonderful when in his bold way, as though his soul is being drawn out of itself and is striding along beside Raphael as in a stream of general development, he breaks out in words that can express more to us than a mere description of world history: 'Raphael is a citizen of world history. He is like someone from the four rivers that, as the ancient world believed, came from paradise.'[101]

When one dwells upon such phrases as this, one indeed knows something quite different about the relationship of Herman Grimm to Raphael than one otherwise knows about the relationship of many other interpreters to particular phenomena.

Thus for Herman Grimm personalities flow together with the total stream of cultural life. One could also say that he brings the highest spiritual sphere down to the most personal element. And a wealth of spiritual experiences come towards us when Herman Grimm speaks the following words from the depths of his soul, as he gives expression to how he relates to the cultural realities with which he is concerned:

> Were Michelangelo called forth by a miracle from the dead in order to live among us again, and were I to meet him, I would reverently stand aside so that he might pass; but if I were to encounter Raphael, I would go behind him to see whether I might find an opportunity to hear a few words from his lips. With Leonardo and Michelangelo one can confine oneself to relating what they were to their times; with Raphael one must speak about what he is to us today. Over those others a gentle veil has been laid, but not over Raphael. He is one of those whose growth is not yet at an end by a long way. There will always be future races of people to whom Raphael will pose new riddles.[102]

This is a characteristic mood, not objective in the sense that one so often demands today but describing the corresponding phenomena in such a way that we feel directly drawn into their proximity when we are able to feel a breath of what was living in Herman Grimm's soul when he could write such sentences. Then one also understands how this spirit was able to struggle with a phenomenon of world history and specifically with Raphael. It is remarkable—as he himself asserts—how he related to Raphael, quite differently to how, for example, he expressed himself when he wanted to give a description of Michelangelo. The portrayal of Michelangelo's life by Herman Grimm is a wonderful book, in spite of the fact that in many ways it can perhaps be regarded as superseded today. How significant the figure of Michelangelo appears in the context of the whole life of the

Middle Ages, how it stands out from the other figures who feature prominently! How it stands out from the wholly unique description of Florence itself, or how it stands out from that tableau that Herman Grimm presents by letting two spiritual forms rise up before our mind, Athens and Florence, thus enabling the interweaving of the three millennia that he has characterized to appear as a mighty background against which figures such as Dante, Giotto and the other painters of that time stand out, then figures such as Savonarola and finally Michelangelo himself.

From all this the impression also arises that Herman Grimm might have related differently to Raphael and his surroundings than he did to Goethe, but that what he has to say to us is no less intimate. With Herman Grimm's portrayal of Goethe we always feel that he grew up as a spiritual grandson of Goethe. Likewise with his portrayal of Michelangelo we feel that he is personally involved in everything, that he—one might say—personally goes to every palace in Florence, walks through all the streets of Florence, personally becomes familiar with other connections and, by placing himself before Michelangelo, then comes to be able to portray what he did. But we feel everything he painted as though as a unified whole.

What he gave about Raphael has a different quality. We feel here a struggle with the subject-matter, with the spiritual image; we feel that Herman Grimm can never do enough as far as he is concerned. He says himself that he had taken up the material again and again, that nothing that he had already published satisfied him. Indeed, what he in the end tried to offer as a portrayal of the personality of Raphael—which nevertheless remained a fragment and then appeared in the collection of essays as 'Raphael as a World Power', from which the sentences that I have already read out derive—was to be among his last works.

Why did Herman Grimm so struggle with the material that he had on Raphael? Because he could only present something to his own satisfaction when he was able to be completely at one with the subject-matter. But in Raphael he saw a spirit whom he characterized in the way that the words previously quoted indicate: 'Raphael is a citizen of world history. He is like someone from the four rivers that, as the ancient world believed, came from paradise.' And so Raphael himself grew for him into someone of giant stature with every sentence that he addressed to him. Thus he could never do enough in his own eyes, because he could not himself capture this 'world power' in a book. If in his portrayals of Homer, Michelangelo or Goethe the breadth and yet the elegance of his mind manifests itself, with Raphael the deep uprightness, the deep honesty of this spiritual personality comes to the fore.

Anyone who takes up his book about Homer may well find it insufficiently erudite. Herman Grimm says on the very first page that this book is not intended as a contribution to research on Homer. Yes, Herman Grimm could in these and similar matters behave absolutely like an intellectual prince, as I have previously related. Thus it also appears to one to be quite natural that when he set about assembling his ideas for what he wanted to say about Goethe, he boldly proceeded from the viewpoint that everything else that he had been able to find about Goethe was inadequate. What may to many appear as brazen audacity seemed in the context of his literary and artistic attitude to be perfectly natural.

This is how he related to all cultural life. Hence to many people who proceed from a scholarly standpoint, Herman Grimm's book on Homer may be insufferable. Everything that has been said with regard to whether Homer lived or not, whether the *Iliad* was put together from all manner of different elements and so on, was of no concern of his. He took it as it was. He therefore made a point of saying how wonderfully it was inwardly composed, how the later part always relates to what goes before, so that everything that reveals this inner composition appears to us to be inwardly coherent. But apart from this, what seems to me of the greatest stature is something that is enormously valuable for a spirit-researcher: his absorption in the soul-life of the Homeric heroes. Everywhere we see Herman Grimm's soul-filled approach to the soul-life of Homer's heroes. Everywhere we see a real understanding—in a world-historical context—of the soul of Achilles, of Agamemnon, of Odysseus and so on. A book that works overwhelmingly as a description of souls despite the intimacy of the stylistic manner of expression! We are throughout led not only to the heights of historical study but we are also led deeply into the souls of the individual Homeric figures. Indeed, many scholars may well say that Herman Grimm has dealt with the *Iliad* by failing to take account of the whole of Homer research and all proper previous work and has then taken everything as it stands! This is indeed what he does, it is all rather 'amateurish', and one might characterize it by means of the dry formula: this man has written a book without any previous study.

Did Herman Grimm write this book without any previous study? Anyone who concerns himself with Herman Grimm's intellectual life will find these previous studies, even though they appear different to all the prior studies of ordinary scholars. Herman Grimm's prior studies lay in studies of souls, in immersing himself in the human soul and its mysteries. And one can come to the conviction that no one else would have so wonderfully been able to shed light on the souls of the Homeric heroes than the one who had undertaken such previous studies. Herman Grimm is seemingly searching for what was uppermost in Homer's imagination. But what he says everywhere shows us a bearer of the most refined psychological insight from whom we can presume to find something really extraordinary, when we see the way that he observes the Homeric heroes from Achilles and Agamemnon to Odysseus. How did he come to write many a word in his book on Homer or in his other works that strikes the spirit-researcher as so remarkably inspired? It was because it was preceded by quite particular prior studies. And the spirit-researcher will look for these prior studies in the works from Herman Grimm's first period.

Here we have above all that wonderful collection of novellas,[103] which are perhaps less read today than many books of this kind but ought to be read by those who are interested in spiritual life, a collection of novellas which can be thought of as an intensive attempt to get to know human souls, to fathom human mysteries, to establish the working of the human soul in the context of the physical world. Here is the first of these novellas, which appeared in the first period of his creative work as an author, *Die Sängerin* ('The Singer'). It shows how a man begins to feel a passionate inclination towards a woman, a woman with an enveloping spiritual nature. We are shown how these two personalities are never able to come together, how the woman dismisses the ardently loving man from her society, how in the soul of this man everything lives on in the form of impulses which on the one hand draw him to the woman, who on the other hand, from her soul, drains the strength from the whole bodily nature of this man. In what one might call a form of spiritual research, we see how he falls into a state of soul infirmity. And then we see him again, when he has been received at the estate of a friend, entangled in the net of the woman. The friend notices that it is high time for that personality for whom his friend yearns with all his soul to be drawn to the scene. She comes—but too late. While she is in front of the house, the person concerned shoots himself.

And now comes something that Herman Grimm has so often touched upon in his artistic expositions but which, at the point where it could well be taken up by spiritual research he always has to let it lapse into indefinite ponderings. It is now briefly and succinctly described how the dead person is living in the imagination of the singer. There is an unforgettable scene where she, who feels her full guilt for the death of this man, sees this person come night after night from the kingdom of the dead, and these visitations of the one who has died now become the soul-content of the woman. This is described not as a mere imaginative construct but as by a man who knows that there are mysteries that extend beyond a person's death. There is a wonderful description where the friend is standing in front of the woman, and where she says that the dead person is coming to her—until the woman's last letter to the friend, in which she says that she now feels herself to be close to death, that the dead person with whom she was so connected has from his realm of the shades drawn her into his domain. Perhaps there is no modern writer who has with such intimacy found the words with which to make contact with the spiritual world.

It is described in spiritual research that when a person goes through the gates of death, that which otherwise remains connected with him also when he is asleep, the so-called etheric body, rises out of the physical body together with the higher soul-members and passes over into the spiritual world. On the basis of spiritual research we form a picture of how the corpse remains behind, how the person then with his etheric body becomes separated piece by piece, section by section from the physical body, and how the etheric body then for a while provides the sheath for the person's higher soul-members. This is an idea that can become ever more familiar to those who have some knowledge of spiritual research. In what follows we shall now consider in what wonderful a way Herman Grimm's artistic soul forms a relationship with these facts of the spiritual world, and this will similarly lead us to the question why for deeper reasons Herman Grimm did not bring his cultural studies to fulfilment in a substantial work.

Apart from his novellas Herman Grimm wrote another artistic work, the novel *Unüberwindliche Mächte* ('Insuperable Powers'),[104] in which—as is generally the case in his writings—we encounter the elevated style that everywhere guides us towards a way of observing life and the world. Moreover, everything else is on a high-flown level. Especially what one might call the collision of two ages of mankind at a microcosmic level. The one world is that which abides only by titles, ranks and official positions and feels itself at one with them. From this world there derives a count from an ancient family who is impoverished but who still lives wholly in the reverberation and residual feeling of his rank as a count. It is wonderful how in this novel the world of old prejudices and ordering of ranks is contrasted with the 'new world'. The outlook of America plays into this situation. It is Americans who encounter the man who lives wholly in his titular prejudices and sensibilities and whom Herman Grimm calls Arthur. This count meets Emmy, the daughter of Mrs Forster, who has American origins, and we see this count inflamed with passionate love for Emmy.

It is impossible to do justice to the rich content of this novel. We are confronted with the whole contrast between Europe and America, the whole contrast between the old Prussian nature and its new qualities engendered as a result of the wars—a hugely significant cultural tapestry within which the characters are imprinted and from which they continue their development. It suffices to mention that through the impulses that come together from these various streams, Count

Arthur dies a tragic death just as he is about to marry Emmy. A person who belongs to his ancestral family but who in his delusion considers himself to be the rightful heir of the count's estate and views the true heir, the Count Arthur, as a bastard, comes to meet Count Arthur spurred on by envy and jealousy, and the circumstances are such that on the eve of his wedding Count Arthur is shot by this man.

One may perhaps never find an opportunity to consider the words 'Insuperable Powers'—which many who want to view this novel purely rationalistically may perhaps regard merely in terms of the impossibility of finding a bridge between the prejudices of rank—to be more justified than when one sees how Herman Grimm, without intending to do so, lets the idea of karma, the idea of the causal linking of destinies that come to expression in human life, form connections knot by knot and brings them to a development, and how he indeed portrays forces that can only exert an influence if they derive from former incarnations, from previous earthly lives. He describes this not by speaking theoretically of 'forces' or of 'karma' but simply by letting the facts speak and giving expression to these powers, so that they seem to us in every way like the ideas of spiritual research. We see a karmic destiny being fulfilled, we see insuperable karmic powers coming to expression, and we see something else.

In a short concluding chapter Herman Grimm shows us how Emmy gradually ails and how she dies. The way that he describes Emmy's approaching death is so utterly characteristic of Herman Grimm's deep sympathy with soul-spiritual problems. She is brought to Montreux. Montreux itself is described in a quite distinctive way, the whole area within which Emmy dies is described. However, he describes Emmy's death not like another writer who is far removed from spiritual life, but as someone who goes to where the mysteries of death and the mysteries of the land beyond death speak to souls, and I would be offering something incomplete if I were not to conclude with the words that Herman Grimm himself includes about Emmy's death:

> And this is Emmy's dream.[105]
>
> Between midnight and morning she believed she woke up.

> Her first glance at the window, through which a subdued brightness streamed in, was free and clear and she knew where she was. She also heard her mother, who was sleeping beside her, breathing. A moment later, however, and with a pressure that she had never felt before, she was seized with an overwhelming fear. These were no longer those particular thoughts that had been tormenting her in recent days but it was as though a giant hand was holding all the mountain ranges of the Earth over her by a thin thread and at any moment the fingers that held it could open and the great weight plummet down, thus remaining lying upon her for eternity. Her attention wandered around both within and outside her, looking for a shimmer of light, but nothing presented itself, the light from the window had faded, her mother's breathing was no longer audible and she was surrounded by a stifling loneliness, as though she would never again return to the land of the living. She wanted to call out, but she could not, she wanted to touch herself, but no limb obeyed her. It was quite still, quite dark, not even thoughts could be grasped in this terrible anxiety, she was even deprived of her memory—then a thought finally came to her: Arthur!
>
> And now, wonderfully, it was as though this one thought had been transformed into a point of light that became visible to her eyes. And in the measure that the thought grew to a boundless longing, this light came and increased in intensity, and suddenly as though became diffused and opened out and took on a new form—Arthur stood before her! She saw him, she finally recognised him. He was indeed himself. He smiled and was close beside her. She did not see whether he was naked or whether he was clothed: but it was he, she knew him too well, he himself, no mere phantom that had taken on his form.

So closely does Herman Grimm draw him who some time before crossed the threshold of death to her who becomes a seeress, draws her in the moment of her own death to the dead person in such a way that she addresses his soul: 'She did not see whether he was naked or whether he was clothed: but it was he, she knew him too well, he himself, no mere phantom that had taken on his form'.

> He reached out his hand to her and said: 'Come!' Never had his speech sounded so sweet and enticing as it did today. With all the strength of which she was capable, she tried to stretch out her arm to him; but she could not. He came still closer and reached out his hand closer to her: 'Come!', he said again.

> It seemed to Emmy as though the power with which she tried to bring at least one word to her lips would have been capable of moving mountains, but she was unable to utter this one word.
>
> Arthur looked at her and she at him. Had there now been the possibility of moving a finger, she would have been able to touch him. And now the most terrible thing happened: he seemed to draw back again! 'Come!', he said for the third time. And feeling that he had spoken for the last time, that the terrible darkness would again engulf his heavenly appearance, now filled with a fear that tore her asunder as frost splits trees she made a last attempt to extend her arms to him. But it was impossible to overcome the heaviness and cold that kept her in bondage. And then as a bud bursts from which a blossom grows before our eyes, from her arms other arms radiated forth, from her shoulders other shoulders shone forth, and these arms reached towards Arthur's arms and he grasped her hands with his hands, and as he slowly glided back he drew her after him, together with the whole glorious form that rose up from Emmy's being.

One cannot more wonderfully describe the departure of the etheric body from the physical body if one undertakes such a description with a pure artistic soul. We may well say of the spirit, the soul that lived in Herman Grimm that it came close to what we seek with such longing in spiritual research. This was a soul, this was a spirit of which we may say that it serves as a proof of how the modern soul in its approach to the twentieth century has sought the paths to the spiritual life.

Thus we gladly turn to Herman Grimm, whom we observe to be on the path that we want to explore further. And so we see how he raises up the creations of Raphael and of Michelangelo, the experiences of Goethe and the Greek soul of Homer to the stream that flows through the millennia for his spirit as 'creative imagination'. Then we know how close Herman Grimm was with his whole feeling and sensibility to the living weaving and working of the soul-spiritual world that is behind all physical realities. For when Herman Grimm speaks of his 'creative imagination', this is not something of an abstract nature. In so far as we are perhaps with him dealing with something in the abstract realm, it is also for us a necessity that we break through the thin wall that separates Herman Grimm from the living spirit, which does not work as creative imagination but lives behind everything of a sensory nature as a direct spiritual influence. It has the aspect of a modesty that does not yet venture to say more than it says when we see Herman Grimm speak of the imagination of mankind working through the millennia, since as an artist he was nevertheless so closely in touch with the living soul that has crossed the threshold of death. Thus it will not be difficult for us to see, where Herman Grimm speaks of the creative imagination, the living spiritual beings that we as spirit-researchers seek behind the world of the senses.

It will then perhaps not appear unjustified if we do assert that, for such a spirit who has so honestly and uprightly struggled for the truth, this creative imagination—when he sought to approach it ever and again—was nevertheless to him something of an abstraction; that his soul had the urge to comprehend the living spirit, and that therefore the great work that he intended could not come into being: because if it had been written, it would have to have become a work that would have had to portray the spiritual world not merely as creative imagination but as a world of creative beings and individualities.

Spiritual research has not been arbitrarily instituted by this or that person in recent times but is demanded by the seeking souls of the modern age, to whom Herman Grimm so clearly and characteristically belonged, as we have seen. Thus in the case of this remarkable personality we can become aware that with spiritual research we are not alien and isolated in modern cultural life. We have been enabled to view a figure such as Herman Grimm as someone to whom we feel related. Even though he does not fully share our viewpoint, we stand—or at any rate could stand—infinitely close to him. And when contemplating such a figure it is also better to take account not so much of every detail but rather of the totality, to look upon it with all that harmony of soul, with all that gentleness and yet also bold sharpness and strength of soul-life, with which it is able to impress us. Even though we may address this or that vital question in a somewhat different way to Herman Grimm, I know that it is not wholly foreign to his style if I summarize what I have wanted to express. One might arrive at the thought—shall we say the delusionary thought—that can then live in the soul as a beautiful delusion: If higher spirits, extraterrestrial spirits, wanted to become acquainted through reading, through lectures, with what happens on the Earth, they would prefer to read writings such as those in which Herman Grimm has recounted the earthly destiny of human beings.

This feeling can sound forth to one from virtually every line of Herman Grimm's writings, and this feeling raises one's whole personality to what one might call an extraterrestrial sphere. One then feels so close to this personality that, were one to want to characterize what has been said today about Herman Grimm, one may become aware of some beautiful words that he himself addressed to a friend who had died, his friend Treitschke,[106] whom he greatly appreciated:

'How gladly this man embraced life. How courageous in battle. How language offered itself in service to him. How his latest book always had the quality of novelty. How little could even those who, in the bustle of cultural communication, had a taste of his pushiness take offence at him. Even they will cry: "Yes, he was one of us!"'

These words were at the same time the last that Herman Grimm wrote and had printed, as we know from the publisher of his works, Reinhold Steig. And I should like to summarize and probably also conclude what I have said this evening with the words: How gladly this man, Herman Grimm, embraced life, how gently—and yet also how individually! And what a harmonious impression his whole life's work makes! How language offered itself in service to him! How his latest book always had the quality of novelty! How little can even those who do not share his ideas and viewpoints distance themselves from him, if only they properly understand themselves! And how close must those who from whatever area of spiritual research seek the path to the spirit feel to him! How close must these people feel to him, and how dearly they would like—if his spiritually so gently radiant form were to appear before them—to burst forth with the words: Yes, he was one of us!

Lecture 9

BERLIN, 30 JANUARY 1913

RAPHAEL'S MISSION IN THE LIGHT OF THE SCIENCE OF THE SPIRIT

RAPHAEL is one of those figures in the history of human culture who appear like a star; such figures emerge all of a sudden, so that one has the feeling that they suddenly appear from indeterminate depths of the spiritual evolution of mankind and then disappear again after they have through mighty creative deeds made their mark upon the cultural life of humanity. On closer observation it becomes evident that a human being of this nature, who first flares up like a star and then disappears again, is linked to the whole of human culture as an integral part of a great organism. One has this feeling especially in the case of Raphael.

Herman Grimm, the eminent art historian of whom I spoke last time, has tried to trace Raphael's influence and fame through the ages subsequent to his own time and right up to the present.[107] He was able to show that what Raphael has created has since his death continued to exert a living influence, that a unified stream of spiritual development has flowed from his life, reaches beyond his death and extends to our own time. If Herman Grimm has shown how the ensuing development of humanity is a living extension of Raphael's creative work, so—on the other hand—could one say with respect to cultural history that the preceding ages can give one the impression that they were themselves in a certain sense pointing towards the later appearance of Raphael as an integral part of a whole organism.

It is appropriate at this point to recall an observation made by Goethe and apply it not to the world of space but to the world of time. Goethe made this significant pronouncement:[108] 'How can a person relate to the infinitude of space if he does not gather up all the spiritual forces that are extended on all sides within the inmost depths of his being, if he does not ask himself: Can you conceive of yourself in the midst of this eternally living order if you do not at the same time distinguish in yourself a persistently moving element around a pure central focus?'

Applying these words to the evolution of the ages one might say that in a certain respect the Gods of Homer, who have been described so masterfully by Homer nearly a thousand years before the founding of Christianity, would as we look back to antiquity lose something of their stature if we were not able to see how they have been reborn in the soul of Raphael and have reached a kind of consummation through the mighty pictorial expression that they have found in his creative work. Thus what Homer accomplished long before the coming of Christianity is linked for us with what originated in the sixteenth century from the soul of Raphael.

Again, if we turn our attention towards the biblical figures of the New Testament and then study the paintings of Raphael, we have the feeling that something would be lacking if the descriptions in the Bible were not augmented by the creative, formative power of Raphael's Madonnas and similar pictures deriving from biblical tradition and legend. Therefore one might say that Raphael does not only live on in the ensuing centuries but his own creative work is integrally related to what preceded him, which itself points towards to the consummation that it should find through him, even though this, it is true, comes to expression only in the course of later historical study.

Thus a phrase used by Lessing, namely 'the education of the human race',[109] appears in a particular light when we see how in this way a unified spiritual essence flows through the evolution of humanity, and how this unified essence streams forth especially in outstanding figures such as Raphael. Moreover, the notion of repeated earthly lives, which has so often been emphasized from a spiritual-scientific standpoint in relation to the cultural evolution of mankind, can be experienced in a quite particular way if one bears in mind what has just been said. One realizes for the first time what it means that this human essence reappears again and again in repeated earthly lives through the ages of human history and bears from one age to another what is to be implanted in the cultural evolution of mankind. Spiritual science looks always for meaning in human evolution.

It does not merely wish to depict the successive events in human history in a continuous straight line but aims to attribute a significance to particular periods, so that when the human soul appears again and again in successive earthly lives it is constantly able to experience something new when it enters earthly existence. Thus we can indeed speak of an education that the human soul undergoes through its various earthly lives, an education through everything that has been created and developed by the common spirit of humanity.

What will be said here from a spiritual-scientific standpoint about Raphael's relationship to human evolution as a whole during the last few centuries is not intended to be a philosophical appraisal of history but something that has emerged quite naturally from an extensive study of his creative work. Moreover, the theme of this evening's lecture has arisen not because of some sort of desire to make a philosophical survey of the cultural life of humanity but because everything that I have experienced after contemplating and reflecting upon various works by Raphael has crystallized quite naturally into what I should now like to say. It will be impossible to make detailed studies of Raphael's paintings; this can be done only if one has the means to display his pictures before the audience.[110] However, Raphael's creative work gives rise to a general impression; and if one has studied Raphael something of an overall impression arises in one's soul. One may then ask: How can this general impression be related to human evolution as a whole?

One's attention becomes focused in relation to Raphael on a particular period with which he is intimately connected, that period which is associated with the development of the Greek people. Indeed, if we study human evolution over recent millennia, we encounter a kind of intermediate age which the Greeks not only created but experienced with their whole being. Greek culture, which in a certain sense coincides with the founding of Christianity, was preceded by an age with a quite different character from the one that followed this Greek period. If we study the people living in the time that preceded Greek culture, we find that the soul and spirit of human beings was far more intimately connected with everything of an outward bodily nature than was the case in the later period. What we refer to today as an internalization, an inner withdrawal, of the human soul when it seeks to turn to the spirit or become conscious of the spiritual foundations of the world, this did not exist to the same degree as today in pre-Grecian times. The situation at that time was that when a person made use of his bodily organs, the spiritual mysteries of existence simultaneously illumined his soul. The detached and aloof observation of the sense-world characteristic of modern science did not exist in this former time. A person beheld objects with his senses and experienced together with the sense-impression what was living and weaving of a soul-spiritual nature in the phenomena. In contemplating the phenomena with his senses he could at the same time perceive the spiritual domain. In these ancient times it was not necessary to withdraw from the sensory impressions, to give oneself up wholly to inner contemplation, in order to advance one's knowledge of the spiritual world.

If we go very far back in the evolution of humanity, we find that what we call in the true sense a 'clairvoyant perception of phenomena' was a capacity that people generally possessed in ancient times, and that this clairvoyant perception was not achieved through special circumstances but was something as natural as sensory perception. Then came Greek culture with its distinctive world, of which it can be said that the cultural life begins to acquire an inward quality but that what the mind experiences inwardly is always seen in connection with what is taking place in the outer world. In Greek culture a balance is maintained between the sensory and the soul-spiritual elements. The spiritual domain was no longer as directly present with sense-perception as was the case in pre-Grecian times. It arose in the Greek soul as a separate inner faculty, but as something that one felt when the senses were directed towards the outer world. The spiritual dimension was beheld not in but through the phenomena. Thus in pre-Grecian times the human soul was, as it were, poured out into the bodily nature. In Greek culture it had to some extent freed itself from this bodily nature, but the balance between the soul-spiritual and the bodily aspects was still maintained. This is why what the Greeks created seems to be as fully imbued with spirit as that which came before their eyes through the agency of their senses.

Then come the post-Grecian times, those times when the human mind becomes internalized, when it was no longer able to receive what lives and weaves in the phenomena in terms of spiritual content together with the sense-impression. These are the times when the human soul had to withdraw into itself and had to experience its struggles and conquests in a state of inward separation if it wanted to reach towards the world of spirit. Spiritual contemplation of phenomena and sensory perception of phenomena became in a certain sense two worlds that the human soul had to experience.

This becomes discernible if we study a figure such as Augustine, who lived at a time that was approximately as distant from the founding of Christianity as our age is from the Reformation. If we compare what Augustine experienced and expressed in his writings with what has come down to us from the world of Ancient Greece, how well this characterizes the progress of humanity of which we have been speaking! All that Augustine sets forth in his *Confessions*,[111] what he shows us of the struggles of the inwardly focused soul, what he shows us of a scene of action which is depicted within the inner soul set apart from the outer world, all this is impossible to envisage in the case of the Ancient Greeks, where we universally see how that which lives in the soul is linked with what is being enacted in the outside world.

It would be true to say that the evolutionary history of humanity shows evidence of a mighty incision. On the one hand there is the world of Ancient Greece, which shows us how humanity maintains the balance with respect to the soul-spiritual and the outward bodily aspects. On the other hand there is the influence in this respect of the founding of Christianity, which had the effect that everything that the human soul was able to experience took the form of inner struggles and conquests; while attention was directed not to the sense-world in order to become conscious of the riddles of existence but to what the human mind could perceive intuitively if it devoted itself wholly to soul-spiritual forces. What a deep gulf separates the infinitely different figures of Ancient Greece—the majestic Greek Gods so perfected in their beauty, Zeus or Apollo—and the Christ dying on the Cross, who is characterized by inner depth and greatness but not by outward beauty. This is the outward symbol of that deep incision that Christianity and the world of Ancient Greece form in the evolution of mankind. And in those figures that follow the Grecian Age we see the effects of this incision as an ever stronger internalization of the soul.

This internalization that has thus taken place characterizes the further progress of human evolution. If one wants to understand this evolution of humanity from a spiritual-scientific point of view, one needs to realize that we live in an age which—to the extent that we observe its immediate antecedents and the prospects that we can see emerging in an eventual future—can increasingly be seen in terms of an intensifying internalization. Thus we envisage a future in which an even greater gulf that can be revealed from a contemplation of the past will open up between everything that goes on in the world without, that takes place in the more or less mechanical, technical life of the outer world, and what the human soul endeavours to achieve if it seeks to scale the heights of a spiritual domain which will become accessible only when in our inner being we try to take the steps that lead to it. We are approaching a time of ever greater inwardness. However, a significant stage in this advance of humanity towards greater inwardness in post-Grecian times is marked by the creative legacy of Raphael.

Raphael is a quite particular figure who represents a kind of watershed in human evolution. What preceded him may be thought of as the beginning of this process of internalization; and what comes after him can be seen as a new chapter in this process. Although much that I have to say in today's lecture may sound like a kind of symbolic study, it should not merely be regarded in symbolic terms but in such a way that the attempt is made to grasp what in comparison to Raphael's immeasurable greatness can only be clothed in trivial human concepts, albeit framed in concepts and ideas that are as broad as possible.

When we try to penetrate into Raphael's soul, we are struck first and foremost by the way that this soul appears in the year 1483 as a spring-like birth, then undergoes an inner development, unfolds its capacities in the most wonderful creations and, as Raphael, dies at the age of 37, thus still quite young. In order that we may focus properly on this soul and follow the stages in its development, we shall for the moment turn our attention away from what was otherwise going on in world history and concentrate solely upon Raphael's own inner life.

Herman Grimm has pointed out certain regularities in the inner development of Raphael's soul, and it may be said that there is no need for spiritual science to apologize for pointing out to a sceptical humanity certain cyclical laws pertaining to a spiritual path in any evolution, including that of a single individual, since so eminent a figure as Herman Grimm has, without acknowledging this spiritual science, been led to identifying such a regular inner cyclic pattern with respect to the soul of Raphael. Herman Grimm has drawn attention to the fact that the painting in Milan that has so enthralled us, the *Marriage of the Virgin*, is like something altogether new in the whole evolution of art and cannot be compared with anything that preceded it; so that one could say that Raphael created something from the infinite depths of a human soul that in the context of the whole of cultural evolution was completely new.

If in this way we gain a sense of what lived in Raphael's soul from his birth, we can—if we continue to follow his development—also feel with Herman Grimm how this development of his proceeds in regular stages, in stages of four years. It is remarkable how Raphael's soul advances in its development in cycles of four years. And if we examine such a four-year period, we find that his soul has reached a higher level. Some four years after the *Marriage of the Virgin* he painted the *Entombment*; four years after this the frescoes of the *Camera della Segnatura*; and then in four-year stages until that work which stood unfinished by his death-bed, the *Transfiguration of Christ.*[112]

It is because everything in this soul unfolds so harmoniously that one has the wish to study it for its own sake. But then one can gain the impression that in Raphael's time such a quality of inwardness had to develop with respect to the art of painting, and that what came to expression in figures which only Raphael could create was born out of the depths of soul-experiences, although it manifests itself in pictures of the sense-world. And does it not also become part of history itself?

Having thus spent a while focusing upon the inner nature of Raphael's soul, let us allow the time in which he lived and all that was around him be the object of our attention. For as long as Raphael was more or less a child and was growing up in Urbino, we find that he was in an environment that had an awakening influence upon significant talents that made their appearance there. It was in Urbino that a palace had been built that aroused the excitement of the whole of Italy. This was something that imbued Raphael's early talents with an element that harmonized with their nature. We then see him moving to Perugia, then to Florence and then to Rome. Raphael's life was essentially confined to a narrow circle. How close these places seem to us today when we study his entire life! Raphael's whole world was confined to this circle so far as the sense-world was concerned. Only in the spirit did he rise to other spheres.

But now we see how in Perugia, where Raphael spent much of his youth, bloody battles were the order of the day. The city was populated by inhabitants who were inflamed with powerful passions. Noble families whose lives were spent in wrangling and quarrelling engaged in conflict with one another. The one family drove the others out of the city. After a brief period of expulsion the others then tried to take control of the city again, and several times the streets of Perugia were bestrewn with blood and corpses. One historian describes an extraordinary scene, and indeed all the accounts that historians give of that time are quite distinctive. Thus we see through the historian's account a nobleman of the city entering it in battle array in order to avenge his relatives.[113] The historian describes him to us as the spirit of war incarnate riding on horseback through the streets, beating down everything that crosses his path; and it is evident that the writer had the impression that the vengeance exacted by the nobleman was justified, in that there comes in to his mind the image of that warrior who casts the enemy beneath his feet. In Raphael's picture of St George[114] we feel this image that the chronicler depicts appearing graphically before us, and we have the direct impression that it could not be otherwise that Raphael must surely have been affected by this scene, and that what must outwardly seem to us as so terrible is internalized and reborn from Raphael's soul and becomes the point of departure for his portrayal of the greatest images of human evolution.

Thus Raphael saw people battling and quarrelling around him, he had to experience much disorder and one battle after another in the city where he spent his early apprenticeship with his first teacher Pietro Perugino; and we have the impression that there were two worlds present at that time: the one where cruelty and terror were being inflicted, and another world that lived inwardly in Raphael's soul and actually did not have much to do with what was going on around him in the physical world.

Then again we see Raphael in 1504 after his move to Florence. What was Florence like when Raphael arrived there? The immediate impression of the inhabitants was of weariness, of people who had passed through inner and outer tumults and were weighed down with a certain sense of exhaustion and tiredness. What was it that had befallen Florence? Struggles similar to those in Perugia, bloody persecutions of various patrician families, to say nothing of battles with external powers; and then the dramatic event that shook everyone in the city, the experience of Savonarola, who shortly before Raphael's arrival had died a martyr's death.[115] This remarkable figure of Savonarola stands before us, denouncing with fiery words the evils of the time and specifically the cruelties, worldliness and pagan nature of the Church. When we call them to mind there still resound within us these thunderous words of Savonarola through which he captivated the whole of Florence, so that the people not only hung upon his lips but revered him as if a higher spirit were standing before them in this ascetic body.

The words of Savonarola transformed the city of Florence with the force of a religious reformer who could influence not only religious ideas but even the social fabric of the city. Thus Florence was under Savonarola's influence as if a city of God had been founded there. And then we see how Savonarola became a victim of those powers that he sought to counter both morally and religiously. There appears before our soul the moving picture of Savonarola being led to the stake with his companions and turning his eyes from the gallows whence he was to fall on to the burning pyre—it was in May 1498—to the people who had formerly clung to his every word but who had now abandoned him and were looking with apparent disloyalty to the one who had for so long inspired them. There were only few—and they were mostly artists—in whom Savonarola's words still resounded. After Savonarola had been martyred, one painter of that time donned the monk's robe in order to continue working in his Order under the influence of his spirit.[116]

One can imagine the weary atmosphere that presided over Florence; and it was into this atmosphere that Raphael came in 1504, bringing with him a spring-like breath of the spirit through the medium of his creative work, which introduced to the city a spiritual fire but in a quite different way from Savonarola. When we contemplate the soul of Raphael, which appears to us in its isolation so utterly unlike the mood of this city, when we see him engaged, together with artists and painters, in creative work in a solitary workshop in Florence or elsewhere, a different picture appears before us which shows us in a historically visible way how Raphael's soul was inwardly isolated from the surroundings with which it was directly in contact. We become aware of the figures of the Roman popes, Alexander VI, Julius II, Leo X, the whole papal system against which Savonarola had directed his anger and against which the reformers also turned. But we also recognize that this papal system was at the same time Raphael's patron, we see his soul in the service of the papacy—although in such a way that it had inwardly very little in common with what we find, for example, in his patron, Pope Julius II, of whom it was said that he gave the impression of someone with a devil in his body and always delighted in showing his teeth to his enemies.

These popes are great figures, but they were certainly not what Savonarola or those who thought like him would have called 'Christians'. The papacy had developed a new kind of pagan quality (in contrast to old forms of paganism). There was little to be seen in these circles of Christian piety, though there was much brilliance, ambition and lust for power in the popes as well as in their environment.

Raphael was, as it were, in the service of this pagan Christianity; but in what way? Something was created from his soul that enabled Christian ideas to appear in a new form. In the Madonnas and in other works by Raphael we see the tenderest and most inward aspect of the world of Christian legend being renewed. What a contrast there is between the living inner quality of Raphael's creations and all that was going on around him in Rome when he entered into the outward service of the popes! But how was all this possible? We see him in his early period as a student in Perugia; we see then in Florence how great a contrast there is between his external surroundings and his inner state of being, and then quite particularly in Rome, where he created his immortal pictures amidst an officialdom of cardinals and priests that was altogether repugnant to Savonarola (whom Raphael did not by any means resemble). Nevertheless, one needs to view Raphael in this way if one is wanting to form a true picture of what was living in his soul.

Let us now explore Raphael's pictures themselves! It is not possible for this to happen in detail this evening, but at least one of his more well-known pictures can be singled out so that we are able to gain some understanding especially of the quite distinctive nature of his soul. The picture in question is one that is very familiar to us, the *Sistine Madonna* in Dresden, which almost everyone knows from the numerous reproductions that are disseminated throughout the world. In this work of art, which is one of the greatest and noblest in human history, the mother appears with the child hovering on the heights of the clouds that cover the earthly globe, hover from the indefinite forms of the spiritual, supersensible world engirdled and surrounded by clouds that form themselves quite naturally into human-like figures, one of which seems to compose itself into the child of the Madonna. It awakens within us quite particular feelings, of which we can say that when they permeate our soul we could forget all the legendary conceptions whence the image of the Madonna has originated together with what Christian traditions say about the Madonna.

I say this not in order to reduce the description to its bare essentials but to characterize as fully as possible what we can feel in relation to the Madonna. Anyone who studies the evolution of humanity in a spiritual-scientific sense reaches beyond a materialistic viewpoint. According to natural science, first the lower living beings developed and then evolution advanced upwards to man. But in spiritual-scientific terms we must see man as a being who transcends everything that is at a lower level to him in the kingdoms of nature. With man, we are concerned with something far older than all the beings that are to a greater or lesser degree close to him in the various kingdoms of nature.

For spiritual science, man existed before the beings of the animal kingdom, before the plant kingdom and even before the mineral kingdom. In a wider perspective we look back to ages when that which now constitutes our innermost being was already in existence; for it was only later that this was incorporated into the kingdoms that are at a lower level than man. Thus we see the being of man hovering in anticipation from a realm beyond the Earth; and we understand that we can form a true picture of this being of man only if we raise ourselves from all that the Earth is able to engender and bring forth out of itself to something of a super-earthly and also pre-earthly nature. Through spiritual science we can know that if we engage fully with all the forces and living entities associated with the Earth itself, we will not be able to form a picture of man's essential being; for we must lift our gaze from the earthly realm to super-earthly regions whence the being of man proceeds. Speaking figuratively we must feel how something is wafting towards the Earth when, for example, we direct our gaze towards a morning sunrise, towards the gold-gleaming light of dawn—and especially in a region such as where Raphael lived; and we can have the feeling that forces must work down into the earthly realm that are inherently associated with the being of the Sun. Then from the golden radiance an image appears before our soul of what is hovering in anticipation of being clothed with earthly substance.

Especially in Perugia one can have the feeling that the eye is beholding the same sunrise that Raphael experienced, and that in such phenomena as the rising Sun one can have a sense of the super-earthly aspect of man's being. From the Sun-irradiated clouds there may—however dimly—dawn upon one the realization that the picture of the Madonna with the child is an image of the eternally super-earthly aspect of man's being which approaches the Earth from extraterrestrial realms; and beneath it, separated by clouds, is everything that can only proceed from the earthly realm. Our feelings may be raised to the highest spiritual heights if we devote our attention with our whole soul rather than theoretically or in an abstract way to the effect that Raphael's Madonna has on us. It is perfectly natural for us to have such a feeling when looking at the world-famous picture in Dresden. As evidence of the effect that it has had on many people, I should like to share some words which a friend of Goethe, Karl August, who was at the time the Duke of Weimar, has written about the *Sistine Madonna* after a visit to Dresden:[117]

> With regard to the Raphael that adorns the collection, I can only say that I felt as if I had been climbing for the whole day through the Gotthard mountains, had come through the Ursel Gap and was looking down upon a green, blossoming valley. As I looked at the picture and again away from it, it always seemed to me like a revelation of the soul; even the most beautiful Corregios were only human pictures; my memory of them imprinted palpably as beautiful forms. But Raphael remained with me merely as a breath, as one of those revelations that the Gods send to us in womanly form for our good or ill fortune; like the pictures that come before us in the hours of sleep in our waking or dream consciousness and whose gaze, once encountered, remains with us day and night and stirs our innermost being.

It is also remarkable that if one studies the writings of those who have been able to express a deep level of emotion as a result of having seen the *Sistine Madonna* and also other pictures by Raphael, it is again and again apparent that when people seek to characterize what they feel there are comparisons with light, with the Sun, with all that is radiant and spring-like.

This gives us an insight into Raphael's soul, into the way that from the circumstances of its environment that have been described it engages in conversation with the eternal mysteries of human evolution. We feel that this soul of Raphael has a unique quality, something that has not grown out of its surroundings but is indicative of an immensity of human history. There is then no need to speculate. Such a soul which gazes out into the widths of the world-periphery and gives expression to the mystery of existence not in ideas but forms it in such a picture, such a soul presents itself through such an inner perfection quite naturally as a very mature soul which in its antecedents bears something of the forces of mankind, a soul that must have passed through other periods of human evolution and especially through many of these periods that have invested this soul with greatness and power, so that these qualities can appear again in what we call the life of Raphael. But how do they re-emerge?

We see the living content of Christian legends and traditions reappearing in Raphael's pictures at a time when Christianity had adopted a pagan quality and had abandoned itself to purely outward forms and splendours, just as Greek paganism was portrayed in its Gods and was revered above all by the Greeks in their intoxication with beauty. We see Raphael depicting these figures of Christian tradition at a time when that which had been buried for many centuries beneath rubble and ruins on Roman soil was again being unearthed. We see that Raphael was himself among the excavators. There is something remarkable about this Rome to which Raphael had moved at this time.

What preceded this time? First we see the centuries when Rome was emerging, founded wholly upon the egotism of particular people whose prime consideration was to establish a human society on the basis of what a person might signify as a citizen of a state, a society in the outward physical world. Then when Rome attained a certain climax in its development in the imperial age, we see how it absorbs Greek culture, which streams into Roman cultural life; and we experience how—whereas Rome indeed conquers Greece politically—from a cultural point of view Greece conquers Rome. Greek culture lives on in Roman culture. We see that Greek art, to the extent that it was absorbed by Rome, lives on in a Roman context, we see that Rome is wholly pervaded by the essence of Greek culture.

But why is it that this essence of Greek culture does not continue to be a characteristic quality in the development of Italy? Why did something entirely different happen? Because shortly after Greek culture had pervaded the Roman world, something else entered into the picture which impressed its signature more strongly upon what developed culturally on Italian soil: Christianity, the internalizing quality of Christianity. This did not have the intention of addressing mankind after the fashion of the sense-perceptible emphasis of the Greek cities, Greek works of sculpture or Greek philosophy, but addressed a quality in the inner human soul that was to enter formlessly into it and which it could take hold of only through inner struggles. This is why figures such as Augustine appear, figures with a wholly inward orientation.

But then, since everything in evolution proceeds and unfolds in cycles, we see that after these people have undergone a journey inwards and have lived as regards their soul-existence for a long time without any connection with the beauties of outward life, that longing for beauty reappears. They behold the inner world again in the world around them. It is something really significant when in Assisi we see the intensified inner life of Francis of Assisi appear before our eyes through Giotto,[118] when in Giotto's pictures we see expressed the inner experiences that Christianity can, as it were, engender in the human soul. And even if we may be justified in feeling that the inner nature of the human soul is somewhat awkwardly and imperfectly expressed in Giotto's pictures, we nevertheless see a direct ascent to the point where that which is most inward, most exalted and most noble confronts us in outward form in the work of Raphael and his contemporaries. Here we are again directed towards a particular quality of this soul of Raphael.

If we try to penetrate into the way that Raphael himself must have felt, we would have to say to ourselves: Yes, when we see works of art such as the *Madonna della Sedia*[119] coming into being, it seems to us that the Madonna with the child, and with John the Baptist in the foreground, appear before us in such a way that when we contemplate them we could forget all the rest of the world, and quite especially that this child who is held by the Madonna can be connected with those experiences which we know as those of Golgotha. When looking at Raphael's picture we forget everything that followed as the 'life of Christ Jesus'. We enter wholly into the moment that is recorded here. We simply look at a mother with a child, of which Herman Grimm has said that it is the greatest mystery that we can meet with in the outer world.[120] Peace surrounds this moment, as if nothing could connect with it, either before or afterwards. We are wholly immersed in the relationship of the Madonna to her child; we separate it as far as we are concerned from everything with which it is otherwise associated. Thus what Raphael created has the quality of inner perfection, making eternity manifest in a moment of time.

What must it feel like to be a soul that creates in this way? It cannot feel as does the soul of Savonarola, which with an inner ardent fire inwardly feels the whole tragedy of Christ when he utters his words of anger or when he speaks religiously uplifting, pious words to listeners of Christian devotion. We cannot imagine Raphael's soul getting worked up after the fashion of a Savonarola or others like him, we cannot imagine that that so-called Christian fire had sovereignty over Raphael's soul. But if we can allow ourselves to be influenced by the true nature of a human soul, we should not think that the Christian imaginations depicted pictorially by Raphael could have come before us with such an inner intensity and perfection if this soul had been so wholly estranged from this Christian fire as it appears to us to be when it is working quite objectively on these pictures.

One cannot create figures with such objectivity and roundness if one is imbued, say, with the fire of Savonarola, if one's soul is burdened by the whole tragic mood of Christ and feels inspired by it. A very different quality of peace and a quite different Christian sensibility must have pervaded the soul. Nevertheless, what came to expression in Raphael's pictures could not have come about if the deepest essence of Christian inwardness had not been living in this soul. Is it, then, not quite natural to say: Yes, we have before us a soul which already brought that fire that we perceive so visibly in Savonarola with it into the physical existence which it embarked upon as the artist Raphael. When we realize that it brought this fire through the portal of birth from previous earthly lives, we understand how it could be so luminous, so inwardly perfect, that this fire does not come forth as something all-consuming and shattering but as the radiance of pictorial creativity. So one can say that in Raphael's innate attributes one senses something living there that in a former life had been able to speak with the same fire that emanated subsequently from Savonarola. And one should not be surprised if in Raphael's soul there were a reborn soul from a time when Christianity was experienced not pictorially, not expressed in artistic form, but from the time of its founding, when the great impulse which then worked on in the course of many centuries had its starting-point.

In order to understand a soul such as Raphael, it is perhaps not too bold to say something of this kind. For anyone who has, through returning again and again to a study of Raphael's works, learnt to revere this soul in its depths, to perceive the fathomless profundity of its influence, cannot fail to understand through such far-reaching study what speaks to us when Raphael has poured his soul into his miraculous paintings.

Thus the mission of Raphael only really appears to us in the right light when in accordance with an expression of Goethe's[121] we look in a 'former life' for the Christian fire that appears in a later life as the radiant quality inherent in Raphael. Then we also understand why this soul had to have so isolated a relationship to the world, and why this soul that we have tried to characterize, which had perhaps to an intensified degree something of a Savonarola quality in a previous existence, was able to sense something new in what had entered into the cultural development of Italy at the time of Raphael.

Whereas, as I have already described, Greek culture had become influential in the development of Rome in the time when the imperial age was approaching and was followed by a period of internalization, we see now in the age of Raphael—the Renaissance—on the one hand the reappearance of this Ancient Greek culture which had long been buried under rubble and ruins, we see Rome filling itself with the remnants of this Greek culture, the reappearance of what through the Greek spirit had adorned and beautified the city, the eyes of the Roman people turning once again to the forms that the Greek spirit had formerly created. On the other hand we also see in this age the spirit of Plato, the spirit of Aristotle, the spirit of the Greek tragedies enter into Roman life. Once again we see the conquest of the Roman world by Greek culture. It is quite possible that a figure who had formerly been devoted in a one-sided way to the morally religious aspect of Christianity, and in a previous life had given itself wholly to these morally religious impressions, must have experienced Greek culture as having a fructifying, renewing influence when it emerged from the rubble and ruins on the Italian peninsula.

Thus whereas one sees the morally religious impulse of Christianity as though residing in Raphael's gifts, one sees that which did not live in him as a natural aptitude appear before his eyes in the resurrected culture of Greece. The statues re-emerging from the rubble and ruins and the Greek cultural artefacts deriving from the rediscovered manuscripts influenced Raphael's soul more deeply than anyone else's. What from his own predisposition, from his Christian sensibility, was united with a super-spiritual devotion to the cosmos worked hand in hand with the Greek culture as it re-emerged in his own time. These were the two things that united in his soul and which enable us to experience in Raphael's works the inward quality of the post-Grecian Age, the quality of inwardness that Christianity poured into human evolution, which was brought fully to outward expression in a world of artistic forms marked throughout by the purest spirit of Greece.

We see, then, the remarkable phenomenon that through Raphael the world of Ancient Greece reappears in Christianized form. In Raphael we see Christianity appearing in a time which in a certain sense exhibits all around him an anti-Christian quality. We see that he represents a Christianity that far transcended all aspects of the Christianity that had preceded him and extended to a broad observation of his contemporary world. And yet it was a Christianity that does not reach out dimly and vaguely to infinite spheres of pure spirit but is united—as formerly the Greeks' ideas of the Gods were united in artistic form—with what formlessly lives and weaves through the world and has been concentrated into forms whence at the same time it delights our senses.

This is what we find when we try to form an overall picture, when we focus on one or another of Raphael's paintings, when we allow all this sublime perfection—and yet this most wonderful superfluity of youth, for Raphael was only 37 when he died—to have an effect on us. Not for the sake of some dull theory and certainly not with the object of constructing a philosophy of history but as something derived from direct experience, it must be said that the laws underlying the cultural life of humanity are truly manifested in a spirit as outstanding as Raphael.

Anyone who conceives of this course of cultural life as a straight line where effect follows cause has little idea of the actual facts. It is only too easy to come out with a saying that is surely one of the golden sayings of humanity: Life and nature do not make leaps.[122] Well and good; but the truth is that in a certain respect life and nature do continually make leaps. We can see this in the development of the plant from green leaf to blossom, and from blossom to the fruit. Everything does indeed 'evolve', but leaps occur as a matter of course.

It is similar with the cultural life of humanity, and this is bound up with many mysteries. One of these mysteries is that a later age must always hark back to an earlier one. Just as male and female have to cooperate with one another, the various spirits of the age must work together in a mutually fruitful way if any further development is to occur. Thus in its imperial phase Rome had to be fructified by Greek culture in order that a new spirit of the age might arise. And this spirit of the age had in turn to be fructified by the Christ impulse so that the inwardness that we encounter in Augustine and others might be possible. Similarly this inwardly so advanced human soul of Raphael had subsequently to be fructified by Greek culture, which had been twice buried and then re-emerged—it withdrew in a twofold sense, from eyes in the works of art that lay buried beneath the soil of Italy and from souls in the buried works of literature that manifested the spirit of Greece. These centuries of the first Christian millennium in Italy were remarkably little influenced by what lived in Greek philosophy, in Greek poetry and drama.

Culture was twice buried and waited in, as it were, a realm beyond the threshold for a time when it could newly fructify the human soul which had in the meantime embraced a new religion. It was buried, removed from the outward sight of human beings; and also for the souls who did not know that it would continue to develop, it was like a river that continues to flow far beneath a mountain, disappears from sight and then comes to the surface again. This Ancient Greek culture was buried both outwardly for the senses and inwardly for the depths of people's souls. Now it came bubbling up again. For sensory perception it was excavated from Italian soil in the form of artistic works; for intellectual experience it reappeared not only through its being extracted from ancient manuscripts but through people developing the awareness in the Greek sense that everything sense-perceptible is a revelation of the spiritual world. Human beings began again to feel what Plato and Aristotle had once thought.

However, the person who was most strongly influenced by this—because the Christian impulse had attained a greater level of maturity in his soul than in any other—was Raphael. In him this previously twice-buried and twice-resurrected Greek culture now worked in such a way that he was able to portray in forms the whole of human evolution. How wonderfully he accomplished this in the pictures in the *Camera della Segnatura* in the Vatican, where we see the struggles of those spirits who emerged in the age of internalization and were not there in the age of Ancient Greece. The whole period of internalization was necessary in order that they could be perceived in the time of Raphael. We now see this tendency towards greater inwardness painted on the walls of the papal chambers.

What the Greeks had conceived of only in forms has now become inward. We see the inner strivings and conflicts which mankind has itself undergone magically adorning the walls of the papal palace with a formative power, artistic mood and beauty wholly characteristic of Greece. The Greeks exhibited in their statues their conception of the way that the Gods worked upon the world. What comes to expression in the painting commonly known as *The School of Athens*[123] is the way that human beings had experienced themselves exploring the very foundations of things. And in the *Parnassus*[124] we see the way that the human soul has learnt to perceive the Greek Gods presented to us in a significant re-interpretation of the Gods of Homer. These are not the Gods of the *Iliad* and *Odyssey* but they are the Gods as perceived by a soul that has already passed through the age of inwardness!

On the other wall we see a picture that, irrespective of one's religious persuasion, must make an unforgettable impression (however slight one's acquaintance with it), a picture which portrays something of a deeply inward nature, the *Disputa*.[125] Whereas the other pictures portray—with a Greek beauty of form—something that one can aspire to through a certain philosophical striving, in the picture in question we encounter the deepest truth that a human soul can experience. And since we do not need to think in terms of a narrowly defined Christian consciousness, this manifests itself to us here if we find the triunity of Brahma, Vishnu and Shiva expressed in a completely different way. We see what the human soul—whatever creed it may adhere to—can inwardly experience as the Trinity appear before us. It appears before us, though not in a purely symbolic form, in the symbolism of the Trinity in the upper part of the picture. It again comes before us in every countenance of the Church Fathers and the philosophers, in every hand gesture, in the whole grouping of the figures, in the wonderful colouring. We see it in the totality of the picture, which gives us an inner insight into the human soul in the beautiful form, pervaded as it is by a Greek spirit. Thus we see the internalization that the human soul has experienced in the course of fifteen hundred years rise again as an outward revelation. We see Christianity not as the paganism of Greece with its wonderful figures—which is nevertheless Christianity—reborn in the pictures of Raphael.

Thus this soul of Raphael appears as a kind of watershed of the ages, pointing back to its antecedents, gathering up the beauty of outward revelations that had accumulated prior to Christianity, and at the same time orientated towards what has been brought about in human evolution in terms of the so-called 'education of the human race' and which the reincarnated soul makes manifest as the internalization of this human soul. Thus we stand before these pictures of Raphael, before these miraculous works of a unique art, in such a way that they appear to us as a converging of two ages which are clearly distant from one another: the pre-Grecian and post-Grecian ages, the age of outward experience and that of inner experience.

But these pictures also offer us a perspective into the future. For who of those who realize the potential significance of the interplay of outward beauty and the inner wisdom-filled urge of the human soul would not feel a hope and an assurance, despite everything that must develop outwardly ever more and more in the outward course of human evolution, that this inward quality must advance further in the course of evolution, that the human soul must come to experience increasingly inward periods in its following lives?

If one turns to literature, one can study—not as an art critic or a mere reader—the work of a scholar like Herman Grimm, who tried with his whole soul to portray the working of human imagination; and one can understand the inner sympathy with which he viewed the creative work of Raphael. If, moreover, one approaches such a figure as Herman Grimm with this same inner sympathy one can understand the significance of a certain passage in his book about Raphael. With regard to this passage it is necessary to gain a sense of what was living in Herman Grimm's soul when he expressed a thought that he merely hints at on the very first page of his book, at the point where he devotes his attention to Raphael's having emerged from ancient times. It is not really possible to see from Herman Grimm's formal description of Raphael's work where this thought comes from. In the middle of broad historical observations within which Raphael is included, a thought occurs to Herman Grimm[126] which he formulates tentatively as follows: 'I see developments of humanity occurring before my eyes that I shall be denied to accompany but which appear to me so radiantly beautiful that for their sake it would probably be worth the trouble to begin human life over again.'

This longing for a 're-embodiment' in the Introduction to his book on Raphael is remarkable and, moreover, deeply characteristic of the feeling living in a person who tried to live fully into Raphael's soul and into his connection with other ages. This makes one feel that works such as those by Raphael are not only an end result. They not only lead to an observation that enables us to say how grateful we must be towards what the past has given to our age, but such works can enable a quite different feeling to arise within us, a feeling of hope; because they strengthen within us a faith in an advancing humanity, and because we are obliged to say to ourselves that these works could not be what they are if progress were not an essential aspect of human nature. So we have a sense of certainty and hope if we truly attend to what Raphael has to say to us, and we can then say: Raphael has spoken to humanity through what he has created artistically!

When we look at the frescoes in the Camera della Segnatura, we feel the transitoriness of the outer work and that because of the frequent overpainting that has occurred we cannot any longer have any idea of the magic that Raphael once painted on the walls. We are aware that at some future time a humanity will live on the Earth which will not have the possibility of perceiving the original works; but we know that mankind will always be developing further.

Raphael's works really began to make their triumphal impact when with devotion and love innumerable copies, engravings and reproductions of these works were made. These works of Raphael continue to exert an influence also in their reproductions. One can understand it when Herman Grimm relates[127] that he had hung a large photograph of the *Sistine Madonna* in his room, and that when he entered this room he always felt as though he had no right to do so, as though it were a sanctuary of the Madonna in the picture. Many people will doubtless have experienced that they almost became a different person when they really devote their attention to a picture by Raphael, even if it is a reproduction. It is true that the time will come when the originals are no longer there. But will they not exist in other realms?

What Herman Grimm states in his book on Homer is quite true:[128] We can also no longer rightly appreciate Homer's originals, because when we read the *Iliad* and *Odyssey* in ordinary life we are—without higher spiritual forces—no longer in a position to enter fully into the subtleties, beauty and power of the Greek language. The originals no longer exist; but nonetheless Homer's poetry speaks to us. But what Raphael has given outwardly will always remain as a living witness that there was once a time in the evolution of humanity when the mysteries of existence spoke to the eyes of human beings on a very broad scale not in printed and written form—for at that time this did not generally happen—but in the creative work of Raphael. The age of Raphael was one when people read less but by the same token saw more. What Raphael will always have to say to humanity will be a witness to this time, which was differently constituted but which will nevertheless continue to exert an influence in all future ages, because humanity is one whole organism. Thus Raphael's creativity will live on in the course of human evolution, also inwardly in the successive lives that his spirit has to live and in which he has ever greater and ever more deeply inward gifts to bestow upon mankind.

Thus spiritual science points towards a twofold continuation of life: that further life which has been described in the previous lectures and will be spoken of further, and another spiritual life towards which we are constantly striving and which becomes our guide when we experience earthly existence in ever new epochs. And Herman Grimm is right to say what he did when he gave expression to what he came to feel as a result of his study of Raphael: Even though a time will come when Raphael's work will have faded and been destroyed, he will nevertheless continue to be alive for humanity; for in him humanity blossomed forth into something which in every respect has been implanted in its spirit and which will forever germinate and bear fruit.

A human soul that is able to immerse itself sufficiently in Raphael will be aware of this. Indeed we will have wholly understood Raphael only if we are able spiritual-scientifically to elevate and deepen a feeling that fully impressed itself on Herman Grimm (we indicated in the previous lecture how close he stood to spiritual science) when he concerned himself with Raphael. We shall understand our relationship to Raphael, we shall understand how the thoughts that have been presented today may become seeds for the future, if we conclude by summarizing what it has been the intention to convey today by means of some words of Herman Grimm:[129] 'People will always want to know about Raphael, about the beautiful young painter who surpassed all others, and who was fated to die young. The whole of Rome mourned his death. When Raphael's works are eventually lost, his name will continue to be engraved in human memory.'

Thus wrote Herman Grimm when he began in his particular way to describe Raphael. We can understand these words. And we also understand him when at the end of his book about Raphael he lets these words sound forth:[130] 'Everyone will want to know about the life's work of such a person. Raphael has become one of the elements upon which the higher development of the human spirit rests. We would wish to draw nearer to him, because we need him for our well-being.'

Lecture 10

BERLIN, 6 FEBRUARY 1913

FAIRY-TALE LITERATURE IN THE LIGHT OF SPIRITUAL RESEARCH

THERE are several reasons why it may appear risky to speak about fairy tales in the light of spiritual research. One is the difficulty of the subject, for the sources of the true fairy-tale mood lie so deep within the human soul that those methods of spiritual research that I have often described have to engage in a long and complicated process if these sources are to be found. The sources whence true, genuine fairy tales flow lie far deeper than one might think, since they speak to us of something magical that derives from many centuries of human evolution.

The second is that, precisely because of this magical quality, one strongly has the feeling that the elemental nature and spontaneity, even the very effect, of fairy tales may be destroyed by studying them, by imposing one's own ideas upon them. It is often said, and rightly so, that explanations and analyses of poetry destroy the immediate aesthetic impression, the living quality, that a poem should be able to make if one has a direct, unvarnished impression of it; and this applies all the more to the infinitely subtle and magical quality of what arises in the form of fairy tales from the deep, unfathomable sources of the popular imagination or of individual human hearts. Indeed, to seek to impose one's judgement on what springs so primordially from the human soul as this fairy-tale literature could be seen as being like destroying the blossom of a plant.

Nevertheless, it seems that on the one hand it is possible for the methods of spiritual research to shed at least some light upon those regions of soul-life whence the substance and mood of fairy tales derive. On the other hand, this also enables something to be placed against the second consideration. Precisely because the sources of fairy tales have to be sought so deeply in the soul, one comes purely out of experience to the conviction that what one has to give by way of a spiritual-scientific explanation remains something that so gently touches those sources that they are not only not adversely affected but, on the contrary, the inherent depth and significance of that region in the human soul whence the fairy-tale mood derives is such that one has the feeling that what can be found there is on each occasion so new, so individual and so primordial for the human soul that it may itself best be spoken of in the manner of a fairy tale; for one feels that it is impossible to speak about these hidden springs in any other way.

Thus it could seem quite natural that when someone like Goethe, who in addition to his work as an artist sought to fathom the sources and foundations of existence, wants to describe what lives in the human soul at its deepest level, he does not embark upon theoretical arguments or destroy the wellsprings of the fairy-tale world through his research but gives expression to his insight into this world by means of a fairy tale. Hence in his *Fairy Tale of the Green Snake and the Beautiful Lily*,[131] Goethe tried to express in his own way the deep experiences of the human soul that Schiller put forward in a more abstract, philosophical way in his letters *On the Aesthetic Education of Man*.[132] The very nature of the fairy-tale mood entails that trying to explain and understand it will probably never destroy its creative quality; for anyone who from the standpoint of spiritual research penetrates to the wellsprings referred to will discover something quite remarkable. If I were to say everything that I should like to about the nature of fairy tales, I would have to give many lectures. Today it will only be possible to mention a few indications and some results of my research.

Anyone who tries to explore the sources of fairy tales from the standpoint of spiritual research will find that these wellsprings of the fairy-tale world lie much deeper in the human soul than the sources of the aspect of the soul which creates and enjoys culture and also finds expression in the most powerful works of art, for example the most deeply gripping tragedies. Tragedy portrays the human soul's experience of the powers of which the poet says that they emanate from the massive destiny-laden forces that both exalt and crush human beings. The shocks of tragedy derive from these wheels of fate and the way they are portrayed, but in such a way that we can say that the tangled threads that are woven and then unravelled through tragedy relate more or less to certain individual experiences of the human soul with the outside world, experiences which are difficult to discern because it is not easy to penetrate into the individual nature of the human soul but which can nevertheless be intuited if one has a sense for what occurs within the human soul through its relation to life. One has the feeling that a soul has in one way or another been caught up within a particular event of destiny when it experiences tragedy, as it is portrayed to us.

The sources of the mood and diction of fairy tales lie much deeper than the entanglements of tragedy. We feel that tragedy, and also much else in the artistic realm, arises when, for example, we see a person exposed to the workings of destiny at a particular time, in a particular period, of life. When a tragedy is being enacted before us, we must presuppose that a human being has been brought to the predicament in question through an individual experience, and we then have the feeling that it is this one person—who comes before us in the tragedy with his particular experiences—whom we must understand. A certain circumscribed sphere of human life is presented to us in tragedy and in other works of art.

When we approach fairy tales and the mood associated with them with understanding, we have a different feeling which contrasts with the one just described; because the effect of a fairy tale upon the human soul has something primordial and elemental about it, so that it remains unconscious. When we try to acquire a feeling for it, we become aware that what comes to expression in the various fairy tales does not lie in what is brought to a person in a particular situation of life, it is not a limited portion of human experience, but is something so deeply entrenched in the experiences of the human soul that it is of universal human significance. We cannot say that it is about a particular human soul of a certain age and life-situation; for what comes to expression in the fairy tale is so deeply rooted in the soul that it can be experienced equally by children in their early years, by people of middle age and by the elderly.

That which comes to expression in a fairy tale reflects our deepest experiences throughout our lives. Nevertheless, the fairy tale is a free and often playful, pictorial expression of these experiences and what lies at their foundation. The aesthetic, artistic enjoyment of a fairy tale is perhaps as far removed for the soul from what corresponds in the fairy tale to one's inner experiences as—to make a bold comparison—the experience of taste on the tongue when we are enjoying a meal, is removed from the hidden, complicated processes that the food undergoes in our bodily organism in order that it may be nourished by it. What happens in this regard is not initially apparent to our observation or understanding, and all that a person has is the pleasure of tasting the food. Both aspects seem initially to have little to do with each other, and no one is able to establish from the taste of the meal anything about the role that this food plays in the whole life-process of the human organism. The aesthetic pleasure that a person experiences in a fairy tale is likewise far, far removed from what happens in the deep, unconscious regions of the human soul when the essence of what lives in the fairy tale unites with the human soul; because this soul has an undying need to have the substance of the fairy tale flowing in its spiritual veins, just as the organism has a need to have the nutriments, the nourishing substance in bodily circulation.

If one uses the methods that have been described here as methods of spiritual research, methods of research into the spiritual worlds, one will at a certain stage of spiritual knowledge discover that spiritual processes are, wholly unbeknown to the human soul, working within its depths. In ordinary, normal life these processes that are at work in the depths of the soul come to our awareness only sometimes as gentle dream-experiences that can also be apprehended on occasion by our waking consciousness. When a person is, under especially favourable circumstances, awakening from sleep, he can have the feeling: You are emerging from a spiritual world where there is thinking and where there are intentions, and where something was happening in the deep, unfathomable foundations of existence that is somehow similar to daily experiences and is intimately connected with your whole being, but which is deeply hidden from your daily, waking life.

When the spirit-researcher has progressed to the extent of being able to experience a world of spiritual beings and spiritual realities, he may often meet with something of this kind. However far he progresses, he nonetheless again and again reaches the shore of a world where spiritual processes or impulses come towards him out of a deep unconsciousness; and he says of these impulses: They are connected with your being, you can apprehend them somewhat as a Fata Morgana which appears before your spiritual sight, but they do not wholly yield themselves up to you.

This awareness of the unfathomable nature of the spiritual relationships in which the human soul is involved is the most remarkable experience that one can have. If one attentively accompanies certain intimate soul-processes, it may, for example, emerge that those emotional conflicts that a person also experiences in the depths of the soul and which he portrays in works of art and in tragic drama are relatively easy to understand as compared with some universally human soul-conflicts of which there is no awareness in ordinary waking life, even though all people of whatever age have to deal with them.

One such soul-conflict that one discovers through spiritual research is enacted—without one's everyday consciousness being aware of it—every day on waking up, when the soul leaves the world where it dwells unconsciously during sleep, when it re-enters its physical body. As said, one's everyday consciousness has no awareness of it—and yet it is a matter of the soul's daily experience that it is engaged in a battle that is all-encompassing and which one may call the battle of the separate, inwardly focused, solitary and spiritually-seeking soul with the gigantic forces of nature, forces which we confront in outer life when we stand there more or less helplessly and experience thunder and lightning and the elements of nature unburdening themselves upon helpless human beings.

But all this, even when it manifests itself with immense power in relation to man in certain rare freaks of nature, is a small thing as compared with the battle that remains in the unconscious, that takes place when one awakes, when the soul—which has an inner experience of its soul-existence—has to unite with the forces and substances of the purely physical body into which it dives down in order to avail itself of its senses (which are governed by nature-forces) and its limbs, in which nature-forces are at work. The human soul has a kind of yearning to submerge itself in this purely natural state, a yearning that is fulfilled every time one wakes up; and at the same time there is a tendency to shrink back, to feel helpless with regard to what exists as an eternal opposition to the human soul, with regard to the purely natural state prevailing in the physical form in which one awakes. However strange it sounds that such a battle is enacted every day within the human soul, it is nevertheless an experience that passes by the human soul in complete unconsciousness. The soul cannot know what it undergoes then, but it experiences this battle anew every morning; and—despite not knowing anything about it—every soul is affected by this battle in all its qualities, in its very nature and in the individual character of its being.

Something else that occurs in the depths of the human soul and can to some extent be apprehended through spiritual research is associated with the moment of falling asleep. When the human soul has withdrawn from the senses and the limbs, when it has in a certain sense left its body behind in the physical world of the senses, what comes towards it is a feeling of its inwardness. Only then does it unconsciously experience the inner battles that are caused by its being tied to outward matter and having to do things that are the consequence of its being entangled with it. It feels itself as an appendage of the sense-world with which it is encumbered, and it feels this affinity as an impediment which holds it back in a moral sense. A moral mood such as cannot be compared with all ordinary moral impulses pervades the soul when it is alone with itself. And there are many other moods that occur in the soul when it is free of the body, when it leads a purely spiritual existence from going to sleep to waking up.

However, one should not think that all these occurrences taking place in the depths of the soul are not present in waking consciousness. Spiritual research can exemplify this by means of a very interesting example. It shows that a person does not only dream when he believes that he does but he dreams the whole day. In truth, the soul is always full of dreams; and it is only because waking consciousness is more forceful than dream consciousness that they are not noticed. Just as a fainter light is made invisible through the presence of a more powerful light, day consciousness extinguishes the dream experience in the depths of the soul that is its constant companion. A person dreams all the time, but he is not always aware of it; and out of the abundance of unconscious dream experiences, which are infinitely greater in number than the experiences of waking consciousness, the dreams that come to consciousness rise to the surface rather as single drops of water emerging from the water of an extensive lake. But these dreams that remain unconscious constitute a spiritual experience of the soul, in whose depths a wealth of experiences are therefore taking place. Just as chemical processes occur unconsciously in the body, there are spiritual experiences taking place in unconscious regions of the soul.

If we now bring what has been said here together with something that has already been mentioned previously, this will shed a different light upon the hidden aspects of soul-life of which we have been speaking. We have often emphasized—and especially in the previous lecture—that in the course of human evolution on Earth the whole of human soul-life has changed. When we look far, far back into the course of human evolution, we find that in ancient times the experiences of the human soul were quite different from those of today. We have already spoken—and will continue to speak in future lectures—of how early man had a certain primordial clairvoyance. The way of perceiving the world that is the norm for the soul today in waking consciousness, where we take in sense-impressions through external stimuli and bring these sense-impressions together in our modern consciousness by means of our reasoning powers, feelings and will, is only that of the present. It has evolved out of older forms of human consciousness which—in the best sense of the word—were of a more clairvoyant nature, when people were—in certain intermediate states between waking and sleeping—able quite normally to experience something of the spiritual worlds. Thus even though a person could not at that time become conscious of himself, he found that those experiences that occur in the depths of the soul were less foreign to his normal consciousness than today's situation would indicate.

In ancient times people saw their connection with the spiritual world outside themselves. They saw that what was taking place deeply within their souls was connected with certain spiritual realities in the universe. This was a quality of the primordial clairvoyance of mankind. And whereas people today can have the feeling that I am going to describe only in quite particular moods, in those former times it was a frequent occurrence, not only for those of an artistic inclination but by virtue of being of their time.

It can happen that in the depths of the soul there resides in however vague and indeterminate a form an experience that does not come to the surface of consciousness, an experience such as has been described occurring in the depths of the soul. Nothing of this experience comes to conscious awareness. But something is there in the soul, just as hunger is present in the physical organism; and just as one needs something to satisfy one's hunger, so is there also a need for something to satisfy this indeterminate mood that originates from this experience lying deeply within the soul. One then feels the urge either to resort to a familiar fairy tale or legend or perhaps, if one is artistically inclined, to create something of this kind oneself, even though one senses that all the words that one can theoretically use replicate these experiences only in a somewhat incoherent way. This is how the images of fairy tales arise. This conscious filling of the soul with fairy-tale images is the soul's nourishment with respect to the hunger that has just been characterized.

Because in former times of human evolution every human soul was still closer to a clairvoyant perception of its inner, spiritual experiences, the simple country folk—in that they sensed this hunger more clearly than can be the case today—were in a position to seek nourishment in pictures that arose from their creative soul-life and which we have today in the fairy-tale traditions of the various peoples. The human soul felt its connection with spiritual existence. It felt more or less consciously the inner battles that it had to endure, without understanding them; and it formulated them in pictures which therefore have only a distant similarity to what was living in the depths of the soul. And yet one can feel that there is a connection between what is expressed in the fairy tale and these unfathomably deep experiences of the human soul.

As one can learn from experience, a child's inner sensibility is often able to create for itself a simple companion, a friend who exists only for the child itself but who accompanies it and participates in all the various things it does. Probably everyone knows children who have such invisible friends as constant companions, friends whom you must imagine as being there when something happens that the children like, who must participate as invisible spiritual or soul companions when the child has an experience of whatever kind. One will not infrequently experience what a bad effect it has on a child's feeling life when a so-called 'intelligent' person appears and, on hearing that the child has such a soul-companion, tries to talk the child out of it and even perhaps considers this to be a beneficial thing to do. The child grieves for its invisible companion; and if it is receptive to soul-spiritual moods, this sorrow will have all the greater significance and may develop into ill-health and infirmity. This is a thoroughly real experience that is related to deeply inward occurrences in the human soul.

Without dissipating the 'aroma' of the fairy tale, we can feel this simple experience in the tale of the child and the fire-bellied toad as related by the Brothers Grimm.[133] The story that they tell is of a child who always shares her food with a toad, although the toad only likes milk. The child speaks with the animal as with a human being. Then one day she wants the toad to share its bread as well. The mother hears of this and comes and kills the toad. The child pines away, sickens and dies.

In this tale we can feel an echo of soul-moods that are truly present in the depths of the soul, and, moreover, not only in particular periods of life but simply through human nature being what it is, irrespective of whether one is a child or an adult. Thus every human soul can feel a reverberation of the fact that what it experiences and does not understand and does not even bring to consciousness is connected with the effect of the fairy tale on the soul in the same way that the taste of food has an influence on the tongue. And then the fairy tale becomes something similar for the soul to nutritious food that is used for the body. It is an appealing thought to search in these deep soul-experiences for what reverberates in the various fairy tales. It would of course be a massive task to examine all the many fairy tales that have been collected from this point of view; and it would take much time to do this. However, what can be discerned in particular fairy tales can be applied to all the genuine fairy tales that one can find.

Let us take another tale that the Brothers Grimm also collected, the story of Rumpelstiltskin. The miller, who claims to the king that his daughter can spin straw into gold, is asked by the king to bring his daughter to the castle to show what she can do. The daughter comes to the castle. She is locked in a room with a bundle of straw in order to test her prowess. When she is in the room she is completely helpless. And in view of her plight a little manikin appears before her. He says to her: 'What will you give me if I spin the straw into gold for you?' The miller's daughter gives him her necklace, and the manikin spins the straw into gold. The king is full of amazement, but he wants more; and he tells her that she should spin more straw into gold. The miller's daughter is again locked in a room with a substantial amount of straw, and the manikin again appears and says: 'What will you give me if I spin the straw into gold for you?' She gives him a little ring, and again he spins the straw into gold. But the king wants even more. And when she is sitting in the room for the third time, she has nothing more to give him. The manikin then says that if she becomes queen she will give him her first child. She promises to do so. And when the child is born and the manikin comes and reminds her of her promise, the miller's daughter asks him to wait. Whereupon the little man says to her: 'If you call me by my name, you can be freed from your promise.' The miller's daughter sends messages far and wide. She wants to know all names and the particular name of the manikin. Finally, after several wrong guesses, she manages to discover the little man's name: Rumpelstiltskin.

There is no other art form that so intensely gives one the feeling that one can experience the utmost inner joy in the directness of the imagery and yet can also be aware of the deep soul-experience out of which such a fairy tale has arisen. Even if the comparison may be somewhat lame, it could perhaps be appropriate to say that just as one may be well familiar with the chemical components of one's food and still take pleasure in something that's good to eat, it is also possible to know something about the deep inner soul-experiences that are felt but not 'known' and which come to expression in the manner indicated in the pictures of fairy tales. Indeed, this solitary human soul—for both in sleep and in waking life (even though it is connected with the body) it is solitary—feels but unconsciously, experiences but does not understand the whole polarity of the situation in which it is placed for its own infinite tasks, for the part it has to play in the world of the Gods.

The human soul is aware of how little it is capable of when it compares its abilities with what outer nature can accomplish, with its capacity to transform one thing into another; it is a great enchantress, which the human soul would so dearly like to be. In one's consciousness one may manage to cope with good grace with this disparity between one's inner being and the wisdom and omnipotence of the spirit of nature. But in the depths of the soul, the matter is not so simple. The human soul would come to grief if it were not to feel within its conscious being a still greater being, a being on whom it can rely and of whom it may say: However imperfect a stage you may be at now, this being that is within you is cleverer, it can raise you up to the highest achievements, it can give you wings so that you see before you an infinite perspective extending into an infinite future. You will be able to achieve something of which you are now not capable, for there is something in you that is endlessly greater than your 'knowledgeable self'. It is a faithful helper to you. But you need to acquire a relationship to it, you need to form a concept of this being residing within you who is cleverer, wiser and more skilful than you are yourself.

As one tries to call to mind this conversation of the human soul with itself, this unconscious dialogue with a more capable part of the soul, one may then also try to feel a resonance of it in the fairy tale of Rumpelstiltskin, in what the soul experiences in the miller's daughter who is unable to spin straw into gold but finds a skilful, faithful helper in the manikin. In images whose aroma is not destroyed if one knows their source, one can find a deeply inward soul-life that lies deeply in the very foundations of the soul.

We can also consider another tale. But first I hope you will not take it amiss if I connect it with things that seem to have a personal aspect, although there is no intention to focus on this dimension. It makes it somewhat easier to explain what I mean if I add this personal association.

In my book *Occult Science* you will find a description of the evolution of the world. I do not wish to speak about this now—this can happen on another occasion. Suffice it to say that in the course of this evolution our Earth, as a planet in the universe, has passed through certain stages which we can compare with the successive lives of an individual human being. Just as a human individual passes through successive lives, our Earth has likewise passed through various planetary stages of life or embodiments. For certain reasons we speak in spiritual science of the Earth's having passed through a kind of Moon existence before its Earth existence began, and before this a kind of Sun existence, so that we can say that in the far distant past there was a Sun existence that was a planetary predecessor of our present Earth existence, an Old Sun, which was still united with the Earth. Then in the course of evolution there was a split between Sun and Earth. Both the Moon and the modern Sun—which is not that primordial Sun but only a part of it—split off from the original Sun, so that we can speak of the primordial Sun and of its successor, the Sun of today. We can also speak of the modern Moon as having been engendered from Old Sun. Now if spiritual research traces earthly evolution back to the point when the second Sun—our present Sun—developed as an independent cosmic body, one would have to say that the beings of the animal kingdom that would have been outwardly perceptible to the senses at that time included only those that had evolved up to the level of the fishes.

These things can be pursued with greater precision in *Occult Science*, but they can be discovered only through spiritual-scientific methods of research. At the time when they were discovered and I wrote them down (to be precise, they were not discovered when

I wrote them down in *Occult Science*, but they were, so to speak, discovered for me and I wrote them down), I was not familiar with the fairy tale in question—this is the personal aspect to which I have referred; and can state this absolutely, since I found it only later in Wundt's *Elements of Folk Psychology*[134]and went on to trace it back to its source.

Before I give a brief outline of the fairy tale, I need to point out that everything that the spirit-researcher can investigate in the spiritual world—and what I have just said has to be researched in the spiritual world, since otherwise it loses its immediacy—is a reflection of the world with which the human soul is connected. We are connected with this world in the deepest foundation of our soul. It is always there; we enter this spiritual world unconsciously when we fall asleep in the normal way. Our soul is connected with it; and it has within itself not only those experiences that it has during sleep but also those which are connected with the whole evolution that has just been summarized. It may seem paradoxical, but one can say that the soul unconsciously experiences itself in the stream of evolution that originated from the primordial Sun and then from the daughter Sun that we now see shining in the heavens, and from the Moon that is also the progeny of the original Sun. And the human soul also experiences that in a soul-spiritual sense it has passed through an existence when it was not as yet associated with earthly processes, for example, the time when the highest animal organisms were the prototypes of fish and when the present Sun and Moon came into being and separated from the Earth. The soul is in its unconscious regions connected with these events.

We shall now briefly and in outline look at a fairy tale that can be found among primitive peoples.[135] There was once a man. However, he was made of tree-resin and could work only at night, for if he had carried out his work during the day he would have been melted by the Sun. One day, however, it happened that he went outside in order to catch some fish; and the man made of resin melted away. His sons decided to take revenge by shooting arrows; and the arrows that they shot formed particular figures towering up one above the other so that they became a ladder reaching right up into the sky.

They climbed up this ladder, one during the day and the other during the night; the one became the Sun, the other became the Moon.

It is not my custom to make abstract interpretations of such things and to play around with intellectual concepts. But it is an altogether different matter to be aware of the result arising from spiritual research that indicates that the human soul is connected in its depths with what happens in the world and can be understood only with spiritual means, that this human soul is connected with everything that goes on and hungers to enjoy its deepest unconscious experiences in picture-form. If one feels this, one will also feel the vibrations of what the human soul experienced as the primordial Sun and as the emergence of Sun and Moon during the time of earthly fish-development through the images of this folk tale. Again to introduce a personal flavour, it was for me a most important experience when—long after these things were described in my *Occult Science*—I came across this particular tale. Even though it would never occur to me to explain all of this in an abstract way, a quite particular feeling that I have when I contemplate world evolution finds its twin in another when I give myself up to the wonderful images of this folk tale.

Or let us take another story, this time a remarkable one of Melanesian origin. Before we speak of this fairy tale, let us recall that according to spiritual research the human soul is also closely connected with the present happenings and realities of the universe. Although this is too pictorial a way of expressing it, it is nevertheless correct from a spiritual-scientific viewpoint to say that when the human soul leaves the physical body in sleep it leads an existence directly connected with the whole cosmos, it feels related with the whole cosmos. One possible way of calling to mind the relationship of the human soul—as exemplified in the human ego—with the cosmos, or at least with something significant in it, is to contemplate the plant world. Plants can grow only under the influence of sunlight and the warmth of the Sun. We say in spiritual science that the plant that we see rooted in the earth consists of its physical body and the life body that pervades it. But this is not enough for the plant to grow and develop; for this the forces that influence the plant from the Sun are necessary.

When we contemplate the human body while someone is asleep, this sleeping human being is in a certain sense equivalent to a plant. It has a similarity to a plant because it has the power to grow that the plant also has. But the human being is emancipated from that cosmic order within which the plant is enmeshed. The plant has to wait for the sunlight to influence it through its rising and setting. It is bound to the outward cosmic order. Man is not. Why is this? Because it is true what spiritual science shows, namely that the human ego—which in sleep is outside the physical body, thus giving it a plant-like aspect—develops for the physical body that which the Sun develops for the plants. Just as the Sun sheds its light on the plants, so does the human ego extend its radiance over the plant-like, sleeping physical body. As the Sun presides over the plants, so does the human ego preside spiritually over the sleeping bodily organism. The human ego has an affinity with Sun existence. Indeed, the ego is itself a kind of Sun for the sleeping human body, it engenders its growth during sleep and enables those forces that have been used up during waking life to be replenished. When we become aware of this, we realize the extent to which the human ego is related to the Sun. As the Sun traverses the vault of the heavens (I am of course speaking of the apparent movement of the Sun), the influence of its rays changes in accordance with the constellation of the zodiac lying behind them; and spiritual science likewise shows us ever more clearly that the human ego similarly passes through various phases of its experience in such a way that it exercises a different influence on the physical body in each phase. As spiritual science indicates, one is aware that the Sun works differently upon the Earth depending on whether it is passing, for example, through the constellation of the Ram, of the Bull or some other constellation. One therefore does not speak of the Sun in general terms but of the Sun's influence from the twelve constellations, of its passage through the twelve signs of the zodiac; and one can then indicate the relationship of the ever-changing ego to the ceaselessly mobile influence of the Sun.

We can understand all that has been briefly outlined here and is further described in *Occult Science* as something that can be acquired in the form of soul-spiritual knowledge; we may regard it as something that takes place in the depths of the human soul and remains unconscious, while nevertheless occurring in such a way that it represents an inner experience of the spiritual forces of the cosmos as manifested in the fixed stars and planets. Let us compare all this that spiritual science imparts to us as the mysteries of the universe with a Melanesian tale,[136] of which I shall give a brief outline.

On the road there lies a stone. This stone is the mother of Quatl. Quatl has eleven other brothers. Once Quatl and his eleven brothers have been created, Quatl begins to create the present world. In this world that he created, there is no distinction between day and night. Quatl now hears about an island where there is a difference between day and night. He journeys to this island and brings some beings from this island back to his own land; and through the influence of these beings, those in his land gain access to the alternation between sleep and waking consciousness, and sunrise and sunset become soul-experiences for them.

It is remarkable what echoes from this story. If one studies it in its entirety, there is in every sentence something of the association with world mysteries, just as what the soul experiences from spiritual science is deeply in tune with it. It is indeed the case that the sources of the mood and diction of fairy tales reside in the depths of the human soul! These tales are narrated in the form of pictures because outward events have to be used in order to help to give spiritual nourishment for the hunger that rises up from the experiences that have been characterized. We also have to say that we are very far removed from the experiences, but we can sense an echo of them in the images of fairy tales.

If we keep this in mind, we no longer need to be surprised that the most beautiful, most characteristic fairy tales have come down to us from those ancient times when human beings still had a certain clairvoyant consciousness and were therefore more easily able to gain access to the wellsprings of fairy tales; and it is also not surprising that in those regions of the Earth where people are in their souls closer to these sources than they are in the West, for example in India and in the East in general, fairy tales can have a far more distinctive character. We will, moreover, not find it surprising that in the German fairy tales that Jacob and Wilhelm Grimm collected in the form that they were able to hear them from relatives or other, often simple, unsophisticated people, we find stories that hark back to those times of European life when the great heroic sagas originated; and that the fairy tales contain features that we also find in the great legends of Gods and heroes. Nor should we be surprised when we hear that it has subsequently emerged that the most significant fairy tales are older than the great sagas; for the sagas are about people at a certain time of life and in a particular situation, whereas what lives in a fairy tale is of universally human concern and relates to the human soul from its first to its last breath through all ages of life. Nor will it surprise us if a fairy tale may, for example, present a picture of something that is familiar as a deep experience of the soul, that overwhelming feeling when awakening of helplessness in the face of the forces of nature, to which one feels equal only if one's soul is comforted with the knowledge that there is within one something greater than oneself that enables one in a certain sense to be victorious over them.

If one senses this mood, one will also understand why giants that people have to deal with appear so often in fairy tales. Why do these giants feature as they do? They are of course a picture of this mood that assails the soul when it wants to enter its physical body again in the morning and sees the—for the soul—'gigantic' nature-forces residing there. The battle that the soul is aware of is from the soul's point of view wholly rightly portrayed in the many battles that people fight with giants (even if it is beyond the intellect's powers of understanding). When it is confronted with these battles, the soul realizes that it has only one advantage in this situation, namely its shrewdness or cunning. For the soul's perception is that it can re-enter its body, but what can it do in the face of these mighty forces of the universe? And yet it is aware that it has one thing that giants don't have, and that is its cleverness, its powers of reason! This lives unconsciously within the soul even when it knows that its strength is small when compared with the mighty forces of the universe; and we understand the position that the soul is in when it expresses the mood that has been characterized in pictorial imagery of the following kind.

A man is going along a road and comes to an inn.[137] In the inn he orders a bowl of milk soup. Flies that were buzzing around fly into the soup. He eats up the soup and leaves the flies on the side of the plate. Then he brandishes the plate and counts the flies that he has killed and boasts: A hundred with one stroke! The innkeeper hangs a medallion around his neck that says: He killed a hundred with one stroke. Then the man goes further along the road, enters another region and comes to a castle where a king is looking out of the window of his castle. He sees the man with his medallion and says to himself: I can make good use of him! He takes him into his service and assigns him a quite particular task. He says to him: 'My country has been invaded by packs of bears. If you have killed a hundred with one stroke, you can surely also get rid of those bears for me.' The man says: 'I'll do it!' But before he encounters the bears he first wants his reward and plenty of food, for he thinks to himself that if he doesn't manage he might as well enjoy himself until then. When the time comes for the bears to approach, he gathers up all the available food and other good things that bears like to eat. Then he prepares to meet the bears and makes everything ready for them. The bears come and eat until they have fully gorged themselves; and as they lie there helpless he kills them one by one. The king comes and sees what he has achieved. The man says: 'Yes, I simply got the bears to jump over my stick and cut off their heads in the process!' The king is delighted with this and gives him another task. He says to him: 'Look, the giants will soon be returning to my country, and you must help me with them.' The man promised to do so; and when the time came, he again took with him plenty of good food, and also a lark and a piece of cheese. He then met the giants and regaled them with a conversation about his strength. One of the giants said: 'We'll show you that we are stronger.' And he took a stone and ground it to powder in his hand. Then he said to the man: 'That is how strong we are! What power do you have to match ours?' The other giant took an arrow, shot it off and it went so high that it was only a long time after that it came down again. 'That's how strong we are,' he said; 'I bet you can't do that!' Then the man who had killed a hundred with one stroke said: 'I can do far better than that!' He took a little piece of cheese and a stone and took pains to smear it with cheese and said to the giants: 'I can squeeze water out of the stone!' And he squashed the cheese so that water spurted out of it. The giants were astonished at the strength that enabled him to squeeze water out of the stone. Then the man took the lark and let it fly upwards and said to the giants: 'Your arrow came back in the end, but my arrow is going so high that it will never come back!' And indeed, the lark did not return. The giants were so astonished that they were agreed that they could only overcome him with cunning, since they no longer thought that their giant's strength was sufficient for the purpose. However, they failed to outdo the man in cunning and instead he outwitted them. When they were all asleep, he put a pig's bladder over his head that was blown up and filled with blood. The giants said to themselves: 'We can't overcome him while he's awake, so we'll deal with him when he's asleep.' When he was asleep, they attacked him and broke the pig's bladder; and when they saw the blood gushing out they thought that they had finished him off. Soon after they went to sleep; and they slept so peacefully that the man was able to put an end to them as they slept.

In spite of the fact that this fairy tale, like many dreams, has some unclear and unsatisfactory aspects, we have here displayed before us the battle of the human soul against the forces of nature, first against the 'bears' and then against the 'giants'. But there is also something else in this fairy tale. Our conception of the man who killed a hundred with one stroke is such that we can feel an echo of what lives in the unconscious depths of our soul, in that he can always be assured through his cleverness of being able to master the stronger forces that he inevitably experiences as gigantic. It is not good if one interprets what has been portrayed artistically in pictures wholly abstractly and in its separate aspects; and this is not the intention here. But nothing of the character of a fairy tale is destroyed if one is aware that it is a reflection of processes occurring deeply within the soul. These processes are such that, however much one can know of them through spiritual research and in other ways, one is aware of their primal and elemental nature when one becomes ever and again entangled in them and experiences them in the manner described. And no knowledge of whatever kind can destroy the ability to transform what one experiences in the depths of the soul into the magic of the fairy-tale world.

Thus it is certainly stimulating for the spiritual researcher to discover in fairy tales what the soul needs on account of these profound experiences. At the same time the fairy-tale mood is not destroyed; for someone who by relating to the essential nature of a fairy tale arrives at a deeper insight into the wellsprings of subconscious life will find there something that is impoverished for ordinary consciousness when it is described purely abstractly, and he finds that the way that these deepest of soul-experiences are portrayed in fairy tales is far more comprehensive.

One can then understand that Goethe expressed what he could experience so richly—and what Schiller presented in the form of abstract philosophical concepts—in the meaningful and multifaceted images of his *Fairy Tale of the Green Snake and the Beautiful Lily*. Hence Goethe, in spite of the intensity of his thought-life, chose to give expression to what he experienced of the unconscious depths of the life of the human soul in the pictures. And because fairy tales have so intimate a connection with the soul and with what is so closely affiliated with its inmost nature, they are of all forms of literature the most appropriate for a child's consciousness. They are able to bring to expression the deepest spiritual wisdom in the simplest form. People may come to feel that in the whole of conscious artistic life there is no greater art than the one that traces the path from the unfathomable depths of soul-life to the charming and often playful pictures of fairy tales.

When what is most difficult to understand can be expressed in the most understandable forms, this is art of the greatest and most intrinsic kind, an art that is intimately connected with human nature. And because in the child man's being is linked in so primal a way with existence as a whole, children need fairy tales as nourishment for their souls. It is also the case that what is imbued with spiritual power can work more freely within the child. If the child's soul is not to lose its vitality, this should not be entangled in abstract, theoretical concepts and must retain its connection with what is rooted in the depths of existence.

Thus there is nothing that brings a greater benefit to the soul of a child than to nourish it with that which links the roots of human life with the roots of existence as a whole. Because the child is still having to work creatively on its own formative processes, because it still has to unfold its formative forces for its growth, for the development of all of its attributes, it experiences so wonderful a degree of nourishment in the pictures of fairy tales, in which it is connected at a fundamental level with existence. And because even when a person is mainly taken up with rational and intellectual matters he can never be torn away from the roots of existence, and because even in the very midst of life he is connected most intimately with them, he will gladly return to fairy tales at any age of life if he is of a healthy, open-hearted mind. For there is no age of life or human situation that could alienate us from what streams from fairy tales. Indeed, we would be abandoning the deepest and most important aspect of our human nature if we no longer had any sense for that part of ourselves which is unfathomable to the intellect but which comes to expression in genuine fairy tales and in the simple, artless, primordial mood associated with them.

One can therefore understand that people such as the Brothers Grimm, who devoted many years to making the culturally veiled fairy tales that they derived from the popular folk tradition available to humanity as a whole, had the feeling from the way that they lived with them—as opposed to anything that they might have learnt through spiritual science—that they were giving to the world something that belongs intrinsically to human nature. It is therefore apparent that, although a narrowly intellectual culture has done so much to alienate the human soul and also the souls of children from fairy tales, such collections of fairy tales as those of the Brothers Grimm have found their way to all people who are receptive to such things, and that they have become the common property of not only every child but of the hearts of everyone. This will become increasingly the case as spiritual science ceases to be a mere theory and becomes a mood that leads the soul increasingly to feel a oneness with the spiritual roots of its existence.

Thus the dissemination of spiritual science will confirm what true collectors, lovers and tellers of fairy tales wanted to achieve. This is exemplified by things that a devoted friend of fairy tales[138] often said in his lectures which I was myself enabled to hear, words that can be a means of summarizing what results from a spiritual-scientific consideration of fairy tales such as has been presented today. We can summarize it in words which that man who understood how to love, collect and value fairy tales spoke in his lectures and was always glad to do so: Fairy tales and legends are like a good Angel who is given to a person from his birth, from his home on his earthly path through life, in order to be his trusted companion and, through this companionship, makes it possible for life itself to be a truly inwardly ensouled fairy tale!

LECTURE 11

BERLIN, 13 FEBRUARY 1913

LEONARDO'S SPIRITUAL GREATNESS AT THE TURNING-POINT LEADING TO THE MODERN AGE

THE name of Leonardo is constantly invoked before the minds of innumerable people through the wide circulation of what is perhaps his best-known picture, the famous *Last Supper*. Who does not know Leonardo's *Last Supper*, and who—on the basis of such knowledge—has not come to admire the mighty conception that comes to expression in this picture? Here we see the pictorial embodiment of a moment filled with significance—a moment which is experienced by countless souls as one of the most significant in earthly evolution: the figure of Christ in the middle with the twelve disciples on either side of Him. We see these twelve disciples in deeply expressive gestures and attitudes. We see the gestures and attitudes of each of these twelve figures individualized in such a way that we may well receive the impression that every kind of human characteristic comes to expression in these twelve disciples, every way in which a particular soul can—as regards its temperament and character—relate to what is expressed in the picture.

In his treatise on 'Leonardo da Vinci's *Last Supper*',[139] Goethe has described perhaps more impressively than anyone else that moment when Christ Jesus spoke the words, 'One of you will betray me.'[140]

In the many reproductions of this picture that exist all over the world, we see what comes so expressively towards us from each of these souls who are so intimately connected with the One who is speaking and look towards Him so reverently, once He has uttered these words.

There are depictions of the *Last Supper* which derive from an earlier time. Without going any further back, we can, for example, explore representations of this event from Giotto to Leonardo; and we shall find that Leonardo introduced what one might call a dramatic element, for it is a wonderfully dramatic moment that he presents in his picture. The earlier representations appear to us as peaceful, expressing merely a sense of togetherness; while Leonardo's pictorial depiction of the *Last Supper* would appear to be the first to conjure up before us an expression of deep psychological insight with full dramatic power. But if from the world-famous reproductions one has formed this impression of the idea of the picture in one's soul and heart and then comes to Milan, to that old Dominican church of Santa Maria della Grazie, and sees there on the wall what can only be described as blurred, indistinct damp daubs of colour, which is all that remains of what has gained world-wide fame through its reproductions, one may perhaps investigate further and thereby receive the impression that it is already quite some time since what the people who saw it after it had been painted by Leonardo spoke about with such enthusiastic and fervently rapturous words has been visible on that wall of the old Dominican church. What must once have spoken to souls from this wall as an artistic wonder, not only through the conception which has just been brought to expression with a certain difficulty but which must have so spoken through Leonardo's highly expressive marvel of colour that in these colours the most intimate aspect, indeed the very heartbeat, of the souls of the twelve figures came to expression, must for a long time have been no longer discernible on this wall. What has this picture not had to suffer over the ages!

Leonardo felt himself compelled to depart technically from the way that frescoes had been painted on such walls before him. He found the sort of colours that had previously been used not sufficiently expressive. He wanted to make emotions of the most delicate kind visible on the walls and therefore tried painting in oils, which had never previously been done for frescoes. This ran into a whole series of obstacles. The state of the wall, and indeed of the whole place, was such that relatively soon these colours were inevitably affected by damp, which emanated from the wall itself. The whole room, which served as the Dominicans' refectory, was on one occasion completely under water in a flood. Many other factors played into the situation, such as the quartering of soldiers in war time. The picture was subjected to all these things.

There was a time, moreover, when the monks of the monastery did not behave with particular piety towards this picture. Thus they found that the door that led beneath the picture to this refectory of the monastery was too low, and one day they had it made higher. This ruined part of the picture. Then on one occasion a coat of arms was placed over the head of Christ. In short, the picture was treated in the most barbarous way. And then there were some people who can only be described as artistic charlatans who overpainted it, so that very little of the original paintwork can be seen. And yet when one stands before the picture, an indescribable magic emanates from it. All the barbarism, all the overpainting and weakening that it suffered, could not fundamentally destroy the magic that proceeds from the picture. Today it is still no more than a shadow extending over the wall, but a magic quality lives in this picture. For the most part this lies only to a certain extent in the painting itself; it is the conception that works on the soul, but its influence is powerful.

Anyone who has to some extent familiarized himself with other works by Leonardo, anyone who has tried to gain familiarity with his creative work through reproductions or by viewing pictures ascribed to him—which have been more or less preserved as he painted them—that are scattered throughout various European galleries, and has, moreover, studied what he wrote in the course of his life, anyone who has become familiar with his life that ran its course from 1452 until 1519, will stand before this picture in the refectory of the Dominican monastery of Santa Maria della Grazie in Milan with quite particular feelings. For it is indeed the case that one feels that—to the same extent that something still remains of the magical creation that Leonardo once painted on this wall—there continues to be present for the universal consciousness of humanity evidence of the immense greatness, of the power and content of this all-embracing personality of Leonardo himself. The extent of the influence of Leonardo's work on people's souls today has a similar kind of relationship to what this great personality brought into world evolution as these faded and blurred colours have to what he once conjured up on the wall. And just as one stands filled with sorrow before this picture in Milan, so does one behold with an equal sorrow the whole figure of Leonardo.

Goethe points out that, if one takes into account the descriptions of previous biographers, one receives the impression that in Leonardo a personality appeared who worked everywhere with fresh energy, viewed and related to life with joy and embraced everything with love, with a tremendous thirst for knowledge that wished to understand everything, fresh in both soul and body. Then one may perhaps turn one's attention to that picture which is considered to be a self-portrait and hangs in the Royal Library Museum in Turin, and one sees this self-portrait of the *old* Leonardo, this face with expressive lines caused by suffering, with an embittered mouth and with features which betray what Leonardo had to feel because of his opposition towards the world and towards everything that he had to experience. Thus this personality appears in a remarkable way before us at the beginning of the modern age.

If we now turn once more to the picture in Santa Maria della Grazie and try to study this shadow on the wall of the refectory together with the oldest engravings, the oldest reproductions that remain of this picture, and if we try, as it were, with 'the eyes of the spirit' (in Goethe's words),[141] to let this picture come to life again within us, a feeling may perhaps arise in us that leads us to ask: When the one who painted this picture put the final touch to it, did he go away satisfied with what he had done? Did he say to himself: 'You have managed to portray what lived in your soul'?

It seems to me that one can arrive quite naturally at this feeling, at this question. Why? If one views Leonardo's life as a whole, one cannot avoid having a feeling of this kind. As one begins to form a picture of his life—how he was an illegitimate child, the son of a father of no more than average ability, Ser Pietro of Vinci, and a peasant maid, who then entirely disappears from his life, while the father marries someone of his own social standing and has the child fostered, so that the child grows up alone, left to the devices of nature and his own soul—one realizes what an immense reservoir of life-forces must have resided in this human being to enable him to remain so vitally alive! For he did indeed retain his youthful energy. Since he showed a talent for drawing at an early age, he entered the school of Verrocchio. His father sent him there because he believed that his talent for drawing might prove useful. The young Leonardo was employed as a painting assistant to the master. An anecdote is related from this time that Leonardo once had to paint a figure and that when the master saw it he decided to give up painting altogether, because he saw that the abilities of his pupil surpassed his own. This would seem to be more than a mere story, if one sees Leonardo for what he was.

We then find him growing up in Florence, constantly raising the level of his abilities as a painter. But we also find something else. If we follow the development of his talent as a painter, we have the impression that every year he embarked upon the greatest artistic plans and was always making new ones. He also had commissions from people who recognized his great gifts and wanted to own something that he had done. Leonardo first formed an idea of what he wanted to create and then proceeded to engage in study. But what was the nature of this study?

It involved entering in a highly characteristic way into all sorts of details that had to be considered. Thus if, for example, he had to paint a picture with three or four figures in it, he set to work in such a way that he did not only study a single model but he went about the city and observed hundreds and hundreds of people. He would often follow one person for a whole day if he observed an interesting feature. Sometimes he would invite all sorts of people of different classes to his home and tell them all manner of things to amuse or frighten them, for he wanted by this means to study facial features for the most manifold soul-experiences. Once when a rioter had been caught and was being hanged, Leonardo went to the place of execution; and the drawing in which he tried to capture the facial expression and the whole gesture of the person being hanged has been preserved—in the bottom corner of the picture is a further head in which the exact expression is recorded.

Some caricatures by Leonardo—quite incredible figures—have been preserved, and we can see from these what he wanted to achieve. He had, for example, drawn a face and proceeded to explore what happens if one makes the chin bigger and bigger. In order to see what significance the various parts of the human form have, he enlarged a particular portion of the body so as to ascertain how this member fits naturally in the whole human organism. We find caricatured forms in all manner of distortions in Leonardo's work. He kept drawings in which he has repeatedly sketched a particular aspect and which he wanted to use for certain projects. Although many are the work of his pupils, there are a number that are his own.

If one takes all this into account, one has the impression that he would often work in the following way. On receiving a commission, he would study the details in the manner described. Then some particular aspect might arouse his interest, and he now no longer focused on the purpose of the picture but sought rather to explore the peculiarities of an animal or human being. If he had to paint a battle, he would go to a riding school to study the details, or he would go somewhere where horses were left to themselves; and in this way he lost sight of the original conception of his explorations. Thus he worked on one study after another, and in the end was no longer concerned with returning to the picture.

Thus we see from some of the more significant pictures from that first Florentine period (although all these pictures have since been overpainted, and the original form can barely be recognized), such as the *St Jerome* and the *Adoration of the Magi*, that he also made studies for these pictures such as has been characterized; and one altogether has the feeling that this man lived in the fullness of world mysteries. He sought to penetrate these mysteries and to reproduce the secrets of nature in an original way; but he never came to the point of being able to say to himself that he had completed anything. One must put oneself in the place of such a soul that was too rich to bring anything that it had undertaken to completion, a soul that was so receptive to the mysteries of the world that no matter where it began it was impelled to pass from one mystery to another and never come to an end. One needs to understand Leonardo's soul as being too great in itself to be able to reveal its full greatness.

As we pursue our study of Leonardo, we note that he was commissioned to undertake two tasks by Duke Ludovico il Moro in Milan, who had received him there in his court; one of these was the *Last Supper* and the other was an equestrian statue for the Duke's father.

We see that Leonardo worked for fifteen to sixteen years on these two projects. However, there was much else going on at the same time; for in addition to characterizing Leonardo as we have done, we must—if we are to understand him fully—add that the Duke had not summoned him only as a painter. Leonardo was also an excellent musician, perhaps one of the best of his time, and the Duke had found particular pleasure in his musical gifts. But the Duke continued to employ him also because Leonardo was one of the leading military engineers, one of the leading hydraulic engineers and one of the best mechanics of his time, and because he was able to promise the Duke that he could supply him with engines of war, which were something of a novelty, machines utilizing steam power and suspension bridges which could easily be constructed and speedily dismantled. At the same time he worked on constructing a flying machine. In order to accomplish this he devoted his attention to observing how birds fly; and he was probably one of the first to investigate this. But when one is perusing Leonardo's writings today one must always remember that these are only copies that contain much that is inaccurate and therefore correspond in their form to what one sees today of the *Last Supper*. Yet in all these instances it is clearly apparent what a great, all-embracing spirit dwelt in Leonardo.

So we can see that Leonardo not only supported the court of Milan on all sorts of occasions through his gifts as a painter and by arranging theatrical events but by developing various military and other schemes and also assisting the builders of the cathedral with his advice and practical help. Moreover, we know that he trained innumerable pupils who went on to work on the most diverse projects in Milan, so that it is scarcely possible to know today the extent of Leonardo's involvement in the development of the city of Milan and its surroundings.

In addition to all this, Leonardo made innumerable studies for the equestrian statue intended for the Duke's father, Francesco Sforza. There was no limb of the horse that he did not study hundreds of times and in hundreds of positions, and in the course of many years he completed the model of the horse. This was then destroyed when the French invaded Milan in 1499 and the soldiers used the model as a target and shot it to pieces. Nothing remains of the immense labour of a personality who, as one can indeed say, sought to investigate one world-mystery after another in order to bring to fulfilment a project where life became manifest within dead material substance, just as life reveals itself in the mysteries of nature.

We know how Leonardo worked on the *Last Supper*. He would often go and sit on the scaffolding and spend many hours brooding in front of the wall. Then he would take a brush, make a few brush-strokes and then went away again. If he wanted to work on the figure of Christ his hand trembled. Indeed, if we piece together everything we know it must be said that Leonardo was happy neither inwardly nor outwardly when he was painting this picture which is so world-famous today. To begin with, there were at the time people in Milan who were displeased that the painting of the picture was taking so long. There was, for example, the Prior of the monastery, who could not see why an artist could not paint such a picture quickly and he complained to the Duke. He, too, considered that the project was dragging on, and he spoke to the artist accordingly. Leonardo answered that as the picture was to portray Christ Jesus and Judas—thus the greatest opposites—it could not be painted in one year; and there were no models for these two individuals in the world, neither for Judas nor for Christ Jesus. He also did not know—he said this after he had been working on the picture for several years—whether he would ever complete it. And then he added that if he ultimately could not find a model for Judas, he could always use the Prior! Thus the picture was extraordinarily difficult to finish. But Leonardo was also not happy inwardly; for this picture exhibited in a particular way the contrast between what lived in his soul and what he was able to depict on the wall.

At this point I need to present a spiritual-scientific hypothesis that may occur to anyone who dwells upon everything that one can gradually come to know about the picture. This hypothesis came to me when I was trying to find an answer to the question that I posed before. If one considers Leonardo's life in this way, one will conclude that there was an immense amount living in this man that he was unable to make outwardly manifest to humanity and for which the outward means were lacking; and so was he able to incorporate to his satisfaction something of the greatest magnitude in the *Last Supper*, as he doubtlessly wished to do? This question arises quite naturally. When one sees how again and again he tried to explore one mystery after another through his studies in order to achieve something that in the end he did not bring about, one is bound to ask such a question. Then the answer comes almost out of itself. If Leonardo, on the other hand, had only progressed with the equestrian statue which he intended to be a miracle of sculptural art to the point of making a model of it which was then destroyed, so that he never even set about the casting process, if, therefore, he completely bade farewell to this statue after sixteen years of unfulfilled work, how—most likely—did he leave the *Last Supper*? One has the feeling that he left this picture with a sense of dissatisfaction! If all that one can see today of this picture is a ruin of blurred, damaged colours, and if for a long time nothing has been visible of what Leonardo once painted on the wall, one may perhaps maintain that what he painted on the wall could not even remotely have represented what lived in his soul.

In order to arrive at such a conclusion, one needs to put together all manner of different impressions that one can receive by looking at the picture. But there are also some outward reasons for it. Among the writings of Leonardo that have survived there is a wonderful *Treatise on Painting*. The essential nature of painting as an art is described, how it must work in relation to perspective and colour, how it must work in accordance with a particular conception. In spite of its being only a fragment, this book by Leonardo about painting is a marvellous work, the like of which has probably not been written. The principles of the art of painting are depicted as only the greatest genius could have presented them. It is, for example, wonderful to read how Leonardo shows the way in which horses must be depicted in a battle scene, giving the impression of bestiality and yet grandeur such as belongs to the portraying of a battle. In short, this work shows us all Leonardo's greatness and also all his frailty. We shall speak about this later. Above all, it reveals how he always regarded his art as a painter as a matter of studying how reality presents itself to the human eye.

The way that light and dark and shades of colour are used in painting is beautifully described in this book by Leonardo about this art. And if we had to confirm that there lived in Leonardo's soul the ardent longing of his conscience never even in the smallest detail to offend against the truth, which as we shall see elsewhere he prized so highly, if we wanted to show how this lived in his soul, we could say that this is everywhere apparent in his treatise about painting, with its injunction never to offend against the truth of the impression, ensuring that this impression is always in accordance with the inner mysteries of nature.

If we contemplate his *Last Supper* there are two things of which it can be said that they do not wholly accord with Leonardo's requirements with respect to painting. One of these is the figure of Judas. From the reproductions and also to some extent from the shadowy image of the painting in Milan one has the impression that Judas is completely covered in shadow, he is quite dark. Now study how the light falls from the different sides, and how in the case of the other eleven disciples the lighting conditions are portrayed to the most exemplary degree in accordance with reality. Nothing really explains the darkness on the face of Judas! We do not receive a satisfactory explanation of the reason of this darkness from the external lighting relationships. And when one comes to the figure of Christ Jesus, a purely outward perception without having recourse to spiritual science can yield no more than a suggestion. For just as little as the blackness, the darkness of the figure of Judas is justified, so is the Sun-like quality of the figure of Christ, standing out from the other figures in the manner indicated, equally without justification. We can understand all the other countenances from the way they are illuminated, but not that of Judas nor that of Christ Jesus.

If, however, one proceeds from a spiritual-scientific point of view, the thought that quite naturally arises is that the painter has striven to make it apparent that in these two contrasting figures of 'Jesus' and 'Judas' light and darkness are governed by inner rather than outer factors. He probably wanted to make us realize that the face of Christ appears to us such that the way that it is lit cannot be explained outwardly but that we are to believe that the soul behind this countenance endows it with a power of light out of itself, so that it can shine in defiance of the lighting conditions. Likewise with respect to Judas one can have the impression that this figure, as it were, conjures up a shadow which is not explained by the shadows woven around it.

It is, as said, a spiritual-scientific hypothesis but one that I have developed over many years, a hypothesis that can be seen to be all the more confirmed the further one enters into the whole problem. According to this hypothesis one can understand how Leonardo, who in his works and studies consistently endeavoured to be true to nature, worked with a trembling brush to depict a problem that could be justified with respect to this one figure. And then one can understand that Leonardo could well be bitterly disappointed, and indubitably so, because it was impossible through the means of the art-forms available to him to bring this problem to expression with complete truthfulness and veracity; for he could not yet do what he wanted and eventually despaired of the possibility of achieving it, and therefore had to leave a picture behind him which did not satisfy him.

And then one can answer the question as to the feelings with which Leonardo felt in accordance with his whole being and spiritual greatness: yes, Leonardo most likely left this picture with the bitter feeling that in his most important work he set himself a task whose execution could never satisfy him with the current means available; and even if no eye in later centuries will see what Leonardo had magically created on the wall in Milan, it was in any case certainly not what lived in his soul. Indeed, if one pictures him in relation to his most important creation, one is tempted to ask: What mystery is actually concealed behind this figure of Leonardo?

When we considered the personality of Raphael a fortnight ago we tried to show that such a personality can be understood quite differently if one bases one's investigations upon spiritual-scientific foundations, if one is clear that the human soul is something that forever returns in many earthly lives, so that a soul that has been born at a certain time does not live only this one life but, in its whole disposition and in the whole manner of its development, brings with it gifts and aptitudes from previous earthly lives and now incorporates what it has brought from previous earthly lives into the present one, finding itself confronted by what the spiritual environment now offers. If one views the soul in this way, recognizing that it enters into existence with an inner spiritual inheritance that derives from repeated earthly lives, and if one accepts that the whole evolution is meaningful and wisdom-filled, if one presupposes that something does not appear by chance in certain epochs but in accordance with rule and law, just as the blossom of the plant appears after the green leaves, if, therefore, one accepts that the history of human evolution is formed through wisdom and the human soul returns ever and again from spiritual regions, it begins to be possible to interpret the figures of particular individuals. However, what can be studied with respect to the lives of human individuals becomes more clearly manifest if one considers such exceptional human souls. If one studies Leonardo in the way that we have tried to summarizse in outline particular moments of his life, one is led again and again to the background from which this soul stands out. This background is the time into which this soul was placed between 1452 and 1519.

What was this time like? It was the time before the ascendancy of the modern natural-scientific world-view, before the world-conception of Copernicus came to prominence, before Giordano Bruno, Kepler and Galileo were active. How do we regard this time from the point of view of spiritual science?

We have repeatedly drawn attention to the fact that the further we go back in the course of human evolution, the more human perception of and interaction with the surrounding world become different from what they are now. In ancient times of human evolution we find in every soul a kind of clairvoyance, by means of which souls had insight into the spiritual world at certain transitional stages between sleeping and waking. This original clairvoyance was lost in the course of time; but until the fifteenth century there still remained a residue of it from former ages. The clairvoyance itself had long since disappeared; what remained was a feeling that the human soul had a connection with the spiritual background of the world. What souls formerly beheld they continued to feel; and although this feeling had already become weak, they nevertheless experienced themselves as connected in the centre of their being with the spiritual influences that live and weave through the world, just as the physical processes in the human body are connected with the physical events of the world.

It forms part of the laws of evolution that the old relationship of the human soul with the spiritual world had to be broken off for a while. Modern natural science would never have been able to blossom if the old clairvoyance had remained. This whole former way of perceiving the world had to be lost in order that souls could devote themselves to what presents itself to the senses and to what can be scientifically established by the intellect that is bound to the brain. The world-conception of natural science which has become established from the time of Leonardo until today was only made possible through the loss of the old spiritual perception of mankind and through man's inclining himself—as one says—'objectively' to outward sensory perception and to what the intellect is able to grasp as a result of it.

Today we again stand at a new turning-point, at the beginning of that time when through modern spiritual science it is again possible for human beings to come to a spiritual way of looking at things. For the development of natural science has a twofold significance. It had first to furnish humanity with a certain wealth of natural-scientific knowledge. In the course of the centuries since the appearance of Copernicus, Kepler and others, since natural science has gone from triumph to triumph, this has been incorporated in a wonderful way into practical and theoretical life. This is the one thing that has been brought about through natural science in the centuries since the time of Leonardo. The other is something that could not arise immediately but which became possible only in our time; for not only can what one has learnt through the Copernican conception of the world, through the observations and research of Kepler and Galileo and through modern spectral analysis and so on, be attributed to natural science but also a certain education of the human soul.

The human soul first directed its gaze towards the world of the senses; in this way natural science was developed. But through natural science new ideas, new concepts were formulated; and where natural science has rendered its greatest service is not through sense-perception but through something quite different. This has already been indicated. In one particular sphere people relied on sense-perception in the time before Copernicus. What resulted from this? They believed that the Earth stood still in space and that the Sun and the other planets moved around it. Then came Copernicus, who had the courage not to rely on sense-perception. He had the courage to say that if one relies entirely on sense-perception one does not make any empirical discovery, and that one arrives at empirical discoveries if one strictly thinks through everything that one has previously observed. Human beings then followed in his footsteps, and it is altogether a failure to recognize the true situation if one were to believe that natural science attained its present heights because humanity relied only on the senses.

What has come to humanity through natural science has, however, also made an impression on human souls; the ideas of natural science live in our souls, they have educated our souls. In addition to what the natural sciences have given in terms of content, they have also been a means of education for human souls; and in that natural-scientific ideas are not merely thought but lived, souls have developed the maturity actively to seek spiritual science purely out of themselves. Mankind first had to become sufficiently mature for this, and accordingly centuries needed to elapse since the time of Leonardo.

Now let us consider Leonardo. He enters into this time with a soul that in an earlier existence had belonged to those initiates who had raised themselves in the old way to the mysteries of world-perception. When he was born in the fifteenth century, this could not be continued. For in earlier incarnations, in so far as these previous earthly lives made it possible, one may have immersed oneself in the mysteries of the world in a great and mighty way; but how one brings them to consciousness in a new existence depends on one's outward physical body. A fifteenth century body could not bring to expression the inner thoughts, feelings and formative powers that Leonardo had received into his being at earlier stages of existence.

What he possessed from earlier times worked only as a power, but he was confined within a body living in the age directly before the blossoming of natural science. The time was coming—its dawn already imminent—when people wanted to perceive the world of sense-existence only with their senses and think only with the intellect that is associated with the instrument of the brain. Leonardo was constantly driven to seek the spirit, for he brought this with him from former lives, and this aspiration that he felt for the spirit was exhibited by him on a grand scale.

Let us now view him as an artist. Art had become something entirely different in the time when Leonardo lived from what it was in the age of Greece. Let us try to imagine what it would have been like for a Greek artist to create, for example, a sculptural form. What kind of feeling do we have when we contemplate, for instance, the statue of Marcus Aurelius in Rome? Those who fashioned something of this kind would never have moulded its individual forms from an external model as, say, Michelangelo or Leonardo did in their detailed studies. The wonderful horse of the statue of Marcus Aurelius was certainly not studied in the way that Leonardo studied his horse for the equestrian statue of Francesco Sforza. And yet how alive these old statues appear to us now! Why is this? The reason is that human souls in Greek times felt themselves to be creators of their bodies, because they felt themselves to be at one with the whole world. In the age of Greek art one felt for example in an arm all the forces that formed the arm. One had an inner sense of the independent, inner being of one's own form. People beheld forms not from without but as knowingly created from within, in that they were still conscious of the power that fashioned them. This can be outwardly demonstrated today. Look at the Greek statues of women: they are all experienced directly. Thus they are all depicted at the time of life when there is an expansion of growth. We always have the sense that the artist is creating from nature because he was within the spirit of nature, because he felt himself connected in his soul with the spirit of nature.

This feeling of being connected with the spirit that lives and weaves in everything was to be lost in Leonardo's time, and it had to be lost because otherwise the new age could not have emerged. This is not a criticism of the age but a representation of the meaning of the facts.

Let us now see how Leonardo sets to work by having an inner knowledge, an inner experience in his soul which, however, does not come to consciousness. There is something that works in a living way on these forms, but Leonardo cannot take hold of it inwardly. He feels as though separated from it; and now nothing satisfies him. He stands there in expectation of this natural-scientific world-conception (for it has not yet come into existence); but he cannot possess it for himself. Take his writings: on every page there are things that people rediscover only in the course of the next three centuries and have sometimes still not discovered. Leonardo had the most wonderful ideas, which in his time could not be made use of. We find them in his writings and also in his artistic creations.

Thus we experience in him the powerlessness that a soul had to cope with in an age when the old kind of world-conception had come to an end and the new one had not yet emerged. This new world-conception led inevitably to the splintering of the former comprehensive human outlook into a perception of details. We see emerging a specialization of specific branches of activity. With Leonardo everything still appears to be united. He is at once a great painter, a great musician, a great philosopher, a great technical expert. He united all this in himself because his soul came over from olden times possessed of great gifts and, in the new age, can touch everything but cannot penetrate it. And so from the human point of view Leonardo appears as a tragic figure, but when viewed from a higher viewpoint can be seen as being of immense significance at the turning-point to a more recent age.

One can see this for oneself if one further examines what Leonardo has created. He brought his most important projects only to a certain point, and his pupils then worked further on them. Even with such pictures as his *John* or the *Mona Lisa* in the Louvre in Paris we see that the way they were executed technically meant that they soon had to lose their brilliancy. But then we also always see that Leonardo could never do enough to satisfy himself. It is not possible without having the pictures in front of us to speak about the details of Leonardo's paintings. If one contemplates them it becomes apparent that Leonardo as an artist was always coming to limits beyond which he was unable to go, and that what lived in his soul could never arrive at the point where it reached from a soul-experience to a conscious insight, so that in a moment something lit up from that stage of soul-experience in such a way that one might rejoice and then sink back in sorrow, because it did not come to clear consciousness. It did not once do so for Leonardo.

We follow Leonardo with feelings of bitterness when we see how in the end he was brought to France by Francis I for the last three years of his life, and spent these years in a dwelling-place assigned to him by Francis I in spiritual contemplation of the mysteries of existence. Then he appears to us as the lonely man who cannot really find anything in common with the world surrounding him, and who must have felt an enormous contrast between what he experienced as the foundations of existence, which can find their form in art, and what he had been able to give to the world in no more than a fragmentary form.

If one thinks of things in this way, one can look at Leonardo and see that here is a soul where much is going on. Much, an infinite amount, is going on. It is staggering to observe what this soul has contributed to human evolution. And what this had outwardly manifested as a gift to human evolution—even by the time of Leonardo's death—is a small part of what lived in this soul! How do we stand before the economy of existence if we were to adopt the view that human existence is fully contained in what becomes outwardly manifest? How senseless and purposeless does the life of a soul such as that of Leonardo appear when we see what went on within it and what it was able to suffer and endure on account of this, and when we compare this with what it could have given to the world! What a contrast there would be if we were to say that this soul should only be regarded in accordance with what it made outwardly manifest in life! No, we should not think of it in this way! We must look at it from another standpoint and say: Whatever it may have given to the world, what it has experienced, what it went through in its inmost being, belongs to another world, a world that—in contrast to our world—is of a supersensible nature. Such individuals are, above all, a proof that the human soul has its place within supersensible existence and that such souls as Leonardo have something to do with supersensible existence; and that what they can give to the outer world is merely a 'by-product' of what they have to go through as a whole.

We only come to a right impression if we add to the stream that manifests itself in outward human events another, supersensible stream and say: Something runs in parallel with the sensory stream, and such souls are deeply embedded in this supersensible stream. They are obliged to live in it in order to form a link between the realm of the senses and that of the supersensible. The existence of such souls becomes meaningful only if we are able to accept a supersensible existence in which they are embedded. Thus we see little of Leonardo if we view his outward creativity; we gain the impression that this soul still has something to sort out in supersensible existence, and we then say to ourselves that we understand! In order that this soul can in the totality of its life that runs its course through many earthly lives always reveal something of its qualities to mankind, it had in its existence as Leonardo to pass through a life whereby it was only able to bring to expression the smallest part of what lived within it. Thus such souls as that of Leonardo are indeed world-riddles and riddles of life, world-riddles incarnate.

What I wanted to present today should not be encapsulated in sharply defined concepts but it should give an indication of how to approach such souls. For spiritual science should not be giving out theories! Spiritual science should through all that it undertakes comprehend man's life of feeling and experience as a whole and should itself become an elixir of life, so that through it we acquire a new relationship to both world and life. Spirits such as Leonardo are quite especially suited to lead to this new relationship to the world and to life that we can acquire through spiritual science coming into the world. When we contemplate figures such as Leonardo, we can say that they enter existence full of enigmas, because they have to live out something greater than their age can give them. Because they bring with them something from their former lives, souls such as

Leonardo not only enter life at an inconspicuous level but in the way that Leonardo himself did. Born of a father of no more than average ability and of a mother who soon completely disappears from view after giving birth to an illegitimate child, Leonardo was brought up among very ordinary people. Thus we see him having to rely wholly on his own resources and giving expression to what he had brought from previous lives. When we consider the unfavourable circumstances of his birth, we recognize that they did not prevent the greatest soul-capacities from coming to manifestation.

Thus we see Leonardo's soul so healthy, so comprehensive in its nature, that we can echo what Goethe says out of his great soul: 'He stood there in all his symmetry and fine proportions as a model of humanity; and just as the power of comprehension and clarity of the eye truly belongs to the mind, so clarity and intelligence were possessed by our artist to the highest degree.' If we apply these words to Leonardo—and they are indeed applicable—we can apply them to the youthful Leonardo, who appears before us with a bodily and spiritual vigour, accomplished, joyous in creating and when meeting the world, and at the same time with a longing for the world—a complete human being, born to be a conqueror, a person who was also full of humour, as he showed on various occasions of his life. And then we turn our attention to that drawing that is considered to be a self-portrait and justly so, to the old man in whose face much experience, much difficult, painful experience, has engraved deep furrows, whose features around the mouth indicate the whole disharmony in which we see the lonely man, far from his fatherland, under the protection of the King of France, still struggling with the world but lonely, forsaken, misunderstood, although loved by friends who had not failed to accompany him.

Thus we are struck quite especially by the greatness of this spirit of Leonardo with all the suffering that it endured, by the way that it accommodated itself to this body, first fashioning it perfectly and then leaving it embittered. We behold this countenance and feel the genius of humanity itself looking out at us. Indeed, we begin to understand this age, the sunset-period in which Leonardo lived, and the age in which Copernicus, Kepler, Giordano Bruno and Galileo lived, who heralded a new dawn; and we see all the limitations and constrictions that Leonardo's great soul had to experience. We understand the age and understand the great artist who stands behind all human means and who ultimately can only work with human means. Having explored the subject through spiritual science, we must bring the whole of our human intelligence to bear as we contemplate Leonardo's face; and we shall see the whole nature of the age gazing out at us from it. Yes, from these embittered features the despondent human spirit looks out at us. We must come to recognize it in order to understand the full greatness of the power which had to be present so that a Copernicus, a Kepler, a Galileo, a Giordano Bruno could arise.

In truth, we only acquire the appropriate reverence for the whole course and evolution of the human spirit if we learn to further intensify our sense of the tragedy that we feel as a result of Giordano Bruno's death at the stake through beholding Leonardo's soul with its sense of powerlessness in the preceding age of decline. Leonardo's greatness becomes clear to us only when we gain an inkling of what he was unable to achieve. And this is connected with something that we want to add by way of a summary of what we have been considering today. It is connected with the fact that the human soul can be satisfied—indeed, filled with delight—at the sight of imperfection (although most strikingly so by great rather than small imperfections), at the sight of that creative activity which because of its greatness fails in its execution. For in forces that are dying away we have a sense of the forces preparing the future, and in the sunset we have the promise and hope of the dawn.

As we contemplate human evolution, we must be constantly aware that the course of all progress is such that when what has been created falls into ruin, we know that from the ruins new life will always blossom forth.

Lecture 12

BERLIN, 6 MARCH 1913

ERRORS OF SPIRITUAL RESEARCH

Just as it is of great importance in every area of human endeavour to recognize not only the paths of truth but also the sources of error, this is especially the case in the realm that is the subject of these lectures, that of spiritual research or spiritual science. In this realm one has to do not only with sources of error that can, as it were, be eliminated through judgement and careful consideration but with sources of error that arise at every stage in the course of a spiritual investigation of truth. These are errors that must not merely be refuted on the quest for truth but fully overcome; and it is only by knowing them, by being able to gain a spiritual understanding of these experiences in their character as error, that one can be enabled to guard against them and protect oneself from them. It is not possible to speak in this realm of particular truths or errors, but it is necessary to become clear as to which activities and misapprehensions of the soul can cause a person to succumb to untruth on the path of spiritual research.

It can readily be understood that anyone wishing to gain access to the supersensible worlds in the sense of what has been presented in the previous lectures first needs a healthy organ of perception, just as healthy senses are needed for outward sensory observation. The second thing one needs in addition to an organ of perception is a proper development and clarity of consciousness, which has the capacity to oversee and evaluate the observations that one makes. Even in ordinary sensory observation of life it is necessary that we not only have healthy senses but that our consciousness is also healthy, that is, a consciousness that is not befogged or confused, nor deadened or paralysed in some way. Both these qualities of soul-life become even more significant at a higher level in the realm of spiritual research.

In order to make myself clear, I shall compare this with a situation from ordinary sense-observation. Suppose someone has, for example, an abnormally developed eye. He will then not be capable of observing the available phenomena in a right and uninhibited way with this abnormally developed eye. Hundreds of other examples could be cited, but we can confine ourselves to this one. A very significant natural scientist of the present time,[142] who is not in the least inclined to submit willingly to any delusion, had a certain eye-condition; and in his biographical sketch he described how this condition caused him to see things incorrectly especially when it was growing dark and, hence, to arrive at false judgements. He describes, for example, that he would often go for a walk when it was dark and because of his eye-condition might see a form of some kind that he considered to be real but which was called forth by the abnormality in his eyes. He then relates that he was once going round a corner in a city that was unfamiliar to him, and because he considered the city to be unsafe his eyes misled him into seeing someone approaching him round the corner who wanted to assault him; and he even pulled out a weapon in order to defend himself. He was, therefore, despite his full knowledge of his eye-impairment, unable to judge the situation rightly and realize that what his eye registered was not there at all. Thus misapprehensions can arise through all our sense-organs. This is merely cited as a comparison.

It has been mentioned in previous lectures[143] that a person can through certain inner developments of his soul become a real spirit-researcher, that he can cultivate spiritual organs through which he can gain insight into the supersensible world. These spiritual organs must also be developed in the right way if it is to be possible, in accordance with the analogy of sensory perception, to see not caricatures and untruths but to behold the true reality of the higher, spiritual worlds. Now the development of higher spiritual organs—which, as we have seen, can be brought about by rightly employed meditation, concentration and contemplation—depends upon making a beginning with ordinary life. Every person who wants to enhance his development towards the spiritual worlds must, as is right and natural, take his starting-point from ordinary soul-development, from what is right and normal for daily life and also for ordinary science. Only from this starting-point, by assimilating into the soul those mental processes that we have characterized as meditation and other similar exercises, can the soul move towards observation of the spiritual worlds.

It is important that at the starting-point, that is, before the beginning of spiritual schooling, the prospective spirit-researcher must have a sound power of judgement, a capacity to discern what is actually going on. Every starting-point that does not derive from a power of judgement that gives itself up wholly to the phenomena is an aberration, for it brings about unhealthy organs of spiritual observation which can be compared with abnormally developed sense-organs. Here we are again at the point that has arisen in previous lectures and which shows how important and significant what one can designate as the soul-life of the spirit-researcher is before he embarks upon his spiritual-scientific schooling, his development as a spirit-researcher. An unsound power of judgement, an inadequate capacity to observe things as they are, leads a person to distort the facts and beings of the spiritual world or—as we shall see today—to view them in a variety of false ways. This is, as it were, the first important principle for all development towards spiritual research. Spiritual-scientific schooling makes it necessary that the starting-point must be made from a sound power of judgement, from an interest in phenomena that always seeks to base itself on the true relationships of existence, before the path to the supersensible worlds is embarked upon. Everything that readily surrenders itself to deceptions, that is content to judge in an arbitrary way and represents a certain unsound logic, also leads to the development of unhealthy spiritual organs.

The other starting-point that is of significant importance is the moral mood of the soul. Moral integrity, moral power is as important as sound logic, as sound intellectual reasoning. For if unsound logic and reasoning power leads to inadequately developed spiritual organs, so does the weak-hearted or immoral mood that a person seeking the spiritual worlds before the beginning of spiritual schooling lead to what we could call a certain nebulousness or stupor, so that when he confronts the higher worlds he experiences a kind of paralysis and even a loss of consciousness. It should be noted, however, that the loss of consciousness or stupor at the stage of soul-development referred to here cannot by any means be compared with the loss of consciousness or paralysis of ordinary, everyday consciousness. In the latter situation there is a certain loss of consciousness in relation to the areas of daily life. In the spiritual domain, the deadening or clouding of consciousness equates to its saturation with all that can derive from the ordinary world of the senses or from the ordinary experience of the day. The spirit-researcher who is in error cannot be beset with a clouding or loss of consciousness as in ordinary consciousness; but he can be unconscious in relation to the spiritual worlds as a result of his spiritual field of consciousness being filled with what has justification only through the nature of its manifestation in ordinary sensory and intellectual consciousness. By taking this into the spiritual worlds, the spirit-researcher dulls his higher consciousness.

One can also portray the matter in the following way. A dimming of consciousness, the impairing of the ordinary nature of the soul in everyday life, is like an infiltration of sleep or dream into clear, waking consciousness. However, the deadening or clouding of higher, supersensible consciousness is like an infiltration of ordinary daily consciousness, the consciousness that we carry around with us in the ordinary world, into that consciousness which should purely and clearly survey and evaluate the facts of the higher, supersensible worlds. Any kind of immoral or morally enfeebled mood, any kind of moral untruthfulness leads to such a clouding of supersensible consciousness. Hence at the outset of a spiritual-scientific schooling a corresponding moral state of being is of essential significance; and if you peruse my book *Knowledge of the Higher Worlds: How is it Achieved?* you will find indications of particular forms of soul-development through which this appropriate moral condition can be cultivated.

Especially harmful in this respect is any kind of vanity, ambition, an ordinary sense of self, or a certain sympathy for experiences of this nature that can afflict a person in ordinary life. Inner composure, impartiality, a loving involvement in things and worlds, an attentive interest in everything that life can offer and qualities of a similar nature—but quite especially a certain moral courage, a willingness to stand up for what one recognizes as true—these are appropriate starting-points for a spiritual-scientific schooling.

It is clear from the previous lectures that all spiritual schooling is dependent upon spiritual forces that are present in the soul, but slumber within it in ordinary life, being awakened and developed; for spiritual organs and supersensible consciousness can only be nurtured through the forces residing in the depths of the soul—which in ordinary life are not developed at all or only weakly so—truly emerging into the light of consciousness. Moreover, the following can also be seen from what has been said hitherto. Two things manifest themselves when through appropriate meditation, through concentrating one's whole life of soul upon particular mental pictures freely summoned into consciousness, one endeavours to draw forth these forces residing in the depths of the soul. Firstly, a quality that is always present in the soul but can be kept in abeyance relatively easily in ordinary life is—together with other qualities that slumber in the depths of the soul—strengthened and intensified; for spiritual development cannot take place unless in a certain sense one makes one's whole soul-life inwardly more active, more infused with energy. That quality which—together with whatever else one is seeking to strengthen—is thus intensified is what one may call the sense of self, one's self-love. Indeed, it could be said that one only really comes to know this quality of self-love when one undergoes a spiritual-scientific schooling; only then does one realize how deeply this self-love that resides within the human soul is slumbering there. Anyone who intensifies his soul-forces through the exercises described in the preceding lectures notices at a certain time of his development that another world enters his life of soul. However, as part of his spiritual development he must at the same time be able to notice and have the knowledge to recognize that the first form of the new, supersensible world that appears is nothing other than a shadow image, a projection of his own inner soul-life. The soul-forces that appear to him as a result of what he has developed in his soul-life initially take the form of a mirror picture. This is also why a materialistic thinker can very easily mistake what appears in the soul-life of a spirit-researcher for illusions, hallucinations, visions and the like that can manifest themselves in an unhealthy soul-life. That an objection deriving from this confusion rests purely upon an ignorance of the facts has frequently been explained. It must again and again be pointed out that an unhealthy soul-life which beholds its own essence as in a mirror picture considers this mirror picture to be a real world and is not in a position to eliminate this perception through inner choice. Whereas by comparison, it must be an integral part of a true spiritual schooling that the spirit-researcher recognizes the first phenomena which appear as reflections of his own being; and that he not only recognizes them as such but he is also able to eliminate and extinguish them from his field of consciousness.

Just as the spirit-researcher on the one hand comes through his exercises to be able to strengthen his soul-forces, so that they conjure up a new world before him, so on the other hand must he be capable of extinguishing this entire world in its initial form, he must not only recognize it as a reflection of his own being but also be able to extinguish it again. If he is unable to do this, he is in a situation comparable with one that, were it to occur in sensory observation, would be completely unsustainable, completely impossible for a real development of the human soul. Let us suppose that in the context of ordinary sense-observation a person were to look at an object and were to be so attracted by it that he could not avert his gaze from it. He would therefore no longer be able to look around freely but would be tied to the object. This would be an unbearable situation with respect to the outer world. In the case of spiritual development it would signify exactly the same in relation to the supersensible world if a person were to be incapable of redirecting his spiritual organ of perception by extinguishing the image that presents itself to it. For only if he can pass the test of extinguishing this image, so that once it accordingly returns after he has overcome himself he can come to know his true reality, does he face reality and not his own fantasy. Thus the spirit-researcher must be able not only to evoke and foster his own spiritual phenomena but must also be capable of extinguishing them again. But what does this mean?

It means nothing less than the need for an immensely strong force that is necessary to overcome the sense of self, self-love. For why is it that an abnormal soul-life which arrives at hallucinations, visions and delusionary notions sees these fabrications as realities and not as the emanations of its own being? This is because a person feels so connected with what he himself brings forth that he would believe himself to be as though destroyed if he were unable to regard this product of his own being as a reality. And if someone leaves the ordinary world and his soul-life is abnormal, self-love is intensified to the point of being like a force of nature.

Within ordinary soul-life we can very easily distinguish between fantasy and reality; for in normal life we have a certain power over our ideas. Everyone is familiar with this power that the soul has over the mental images that it engenders, in that it has the capacity to get rid of notions if their erroneous nature is recognized. We are in a different situation in relation to the outer world when we confront the forces of nature. When lightning flashes, when thunder rumbles, we have to allow these phenomena to take their course; we cannot forbid the lightning from flashing or the thunder from rumbling. But when we depart from ordinary soul-life, the sense of self appears within us with the same inner force; and just as one cannot forbid lightning from flashing, one cannot prevent the self-love that has developed into a force of nature if it is only a reflection of one's own being, that which presents itself to the soul as an image of its own being in such a way as to be perceived as a real outer world.

From this one can also see that the self-education of the spirit-researcher must be directed above all else towards overcoming by degrees this self-love, this sense of self; and only when this is attempted at every stage of spiritual development through strict self-observation does one finally come to be able to erase from consciousness a spiritual world that has appeared to us in the manner described, that is, to be in the position to let what one has brought about with all manner of exertions to sink into oblivion. As is described more fully in *Knowledge of the Higher Worlds*, something must be developed here with respect to spiritual schooling which in ordinary life the untrained human will cannot encompass.

If someone undertakes to do something in ordinary life, he wants to do it; if he neglects to do something, he does not want to do it. In ordinary life, people are accustomed to applying their will impulses. But in order that the spiritual world that appears in the manner described can be extinguished, the will must not only have the faculty in question but it must, once the spiritual world appears, be able slowly and gradually to diminish itself to the point of utter will-lessness, even to the extent of extinguishing itself altogether. Such a cultivation of the will is achieved only if the exercises described in the book referred to are systematically carried out by the soul.

This is, on the one hand, what is intensified in our soul if we want to energize the forces slumbering within it: self-love, the sense of self; and this intensification constantly leads us under certain circumstances to regard what we actually are ourselves, what lies only within us, as an outward reality. Something else that manifests itself when the soul undertakes the corresponding exercises for spiritual schooling is that, at a certain stage of this development, the person concerned must actually abandon with his consciousness everything that has hitherto in outer everyday life and in ordinary science given him the substance and certainty of truth, that gives him the possibility of recognizing something as reality. It has already been indicated in the previous lectures that all supports that we have for our judgements in ordinary life, that all basic reference points that the sense-world gives us and that teach us how we have to think about reality must be abandoned. For through spiritual schooling we are wanting to enter a higher world. When the spirit-researcher sees at an appropriate stage of his development that in the world that he is wanting to enter he can no longer have any support through outer sense-perception, that he can also no longer have the support of the intellectual judgement that he has acquired which has otherwise guided him rightly through life, then comes the serious and significant moment in the life of the spirit-researcher when he feels as if the ground has been taken from under his feet, as if all certainty has been lost and as if with every further step he must surely fall into an abyss that he is approaching. That this experience is not associated with all manner of dangers is something that a true spiritual schooling that belongs expressly to the present time is concerned to ensure.

The endeavour to explain this further has been made in the book *Knowledge of the Higher Worlds*. If one undertakes the exercises given there, one arrives step by step at a point where one experiences what has just been described, where one feels as though one is hovering over an abyss. But one has already become so calm in one's soul that one views the situation with a newly acquired, special faculty of judgement, so that what would otherwise inevitably manifest itself in the human soul by way of terror and horror (though not fear of the ordinary, everyday kind) does not arise. One comes to know the foundations of fear, terror and horror, but one has progressed to a state of mind where one can endure it without fear.

Here we are again at a point where it is necessary for the soul to acknowledge the truth and avoid falling into error, because the support that one has in ordinary life disappears and the soul feels itself as though positioned over an abyss. This must happen in order that out of the emptiness the full spirituality of the world can approach the soul. What in ordinary life is called anxiety and fearfulness is through such a schooling intensified and expanded in the same way that the sense of self and self-love are also intensified and expanded. They grow somewhat as a force of nature. And here something must be said which might perhaps sound paradoxical. If we have not achieved a certain level of courage and are in a certain respect cowards, we may in ordinary life be frightened by an event of one kind or other; but if we are not cowards, we can endure it. In the region of soul-life that has been described, we are approached by fear, horror and terror, but we must manage not to be frightened by fear, not to be horrified by terror and not to be worried by anxiety. This is the paradox, but it wholly accords with a real soul-experience that appears in this realm.

Everything that a person experiences on entering the spiritual world is actually associated with what is referred to as an experience with the Guardian of the Threshold. I have tried to explain something in concrete terms about this experience in my Mystery Play *The Guardian of the Threshold*. Here I shall just mention that at a certain stage of spiritual development a person comes to know his own inner being as it can love itself with the force of an event of nature, as it can be frightened and fearful upon entering the spiritual world. This experience of one's own self, of the intensified self of that inner being that does not otherwise come before the soul, is the shattering event that is called the meeting with the Guardian of the Threshold; and it is only by having this meeting that one forges the faculty to distinguish truth from error in the spiritual world.

It is easy to understand why this experience is called the meeting with the Guardian of the Threshold. It is, after all, clear that the spiritual world into which a person enters is always around us and that the only reason why he does not become aware of it in ordinary life is that he does not have the corresponding organs of perception for it. The spiritual world always surrounds us, and it is also always behind what the senses perceive. But before a person can enter it, he must strengthen his ego. However, with the strengthening of the ego the qualities referred to earlier appear. He must therefore above all else come to know himself, so that when he is able to confront a spiritual outer world in the way that he can confront an objective being he has the capacity to distinguish himself from what is truth. If he does not learn to make this distinction, he will constantly confuse what is only in him, and what are only his subjective experiences, with the spiritual world-picture; and he will never arrive at a real understanding of spiritual reality.

The extent to which fear plays a certain role on entering the spiritual worlds can be seen especially in people who deny the existence of such a world. Among these people there are many who also have other reasons for denying its existence; but a large portion of them, who are theoretical materialists or materialistically inclined monists, do so for a specific reason that is clearly visible to someone who understands the soul. In this connection we must now emphasize that the soul-life of man is of a twofold nature. There is not only that aspect of which a person is ordinarily aware but processes are enacted in the depths of soul-existence that cast their shadows, or their lights, upon ordinary consciousness. But ordinary consciousness does not extend to this level. We can have hatred and love, joy and fear and excitement in these hidden depths of the soul without these emotions manifesting themselves in the conscious life of the soul. Hence it is entirely correct to say that a particular manifestation of hatred consciously expressed by one person towards another can have its origin in a love residing in the depths of the soul. A person may have a sympathy, a deep sympathy, for another person in the depths of his soul; but for reasons of which he may be entirely ignorant he becomes totally oblivious of this love, this sympathy, and appears instead to be full of hatred and antipathy.

This is something that is rooted in the depths of our soul, so that things appear quite differently in this region from in that of our everyday consciousness. Thus there can be states of fear and anxiety in the depths of the soul without the person concerned having any awareness of this in his ordinary waking consciousness. He may have that fear, that anxiety in the face of the spiritual world in the depths of his soul—because he must cross the abyss that has been described before he enters it—but not notice any of this in his waking consciousness. Instead, all those who have not as yet entered the spiritual world but have acquired an understanding of doing so have this terror, this fear of the spiritual world to a certain extent. Regardless of what one may think about this fear and anxiety that reside in the depths of the soul, they are indeed present, though more strongly in the case of some people than with others. And because the soul could be harmed by this, human individuals are protected by the wisdom inherent within them from being readily able to perceive the spiritual world; and the experience of encountering the Guardian of the Threshold is one that they can have only when they are ready for it. One therefore speaks of the experience with the Guardian of the Threshold.

In the case of materialistically or monistically inclined people, we can observe that they know nothing of this experience but that this fear of the spiritual world is present in the depths of their souls. There lives in them a certain antipathy towards the threshold that one has to cross. Materialists or monists endeavour to dispel this fear, this anxiety residing in their souls by thinking out their theories and denying the spiritual world; and this denial is nothing other than an attempt to stifle their fear. This is the real explanation for materialism. However unsympathetic it may sound, for someone who has an understanding of the soul it is apparent that in a gathering of materialistic monists, of those who deny the soul or spirit, their souls are dominated by a fear of the spiritual world. One could say mockingly that fear-mongering is the basis of materialism; but even if one proclaims this mockingly, it is nevertheless true. In materialistic writings and world-conceptions, the spirit-researcher always discerns between the lines a fear and anxiety in the face of the spiritual world.

However, the materialism that is present in ordinary life when people are materialists or materialistically inclined monists can also be present when through specific means they arrive at a certain degree of spiritual perception; for it is possible to pursue certain exercises in one's soul. One can also on the basis of a more or less unhealthy soul-life arrive at some degree of spiritual understanding, but that does not mean that there will be any real insight into the nature of the spiritual world. In a certain sense one can also raise what has just been characterized—namely, what is embodied by materialistically inclined people in the ordinary world—into the spiritual world, something that is like the fear of which one knows nothing. If one does not perceive the connection, one may carry up into the spiritual world something that is widely disseminated in ordinary life: comfortableness in thinking, comfortableness in feeling.

Fear is related to a love of ease, to clinging to habits. Why are people fearful of change? Because they are comfortable with things as they are! This comfortableness is related to fear. Just as we were previously describing what can sometimes be the ground for hatred, one can also say of fear that casualness and love of ease are related to it. But one can carry this attitude of comfortableness up into the spiritual world. No one should now object that the people who are being referred to show no evidence of fear or love of ease, for it is thoroughly characteristic that the ordinary mood of soul knows nothing of the way that these things are rooted in the subconscious. If a person brings fear into the spiritual world once he has developed to the point of acknowledging the spiritual worlds, an aberration arises in a spiritual realm which it is of the greatest importance to be aware of: the inclination towards phenomenalism.

People who are drawn to this inclination become not spirit-researchers but—to put it bluntly—beholders of spectres; they are possessed by an inclination towards phenomenalism. This means that they want to perceive the spiritual worlds in the way that the sense-world can be beheld. They do not want to perceive spiritual phenomena or spiritual beings but something similar to a being that the sensory eye can behold—in short, they want to behold not spirits but spectres. The aberrations of spiritism—which is not to say that all spiritism is unjustified—rest unequivocally upon this inclination towards phenomenalism. Just as the ordinary, everyday materialist wants to see everywhere only matter and not the spirit behind matter, so does a person who brings to the spiritual worlds the same state of soul that is actually present in materialism see everywhere ghostly, condensed spirits.

This is one extreme form of dangerous error that can arise. It has to be said that this tendency to bring the ordinary fields of consciousness into the supersensible field of consciousness is also very widely present in those who have full recognition of a spiritual world and would even want that proofs be provided for such a world. But the error here lies in that they want to permit only such proofs as are valid in the realm of phenomenalism, that everything should be condensed to a spectral quality. Here something arises that at the beginning of our considerations today was referred to as a stupor, a loss of consciousness with respect to the spiritual world. Whereas a loss of consciousness in ordinary life is an infiltration of a sleep- or dream-like state, with respect to the spiritual world attributing validity only to that which appears in the same way as the phenomena of the ordinary world signifies a loss of consciousness in relation to it; for it is being demanded that proofs be provided that are to be taken wholly in accordance with the nature and qualities of the ordinary world. Just as one brings sleep into the ordinary world if one loses consciousness, so does one suffer a loss of consciousness towards the beings and processes of the spiritual world if one takes into the supersensible world that which is only bound up with the world of the senses.

Anyone who is a real spirit-researcher also knows these regions of the spiritual world that are condensed to a spectral quality, but he knows that everything that becomes condensed in this way is merely the dying, withering aspect of the spiritual world. Thus if, for example, something is with the help of a medium brought to light that represents the thoughts of a dead person, we are being presented only with what has been left behind by the one who has died. We are not being confronted by what passes through the portal of death, journeys through the spiritual world and reappears in a new earthly life; and we are then not dealing with what is present in the individuality of the deceased person but with what is in the sheath that has been cast off, like the wooden part of a tree or the shell of a shell animal or the skin of a snake.

Such sheaths, such things as can no longer be used are continually being cast off by the beings of the spiritual world, and through the intervention of a medium they can be made visible and perceptible, albeit as something unreal. The spirit-researcher knows that he is not dealing with unrealities. However, he does not abandon himself to the error that these phenomena represent something fruitful, something budding and sprouting, but something that is dying and withering. Moreover, it must be emphasized that whereas in the realm of the sense-world one has to do with something that must be left well alone if an error is involved, that must be eliminated as soon as one discerned an error, in the spiritual world one cannot deal with an error in the same way. For there, an error corresponds to what is dying and withering, and the error consists in considering this dying and withering element in the spiritual world to be fruitful or significant. Thus even in the lives of ordinary people, an error is something that one rejects. In the spiritual world error arises through the dead and dying being regarded as something sprouting and fruitful, in that one considers what has been cast off by the dead as destined for immortality.

We can see how deeply even the best minds of our time are obsessed by phenomenalism and want only such proofs as have been characterized to be valid especially in one individual, who has written so many fine things about the world and who has now written a book about these various phenomena of spiritual research. I am referring to Maurice Maeterlinck and his book *On Death*.[144] We read there that he is fully inclined to acknowledge the existence of a spiritual world, but he will only accept as proof what appears in phenomenalism. He does not notice that he tries to find in phenomenalism what can never be permitted in it. Then he criticizes the 'phenomena' very acutely and succinctly. But he notices that all this is actually of no particular significance, and that the human soul after death does not exhibit vitality on a deep level, that it behaves awkwardly, as though groping in the dark. Moreover, since he wants to acknowledge only proofs of this sort, he does not arrive at a recognition of spiritual research but remains stuck. So we see how the possibility of error opens up to someone who would dearly like to acknowledge the spiritual world but who is unable to do so because he demands not spiritual research but spectral research and does not want to direct his attention to what reality can give. Especially his most recent book is extraordinarily interesting from this point of view.

Thus in the inclination towards phenomenalism we have the one extreme of the possibilities for error in spiritual research. The other extreme of these possibilities is ecstasy; and between phenomenalism and ecstasy—if one knows both—lies the truth, or at least it can be reached if one knows both. But the path to error lies both from the side of phenomenalism and from that of ecstasy. We have seen what state of soul leads to the wish to acknowledge only phenomenalism. It is fear, terror, which a person does not admit and seeks to suppress. Because he shrinks from forsaking everything of a sense-perceptible nature and making the leap across the abyss, he embraces the sense-perceptible, invokes the spectral element and thereby arrives only at the dying, at that which destroys itself. This is the one source of error.

The other power of the soul which is intensified through the exercises that have often been described here is self-love, the sense of self. Self-love has as its other pole that of 'standing outside oneself'. The tendency to 'find pleasure in oneself' (if you will forgive the somewhat radical expression, but it does express what is meant) is only the one side. The other consists in 'losing oneself in the world', in surrendering oneself, becoming absorbed and feeling at ease in the other; and the corresponding intensification of this self-seeking tendency to stand outside oneself is an extreme degree of ecstasy. That is the cause of a state whereby a person can in a certain sense say to himself that he has broken free of himself. But he has become free of himself only by feeling at ease in being outside himself.

If someone who understands the soul considers the evolution of mysticism in the world, he finds that a large part of mysticism has its foundation in the phenomenon that has just been characterized. However great and powerful, however profound and meaningful mysticism may be in terms of soul-experience on the one hand, the possibilities for error of ecstasy are actually rooted in a false cultivation of man's mystical sense. When a person strives to enter increasingly into himself when he endeavours through what he calls the deepening of his soul-life to 'find God within himself', this God that he finds within himself is often nothing other than his own ego turned into God. With many mystics who speak of the 'God within', we find nothing other than their own ego branded with God's name. Mystical immersion in God is sometimes nothing other than immersion in one's own beloved ego, especially in parts of one's ego into which one does not penetrate with full consciousness, so that one surrenders oneself, loses oneself, comes out of oneself and yet remains only within oneself. Much that manifests itself to us as mysticism shows how in the case of false mystics a love of God is often merely disguised self-love.

The true spirit-researcher, who must on the one hand guard against bringing the outer world of the senses into the higher worlds, must also on the other hand protect himself from the other extreme of false mysticism, of standing outside oneself. He should never confuse love for the spiritual nature of the world with self-love. In the moment when he does so, the following situation arises (as a true spirit-researcher who has pursued a rightful path of development can confirm). Just as someone who is driven by phenomenalism perceives only the residual or dying element of the spiritual world, a person who devotes himself only to the other extreme sees not spiritual actualities and beings but only particular parts of them. What he does in the spiritual world is not in accordance with someone who observes the flowers in a meadow but, rather, with someone who takes what is growing in the field, chops it up, cooks and eats it. The comparison is indeed strange but entirely appropriate. Through ecstasy, spiritual phenomena are not grasped in their totality or wholeness but only in a way that pleases and benefits one's own soul so that it can consume them spiritually. It is actually a consuming of spiritual substance that is cultivated within human beings by ecstasy. And just as little as one comes to know the inner nature of the things of the sense-world by eating them, one cannot understand the forces and beings of the spiritual world by abandoning oneself to ecstasy solely to make one's own self glow with what gives one pleasure. In such a situation one merely arrives at a certain knowledge of one's own self in relation to the spiritual world. One lives only in a heightened sense of self; and because one only takes from the spiritual world what one can spiritually consume, one forfeits what one is unable to deal with in this way, that which lies outside what can be enjoyed through ecstasy. But this is the greater part of the spiritual world. As a result the mystic who inclines towards ecstasy becomes increasingly impoverished; and we find that mystics who ascend to the spiritual world through ecstasy tend to indulge themselves in constantly repetitive feelings and sensations. Many presentations made by such mystics do not sound like objective descriptions of what is going on in the spiritual world but more like the indulgence of the one who has given the presentation in what he is describing. Many mystics are actually none other than spiritual gourmets; and the rest of the spiritual world which is not to their taste does not even exist for them.

We see again how concepts change when we ascend from the ordinary world into the higher worlds. If in the ordinary world we concern ourselves only with our own concepts, we become increasingly impoverished, as does our logic. Ultimately we find that we are no longer able to cope, and anyone who knows the facts is able to correct us. In the ordinary world we compensate for this impoverishment by expanding the range of our concepts. In the spiritual domain that which corresponds to ecstasy leads to something else. By apprehending realities and not things that are unreal, but selecting only particular parts having picked out elements that suit us, we acquire a view of the spiritual world that is suited only to ourselves.

We bear *ourselves* into the spiritual world, just as on the other hand, in phenomenalism, we bring the sense-world into the spiritual world. In the case of someone who arrives at a false picture of the world through ecstasy, it can always be shown that his starting-point was an unsound power of judgement, an incomplete knowledge of the facts.

Thus we see that the spirit-researcher must avoid the two extremes that cause him to encounter all possible sources of error on his path, phenomenalism on the one hand and ecstasy on the other; and there is no better way of avoiding the sources of error than if the spirit-researcher cultivates one particular mood of soul which, when he wants to transport himself to the spiritual world, will enable him also to be in this spiritual world, to be able calmly to engage in observation there. However, because one cannot always be in the spiritual world as long as one is in a physical body but must also live with the physical world, this mood of soul that the spirit-researcher must cultivate enables him to strive to the best of his ability in the physical world to understand the realities of life with sound common sense, without emotional wallowing or untruthfulness.

The spirit-researcher needs a healthy sense for facts, a genuine feeling for truthfulness, to a far higher degree than is ordinarily the case. All rapturous enthusiasm, all lack of precision which make it so easy to slip away from what is really there are harmful to the spirit-researcher. As one can already see in ordinary life, it immediately becomes transparently clear in the realm of spiritual schooling that anyone who allows himself to venture only a little in the direction of imprecision will notice that only a tiny step separates imprecision from falsehood and untruthfulness. The spirit-researcher must therefore endeavour to feel himself obliged to hold firmly and uncompromisingly to the unconditional truth that exists in ordinary life; for any compromise in this respect leads in the spiritual world from one error to another.

In those circles that want to have something to do with spiritual research, there should be a strong justification for thinking that an outward sign of the true spirit-researcher must be his truthfulness, and that in the moment when the spirit-researcher shows that he feels no obligation to test what he says but makes pronouncements about the physical world that he cannot verify, he also becomes flawed as a spirit-researcher and can no longer merit complete trust. This is connected with the conditions of spiritual research itself.

When the realms of spiritual research and spiritual science are spoken of today, it must constantly be emphasized that there is no justification for the kind of judgement that claims that only the spirit-researcher can gain insight into the spiritual world and that someone who has not yet become a spirit-researcher cannot know, understand and make sense of it. You can see from the descriptions in my book *Knowledge of the Higher Worlds: How is it Achieved?* and also from *An Outline of Occult Science* that in our present age every person who makes the necessary effort can to a certain degree become a spirit-researcher, whatever his life's situation may be; but it is also possible for someone to understand descriptions of the spiritual worlds without being a spirit-researcher.

It is necessary to be a spirit-researcher not in order to understand communications from the spiritual worlds but so as to discover them, to investigate what is present in the worlds of spirit. Just as one must be a painter in order to paint a picture but does not need to be a painter in order to understand the picture, sound common sense is sufficient for understanding communications from the spiritual worlds. Research of the spiritual worlds entails that a person is equipped with higher organs of observation; but when what is researched is formulated in concepts of the ordinary world, as is often attempted here, plain common sense can—if it is sufficiently unprejudiced and does not create obstructions for itself—grasp what is brought to light through spiritual research. One could say that what is sought through spiritual research is similar to what grows beneath the Earth's surface and is found only if one excavates it like a miner. What one finds there can arise in the way that it is present only if it flourishes within the layers of the Earth that are covered by what lies above them. What is down in the depths could not come into being and flourish on the surface of the Earth; but if we make an opening and let the sunlight in, the Sun can illumine what is underneath and everything can appear in its light. It is similar with what can be discovered through spiritual-scientific research: it can be revealed only if the soul has transformed itself into an organ of perception for the spiritual world. But if it has been formulated in the concepts and ideas of ordinary life, the human intellect can, provided that it is sufficiently imbued with sound common sense, illumine and understand everything as a kind of spiritual sunlight. Thus the whole of spiritual science is available to be grasped by healthy human reason. Just as the art of painting exists not only for those who are themselves painters, so are communications about the spiritual world not merely for the spirit-researcher—even though pictures can arise only through painters, and the spiritual worlds can be explored only by spirit-researchers.

Anyone who believes that what derives from the communications of the spirit-researcher cannot be understood by means of the ordinary intellect does not have a correct view of the nature and essence of the human capacity for thinking. In man's capacity for thinking there are faculties that have a direct connection with the nature of the higher worlds; and it is only because man is accustomed to approach only sense-perceptible phenomena with his concepts that he believes that the ordinary faculty of judgement will elude him if supersensible phenomena are presented to him. However, if one develops one's thinking potential one can cultivate it in such a way that it is capable of comprehending what is made manifest through spiritual research. The only reservation is that one should not form a prior conception of how one may comprehend something of this kind. This arises from the exercise itself. If one forms a definite notion of how one should comprehend these things, one opens oneself up to a problematic error with respect to spiritual research.

This is the second aspect that comes across particularly blatantly in Maurice Maeterlinck's new book; for it is especially striking that an individual who wants to direct his attention towards the spiritual world, who has made some sensitive observations about various things and has also himself tried to portray the mysteries of the spiritual world dramatically, should prove so inadequate when he should be approaching true spiritual science. He asks to understand things in a particular way—not a way that arises out of actual phenomena but one that he dreams up for himself, which he believes will prove authoritative. Thus the strangest thing is that Maeterlinck considers what theosophy or spiritual science has to say to be only a sort of belief when it speaks today about repeated earthly lives (even though it speaks with a certain outward justification and not with a merely inward conviction, which would be similar to a certain primordial belief of humanity). He calls it a belief because he cannot see that there is no question here of belief but, rather, of knowledge. Thus he finds that the evolutionary course of an individual human being which goes from one life to another cannot be proved, because he has a particular notion of what constitutes a proof.

Certain other people resemble Maeterlinck in this respect. Until recently there was a kind of belief, a certain geometrical, mathematical belief, which was summarized in the words the 'squaring of the circle'; that is, people employed a certain analytically mathematical, constructive thinking in their search for that square which equalled the circle in area or circumference. Now, no one will doubt that there can be a square that is exactly as large as a circle. In reality, this can perfectly well exist. But it is impossible to show with mathematical constructions or with analytical computations exactly what the diameter of a circle would have to be to equal a particular square. That is to say, mathematical thinking does not suffice to prove something that can indeed exist physically. There have been countless people who have worked on the squaring of the circle, until recent mathematicians have provided the proof that it is impossible to solve the problem in this way. Today anyone still trying to solve the problem of the squaring of the circle is considered to be ignorant of mathematics in this realm.

Just as such people have related to the squaring of the circle, so does Maeterlinck relate to what he seeks to prove. One can understand the spiritual world, one can comprehend that what is brought to light through spiritual research is real; but if out of a preconception one demands a particular kind of proof, one cannot prove the existence of this spiritual world any more than one can prove the squaring of the circle by mathematical means. One would therefore have to reply to Maeterlinck that he is trying to square the circle in the spiritual domain. Or he would have to be shown that the concepts through which he would seek to prove the existence of a spiritual world disappear when human beings pass through the portal of death. How is one to be able to verify the existence of such a world with concepts derived from the world of the senses? But this is what Maeterlinck is trying to do; and it is extraordinarily interesting that when he allows his healthy feeling for truth take the upper hand, he cannot avoid acknowledging repeated earthly lives. The way that he writes about a knowledge that he calls a belief is highly interesting, and I should like to read you a translation of what he says:[145]

> ...Never was there a belief more beautiful, more just, more pure, more morally fruitful, more comforting and in a certain sense more probable than this. With its teaching of gradual redemption and purification, it alone gives meaning to all bodily and spiritual inequities, all social injustice, all outrageous injustices of destiny. But the goodness of a *belief* is no proof of its truth. Although six hundred million people devote themselves to this religion, although it is very close to those origins that are enshrouded in darkness, although it is the only one that is not hated and is the least tasteless to all, it should have done what the others have not done: bring us incontrovertible evidence; for what it has given us hitherto is only the first shadow of the beginning of a proof.

This means in other words that Maeterlinck is trying in this realm to square the circle. We see from this example with the greatest clarity how someone who can only think that the salvation of spiritual science lies in the one extreme, in phenomenalism (all his writings show this) is totally incapable of grasping the significance and true nature of spiritual-scientific research. Much can be learnt from such a phenomenon as Maeterlinck, specifically that the truths that have to be incorporated in the world evolution of humanity are, when they first appear, in the position that Schopenhauer characterized with words that have already been cited here:[146] In all centuries, poor truth has had to apologize for its paradoxical qualities—and to Maeterlinck, truth even appears 'unbelievable'; and yet it is not the fault of truth. It cannot take on the form of error which so universally holds sway.

It therefore looks with a sigh at its protective God, time, which nods to it the promise of victory and glory but whose vast wings beat so slowly that the individual perishes in the meantime.

So it goes with the course of the spiritual evolution of mankind; and it should be both interesting and instructive to us that the best people in the present, those who wish with every fibre of their being to form a connection with a spiritual world, are not capable of grasping the central aspect of true spiritual science. Instead, precisely where it is a question of identifying the path to the two possibilities of error they stumble, because they do not dare to leap over the abyss, because they want to cling to the ordinary world of phenomenalism. Or else, even if they are not aware of this, they seek an intensification of the sense of self in ecstasy.

It cannot only be a matter of recognizing the character of particular possibilities for error but of learning what one needs to avoid if one is to recognize and block up the sources of spiritual-scientific error. From the way in which today's studies have been undertaken, one conclusion to be drawn is that one must know the sources of error. For there is always the temptation in the soul either to err in the direction of phenomenalism, thus to confront the spiritual world in a spiritually unconscious state of mind, or to err in the direction of ecstasy, that is, wanting to enter the spiritual world with inadequate organs of spirit. The path lies between the two extremes. One must know the possibilities for error. But because they can appear in spiritual life with every step, one must not only know them but overcome them; for the results of spiritual science are not only the results of research but they are also conquests, victories over errors, victories over perceptions that have previously been gained, victories over the sense of self and other things besides.

Anyone who enters more deeply into what has today been only briefly outlined will notice that, even if the possibilities for error can lurk to a frightening degree whenever we embark on research of spiritual life, we have nevertheless to be constantly overcoming errors. He will notice that spiritual research not only accords with an indomitable yearning for what he needs for confidence and certainty in his life but also that, for anyone who really understands it as a movement, its aim must appear thoroughly accessible to sound common sense. To summarize what today's lecture was intended to convey on the level of feeling, I should like to say that in spite of all opposition, in spite of all the things that can stand in a hostile way in the path of spiritual research, anyone who enters with a healthy understanding into the results of spiritual-scientific research can feel and experience that the fruits of this research thrust their way through weighty hindrances of the soul, through confusing darknesses of the spirit, to an earnest clarity, to a radiant truth.

LECTURE 13

BERLIN, 3 APRIL 1913

MORALITY IN THE LIGHT OF SPIRITUAL RESEARCH

WHEN Plato, the great Greek philosopher, wanted to give some kind of a definition or characterization of the divine, he described it as the 'good'.[147] And Schopenhauer, who in many respects followed Plato, once said in his writings[148] that he was far more entitled to refer to his philosophical outlook as an 'ethic' than was Spinoza, for the reason that he, Schopenhauer, based his whole world-conception on the primal force of the will, hence something that is at the same time connected with the innermost moral impulses of the human soul that formed the basic creative force of the universe; whereas Spinoza—so thinks Schopenhauer—built up his system in such a way that morality, the ethical, is not as such included in the highest world-principles.

Like Plato, Schopenhauer wished to indicate—as have the representatives of many philosophical world-conceptions—that everything that we call morality in human evolution is so intimately and so deeply embedded in this evolution of humanity that one could scarcely conceive of the moral realm other than as ultimately encompassing also all purely natural occurrences and as lying at the foundation of everything that man can ascertain as the fundamental principle and basic essence of things in the natural or spiritual world. Thus in the view of such philosophers, the moral element within man is the result of apprehending and being illumined by the divine morality that irradiates the whole world; and it is already implied by this that every development in terms of world-views concerning the primal foundations of existence must always, as a matter of course, bring human beings ever closer to the sources of the moral impulses of the world.

Even though one does not need to be fully in agreement with such philosophical world-conceptions, one will nevertheless be able to say that proponents of such views arrive at the kind of opinion exemplified in both Plato and Schopenhauer because they sense the value and significance of the moral element in the evolution of mankind and therefore would not want to be without moral impulses in the primal foundations of world existence. Even without being theoretically in complete agreement with such world-conceptions, one will nevertheless be able to learn from them and find it established that every world-conception that seeks to be influential in human life and human affairs must in a certain sense appear justified before the judgement seat of morality, that morality must be able to say an unconditional 'yes' to it. Thus it is a necessity to be able to relate every world-conception to the moral impulses of existence. The theme of today's lecture, the intention of which is to consider the relationship of what is meant here by spiritual science to the moral principles and impulses of the human soul, has arisen from foundations such as these.

Now when questions of morality are being addressed, a certain—one might say—holy awe of the territory that one is entering is necessary from the outset for something approaching a sensible way of considering the matters involved. Once one ventures into this territory, where one has to give consideration to judgements which want to pronounce in the most intensive way upon the worth or lack of worth of the human soul, one immediately senses upon entering this realm that one is plunging into unfathomable depths of human soul-existence, into such depths that one would not wish lightly and carelessly to come to conclusive judgements in this domain. Schopenhauer has also in this respect formulated a meaningful and much-quoted remark: 'To preach morality is easy but to implement it is difficult.' What does Schopenhauer mean by this?[149]

That it is easy to preach morality is apparent as soon as one devotes even only a little attention to human life; for there can hardly be anything that people preach about as much as morality, there is nothing that is so subjected to judgement as the soul's moral status or the lack of it. And if one makes a thorough study of human life, one has to reiterate that moral preaching actually makes very little headway towards enabling human souls to grasp that the moral principles that are imparted to them by this or that philosopher—even if they are clearly understood—can also be real moral impulses living in people's souls! Yes, how easy it is for many people to preach morality who find it really difficult to put moral impulses into practice. Schopenhauer's meaning is that all the preaching that is done about principles, moral formulations or moral edicts is actually without significance. There is in his view significance only if one can exhibit in one's soul a soul-force, a soul-impulse that becomes a reality in the soul and out of which moral actions arise. One would then be able to say that one has referred to something in the human soul that, if left to its own devices, results in moral action; one would then have found the ground for moral action in the soul. One will then have implemented a moral deed, because one has laid bare the moral impulse in the soul. This goes far beyond the mere preaching of morality.

One can see directly from such a challenge, which is as justified as it can possibly be, how difficult it is to penetrate those depths of the human soul where moral impulses are indeed slumbering, where those impulses that give rise to morality or immorality reside. It is difficult to enter with our judgements into those depths. Let us take a particular instance, one that can teach us how difficult it is for an ordinary soul to make a judgement about the moral worth or worthlessness of a human action. Let us suppose that a person of some significance sets off for a ride on a horse. On his way this person comes across a poor woman crouching by the roadside. The important person galloping by on the horse sees the woman, reaches into his pocket and, taking from it a purse full of money, throws it to the woman.

This is the scenario that is enacted before us. Now it is a question of asking ourselves how we should judge such an action in the light of morality. Herman Grimm, of whom I have also already spoken, says the following about this event, which was an actual occurrence in the life of a well-known individual.[150] Suppose the woman was superstitious, and that the situation was that she had intended in the near future to commit a crime in order to provide for her children, who were in desperate need. Because of the purse of money that this man threw at her, she no longer had to steal and thereby add still greater misery to her family's plight. But she is superstitious, says Herman Grimm. Why should the woman not say: Through this man an Angel of the higher worlds appeared to me and I was rescued from the abyss?

Thus through what this woman experiences in her soul, we would appear to have some kind of moral action displayed before us. But Herman Grimm goes further and makes the supposition that this person who threw the purse full of money to the woman afterwards comes into the company of some other people. The first of these people, who hears the original person relate what he has done, thinks: I have always heard that this person is remarkably mean; I now see how worthless such judgements always are! Herman Grimm then goes on to say that this man furthermore does his utmost for the bestower of the gift, contributing towards dispelling the rumour about his meanness by speaking everywhere about his 'magnanimity'. But suppose—says Herman Grimm—that a second person were to hear the same story and felt himself affected by it in a quite particular way; for he had—so we understand—not long before wanted to borrow a much smaller sum than was in the purse from that same man, who refused to loan it to him. Will this second person not arrive at a different judgement? Or—continues Herman Grimm—there could be a third person who at the moment when he hears what has happened is prompted to say: 'I am in need of money: can I not have something too?' Such a person could likewise arrive at a judgement that would be quite different both from that of the woman and from that of the others. A fourth person might perhaps know when this incident is related that the man in question had considerable debts at the time, and this person will again say that it is thoroughly wrong to give money away so readily when one has the obligation to pay debts that trusting people are expecting to be honoured. A further person, says Herman Grimm, might know that the purse of money did not belong to the man himself but to his wife and that the man carelessly threw away the purse of his wife, who might therefore well complain about this man's reckless behaviour. Several other points of view are also possible.

Thus we see that people with differing viewpoints might judge such an action entirely differently and would not see the need to have a direct experience of the actual impulse living in the soul of the person performing the deed. Herman Grimm places particular emphasis upon this instance because he wants to demonstrate the extent to which moral judgements should be treated with a certain reserve when they appear in, the example, the memoirs of a famous person. Judgements of all these different kinds could indeed appear in memoirs, for the whole affair that I have presented here did indeed occur in a comparable situation with the great poet Lord Byron; and Herman Grimm came to speak about this incident through speaking with one of his biographers who had known Byron personally. He has been cited here because his account clearly shows what is involved in making judgements about real life—which can be arrived at in a variety of ways—when we try to form a judgement about the moral worth of a person's deed. Just as one must indeed say that it is, as Schopenhauer indicates, difficult to implement morality, so is it well-nigh impossible in any particular case to approach the soul-life of a human being with a conclusive moral judgement such that this conclusive moral judgement truly reflects the actual state of affairs.

However, considerations such as these should not lead to the view that we should be indifferent with respect to matters of morality. On the contrary! Anyone who understands life in its totality will nevertheless regard morality as the holiest aspect of human life and, hence, come to the view that what is most holy in human life should also be approached with a reverent awe; for it is in many ways presumptuous to form a moral judgement of another person in view of the extent of the differentiation between one human being and another.

On the basis of what has been said, we now need to recall what has been presented here in these lectures about the character of spiritual science. Spiritual science leads us on the one hand more deeply into the spiritual foundations of things. But we have also seen that this is made possible in that we uncover deeply hidden forces of our soul-life, so that we comprehend the spiritual foundations of the world only by drawing forth forces that slumber in the depths of the human soul. With the methods of spiritual research we therefore approach the deeper foundations of human soul-life whence moral impulses stream forth in what is often so mysterious a way. The question that must now arise is: What happens when those explorations seeking to illumine these inner depths of the soul encounter the moral impulses that reside there? In the ordinary everyday life of the physical world it is probably true to say that, amongst the simplest of human souls and people of least education, moral impulses are able to speak forth from the depths with great certainty. While on the other hand, it is also true that many highly educated people, including some philosophers and scientists, can on a moral level be put to shame by people who have little knowledge to call their own but who nevertheless are able to accomplish the most sacrificial deeds of true human love out of the depths of their souls. Ordinary knowledge, outward physical understanding clearly cannot furnish the means of gaining access to the depths whence the impulses derive from which morality can become a living reality.

Now if spiritual science seeks to encompass the spiritual sources of existence, it immediately transpires that a human soul that wants to become a spirit-researcher must develop in a threefold way. This threefold path has been presented in the course of these winter lectures[151] as the three stages of supersensible knowledge. The first of these is what we call imaginative knowledge, that is, that knowledge which manifests itself to the human soul when it has freed itself from all sense-perception and all intellectual activity that is linked to the instrument of the brain. Once the soul has achieved this, it feels a world of pictures rising up from its depths; and with further development on the part of the spirit-researcher these pictures become images of the actual spiritual realities that lie hidden behind the outward world of the senses. Imaginative knowledge is the first of these stages which one will find explained in my book *Knowledge of the Higher Worlds: How is it Achieved?*

The second stage that the human soul needs to attain—and even though it has already been mentioned that these things can only be expressed in a more or less pictorial way, it is as well to refer to this again briefly to avoid any misunderstandings—consists in that what has manifested itself only pictorially (though this is not to be compared with the images apprehended by a particular sense) appears by means of a 'cosmic speech' as though out of itself as inspired knowledge. That is, if the spirit-researcher's faculty of Inspiration has been awakened, the spiritual beings and realities that lie beyond the world of the senses speak to him.

The third stage, which enables the spirit-researcher actually to enter into the essential nature of spiritual realities and beings, is called Intuition. Not that intuition which is sometimes referred to by means of this word in casual conversation but something that is a real stepping across of one's own soul-life into the being of another, through which a person's capacity to connect his own being with another being enables him to enter into the inner nature of spiritual beings outside of himself. Thus in contrast to knowledge of a sense-perceptible and intellectual nature, Imagination, Inspiration and Intuition arise at different stages of knowledge.

The human soul enters into the spiritual world by means of these three stages of knowledge. The forces of Imagination, which are for perceiving pictures of the supersensible world, the forces of Inspiration, which apprehend what the spiritual realities and beings of the supersensible world have to reveal, and the forces of Intuition—all these slumber in every human soul. Through the methods that have been described here, they can be brought into activity. Thus the human soul must enter as a spirit-researcher into its depths in order to come to the primal ground of existence.

Now it has already been pointed out, especially when the 'errors of spiritual research' were being discussed, that the starting-point from which the soul attains to those stages of its existence where it is able to gain insight into the spiritual world is of great importance. It was especially emphasized that a kind of loss of consciousness with respect to knowledge of the spiritual world manifests itself in a soul that does not have as its starting-point a moral mood of integrity. Such a soul will manifest a certain benumbed quality towards the higher worlds and will be able to reveal from these higher worlds what is seen through such a veil and, hence, what is distorted and falsified. Thus an indication has already been given of the connection of the initial moral soul-mood with what the soul can attain when it actually enters the spiritual world through Imagination, Inspiration and Intuition. But we can characterize the significance of one's moral state of soul for the higher stages of knowledge even more precisely than this.

Imagination manifests itself in the spirit-researcher in such a way that pictures arise as though on the horizon of his consciousness, initially from his soul-life and then from his spiritual life as a whole. These pictures that thus appear, and whose significance we have already described, will inevitably differ in accordance with the particular state of soul that a person has already here in the physical world. A soul that has developed a sense for the right and true connections between facts here in the physical world will bring with it into the higher worlds an inner capacity to discern the true relationships of things when, through the methods described, it ascends to Imagination. Thus we can say that a soul that truly understands how to live amongst the phenomena of the physical, sense-perceptible world carries its sense for truth with it into the spiritual worlds; whereas a soul that through inexactitude (as is characterized with respect to the sense-perceptible phenomena of the physical world by untruthfulness)—and it has already been noted that from inexactitude to error and even to mendacity is only a small step—such a soul brings with it an inner capacity for untruthfulness in the world where imaginations, the pictures of the spiritual world, are to appear. The consequence of this is that from its untruthfulness, which is not in harmony with the world but derives only from its own inner nature, a world of pictures is built up which is only an outpouring of the human individual concerned.

When a soul attains to imaginations, untruthfulness will therefore bring it about that such a soul is unable to reveal anything from the spiritual worlds other than the reflection of its own untruthfulness. Thus in all spiritual schooling the soul must, as part of its preparation for imaginative knowledge, before its entry into the world of imaginations be firmly grounded here in the physical world in what one may call a sense for facts or realities; and it should be strongly emphasized that anything that detracts from a sense for facts cannot provide a right preparation for perceiving the spiritual world.

For anyone wanting to become a spirit-researcher, it will be a good preparation if he holds himself back as far as possible from all personal and subjective criticism, from judging things from his own standpoint, from always asserting: 'I think this is right', 'I think this is wrong'. For someone wanting to become a spirit-researcher, a much better preparation for spiritual knowledge is if one tries one's best to avoid making judgements about, or assert the validity of, things in the physical world purely from a personal standpoint, if one endeavours as far as possible to allow the facts of life to speak for themselves. We shall therefore find that someone who is on a right path to the spiritual world makes every effort in what he relates or describes not to present his own judgements about things but to let things speak for themselves, in that his endeavour will, rather, merely be to juxtapose and combine the facts.

Thus when we come across someone who says at every opportunity: Such-and-such has happened, I find it not to my liking; such-and-such has happened, I find it to be a poor show; such-and-such has happened, I find it repulsive, I find it splendid—however the shades of meaning may develop, such a person is not on a good path for approaching the spiritual worlds. A person is far more likely to be on a good path if he tries to suppress such judgements and purely and simply relates the facts, if he looks at the facts and lets them speak for themselves and is guided by the principle: If I impose my opinion on someone, it is after all only my opinion—and then I am not only telling him to believe me that it is true but also that I have an opinion; but if I set out to tell a person what I have encountered, he can form his own judgement for himself. The more that one inclines to the latter policy of looking at the world and speaking about what one has seen, the more one equips oneself with a sense for the facts and prepares oneself for imaginative knowledge. Anyone who wants to prepare himself for imaginative knowledge should above all become accustomed to say with respect to every experience: This is how things are. He should consider it to be unimportant what he thinks about things and should endeavour to be merely the instrument through which they themselves can speak.

If one takes this into consideration, it becomes clear that a quite fundamental virtue, that of truthfulness, forms from the outset part of the right means of preparation for a methodical schooling leading to knowledge of the higher worlds. One will not then come into the embarrassing situation of doubting that a right schooling for knowledge of the higher worlds is or at any rate should be something that leads to an enhancement of morality. Indeed, one can view this from another perspective. One can envisage a situation where someone has not prepared himself for the higher worlds through this virtue of truthfulness. The slumbering forces of his soul will then indeed be awakened if he carries out the corresponding exercises, and he will eventually be able to gain access to an imaginative world. But what will this world then be? It is none other than a reflection of his own being. And because at the moment when one disregards the sense-world and also the brain-bound intellect, one is confronted by this imaginative world as something real irrespective of whether it expresses a genuine reality or is only the reflection of one's own being, anyone who is not rightly prepared through truthfulness will also find an imaginative world displayed before him which he is led to believe that it is the real imaginative world—and yet it is only the reflection of his own soul, his own inner being. This world represents a constant temptation of untruthfulness. One can therefore say that someone who does not enter the spiritual world by practising truthfulness places himself in a situation where the enticements to untruthfulness and lies are constantly present around him when he perceives the supersensible world. From this the only possible conclusion is that any ascent into the supersensible world must be associated above all else with the cultivation of a sense for factual realities; for only if we have a sense for the connection between the realities that we find around us in the physical world can we develop ourselves towards truthfulness.

The same situation applies in a similar way to Inspiration, although in this realm it is even more discernible and meaningful. Through Inspiration the things that exist spiritually around us speak to us, as it were, they display, reveal their being to us. We do not hear them by means of voices and sounds that resemble external sounds, but we hear them spiritually.

A different kind of preparation is necessary if a person is not merely to apprehend what his own being reveals but is to come to know a real, objective world. For this it is necessary to enhance a quite particular virtue of the soul. Such things can only be ascertained through experience. Anyone who wishes to attain to Inspiration must develop within himself—in a higher way than is necessary for the ordinary world—the virtue of moral courage, steadfastness and fortitude. For anyone who has moral courage, who does not shrink from what may under certain circumstances endanger his own being, will be able to withstand what speaks to him from spiritual realities through Inspiration. And someone who has developed too little fortitude and moral courage before he enters the spiritual worlds will very soon notice—or rather, he will not so easily notice it himself, but the others who understand something of the matter will notice it—that certain things speak to him from the spiritual world, but that everything that speaks to him is only an echo of his own being. Because his soul is not strong enough, because it does not have full hold of itself, it is unable to retain what it is within itself but lets it stream forth, and what it is itself then returns to it. A soul which has not been prepared for Inspiration through moral courage will very soon present itself as one that hears something like 'spiritual voices', but these spiritual voices will be none other than what it bears within itself, which is only an echo of its own being. A soul that arrives at this situation will most certainly be crushed by what is impressed upon it from the spiritual world.

So we see again that an important quality of the soul, a quality of which the moral character cannot be deprived, must be strengthened and consolidated if this soul wishes to enter the supersensible world—moral courage, fortitude. This is necessary as a preparation for true Inspiration. From this it can easily be concluded that it is of primary importance to strengthen one's moral courage in the physical world before one seeks to become a spirit-researcher, so that the soul can indeed perceive the revelations that have been given by way of imaginations also through inspirations.

Many who have not understood these matters sufficiently thoroughly have thought that being able to depend upon the moral courage of another soul gave them the means of ascending into the supersensible world and that sooner or later they would manage to get there—and they merely showed that they were reflecting their own being, which they interpreted as 'sounds' and 'words' [from the spiritual world].

Thus spiritual schooling is intimately connected with the enhancement of moral forces; and therefore every rightly imparted spiritual schooling will seek to strengthen and consolidate these powers. For this reason, you will find that wherever methods through which one can ascend to the spiritual worlds are described—for example, in my book *Knowledge of the Higher Worlds*—indications are given regarding the necessity of strengthening one's moral forces; for they cannot simply remain as they are in the ordinary life of the physical world but they must be enhanced and consolidated.

However, what is needed in this connection strikes us with particular clarity when we advance towards Intuition, through which a soul that has become a spirit-researcher is enabled to place himself within another spiritual being or another spiritual reality. We shall find that it is virtually impossible to incorporate oneself in other beings after spiritual schooling if one has not ensured in the physical world that the quality which can be referred to as having a free, open interest in everything that surrounds one is enhanced. All petty reserve, all withdrawal into oneself, everything that does not guide the soul's attention towards sharing in the sorrows and joys of fellow beings and of everything that surrounds us in the world of the senses—all this prevents the soul that has ascended into the spiritual world from attaining true Intuition, from arriving at true knowledge of higher beings. And here we stand within the realm where our considerations have an affiliation with what Schopenhauer calls his 'reason for morality'.

Schopenhauer was no spiritual scientist in the sense intended here. Thus for him the soul that descends into its depths does not enable one to see that it develops a threefoldness of forces that corresponds to the three stages of knowledge (Imagination, Inspiration and Intuition) but everything is merged together for him. The 'soul' is a nebulous mixture of all forces living within its depths. Thus Schopenhauer is also unable to explain the moral virtues, the development of which must be the preparation for a spiritual schooling: a sense for facts and actualities as a foundation for the virtue of truthfulness with respect to Imagination, fortitude as a foundation for what leads to Inspiration, and the third—of which Schopenhauer gives a full explanation—that slumbers in the depths of the soul and which one can in general refer to as interest in the surrounding world and its beings. But Schopenhauer draws attention to something else, and here he exhibits a quality of real inspiration. He draws attention to what in fact is one of the few soul-qualities and soul-impulses that show already in the physical world that there exists a kind of sub-earthly connection between one soul and another. Schopenhauer draws attention to compassion,[152] or rather sympathy. One only needs to mention the word compassion (or sympathy), of which Schopenhauer says that it must be present in every soul that can be called moral; and one will initially feel that with this word sympathy something is indicated that is in fact connected with the innermost moral impulse, with what can be a true foundation for morality. On the other hand one will feel that with the word sympathy one has touched upon something that is an Intuition that is already present in the physical world, a translation of one's own soul into that of another. For anyone who is able to contemplate the world with any degree of intelligence, that which is denoted by the word compassion represents a proof that there is a sub-physical connection between one soul and another, a proof that the spirit with its forces is actively present between different souls.

Thus Schopenhauer—and the same applies to others who have looked into these things—is right to call compassion or sympathy the true mystery of the human soul which can be observed here in the physical world; for there is something infinitely profound about a soul that is incarcerated in a body feeling something concerning which another soul rejoices or through which another soul suffers, so that in the toing and froing of forces of one soul to another soul a kind of spiritual mystery is enacted already here in the physical world. Thus Schopenhauer says that one can preach morality as much as one likes, but morality is actually based upon sympathy, or upon compassion. One can therefore indeed say along with Schopenhauer that there is only as much morality in the world as there is sympathy. There was a certain justice in Schopenhauer's having pointed out that it would be intolerable to hear the words: 'This person is virtuous, but he has no compassion'.[153] Schopenhauer means that everyone will sense the impossibility that such words could be expressed, that virtuousness and an absence of compassion could be combined in a single soul. Thus Schopenhauer also implies that it is intolerable to hear the words: 'He is an unrighteous and wicked person, but he is very compassionate', even though one may well say that the inner nature of the human soul is sometimes so confused that one can also experience how someone may perform deeds that are without doubt wicked and lacking in virtue and yet can develop a certain feeling, for example for doves and similar creatures. All in all, however, one can say that Schopenhauer is touching here on the very foundations of morality.

If one is speaking in the sense of spiritual science, one must extend the principle of compassion somewhat further; and there then appears before our soul what one can characterize as a participatory interest, as a participatory attentiveness with respect to everything that is happening around us. For someone who cannot share in a joy that is being experienced does not have a real, inner interest in it, and a person who cannot share in the sorrow of another being has no deep, genuine interest in it. In many respects, compassion, sympathy and interest are linked together. To have real, true interest means to have love; for one cannot have interest without having love in the true sense of the word, without having sympathy.

So the right preparation here in the physical world for intuitive knowledge is to strengthen the soul by getting it used to having an interest in everything that lives, breathes and is, to cultivating an attentiveness for everything that surrounds the soul. The deeper our interest can be, the better we prepare ourselves as spirit-researchers for intuitive knowledge of the higher worlds. Thus one can say that, for spiritual science, the radiating of compassion in the physical world is like a reflection of the fact that those deep forces of the soul that lead to Intuition can only develop rightly and truly if the soul is prepared for this through having a genuine interest in the surrounding world, that is, through having love and sympathy.

Thus whenever there is any discussion of the true path of spiritual schooling, we see that this true path is inseparable from what is at the same time the most important of human virtues; for these most important, most crucial moral virtues are fully encompassed by an interest-filled love, by an attentive awareness of all sorrow and all joy and, indeed, all existence, by a steadfast surety of purpose and by truthfulness. If anyone wishes to understand a virtue such as faithfulness, he will be able to come to know it most easily as a particular form of steadfastness. A person who is steadfast will also, correspondingly, understand the importance of keeping faith. All virtues, one might say the totality of all virtues, can be traced back to these three qualities of the soul.

Now if one is to describe the relationship of spiritual science to morality, one must also point out that a person who actually arrives at a contemplation of the spiritual world, whether through spiritual schooling or whether he merely accepts without prejudice what spiritual research has to offer him, comes before a world that places quite particular demands on him, demands which will quite certainly call upon the soul's reserves of confidence, hopes and inner forces. But the human individual also arrives at the point where he confronts himself, where he has in full self-knowledge, as it were, stepped forth from his personal limits, where he has entered a world that no longer bears within itself only his personal interests and intentions. Our soul comes to that point on the path of spiritual research when it confronts its own personality, when it confronts the being that it has been hitherto. It has already been pointed out that this confrontation with the being that one has previously been is referred to in spiritual research as the meeting with the Guardian of the Threshold, that threshold which separates the supersensible world from the ordinary physical world. In this Guardian of the Threshold one observes for the first time what one is, what one has hitherto called one's personality, one's interests, what one has willed, what one has felt as something that was connected with sympathy or antipathy. All this comes before one as a stranger, and yet it comes forth from oneself. One beholds it as a stranger and learns to say: This is all that you have previously said. Now you have it before you, and it shows itself to you as another being; you are outside of yourself. It is similar with a person's feeling and willing at the moment of meeting the Guardian of the Threshold. When one experiences this, one also knows how strongly all the magnetically working forces are that draw one towards the personality that one was, and which one must abandon.

That is the most important thing about this shattering experience—that one is aware that one must get away from oneself; but this being that one was and which one confronts does not want one to get away, it draws one with overwhelming forces towards itself. And if one succumbs to these forces, one will not be able to enter the spiritual world. By coming to know oneself, one learns to know the bond between the higher worlds—between the higher powers of knowledge that slumber within a person—and what one is in the physical world. On a theoretical level this becoming free from oneself may appear quite simple. However, if one experiences this event, not only through spiritual schooling but through what a person can understand through what spiritual schooling can impart, it becomes clear that these magnetically working forces are not to be overcome so absolutely through making a judgement but that with the process of freeing oneself the strength of the forces of bondage grows so that one feels: everything that seeks to draw one back becomes stronger the more one gets away from oneself. One notices increasingly what draws one to the ordinary personality, and one is also aware how necessary it is that one has previously acquired the strength to resist these magnetic forces. This means that one must indeed precede the actual entry into the spiritual world with such a strengthening of one's soul-forces with respect to what is good and moral, with such a dedication to what the spirit demands of us, that one can resist the enticements of the lower personality with a stronger power than is necessary in the physical world.

Thus when one faces the shattering events that have been characterized, one becomes aware for the first time that every approach to the spirit is at the same time a matter of drawing closer to moral challenges. So one has learnt through experience something that justifies what Plato, the great Greek philosopher says when he refers to the divine as 'the good'. When one confronts natural phenomena, one's judgement of them will be correct to the extent that one refrains from making moral judgements about them. Who would want morally to judge, say, a salt crystal or a plant for being stunted in their development? In the ordinary physical world, the natural and the moral world-order are intertwined, so that one only feels the depths of the moral world-order when one is aware that one will actually be admitted to the spiritual world through moral strength alone. Hence it is a principle of the spiritual world, and it is also a matter of experience, that anyone can come to the Guardian of the Threshold; but only someone who passes by him through moral strength is able to do so. However, those who approach him and then have to withdraw are then confronted by a spiritual world that is only the reflection of their own inner world. Thus anyone can believe that he has a whole spiritual world before him; he can also show other people what he means by saying that he has a spiritual world before him. And the other people may believe that there is a spiritual world that corresponds to the truth. But if he has not been able through his moral power and through his moral state of soul to pass by the Guardian of the Threshold, his spiritual world is not pervaded with truth or objectivity. It will therefore arise out of itself that any real knowledge of the spiritual world will present a picture of spiritual relationships such that the way that it is presented will at the same time not merely preach morality but will implement morality in the soul.

This is especially the case when one considers what has often been described here from a variety of points of view as a necessary fruit of spiritual research: the life of the human soul through repeated earthly lives. Everything that we are in one life forms the causes of the qualities that we have in the following life; and the qualities that we bear within us represent the influences deriving from previous earthly lives. A soul that does not develop a sense for what is factual will through this inadequately developed sense prepare causes that in the next earthly life form the predispositions for a soul that has a prior tendency towards untruthfulness. Untruthfulness that has, so to speak, been cultivated in such a life gives rise to a predisposition towards untruthfulness in the next life. Truthfulness alone, when cultivated in one life, gives rise in the next earthly life to the predisposition, to the outward talent of truthfulness; so that when one speaks of truthfulness as a necessary preparation for spiritual schooling, one is at the same time referring to something that forms within the soul the inclination towards a greater degree of morality than in the past.

If instead of fortitude, instead of moral courage, a certain inner indifference is developed, an easy-going attitude, a shrinking back from being true to oneself in one's soul, from bringing to fulfilment what one has recognized as true and right, because this works upon Inspiration, such a soul-life in which this cultivation of fortitude has been neglected will thereby be the cause of influences that will have an effect upon the next life and make the soul into a self-serving egotist. Egotism in one life is, as it were, inspired from the previous life through the soul's lack of moral courage in that life. And the effect of being indifferent towards the outer world, lacking interest and attentiveness and being selfish and reserved is that—as a kind of Intuition—this present being sends its influence to the next earthly life, where it bears the fruits that it has engendered, that is, that it engenders a tendency towards alienation from the surrounding world, towards a non-relationship with it.

What does it mean for the human soul to be alienated from its surroundings? Oh, it means a great deal. Someone who is alienated from the surrounding world and does not fit into it finds that its effect on him is such that it makes him continually ill, and this works not only upon the soul but also right into the body. Pathological, unhealthy dispositions are transmitted as a kind of Intuition from a previous earthly life to a following life through this soul having journeyed inattentively and without interest through life. What in one incarnation is more of a soul nature—a lack of interest in, a lack of sympathy with one's surroundings—reaches more deeply into the next incarnation right into the bodily nature and appears in the form of ill health.

Thus if we study the moral foundations of the human soul in a spiritual-scientific sense, we see that we do indeed touch upon what is active within it as impulses, in that the soul migrates from the one life to the other and builds up the new life in accordance with the causes that it has brought with it from the previous one. Thus morality becomes the formative power from one life to another; and we do not then merely preach morality but we show what morality does, how it works as a power within the human soul. So all those objections that are with a seeming justification made against spiritual science fall away. When spiritual science speaks of repeated earthly lives in the sense that what a person has experienced in terms of joy or sorrow will be balanced out in a following life through karma, it is often said that this is the basis for a certain egotism. But if one does not haggle over niceties but sees the point of the matter, if one wants to speak not only about preaching morality but about implementing it, it must be said that in order to become more and more moral, the soul must become more and more perfect, that is, the inner impulses must be shown for it to become more perfect. Thus it must be shown how moral impulses are connected with the perfection or imperfection of the soul. So when it is a matter of demonstrating the relationship of spiritual science to morality, we can say: Spiritual science is quite certainly validated by the justified demands of morality, for it must at the same time incorporate moral demands into its own most significant demands. Indeed, in a certain way it justifies those impulses that lived in a thinker such as, for example, Plato, who referred to the divine-spiritual as 'the good', in that it shows how the spiritual tolerates only the good, that is, it must be intimately related to the good.

Thus spiritual science may be regarded as something that, not in an outward but in an inward way, contains within itself the principles on which morality is based. And in addition to much else of which we shall speak in the next lecture concerning what spiritual science may give human beings for the inner support and health of their souls, for everything that they need by way of strength for work, of confidence in order to maintain themselves in outer life and to fulfil their task in life, spiritual science can give us something further which is an important addition to the understanding of human life and which may satisfy the human soul. We have, after all, at the beginning of this lecture drawn attention to the fact that morality and moral judgement are indicative of those depths of the human soul where the soul relates silently and with reverence to other souls, because it is aware of the difficulty of intervening where moral impulses reside within the soul. We have therefore seen that someone who speaks of moral principles in life touches upon those unknown depths of the human soul before which we must stand with the highest respect; so that we must say to ourselves that any unjustified interference in this human soul is itself an immoral act, and we sense as a result of our moral relationship to our fellow human beings that in our moral judgements we stand before the depths of their souls. And spiritual science shows us that when these depths of the human soul have been strengthened, when they have been reinforced and consolidated, they do indeed lead to the objective spiritual world, through which alone the soul can become a fellow citizen of the spiritual worlds.

It is therefore the case that what we stand before with reverence in moral judgement is at the same time that which is alone the 'permit' for crossing the threshold, behind which the spirit together with its mysteries holds sway. However, this makes us aware of the essential nature of the human soul, of the relationship of the human soul when it is comprehended in that deep sense that enables us to say—even when we are unable to agree with the moral behaviour of a human soul whom we encounter—in that we take into account the human soul's passage through repeated lives: Yes, even in the depths of the human soul that we are obliged rightfully, morally to condemn, there lives something that makes it related to the spiritual world if it but wills to penetrate into its depths and become conscious of the sources of morality residing there!

Thus the spiritual-scientific understanding of morality reconciles us with what we may call the true value of the human soul. It puts the words into our mouth which we need—in order to give strength for joy and abundance, to give strength for the spirit and the soul, to give consolation for life's many sorrows—to acknowledge, that in every situation of the human soul, even when this soul is not conscious of this or that, there is much about which the soul may say: Even if it is very hidden, there is something within me that professes goodness! This is especially helpful when the soul needs strength in order to keep going, when strength is needed for life and work, when, in spite of errors in the moral realm, the human soul can nevertheless say to itself—and it can do so when it comes to know itself through spiritual science—what Theone says in the Greek poet Euripedes's play *Helena*: I want to do the good by nature, and love it, because I must respect myself![154]

Lecture 14

BERLIN, 10 APRIL 1913

THE LEGACY OF THE NINETEENTH CENTURY

This winter's lecture cycle has sought to characterize from a variety of points of view the spiritual stream that has as its aim that of leading the human soul through a process of self-exploration to that knowledge which it must yearn for in connection with the most important riddles of life and existence. The attempt has been made to show that a study of present or future-oriented spiritual and intellectual streams makes it clearly apparent that the spiritual science referred to is the right instrument to guide the human soul in the context of the present and the immediate future time. For this reason, it has been a kind of undertone of these winter lectures consistently to emphasize the achievements and results of the intellectual life and aspirations of humanity in the nineteenth century; for if one considers the way that the intellectual life and aspirations of the nineteenth century have taken hold of humanity and have brought about the great triumph of material existence, it can truly be said that it would necessarily seem to be a hopeless undertaking if this spiritual science under discussion here were to reject or set itself in opposition to the justified requirements of natural science or, indeed, the intellectual and spiritual achievements of the nineteenth century.

Thus it will perhaps be seen as an appropriate way of concluding this cycle of lectures that we turn our attention briefly to what we can call the spiritual legacy of the nineteenth century, in order through considering this legacy to be able perhaps to indicate the extent to which the spiritual science that has been spoken of here belongs fully to the present evolutionary cycle of mankind.

What does this spiritual science endeavour to be for the soul? Its endeavour for the soul is to be a source of knowledge of its origin in the realm of spirit, to be a source of knowledge of those supersensible worlds to which the soul belongs as a spiritual being, notwithstanding the fact that the soul lives in the physical world of the senses by virtue of the tools and instruments of its body. Its endeavour is, therefore, to demonstrate conclusively that this soul is a citizen of the supersensible worlds. It endeavours to show that, if the soul applies to itself those methods that have been spoken of here in the course of this winter, it can undergo a development whereby cognitive forces are awakened within it which are not exactly on the same wavelength as the rest of a person's life but which, when they are developed, do indeed enable this soul to find its place in the worlds to which it actually belongs with its higher being. To the extent that the soul discovers these forces within itself, it comes to recognize itself as a being with respect to which birth and death, or, shall we say, conception and death, represent limits in the same sense that the blue firmament of heaven has represented a boundary or limit for the scientifically oriented cognitive soul since the dawn of modern natural science, approximately since the time of Giordano Bruno and those who were of a like mind to him. Through the soul becoming conscious of the forces that slumber within it, something similar emerges in it as regards the spiritual domain of time to what arose in it with respect to outward knowledge of the material domain of space in the time of the dawn of modern natural science, when for example Giordano Bruno[155] indicated that this blue celestial vault, which for many centuries had been regarded as a reality, is no more than a limit that human knowledge places upon itself through a kind of incapacity and which it can overcome when it understands itself.

Just as Giordano Bruno showed that behind this blue vault of heaven the infinite sea of space opens up with infinite worlds encompassed within it, so is it the task of spiritual science to show that that limit or boundary that is placed by conception and death exists only because the faculties of the human soul are no less limited than they were when limited spatially by the blue celestial vault, and than when one's conception of the spiritual realities in which the soul is involved is enabled to extend towards the infinity lying beyond birth and death, the soul recognizes itself as passing through repeated earthly lives. So the life of the soul takes its course on the one hand between birth and death, and on the other hand in the time from death until a new birth.

When we devote our attention to the spiritual widths of time in the way that natural science has ventured into the widths of space, the human soul—in that it enters the life between birth and death from the life that it has pursued between death and the last birth—recognizes itself both as the co-creator of the finer organization of its own body and as the fashioner of the shaping of its own destiny. It has, moreover, been said—it has been less emphasized this winter than in previous years, but it can be studied in spiritual-scientific literature—that when the soul comprehends itself in its deeper aspects, it also traces its life back to those times when life in bodily forms of existence had its origin; that it can trace itself back to those times when it was already in existence before our earthly planet had acquired its material form, before the Earth as a material form itself originated from a purely spiritual primal essence in which the human soul was already present in its earliest condition, even before the arising of the kingdoms of nature—the animal, plant and mineral kingdoms—that surround us. And the perspective of a future opens up that the human soul has to enter, when earthly incarnations will have come to fulfilment, a future in which it will pass over into a purely spiritual world which will come in the Earth's stead; so that one can look towards a future that the human soul will enter purely spiritually, and in such a way that it has to bring the fruits of the forms of earthly life to what it will attain as a spiritual domain as though in a primal condition of existence. However, it will not reach it in the same form as it left it but with the result of everything that can be acquired in earthly incarnations.

If the soul takes hold of itself in such a way that it intensifies within itself the forces slumbering within it, it also recognizes itself in connection with worlds that are themselves the source of our earthly planet; it recognizes itself as a citizen of the whole universe. Spiritual science can widen its awareness from the successive earthly lives of the individual soul to the successive lives of the planets, and even of the Sun, in the universe. The method is, therefore, one that consists in the self-education of the soul down to its deeper forces. The result is the knowledge of both the origin and the direction of the life of soul, the knowledge that the primal source is the spirit to which the soul belongs, that it is the spirit which causes matter to arise from it and which brings it into its various forms, and that the most important form that initially evokes our interest is that of the human body. This knowledge will, therefore, have to become part of human consciousness in the near future—that the spirit is the first and highest aspect, that the spirit releases matter from itself as water gives rise to ice, that it is the spirit that adopts its outward form in the human body, that the spirit has a connection with the spiritual influences, realities and beings of the world, and that the human soul is a citizen of this world of spiritual realities and beings that give rise from themselves to all outward material existence, pour it into the corresponding forms that make up the surrounding universe that we can perceive with our senses. This is how I would briefly characterize the methods and results that constitute what is here referred to as spiritual science.

This spiritual science is only in its beginnings at our present time. It has frequently been emphasized that it must be thoroughly understandable if enemies and opponents of this spiritual science still rise up today from every side. This must be especially understandable for someone who does himself stand firmly on the ground of this spiritual science and is aware of its particular nature in the context of present-day cultural life as a whole. It is not surprising that this spiritual science finds enemies and opponents, that people view it as fantasy, daydreaming and perhaps sometimes as something much worse. It would be far more surprising if, bearing in mind the particular nature of this spiritual science, there were at present more voices of recognition and encouragement than is the case; for it certainly seems as though not only the results of this spiritual science but also the whole way of thinking and imagining that must be cultivated here are at variance with all the habits of thought and ways of understanding things that have arisen for mankind through the legacy of the nineteenth century. However, this only appears to be so. And one may say that it appears thus most strongly to those who believe that they must stand on the firm foundation of this legacy of the nineteenth century in such a way that they consider only a materialistic—or a materialistically inclined—way of viewing the world to be compatible with this legacy of the nineteenth century.

To the spiritual scientist himself, what he must recognize as this spiritual science is by no means at variance with the legacy of the nineteenth century; for one can also say from the standpoint of this spiritual science that what this nineteenth century has bestowed so hopefully and also so fruitfully upon mankind in the most diverse realms of evolution will in a certain way shine as a light over all future epochs of human development. It is naturally impossible to speak exhaustively about the entire world with regard to this question of the legacy of the nineteenth century. But even if one were, for example, to confine oneself to what the structure of the spiritual and intellectual life of Central Europe or the West shows, one would have to say that much, much light emanates from a real understanding of the significance of what is presented there. But there has also been an inordinate amount of what one might often describe as a dizzying quantity of changes and diversity in the cultural development of the nineteenth century, so that the observer could sometimes be so fascinated by something or other that he could easily be led to become one-sided and thus overestimate its significance. He will perhaps only be rescued from this predicament through the fact that the achievements of the nineteenth century and the different pictures of cultural development are such that one picture is succeeded by another and a great degree of diversity presents itself. We can of course select only some of these, and we shall turn our attention now to the following.

Such a sense of hope for what may arise within the human soul and for what it can become if it becomes conscious of and makes use of its powers is represented at the turn of the eighteenth and nineteenth centuries by the great philosopher of the West, Johann Gottlieb Fichte, who at that very time wrote his famous book *The Destiny of Man.*[156] If one examines how he expressed himself to his most trusted friends and to those closest to him during his work on this book, one finds that he was enabled to look into the deepest mysteries of man's cognitive and religious sensibilities. If one then peruses this book, one may be fascinated by a kind of personal testimony that the human soul is seeking in this book for the sake of its certainty, for the sake of its hope. One receives still more from the way that Fichte, in a first chapter, begins by saying that the knowledge gained through the outward observation of nature and the physical world presents one with little more than a dream, from the way that he wants to show in later chapters how the soul takes hold of itself in its will, how it becomes certain of its own existence, than through the particular explanations that he gives and through the composition of the book as a whole, an impression that can be characterized as follows. This human soul has tried to pose to itself the question: Can I stand firm in my own existence if I have no trust in all the knowledge that is presented to me through my senses and through what my outward intellect beholds? In the style of his time, Fichte answers this resoundingly in the affirmative. What is most impressive about this book is precisely what it can become for the soul through its manner of expression, through the inward surety of tone, which is sure of itself in spite of the refusal to rely on a knowledge of appearances.

Now this book appeared in the midst of a striving on the part of Western cultural life for the sources of human confidence and human knowing. It was preceded by a time when Fichte was summoning up the forces to comprehend the human soul in so powerful a way, the so-called high-point of philosophical endeavour. What Fichte himself attempted, what Schelling, what Schopenhauer endeavoured to do, what has been attempted in the philosophical domain in the first third of the nineteenth century in order to enter into the mysteries of the world with the power of human thinking, all this—and one can today make whatever one wishes of the results of this intellectual upsurge—had a powerful influence upon every feeling and sensing human soul through the whole way that people felt and willed in this entire endeavour.

If one is aware of what Schelling—out of a conception of the world given substance through the intellect but then conceived more imaginatively—seeks by way of a world-picture that is able to bear him beyond all matter into the spiritual evolution of the world, if one then turns to Hegel's intellectual striving, which entrusts to man the power to penetrate into the inner nature of things solely through the power of thought, so that Hegel wanted to make it clear to the human soul that in the power of thought it has the sources wherein all forces of the world flow and wherein one has everything in order, as it were, to comprehend oneself in the realm of the eternal, one will indeed be conscious of a powerful struggle being enacted within humanity. One only needs to maintain the hope and the confidence that were linked to this powerful struggle.

And again, when one looks back, one may perhaps become aware of something that, for those contemplating this whole period of time that is being briefly referred to here more deeply, can shed light upon its origin. Thus in considering the year 1784 one comes across a little characteristic treatise by Kant which bears the title *Was ist Aufklärung?* ('What is Enlightenment?'). The almost pedantic style does not always enable one to sense how deeply the sometimes thoroughly intellectual thoughts of this treatise are rooted in the whole struggle of the human soul in the modern age. What is enlightenment? Kant posed this question, the same Kant who through the often chaotic but nevertheless forceful striving of the human spirit, as came to manifestation for example in Rousseau, was so moved that when he became acquainted with Rousseau's writings—and this is no mere anecdote—he had no peace but put his whole daily routine in complete disorder and at a completely irregular time (and this was a person according to whose daily walk one could set one's clock) went for a walk in Königsberg![157] But one knows how Kant's soul was shaken by the freedom movement of the eighteenth century. In the statements that we read when we take this little book of his into our hands, this becomes—one might say—monumentally apparent to us. Enlightenment, says Kant, is the human soul's freeing itself from its self-inflicted dependence. Dare to make use of your powers of reason! This pronouncement appears in Kant's book from 1784.[158] One really only properly appreciates the other statements in the book if one is clear that something of the nature of a first coming of the human soul to itself comes to expression in them. Let us try by means of a simple thought to see Kant's two pronouncements from his essay of 1784 in their true light.

Descartes, who as a philosopher did not long precede Kant (the 'not long' should be viewed in the context of world evolution), reduced everything to a striking, significant proposition. He referred the human soul to its own thinking and did something of the kind that Augustine had already done in the early Christian centuries. The aphorism that resounded like a ground-tone of the soul-life of Descartes was 'I think, therefore I am';[159] and with this he was saying something similar to what Augustine had previously said: One can doubt the entire world, but in doubting one is thinking, and in that one thinks one is, and in that one understands oneself in thinking, one has understood the nature of existence within one's own being.[160]

According to Descartes, it is impossible for a person of sound mind to know himself as a thinking soul and to doubt in his existence. I think, therefore I am—in spite of the fact that Augustine preceded him in formulating such a proposition, for the century of Descartes and for what continued to resound into the eighteenth century this aphorism was of the greatest significance. But if one now follows the way that Descartes proceeds to form a world-conception with this aphorism as a foundation, one sees that he consistently excludes what has been handed down as traditions from previous centuries. One sees that with his thinking, with what seeks to spring forth from the human soul itself, he calls a halt to what has accumulated over the centuries, he makes a stop to spiritual truths, to questions regarding the destiny of the human soul after death and so forth. Descartes calls a halt to real spiritual truths.

If one ponders this, it dawns upon one what it means that in the midst of the Age of Enlightenment in the eighteenth century Kant's pronouncements resounded: Enlightenment is the human soul's freeing itself from its self-inflicted dependence, and: Dare to make use of your powers of reason! This means that one has now ventured to attempt—and Kant's pronouncement is characteristic of this—to entrust the human soul with the capacity to come to the sources of its existence, to the sources of its forces through its own power, through its own greatness.

Everything that lies in the bold propositions of Fichte's book that have been cited, together with that bold intellectual work that shines forth so magnificently in Western philosophy from the first third of the nineteenth century, derived from this source. If one contemplates this upsurge of the human spirit, which we want to consider today not in terms of the truth or falsehood of its content but with respect to what the human soul hoped to gain by way of inner confidence and surety of hope, and if one directs one's attention further to the middle of the century one will perhaps be somewhat wistfully touched by the words of someone who was both a historian of philosophy and also a philosopher in his own right, namely Hegel's biographer, Karl Rosenkranz. This is what he writes in his Foreword to his book *The Life of Hegel* (1844)[161]: 'It is not without a certain melancholy that I part company from this task, out of the necessity that what has been in process of becoming must also come into existence! For does it not seem as though we people of today are merely the gravediggers and memorial makers for the philosophers who were born in the second half of the last [eighteenth] century and died in the first half of the present century?' One feels perhaps more from such a remark than from other accounts how around the middle of the nineteenth century the whole splendour of the philosophical striving from the turn of the eighteenth to the nineteenth century and from the first third of the nineteenth century was rapidly extinguished.

But a splendour of another kind immediately emerges. Whereas in the 1830s and 1840s the brilliance of philosophical activity rapidly faded, there arose a new confidence, one could say a new blissful sense of hope. This was already prepared by the great scientific perspectives of a physiologist like Johannes Müller and through everything that people like Alexander Humboldt and others had done. But then came such significant achievements as the discovery of the cell and its activity within the living organism by Schleiden and Schwann. In this way a new brilliant age of scientific knowledge was introduced. And now we see that what has been achieved is followed by everything that will shine immortally in the evolution of the nineteenth century. We see how the great achievements of physics ensue: already in the 1840s the discovery of the law of the conservation of energy and of the conversion of heat by Julius Robert Mayer and by Helmholtz. Anyone who knows the physics of the present knows that physics in its modern form only became possible through this discovery. We see how physics is led from triumph to triumph, how through the discovery of spectral analysis by Kirchhoff and Bunsen attention is directed from the material conditions of the Earth to contemplation of the material conditions of the heavens, in that it is recognized that the same substances manifest themselves in the conditions prevailing in the heavens. We see how physics manages to connect its theoretical foundations with the practical exploitation of its principles, how it succeeds in translating itself into technology and how it changes the culture of the earthly planet. We see natural forces such as electricity and magnetism becoming hugely significant through being harnessed by technology. We see promises of the future following on a grand scale from studies of the living, organic world that Darwin has made and which Haeckel has further developed.

All this we see being incorporated in the cultural life of mankind. We see how Lyell's research from the beginning of the nineteenth century gives rise to modern geology, which tries to give a picture of the course of earthly evolution in a material sense. We see, too, how immense efforts are constantly being made to integrate human evolution with earthly evolution by means of purely material laws. All this that has led to the position that confidence in the power of thought has come to occupy in the first third of the nineteenth century has, however, had a deep influence not merely upon theoretical world-conceptions; for if only this had been the case, one could say: All this has been enacted on a kind of higher horizon of cultural development; but below this is the horizon of the rest of the population who is not concerned with it. No, there is nothing in the evolution of humanity that has not been affected by the impulses that have been delineated here with fleeting strokes. We see them extending their influences everywhere into the mysterious forms of this cultural path of mankind.

The human soul itself has in its innermost nature and essence by no means remained unaffected by what has happened. What has taken place over this time could, as a way of characterizing the legacy that the nineteenth century has left behind, be summed up in a soul that had still been able to listen to what came from Fichte's mouth, as exemplified in his book *The Destiny of Man*. Such a soul would have had certain feelings and experiences regarding its own being, regarding the way that it is able to experience itself. This inner structure with respect to the soul's experience of itself at the beginning of the nineteenth century would be portrayed significantly differently if we were to consider a soul that did not confine itself to a materialistic way of looking at things but devoted itself with open senses and with interest to everything that justifiably flows from the legacy of the nineteenth century. This human soul did not remain unaffected in its innermost being by what was developing around it from the centres of great cities, it was not untouched by the cultural achievements that represented an embodiment of the new intellectual spirit, which had been arrived at through the views regarding the new laws of the mechanistic world-order. A soul that had been able to devote itself with its whole heart to a book such as Fichte's *The Destiny of Man* was still free from these views that tend towards regarding the universe and its laws in a similar way to the laws that also govern machines such as locomotives. It has been rightly emphasized that this human soul had to undergo its own changes and developments under the impression of everything that has arisen as of a necessity as a material cultural fruit of the changes in thinking, feeling and experiencing taking place in the nineteenth century.

One should but try to understand through particular symptoms what happened as a consequence of the insights furnished by the natural-scientific thinking of the nineteenth century. Consider, for example, how a painter stood in former times before a canvas, how he mixed his colours, how he knew that they would last; for he knew what he had made them with. The nineteenth century, with the great achievements and advances of technology, instructs the painter to buy his paints. He no longer knows what his senses present to him, he does not know how long the impression of the lustre that he has evoked on the canvas will last. To be sure, it is only under the influence of the technology that has arisen from the achievements of natural science that it is possible for us today to have our publishing networks, our modern newspapers and everything that is then able to make its impression on the human soul and which has above all changed the whole tempo of the human soul and, with it, thought-forms together with the influence on feelings and, hence, also the structure of feelings. One needs not only to call to mind the speed with which the achievements of modern technology make things available to people but it must also be indicated how quickly that which the human mind discovers is impressed upon other human minds through publicity, and with what degree of abundance.

One may compare what someone learns today through publicity about what goes on in the world, also about what human minds are researching, with the way that a person was able to experience all that was taking place at the beginning of the nineteenth century. Let us focus on Goethe, for example! It is indeed possible for us to consider him, because from the careful way that he maintained his correspondence we know more or less exactly what he was doing from one hour to the next, what he was discussing and doing with a particular scholar or writer. The achievements of human intellectual life flowed only gradually into his solitary room in Weimar. But it was of central importance for Goethe that what everyone can receive today through publicity should be able to find its fulfilment. However, this changes the whole of the human soul, the whole relationship of the human soul to its surroundings.

Let us approach this in another way. People in our time write books or read them. Anyone who writes a book today knows that after possibly sixty years it can no longer be read if it is printed on the kind of paper which we owe to the great achievements of technology, for it will have fallen to pieces. Thus one knows if one is not under any illusion how greatly what is available today falls short of the way that things used to be done.

In one of the lectures in this cycle I tried to characterize a figure who, even though he is connected with the whole spirit of the first half of the nineteenth century nevertheless belongs to its second half: Herman Grimm. We have seen that he presents himself as a guardian of the legacy of the first half of the nineteenth century into its second half. However, anyone who reads Herman Grimm's essays on art with inner understanding will notice two things among others. Especially through his most worthwhile essays there is everywhere evidence of a certain school that he passed through, a school that one can hear resounding from every essay. This is the school in which he could participate only because in relatively early times, through what one may call chance, he became acquainted with a figure of great stature, namely Emerson,[162] a great preacher and proponent of world-conceptions not in the sense of former times but in the most modern sense. If we try to form a conception of Emerson and try to immerse ourselves in him, we will find a true spirit of the nineteenth century appearing before us. We can try to sense the pulse of thoughts that appear with the colouring and nuance of the nineteenth century when they relate to Plato, the philosopher, or to Swedenborg, the mystic. Even if they are still so free from prejudice, they are thoughts of the nineteenth century that one can only think in a century that was destined to make the telegraph into a means of communicating with the world. In Emerson one has a figure who, being completely rooted in the culture of the West, raises this culture of the West to what it has eminently become; one has in him a figure who represents the speeding up of thinking. One can try to compare a side in Emerson with a side in Goethe, where one may also gain some insight into Goethe. One may then try—and this is a perfectly natural approach to Goethe—to compare the image of the leisurely Goethe who was still in accord with the pace of the eighteenth and early nineteenth centuries with the rapidly hurrying nature of a person of the nineteenth century, a quality that works on in the pulse of thoughts of Herman Grimm.

Then we have seen how, in his wonderful novel *Unüberwindliche Mächte* ('Unconquerable Powers'),[163] Herman Grimm has even referred to the existence of the human etheric body or life-body, how he referred to much that has found its full expression only in spiritual science. However, one can also see how Herman Grimm enters into everything artistic in a really outstanding way and with great personal interest, how he is able to relate more distant periods of time to one another artistically, how he is able to give an interesting, sensitive observation about art. It is impossible for someone who can have insight into such things to think that the thoughts that Herman Grimm's finest essays present could have been composed in any other age in the way that it was possible for him to do so, namely when travelling in the express train from Berlin to Florence or South Tirol; for this is the assumption than can in many respects be formed from his creative work. Just to imagine that someone like Herman Grimm could have been able to say in previous centuries: The most important parts of my book on Homer[164] were always written in Gries near Bozen in the weeks of spring, because I sense there the influence of spring! That something like this becomes a factor in human life is only possible in the whole atmosphere of the nineteenth century. In this situation we feel a streaming together of what springs forth in Herman Grimm in the form of a wonderful study of art, of what enters fully into the soul of the cultural impulse of the nineteenth century, with what arises from technology, and streaming into it again out of the triumphs of the nineteenth century.

It is impossible to understand something of the deepest issues of the nineteenth century if one is unable to connect them with the most important legacy of the nineteenth century: with the natural-scientific thoughts with which the nineteenth century sought to comprehend the world. We can today not do otherwise than admit that within our soul something is living as one of its most important instruments that would not be there without the structure of natural-scientific thinking as we have it as a legacy of the nineteenth century. This is the one side, the side that presents itself to us in what the human soul has made out of itself once it has implemented what Kant characterized in so monumental a way when he said: Enlightenment is the human soul's freeing itself from its self-inflicted dependence, and: Dare to make use of your powers of reason! This tendency of Enlightenment, that is, making use of the means of research available to the human soul in the way that it is now, passed through the philosophical upsurge and on into the age of natural science. But how has all this come about?

From a spiritual-scientific point of view, we must envisage a greater degree of connection if we want to understand what has come to expression here, if we want to understand the configuration, the structure of our soul, in which we see on the one hand the effects of the will towards Enlightenment and, on the other, everything that natural-scientific culture has brought about. We must juxtapose at least three successive cultural epochs of human evolution. Reference has already been made to these cultural cycles in connection with these lectures in the sense of that observation arising from a knowledge of the life of the human spirit which endeavours to establish how the human soul returns through the ages in successive earthly lives and brings from former ages into later ones not only its own faults, in order to atone for them in the sense of the great law of destiny, but also what it has inwardly experienced by way of cultural achievements. In the sense of this spiritual knowledge we shall initially distinguish three ages. Other ages precede these three; but it would not be appropriate to enter into these today.

The age that is important for us initially can be called the Egypto-Chaldaean Age, which came to an end roughly in the eighth century BC. If one seeks to characterize it, one can say that in this age the human soul lived in such a way that it still had an inkling of its connection with the whole universe, with the whole of the cosmos. It still felt itself in its destiny on the Earth to be dependent on the course of the stars and on the events of the great universal whole. Observations of the dependence of human life on the starry worlds, on the universe as a whole, fill this age of former centuries lasting until approximately the eighth century BC. The soul felt itself affected in a wonderful way when it immersed itself in the wisdom of Ancient Egypt and Ancient Chaldaea, when it saw how everything depended on feeling the soul's connection with the cosmos that extends beyond the narrow limits of human existence. Something that was important in order to feel this connection of the soul with the cosmos was in this cultural epoch the appearance of, for example, Sirius; and with respect to what a person did for the culture of the soul, to what he utilized for the soul or himself accomplished, was the observation of celestial laws. People felt themselves to be born out of the whole universe, they felt just as much a connection with the extraterrestrial world as with the earthly world; they felt as though they had been transported to the earthly world from the worlds of spirit. This feeling was a last echo of the ancient clairvoyance from which the human soul has originated, as has frequently been mentioned here. This ancient clairvoyance existed in earliest times, and man has lost it in the course of his evolution in order that he can behold the world in the way he does now. At that time in the Egypto-Chaldaean Age, there was still an echo of this ancient clairvoyance. People could still understand the spiritual relationship of soul-spiritual laws to all natural phenomena and wanted to do so. The human soul was in a certain sense not isolated within itself at that time. It was, in that it felt itself to be on the Earth, connected and intertwined with the forces that streamed down to the Earth from the universe.

Then came the Graeco-Latin time, which as regards its essential nature and its influences we can reckon as lasting from the eighth century BC until the thirteenth, fourteenth and fifteenth centuries AD; for the after-effects of this cultural epoch last until then. When one considers this age, and especially in its initial phase, one finds the distinctive quality that the human soul has freed itself in a higher sense from the universe, freed itself in its knowledge, in its beliefs, in the recognition of the forces working within it. And when one observes the Greeks themselves, one is particularly aware that the way that healthy human beings developed themselves inwardly and related to the Earth was that they felt themselves to be in connection with their physical, bodily nature. This is what the Greek soul felt and expressed in the second of the periods that we are now considering. It is really difficult today to characterize what is meant by this. We tried to bring it closer to our understanding when considering Raphael and Leonardo da Vinci. The Greek lived quite differently with respect to the soul-spiritual realm. This was especially the case, for example, with Greek artists. People today do not even want to acknowledge that there was something particular about the feeling and experience of the Greek soul. That a sculptor who was representing the human form in the true sense could have before him what we would call a model today was inconceivable for a Greek artist. That is not how it was done. The relationship of the modern artist to his model would have been unthinkable in Ancient Greece. For the Greek knew: My soul-spiritual nature lives in my entire body. He experienced how the forces of this soul-spiritual nature flooded into the forming of the arm, the forming of the muscles, the forming of the whole human form. And he knew that just as it flooded into the human form, so did he have to bring it to expression in his sculptural work. He knew to fashion what he himself could experience in the outward material domain in accordance with the inner knowledge of the bodily nature. Thus he was able to say to himself: I am weak, but if I were to develop my will I could enable this will to work into the forming of the muscles, into the forming of the arm and thereby become stronger. What he thus experienced he poured into the forming of the figures that he created. The perceiving of the outward forms was not for him the essential aspect, but rather the feeling of man's having been placed into earthly culture and the reproducing of what was experienced outwardly.

This was also the experience of the whole personality in Ancient Greece. To think of a Pericles or any other statesmen like modern statesmen is completely impossible. We see today a modern statesman basing what he thinks and does upon universal principles. When Pericles in Ancient Athens appears before the people and carries something out, it is not because he says to himself: Because I see it like this, it must be done. That is not the case. But when Pericles appears before the people and asserts what he wishes, this is his personal will. And if it is agreed to, this happens because Pericles can will what is right, because he experiences it as a personality. In this way the Greek is of a nature that is complete in itself, he lives thinking of himself as a unified being. He can do this because unlike someone belonging to the Egypto-Chaldaean Age, he no longer feels the connection with the Gods and so on. This connection is still present only as a reverberation of former times. What he directly experiences is, however, that he feels his bodily nature to be connected with the world of soul and spirit. In this way, therefore, while he has a stronger experience of himself as a solitary individual than a person of the Egypto-Chaldaean Age he is nevertheless connected with the whole of the rest of nature, because his body, his physical organism has given him this sense of belonging. One has to feel that in the Graeco-Latin Age the soul was already more free from the totality of the universe than in the previous period, but it still necessarily felt connected with everything that surrounded it in the kingdoms of nature; for the soul felt itself connected with that which has derived from these kingdoms, the physical human body. It is this feeling that one must see as characteristic of this Graeco-Latin Age in which the Mystery of Golgotha occurred.

Now we see emerging—and with our thinking and feeling we stand in the midst of it—the third period that we have to consider. How does it differ from the Graeco-Latin period? The human soul is again much more alone, for the Greek felt himself connected with nature through what he was in his body. Let us imagine that a Greek had the possibility of gazing at the most minute living beings through a nineteenth-century microscope and of thinking of cell theory. This would have been an impossibility for the Greek soul! For once it had gone beyond its initial curiosity, it would have experienced with regard to these observations through the microscope that it is completely unnatural to devise instruments through which one sees things differently from the way they appear to the natural eye of the body. The Greek felt himself so connected with his own nature that it would have seemed unnatural to him to see things other than the way they present themselves to the eye. And to make cosmic phenomena visible through the telescope would have seemed to him equally unnatural. The way that the Ancient Greek thought was in this regard in many respects similar to the sensibility of a personality who was inspired by this way of thinking and who coined the beautiful expression: What are all the instruments of physics in contrast to the human eye, which is such a wonderful apparatus![165] That is, the Greek picture of the world was the most fully in accordance with nature, which one attains if one arms the senses as little as possible with instruments and, hence, with making things different from the way one sees them when one perceives nature directly as it is incorporated in the surrounding world.

It is quite different in our time! In our time it has been perfectly natural—and it has been all the more so throughout the cultural development since the period in question began—that what people have sought to identify as an objective natural-scientific picture of the world they completely separated from what lives in the human soul. Thus the view could arise that one can only experience the truth about the human organization if one directs one's suitably equipped eye towards things, if one investigates living beings with a microscope and uses a telescope to view the heavens, if one uses an instrument which makes up for the imprecision of the eye. But if one considers this whole mental outlook that comes to expression here, one has to say that people are now drawing what lives within them, and what is connected with their ego, completely away from their picture of the world. The human ego, the human self is even more alone and solitary than in the age of Greece. If we try to compare the Greek world-picture with our picture of the world as it is given to us by natural science, we must say: The endeavour has been made also in practice to render this picture of the world independent from what goes on in the depths of the human soul, from what lives and weaves and is within the human ego. Thus in the age of Ancient Egypt and Chaldaea, soul and world were—for human experience—one. In the age of Greece the human soul and the human body were one, but through the human body man was still connected with his world-picture. Now the soul-spiritual dimension has become more and more separate, wholly separate from what it regards as the justified content of the world-picture. The human soul is solitary, contained within itself.

We now contemplate the remarkable polarity that appears before us when we approach our own cultural period from the Egypto-Chaldaean era by way of the Graeco-Latin Age. In contrast to the earlier Greek epoch, what a person in our epoch strives for above all else is to arrive at a natural-scientific world-picture that is independent of his soul-nature. The necessary consequence of this is to separate the human soul from what it was connected with in former ages, to cause the soul to fall back upon itself and upon its own consciousness. In the Egypto-Chaldaean Age the human soul still directed its soul-spiritual gaze into the cosmic expanses and let itself be inspired by them, let what lived in them flow into it. Even in the age of Greece man still took what was given to his world-picture and imprinted it into art. In the modern age the world-picture is there in its own right, separated from a person's soul-experience. And yet we must say that when in modern times the human soul has thrust itself out of the objective world-picture, when it no longer finds itself in a soul sense in what is enacted without in mechanically objective terms, when it has broken off the connection with outward world-existence, it wants nevertheless to achieve within itself the power for knowledge, as a world-picture, for its whole existence. To a Greek it would have been incredible if someone had said to him: Dare to make use of your powers of reason! or: Enlightenment is the human soul's freeing itself from its self-inflicted dependence. Socratic words were spoken in Greece, but not these words; for a Greek would not have understood them. He would have felt: What do I want to do with my powers of reason? Most importantly, to gain a picture of the world. But this picture of the world lives constantly within me, in that the world streams into my forces and my soul-spiritual nature. It would be unnatural to make use of my reasoning powers with all that is streaming into me. And someone belonging to the Egypto-Chaldaean Age would have experienced the demand to make us of his powers of reason to be even more extraordinary and unnatural. His response to the proposition: Dare to make use of your powers of reason! would have been: Then my best intuitions and inspirations that have streamed towards me from the universe will have forsaken me. Why should I use my reasoning powers, which would impoverish me in my experience if I availed myself of them, in the face of what streams to me from the universe?

Thus as the human souls that have come from previous epochs, we encounter every time a different age. They are, therefore—in Lessing's words[166]—educated in the Egypto-Chaldaean Age in such a way that the soul feels at one with the world, then in the Graeco-Latin Age, when the soul feels at one with its own bodily nature; and now souls are passing through the time when they must find themselves within their own being, because they have taken themselves out of the objective picture of the world.

So we find that it is thoroughly appropriate if this age must bring forth a Fichte together with his book *The Destiny of Man* and if he poses the question: What if this world-picture is perhaps only appearance, an illusion, if it is only a dream? How can the ego that now feels itself impoverished—this is an experience that comes from the age—come to an inner confidence? How can it find itself?

Thus we see Fichte's teaching of the ego as a necessary result of the whole of evolution. We see how in the nineteenth century because of the world-picture of natural science—how in Fichte's time, when the power of thought was still blossoming—the ego wants to create for itself clarity through its own forces. And we can characterize the endeavours of Schelling and Hegel that followed Fichte in such a way that we see in them the aspiration on the part of the ego emancipated from the world-picture to gain a connection with the world through thought. But we see how, in this third period that has been characterized, the natural-scientific world-picture gradually, as it were, also detracts from the ego, in that it causes all reverberations of the old world-pictures to become impoverished. Such things are not normally sufficiently attended to in our time.

If we look back at one of those individuals who have made significant contributions to our natural-scientific picture of the world, to Kepler, who has brought about so infinitely much of what now lives on in our scientific view of the world, we find a remarkable idea in his *Harmonices mundi*. He extends his gaze from the harmony of the cosmos to the Earth as a whole. But this Earth is for Kepler a gigantic organism that lives in a somewhat whale-like way.[167] At least he finds when he looks beneath its living aspect an organism that has a similarity to the earthly organism of a whale, and he says: This giant animal on which we walk breathes, breathes not in the way that a human being does in the times that are defined by the course of the Sun; and the rising and falling of the ocean is the sign of the in-breathing and out-breathing of the Earth's organism. Kepler finds the way that people envisage how this process takes place to be too limited.

With Kepler, one should not forget—if one is putting forward the connection with Giordano Bruno as a one-sided way of looking at the world—that Giordano Bruno again and again indicated that the Earth is a giant organism[168] that has its in-breathing and out-breathing in the ebb and flow of the ocean. And we do not need to go far back in order to encounter the same thought in modern times. There is a beautiful aphorism of Goethe's where he says something like this in a conversation with Eckermann: I see the Earth as a giant animal that has its process of inhalation and exhalation in the rising and falling air currents and in the ebb and flow of the sea.[169] That is, the view that conceives of the Earth in the way that modern geology does arose only very gradually; and another one that we feel still reverberating in Goethe, and which comes towards us in a very living way in Kepler and Giordano Bruno, was lost. What Kepler, Giordano Bruno and also Goethe thought and felt was something that people experienced very vividly in those ancient times when the soul felt at one with the world. However, it was the natural course of evolution for this sense of being at one with the world to become obscured in the course of time.

If we wish to characterize what has been presented in the sense of spiritual science, we arrive at the following picture. Further elucidation of this can be found in my book *Occult Science*.

If we contemplate the human soul, not in the chaotic way that modern science does but with the insights of spiritual science, we find that it is divided into three parts. There is firstly the lowest member of our human soul-nature which, as one might say, still exhibits the most chaotic depths of the human soul to which the upper parts of human nature do not fully extend: the sentient soul. This is the source of the drives, emotions, passions and all the undefined feelings that hold sway within the soul. Then we have a higher member of the human soul: the intellectual or mind soul. This is the soul that lives more consciously within itself, which takes hold of itself within its own being, which experiences itself not only in the waves of impulses, longings and passions that it feels rising up from the depths but which feels compassion and shares in the joy of all things and which develops within itself what we call intellectual concepts and so forth. And then we have that soul-member that we call the consciousness soul, whereby the human soul fully experiences itself.

In the course of human evolution these different parts have developed in succession. If we go back to the Egypto-Chaldaean

Age, this was primarily the education for the sentient soul which human beings were undergoing at that time; for the connections from the great cosmos that lived into human souls without a person accompanying this with his consciousness could speak to the sentient soul. The wisdom of Egypt and Chaldaea was therefore arrived at unconsciously. If we proceed to the Graeco-Latin Age, we have there the particular development of the intellectual or mind soul, where through intellectual and mind forces—we can see that this soul-member has two parts—an inwardness is expressed which is imbued to a greater extent with consciousness. And in our time we now have—and this arises directly from what has been described—that culture of the human soul whereby this human soul is to come to a full consciousness of itself, that is, to develop the consciousness soul. This is what has come to its highest climax, to its highest level of development in the nineteenth century: the objective world-picture, which leaves the soul alone with itself in order that it can take hold of its self, its ego, with its consciousness soul. It was necessary precisely for inwardly grasping man's innermost essence that the soul related to the world not in the half-conscious way of the Egyptian world-picture or in the way that we have described it for the Graeco-Latin world-picture but that it broke free from the world-picture in order to develop within itself what had to become the strongest part of its nature, the ego, the consciousness soul. Thus in successive earthly lives the favourable opportunity has gradually arisen for man to develop the sentient soul, the intellectual or mind soul and the consciousness soul in successive earthly cultures.

But now let us look at this legacy of the nineteenth century, this consciousness soul: it has struggled—we can discern this as a basic feature especially of the nineteenth century—struggled in the philosophy of a Fichte, in subsequent philosophical statements and propositions, it has struggled even in the case of the more materialistic philosophies, for example of a Feuerbach,[170] who said: The idea of God is only man's portrayal of himself projected into space.

Man placed the idea of God outside himself because he needed to find security in the solitude of his consciousness soul. And if one follows the most radical philosophers such as Feuerbach and culminating in Nietzsche, one sees the human soul seeking its sovereignty and inner certainty once it has wrested itself free from the world-picture that has become objective. Through this process we see the human soul develop in a wholly regular way what arrived at its culmination in the nineteenth century: the emancipation of the consciousness soul and its inner grasping of itself through its own power.

What is to predominate in a future age is already being prepared at an earlier time. One can verify quite precisely how the development of the intellectual or mind soul plays into certain cultural phenomena of the Egypto-Chaldaean Age; and one can see in the Graeco-Latin Age—especially in its Christian phase, for example in Augustine—how mankind is struggling to prepare the consciousness soul. We must therefore say that our human soul only rightly takes hold of itself when in the midst of the age of the consciousness soul it prepares what is to unfold after the consciousness soul. What must this be?

The inner evolution of the human soul presses towards what must be developed, as does the so-called objective world-picture itself. We shall conclude by considering several symptoms of this. What has the nineteenth century, with its brilliant culture, brought about? Let us look at one of the most brilliant scientists of the nineteenth century, Du Bois-Reymond,[171] with his objective world-picture. As one may read in his *Concerning the Limits of a Knowledge of Nature*, he wants to rescue for the human soul what it needs for its inner security; and he tries to deal with this by means of the idea of the 'world soul', because this consciousness soul that has become solitary and set apart from the objective world-picture is inexplicable to him. But the objective world-picture stands in his way. The human soul makes its experience manifest in the brain, in the nerve fibres and other instruments. Now Du Bois-Reymond stands at the frontier of a knowledge of nature. What does he demand if he is to acknowledge a world-soul? He demands that one shows him an instrument also in the universe comparable to what exists within man when the human soul thinks, feels and wills. He says something of this kind: Show me a convolution of ganglia and nerves embedded in the nervous system and nurtured with warm arterial blood under the correct pressure appropriate for the heightened capacity of a world-soul. This he does not find. The same Du Bois-Reymond demands this who in the same address said among other things: When one observes someone when he is asleep from going to sleep to waking up, he can be explained scientifically; but when one observes someone between waking up and going to sleep, together with all the impulses, desires and passions, the ideas, feelings and will-impulses that flood around him and within him, he can never be explained through a scientific mode of thought.

He is right! But let us trace where the legacy of the nineteenth century has led us here. Du Bois-Reymond says: When I observe a sleeping human body scientifically, I can find nothing that makes the interplay of those forces that are engaged in ideas, feelings and will-impulses explicable to me. For it is illogical to want to look for an explanation for the inner nature of soul-phenomena in bodily processes, just as it would be meaningless if one were to seek an explanation for the organ of the lungs from the inner nature of air.

This will be the legacy of the nineteenth century, that natural science will show that if it stands strictly on its own ground, it *cannot* explain the involvement of the soul-spiritual domain within man. Rather must it say: When this human body has awakened from sleep, the realm of soul and spirit is something that it breathes in, just as the lungs breathe in oxygen or the air; and when it goes to sleep the soul-spiritual dimension is something that it breathes out, as it were. In the state of sleep the soul and spirit constitute a wholly independent entity outside the human body.

The legacy of the nineteenth century will be that natural science will be fully united with a spiritual science which says: Man has an ego and an astral body, with which he leaves his physical and etheric body in sleep, is during sleep in a purely spiritual world with his ego and astral body and gives the physical and etheric body over to their own laws. Thus natural science will itself mark out its territory, and through what it has to give it will show how spiritual science must be added to it as a completion. And if natural science will have a right knowledge of itself, as for example belongs to its greatest achievements (as with the natural evolution of organisms from the most imperfect to more perfect states), it will see that precisely in this evolution of natural phenomena in the sense of the Darwinian theory there is something in which the evolution of the human soul is not contained but which must first be grasped by the soul and spirit if the purely earthly aspect is to be welded into the totality of man's being. It is precisely a rightly understood natural science that will be a wonderful legacy of the nineteenth century, in that it will show how spiritual science is necessary for the completion of natural science. Then as a necessary consequence there will be complete harmony between these two. And the human soul will come to understand itself, in that it awakens the forces that slumber within it and comes to know itself. How?

In the Egypto-Chaldaean Age people were still in connection with the cosmos, which made manifest to human beings their spiritual background. In the Graeco-Latin Age man was still indirectly connected with the cosmos through his body. He still felt the cosmos, because he felt the unity between the soul-spiritual realm and the body. Now the objective world-picture has become merely a sum of outward processes. Through spiritual science, however, in that the soul finds itself in its own spiritual depths it will come to recognize itself as being connected in a new way with the universe. The soul will be able to say: When I look about me, I feel myself connected with all living things, with all kingdoms of nature that are around me. But now that I have passed through the culture of the sentient soul of the Egypto-Chaldaean Age, through the culture of the intellectual or mind soul of the Graeco-Latin Age and after I have taken up the culture of the consciousness soul, in which the attention of the ego has been directed towards material culture, I feel myself linked to a sequence of spiritual realms: downwards to the realms of animals, plants and minerals if I look out in a material sense, upwards to the realms of the spiritual hierarchies, to which the soul belongs no less than it is accustomed to see its affinity to the kingdoms of nature. A perspective of the future opens up to the soul which is fully linked to perspectives of the past. Man has undergone a process of development from the spiritual connections of the past; he will in the future work his way into the spiritual realms. The soul will feel itself drawn towards a connection with the kingdoms of nature through its soul-spiritual forces, and it will feel itself to have a connection with the spiritual realms through the Spirit-self. For just as our age is characterized as the time of the development of the consciousness soul, so for the future of human spiritual culture preparations are being made in our time for the development of the Spirit-self, which will gradually come to maturity.

If we view evolution in a spiritual-scientific way, we see it as an organic necessity that this legacy of the nineteenth century should most characteristically bring to expression the task of referring the soul back to itself, of casting it out from its natural environment, in order to compel it to develop its own soul-spiritual forces. And it will be the best legacy of the nineteenth century if the soul will behold itself as separate from everything, while therefore feeling all the more inspired to unfold its own forces. While the Age of Enlightenment has wanted to make use of its own powers of reason, the coming time must draw forth from their slumber in the depths of the soul the still deeper forces through which the perception of a spiritual world that the soul must achieve in the future will come about.

Thus the future will come to be grateful to the nineteenth century that it has placed the soul in the situation where it has the possibility of developing out of itself the higher forces of objective knowledge. This is also a legacy of the nineteenth century. If one considers the inner evolution of the human soul, it must proceed from the unfolding of the sentient soul through that of the intellectual or mind soul and that of the consciousness soul to the development of the Spirit-self. But man will only find the Spirit-self if, through the natural-scientific way of looking at things that is the legacy of the nineteenth century, he has first been separated from all aspects of the outer world.

When one views the legacy of the nineteenth century and then enters further into the details, one will see that the best of the positive results of the scientific legacy of the nineteenth century is the strengthening of the soul, because it then finds itself in what this science is unable to give it. The soul will come to feel with

Du Bois-Reymond: Yes, the sleeping human body can be explained with the laws of physiology, but not what is breathed into it in the form of the soul and spirit. The soul will feel that it must through spiritual-scientific methods raise to consciousness what is bereft of consciousness in sleep, in order to have a perspective of the spiritual worlds. And then, a later Du Bois-Reymond will no longer stand there baffled when he wants to explain the human body scientifically, for he will say to himself: The human soul is not to be found in the nervous system and the ganglia; so why should I demonstrate the presence of nervous systems and ganglia in the giant world-soul?

An outstanding figure of the nineteenth century who only wanted to use what the nineteenth century could give him for a knowledge of the origins of existence, namely Otto Liebmann,[172] who for a long time lectured in philosophy in Jena, expressed the following thought: Why should one not be able to accept that our planets, moons and fixed stars are the atoms or also the molecules of a giant brain which is spread out in the universe in a macrocosmic way? However, he thinks that the human intelligence will never be able to gain access to this giant brain, and that therefore it will also be denied the possibility of acquiring knowledge of a spiritual world-soul. Spiritual science, however, shows that Otto Liebmann is perfectly right; for that intelligence of which he speaks will never be able to succeed in satisfying human longings in this realm. Because this intelligence has initially become great through emancipating itself from the objective world-picture, it should not be a matter of surprise but, rather, regarded as quite natural that a philosophy founded upon this objective world-picture cannot find anything by way of a world-soul. If a scientist such as Du Bois-Reymond is unable to find the world-soul in the ganglia and nervous system of a sleeping human being, why should something of the nature of the world-soul be found in the giant ganglia of a giant brain? No wonder the physiologist has to despair of doing so!

But these foundations are the best legacy of the nineteenth century. They show that the human soul has been led back to itself and must seek and find the connection with the spiritual worlds not through observation but through the development of its inner forces. If the human mind considers that world-picture which it knows as the Darwinist theory of evolution, it will find that the greatness of this theory rests on the fact that it (the human mind) has taken itself out of it. Man would not have arrived in his evolution at the point where he has come if he had not taken himself out of the world-picture. When he understands this, he will understand that he cannot find in this theory of evolution what he first had himself to take out. If one rightly understands Darwin's theory of evolution, one will find that it is not in contradiction with it to believe the spirit-researcher when, as he looks behind sense-perceptible phenomena, he beholds a spirit in which the human soul is rooted as a spirit.

So this concluding lecture is intended to show that there is in truth not the slightest contradiction between what is here meant as spiritual science and the true, genuine achievements of natural science, and that if one rightly enters into what the world-picture of natural science had to become in accordance with the course of human evolution which spiritual science has identified, one knows that this cannot be otherwise, and that, because it has become what it is, the natural-scientific world-picture is the most perfect means of education for what it—the human soul—is to become: an essence that from the consciousness soul is aspiring towards the Spirit-self.

With this, spiritual science is being referred to as that which belongs today to the culture of our time. What has been prepared in the Egypto-Chaldaean Age with the culture of the sentient soul, what was further developed in the Graeco-Latin Age through the culture of the intellectual or mind soul, has found its further unfolding in our time in the culture of the consciousness soul. But everything that comes later has been prepared previously. So just as it can be said that a culture of the consciousness soul, which still has long to last in our time, already existed in Socrates and Aristotle, so must it already be the case that here, within our own age, there can be the source for a true teaching of the Spirit-self. This is how the human soul may understand itself in connection with those worlds in which it, as a spirit in the spirit-world, is rooted.

In addition to everything else that it represents, the natural science of the nineteenth century is a means of education, and the best means of education for spiritual science. From these winter lectures it may perhaps emerge that, from the spiritual-scientific views that have been presented here about the legacy of the nineteenth century, a sure foundation will be found for spiritual science, which should not become a conglomeration or chaos of something arbitrary but something that rests on just as secure a foundation as the natural science that is so admired. If one believes that there must necessarily be a break between what natural science is and has made possible and spiritual science, one would be mistaken about this spiritual science. If, however, one sees how natural science had to become entirely what it has indeed become so that the human soul finds the path to the spirit in the new way that it must find it, one will recognize it as that which must necessarily be placed within evolution as something that has within it the seeds for that period that will follow ours in the same way that our present period follows on from the previous one. Then the apparent conflicts between the natural-scientific and the spiritual-scientific world-pictures will be reconciled.

Of course I do not even remotely believe that in the brief time of this lecture—which has lasted so long—I shall have been able to say more than a very little of what can be discerned from spiritual science about the continuing significance of the natural-scientific path of the nineteenth century in all its many forms. But perhaps through the extension of what has been presented in the souls of the esteemed listeners, through following up what has been indicated today especially by comparing spiritual-scientific results with the rightly understood results of natural science, it will be seen that the necessity of an involvement on the part of spiritual science in the future of human evolution is a clear conclusion from a spiritually oriented study of the evolution of mankind. These lectures were formed from, and their basic tone always informed by, this awareness of an inner evolutionary necessity. This lecture in particular has sought to evoke the feeling that it may appear justified that the mere confidence that figures such as Fichte wanted to gain from the consciousness soul cannot be achieved out of the consciousness soul as such that lives enclosed within their thoughts but, rather, when the soul sees and recognizes that it finds something in itself quite other than its mere intelligence and reason: when it finds within itself the forces that lead to Imagination, Inspiration and Intuition, that is, to life in the spiritual world itself, and when it realizes that this may—through the rightly understood legacy of the nineteenth century—again be spoken about out of a truly inward certainty also in the first third of the twentieth century.

Hegel,[173] boldly building upon what he believed he had understood purely out of the consciousness soul, once spoke some significant words in his lectures about the history of philosophy; and we may conclude with a paraphrase of what he said in order to characterize not so much a conceptual summary but, rather, a feeling that arises like an elixir of life from spiritual-scientific observations. We shall with some changes bring to expression in Hegel's words what the soul can experience for its sense of certainty by way of resources necessary for existence and for its life's work, what it can experience with respect to the great riddles of existence, concerning destiny and immortality. All this is so that the soul is met with the right cosmic light when it—though now not out of an indefinite and abstract quality of the consciousness soul but out of a knowledge that cognitive forces slumber in the soul that make it a citizen of spiritual worlds—when it is wholly pervaded with a feeling such that this feeling becomes the direct expression of the spiritual science that is intended, which makes the soul sure in itself and full of hope:

The human spirit may and should believe in its greatness and in its power; for it is a spirit from the spirit. And with this belief there can be nothing in the universe, in the totality of existence, that is so hard and impenetrable that it should not be made manifest to it in the course of time, in so far as it has a need for it. What was initially held in hidden secrecy in the universe must become ever more manifest and become available to the seeking soul as its knowledge increases, in order that it can develop it to an inner power, to inner certainty, to the inner valuing of existence and life.

Notes

These lectures were taken down in shorthand by Walter Vegelahn and also transcribed by him. This transcription forms the basis for the German text from which this translation has been made. There are places in the text where there are gaps or the meaning is unclear; however, the original shorthand records have not been preserved. For the second German edition of 1988 this volume of the Collected Works of Rudolf Steiner, which was originally published in 1960, was revised by David Hoffmann and provided with additional notes and summaries of the content of the lectures. The lectures had previously been published as a series of single lectures in 1941 and 1942.

The titles of the individual lectures are as given by Rudolf Steiner. The title of the volume was chosen by the editors.

Only three of the lectures have previously been published in English translation: those of 9 January 1913, *Jacob Boehme*, Anthroposophic Press, New York and Rudolf Steiner Publishing Company, London, 6 February 1913 (in *The Poetry and Meaning of Fairy Tales,* Mercury Press 1989) and 6 March 1913, *Errors in Spiritual Research*, Mercury Press 1983). Translations of three other lectures, those of 30 January 1913, 13 February 1913 and 3 April 1913, exist in typescript form. lectures 1–6, 8 and 14 have not previously been translated.

1 Life-force, life-principle *'vis vitalis'*: the specific, inner cause—universally accepted since Aristotle until the middle of the nineteenth century—of life-functions, an unconsciously working, organizing and regulatory force. This view was called vitalism. The 'neo-vitalism' of the eighteenth and nineteenth centuries to some extent took into account the results of 'mechano-chemical biology'. Those who came to oppose the idea of a life-force in the nineteenth century were the representatives of mechano-chemical science and materialistic philosophy such as Jakob Moleschott, Karl Vogt, Wilhelm Wundt, Ernst Haeckel, Wilhelm Preyer, David Friedrich Strauss, Emil Du Bois-Reymond and Wilhelm Ostwald, who formulated criticism regarding the life-force in the following words: 'An organism is essentially a complex of chemical energies'. (*Vorlesungen über Naturphilosophie*, second edition 1903, p. 317, 319.)

2 Justus von Liebig (1803—1873), groundbreaking German chemist. His research together with Wöhler laid the foundations for organic chemistry.

3 Friedrich Wöhler (1800—1882), chemist and doctor. In 1828 he became the first person to manufacture urea artificially.

4 Self-renewal of the organism: see, for example, Max Verworn, *Die Mechanik des Geisteslebens*, Leipzig 1910, p. 85. There is a discrepancy between '*Selbststeuerung*' (rendered here as 'self-regulation') in the text and '*Selbsterneuerung*' (self-renewal') in the note which I have tried to overcome by using both words. (Translator)

5 Emil Du Bois-Reymond, *Über die Grenzen des Naturerkennens*, Leipzig 1872, and *Die sieben Welträtsel*, Leipzig 1882.

6 The source of this reference has not been found.

7 Moritz Benedikt, *Die Seelenkunde des Menschen als reine Erfahrungswissenschaft*, Leipzig 1895, p. 35.

8 Probably Anselm Feuerbach (1829—1880), a painter who was famous in the nineteenth century. He was the grandson of the lawyer Anselm Feuerbach and the nephew of the philosopher Ludwig Feuerbach.

9 Jean Reynaud, *Philosophie religieuse, Terre et Ciel*, Paris 1854.

10 Louis Figuier, *Le lendemain de la mort, ou la vie future selon la science*, Paris 1871.

11 See, for example, Friedrich Schlegel, *Philosophie der Geschichte*, in eighteen lectures held in Vienna in 1828, volume one, Vienna 1829, p. 150f. (fourth lecture).

12 Jacob Frohschammer, *Die Philosophie des Thomas von Aquino, kritisch gewürdigt*, Leipzig 1889, p. 418f.

13 Eduard von Hartmann, *Die Philosophie des Unbewussten*, Berlin 1869.

14 *Das Unbewusste vom Standpunkt der Deszendenztheorie, Eine kritische Beleuchtung des naturphilosophischen Teils der Philosophie des Unbewussten aus naturwissenschaftlichen Gesichtspunkten* ('a critical study of the part of *The Philosophy of the Unconscious* relating to the philosophy of nature from a natural-scientific standpoint'), Berlin 1872. The second edition, this time with Eduard von Hartmann's name as the author, appeared in 1877.

15 In his essay *Die naturwissenschaftlichen Grundlagen der Philosophie des Unbewussten* (Leipzig 1877) Schmidt criticizes Eduard von Hartmann and praises the anonymous essay (see the previous note), which—he says—'has fully confirmed those who have not sworn allegiance to the unconscious in their conviction that Darwinism is in the right' (p. 3).

16 *Faust*, Part 2, Act 5 (palace, midnight), line 11404

17 Etienne Geoffroy de Saint-Hilaire (1772—1844). The source of this reference has not been found.

18 Fichte's actual words are as follows: 'The kind of philosophy one chooses depends, therefore, on the kind of person one is, for a philosophical system is not a dead collection of household goods that one might cast off or accumulate at

one's whim but it is ensouled through the soul of the human being who possesses it' (first Introduction to the *Wissenschaftslehre*, 1797).

[19] The Italian doctor and naturalist Francesco Redi (1626—1697) demonstrated that, in a stagnant liquid, worms and maggots do not arise 'spontaneously' provided that one knows how to keep the insects away that otherwise lay their eggs in the liquid. From this he coined the principle '*Omne vivum ex vivo*'. (See *Osservazioni di Francesco Redi accademico della crusca. Intorno agli animali viventi che si trovano animali viventi*, Florence 1684.) See also Rudolf Steiner's observations in this connection in the lecture of 5 December 1912 in the present volume.

At a later time the chemist Louis Pasteur (1822—1895) expressed his disagreement with the theory of so-called 'spontaneous generation' on the basis of his studies of the fermentation process and the yeast bacteria active within it. See his article *Nouvel exemple de fermentation determineé par des animacules infusoires pouvant vivre sans oxygène libre*, 1863.

See in this connection Rudolf Steiner, 'Reincarnation and Karma—Some Necessary Ideas from the Standpoint of Modern Science' (GA 34, p. 67 Ger.), first published in the journal *Lucifer-Gnosis*.

[20] See Charles Darwin, *The Expression of the Emotions in Man and Animals*, first published in November, 1872, Chapter 2, 'General Principles of Expression'.

[21] An article by Fritz Mauthner entitled 'Die Theosophen', in *Berliner Tageblatt*, no. 562, 3 November 1912.

[22] Motto for a prize-essay entitled 'Über die Grundlage der Moral' in Arthur Schopenhauer, *Sämtliche Werke in zwölf Bänden*, with an Introduction by Rudolf Steiner, Stuttgart and Berlin 1894, vol. 7, p. 133.

[23] A scene that represents events which happen several years after the time of 'The Portal of Initiation' (1910), in *Four Mystery Plays* (GA 14), first scene, 'A library and study belonging to Capesius'.

[24] From *Die Anweisung zum seligen Leben*, 1806, second lecture.

[25] Ibid.

[26] See note 23.

[27] In his writings *Mysterium cosmographicum* (1596) and *Harmonices mundi libri VI* (1619).

[28] Herman Grimm, *Goethe, lectures*, two vols., Berlin 1877, vol. 2, 23rd lecture.

[29] 'What is the point of the whole extravagance of suns and planets and moons, of stars and Milky Ways, of comets and dust particles, of worlds already existing and in the becoming, if a fortunate human being should not in the end unconsciously rejoice in his existence?' *Winckelmann und sein Jahrhundert*, the section entitled 'Antikes'.

[30] Wilhelm Wundt (1832—1920), physiologist, psychologist and philosopher. *System der Philosophie*, Leipzig 1889, third edition in two volumes 1907.

31 Charles Darwin, *On the Origin of Species by Means of Natural Selection*, 1859.

32 John Emerich Edward Dalberg, Lord Acton (1834—1902), 'Inaugural Lecture on the Study of History', given on the occasion of his taking up his post as Regius Professor of Modern History at the University of Cambridge, 11 June 1895: 'But I hope that even this narrow and disedifying section of history will aid you to see that the action of Christ who is risen on mankind whom he redeemed fails not but increase; that the wisdom of divine rule appears not in the perfection but in the improvement of the world; and that achieved liberty is the one ethical result that rests on the converging and combined conditions of advancing civilisation.'

33 The source of this reference has not been found.

34 Goethe, 'Prose Maxims', in *Naturwissenschaftliche Schriften*, edited with a commentary by Rudolf Steiner in Kürschner's *Deutsche-National-Literatur* (1883—1897), 5 vols., Dornach 1975, GA 1e, p. 368. See also Goethe, *Maximen und Reflexionen.*

35 *Die Kunst im Zusammenhange der Kulturentwicklung und die Ideale der Menschheit*, 5 vols., Leipzig 1863—74.

36 Zeuner's letter and manuscript are printed in Moritz Carrière, *Religiöse Faden und Betrachtungen für das deutsche Volk*, Leipzig 1894, p. 152—172, under the title 'Christus in der Weltgeschichte. Kerkergedanken eines deutschen Republikaners'. (Carl Zeuner, born 1813 at Butzbach in the Wetterau, died in advanced years in Cincinnati, America.)

37 Saint George Mivart, *Man and Apes*, London 1873.

38 Alfred Russel Wallace (1822—1913), colleague and friend of Darwin.

39 Gotthold Ephraim Lessing (1729—81), *Die Erziehung des Menschengeschlechts* (1780), sections 91—100.

40 See Lecture 8 in this volume together with the relevant notes.

41 Jacob Frohschammer, *Die Phantasie als Grundprinzip des Weltprozesses*, Munich 1877.

42 *Zur Kritik der Zeit* by Walther Rathenau, Berlin 1912, p. 148—150.

43 Charles William Eliot, 'The Religion of the Future'. A lecture delivered at the close of the eleventh session of the Harvard Summer School of Theology, 22 July 1909, in *The Durable Satisfaction of Life*, New York 1910, p. 172.

44 In Rudolf Steiner's library there is a copy of the following book which describes this experience of Galileo: Laurenz Müllner, *Die Bedeutung Galileis für die Philosophie*, inaugural address given on 8 November 1894 in Vienna, published independently by the K.K. University of Vienna 1894, p. 39f. The relevant passage may be cited here: 'When the anatomist [Galileo] showed how the main bundle of nerve fibres issuing from the brain runs along the neck, extends through the spinal cord and branches out throughout the body, and how only a delicate weft of connecting threads reaches the heart, he turned to a nobleman who was known to him as a

peripatetic and for whose sake he had with great care revealed and demonstrated everything, with the question whether he was now satisfied and was convinced that nerves originate in the brain and not in the heart. Whereupon our philosopher, having stood there for a while in thought, explained: You have shown me so clearly and strikingly that—contrary to Aristotle, who clearly says that the nerves have their origin in the heart—one is compelled to concede that you are right.'

45 See note 19, and the lecture of 5 December 1912 in the present volume.

46 See *De l'infinito universo et mundi* (1584).

47 *Arthur Schopenhauers sämtliche Werke in zwölf Bänden* (Arthur Schopenhauer's Collected Works in twelve volumes, edited with an Introduction by Rudolf Steiner, Stuttgart and Berlin, no date). (Schopenhauer lived from 1788 to 1860.)

48 In Schopenhauer's words: '"The world is my mental picture"—this is a truth that applies in relation to every living and cognizing being'. See *Die Welt als Wille und Vorstellung*, I, section 1.

49 Goethe, 'Zahme Xenien', III. Goethe includes this verse in the didactic Introduction to his *Zur Farbenlehre* ('On the Theory of Colour'). See GA 1c, p. 88 (ref. note 34).

50 The reference is to the pre-Socratic philosopher Empedocles (c. 492—432 BC). See Diels/Kranz, *Fragmente der Vorsokratiker*, fragment 31 B 109.

51 See the Introduction to his treatise *Über das Sehn und die Farben* ('Regarding Seeing and Colours'). Schopenhauer explains 'that the colours with which objects appear to be clothed are only in the eye' and in another context: 'But then how the Sun needs an eye in order to shine, music an ear in order to sound...' (*Palerga und Paralipomena*, vol. 2, ch. 20, section 240). See also note 48.

52 See *Das Wesen des Christentums* ('The Nature of Christianity'), Leipzig 1841, first chapter and appendix, first section. Also *Das Wesen der Religion*, 1851, 20th lecture.

53 *Psychologie vom empirischen Standpunkte*, Leipzig 1874, vol. 1, p. 21f.

54 Thomas Henry Huxley (1825—95), *Lessons in Elementary Physiology*, London 1866, Lecture 1.

55 *Hamlet*, Act 5, Scene 1.

56 See note 19.

57 'Every age of man has a certain philosophy answering to it. ...Yet when he grows old he will always acknowledge himself as a mystic; he sees that so much seems to depend on chance; that folly succeeds and wisdom fails; that good and ill fortune are brought unexpectedly to the same level. So it is and so it has been, and old age acquiesces in that which is and was and will be' (Goethe, 'Prose Maxims', see note 33; also included in his *Maxims and Reflections*). Friedrich Förster recalled a conversation with Goethe in connection with *Faust* (probably

in 1828): 'I only recall that when I expressed the supposition that the final scene would probably be set in heaven and Mephisto would be acknowledged by the audience as overcome, "that a good person is doubtless aware in his heart of the right path", Goethe said shaking his head: "That would indeed be a revelation. Faust ends as an old man, and when we are old we become mystics".' From *Goethes Gespräche*, based on the edition by Flodoard von Biedermann, edited by Wolfgang Herwig, vol. III/2, Zurich 1972, p. 295 (conversation no. 6187).

58 See the first two lectures in this volume.

59 In the lectures given in the Architektenhaus in Berlin during the winter of 1913/14, assembled in GA 63, especially Lectures 4, 5, 7 and 10.

60 By John Tyndall (1820—93), an Irish physicist. The book concerned was first published in London in 1863.

61 Head teacher or principal of the *Realschule* (secondary school) in Wiener Neustadt, Lower Austria (1868—1874), regional school inspector, specialist mathematics teacher. Cf. Rudolf Steiner's description in Chapter 2 of his autobiography, *The Course of My Life* (GA 28). His paper entitled *Die Anziehungskraft betrachtet als eine Wirkung der Bewegung* ('Attraction considered as an Effect of Motion') was published in Vienna in 1873, and he wrote a book that he had previously published under the title *Die allgemeine Bewegung der Materie als Grundursache aller Naturerscheinungen* ('The General Motion of Matter as the Fundamental Cause of all the Phenomena of Nature'), Vienna 1872.

62 Matthias Jakob Schleiden, *Die Pflanze und ihr Leben*, 1848. Theodor Schwann, *Mikroskopische Untersuchungen über die Übereinstimmung in der Struktur und dem Wachstum von Tier und Pflanze*, Berlin 1839.

63 See Ernst Haeckel, *Natürliche Schöpfungsgeschichte* ('The Story of Creation'), described by the author as generally comprehensible scientific lectures about the theory of evolution, two parts, Berlin 1868; and *Anthropogenie oder Entwickelungsgeschichte des Menschen* ('Anthropogenesis or an Evolutionary History of Man'), two parts, Leipzig 1874.

64 *Grundzüge der vergleichenden Anatomie* ('Principles of Comparative Anatomy'), Leipzig 1859, second edition, Leipzig 1870, p. 18f.

65 See note 31.

66 Hermann Ludwig Ferdinand von Helmholtz (1821—1894), outstanding scientific researcher. In 1850 he invented the ophthalmoscope and summarized his considerable research about the eye and vision in his *Handbuch der physiologischen Optik* ('Handbook of physiological optics'), Leipzig 1856—66. He presented his physiological studies of the ear and hearing in his book *Die Lehre von den Tonempfindungen* ('The science of tonal sensations'), Braunschweig/Brunswick 1862.

67 *Psychologie vom empirischen Standpunkte*, vol. 1, Leipzig 1874. (Brentano died in 1917.)

68 Alfred Percy Sinnett, *Esoteric Buddhism*, 1883.

69 Helena Petrovna Blavatsky (1831—91), *The Secret Doctrine. The Synthesis of Science, Religion and Philosophy*, 3 volumes, London 1888.

70 Rudolf Steiner took issue with Paul Deußen (1845—1919), because in his *Allgemeine Geschichte der Philosophie* ('General History of Philosophy') in 7 volumes (1894—1917) he already treats Indian wisdom as philosophy, whereas according to Steiner philosophy as such begins only with Aristotle and all earlier thinking must be referred to as seership. Cf. the explanations given in lectures held in Berlin on 14 March 1908 (GA 108) and on 8 January 1914 (GA 63).

71 See note 67.

72 The source of this reference has not been identified.

73 William Harvey (1578—1657), *De motu cordis et sanguinis* (1628).

74 Marcello Malpighi (1628—1694) supplemented Harvey's discoveries of the circulation of the blood through his microscopic studies.

75 See note 19 and Rudolf Steiner's observations in the lecture of 5 December 1912 in this volume.

76 Galileo, who in his intellectual freedom preferred to trust his own observations and insights rather than the opinions that had been handed down to him, opposed Aristotle's views on physics, astronomy, anatomy etc., which earned him the bitter enmity of orthodox, dogmatic philosophers (cf. Rudolf Steiner's remarks in the lecture of 14 November 1912 in this volume). In 1633 the Inquisition forced Galileo to retract the most heretical of his views, the knowledge of the heliocentric nature of the solar system.

Through his intrepid advocacy of what he recognized as true and through his criticism of Aristotle's teachings about nature and his cosmology, Giordano Bruno drew upon himself the hatred of the Church. Since, unlike Galileo, he was not prepared to retract his views, he was burnt in Rome as a heretic in 1600.

77 See the first lecture in this volume.

78 See Lecture 1.

79 Goethe, 'Anschauende Urteilskraft', *Naturwissenschaftliche Schriften* ('Writings on Natural Science'), see note 34.

80 Immanuel Kant, *Kritik der Urteilskraft* ('Critique of Judgement'), part 2, 'Kritik der teleologischen Urteilskraft', appendix, section 80, the note appended to this.

81 See the paradox about movement of Zeno of Elea (c. 490—c. 430 BC).

82 Goethe, *Zahme Xenien*, III.

83 See Boehme's biography: 'Herrn Abraham von Franckenberg, auf Ludwigsdorf, eines gottseligen Schlesischen von Adel und vertrauten Freundes des sel. Autoris gründlicher

und wahrhafter Bericht von dem Leben und Abschied des in Gott selig ruhenden Jakob Böhme, dieser theosophischen Schriften eigentlichen Autoris und Schreibers' ('A true and accurate report of the life and death of the blessed Jacob Boehme, author of these theosophical writings, by Herr Abraham von Franckenberg at Ludwigsdorf, a devout and noble Silesian and faithful friend of the blessed author'), included in *Schriften Jakob Böhmes* ('Writings of Jacob Boehme'), selected and edited by Hans Kayser, with the biography of Boehme by Abraham von Franckenberg and the short extract by Friedrich Christoph Oetinger, Leipzig 1920, p. 20f. (section 4).

84 *Aurora or Dawn in the Ascendant*, Chapter 23, verses 1—6. First English edition 1656, with the title *Aurora, that is the Day-Spring.*

85 See, for example, his *Mysterium Magnum or an Explanation of the Book of Genesis*, ch. 3, 'How from the Eternal Good an Evil has come into being, which in Good has no Proclivity towards Evil; and of the Origin of the Dark World wherein the Devils dwell', and ch. 4, 'Of the Two Principles, as of God's Love and Anger, of Darkness and of Light, which are very necessary for the Reader to consider', and ch. 8, 'Of the Creation of the Angels and their Regiment' and ch. 9, 'Of the Fall of Lucifer with his Legions'.

86 *Theosophical Questions, or 177 Questions of Divine Revelation*, the third question and answer.

87 Wem Zeit wie Ewigkeit,
und Ewigkeit wie Zeit,
der ist befreit
von allem Streit.

In an earlier translation by Margaret W. Barnetson, these lines are rendered as follows:

To whom time is like eternity
And eternity like time,
He is freed from all strife.

Jacob Boehme had the habit of writing lines of poetry in the family-albums of good friends. See Abraham von Franckenberg's biography of him referred to in note 83.

88 This was the name given to Boehme by the much-travelled doctor and linguist Dr Balthasar Walther von Großlogau from Silesia. See Abraham von Franckenberg's biography cited in note 83.

89 Abraham Calov, *Antiboehmius*, Vitebergae 1684.

90 The following passage is paraphrased from Adolf von Harles, *Jacob Böhme und die Alchymisten. Ein Beitrag zum Verständnis J. Böhmes*, second enlarged edition, Leipzig 1882, p. 113.

[91] Louis Claude de Saint-Martin (1743—1803) learnt German in his 50th year in order to be able to translate Boehme's writings into French. Matthias Claudius for his part translated a book by Saint-Martin from French into German, *Des erreurs et de la vérité* ('Of Errors and Truth, or a Retrospective Examination for Human Beings of the General Principle of All Knowledge'), Breslau 1782.

[92] Wilhelm Grimm (1786—1859) and his brother Jacob Grimm (1785—1863) are considered to be the founders of German philology and early historical studies. They were tireless collectors of gleanings from the linguistic heritage of Germany and also editors, and were the authors or compilers of the *German Dictionary* (1854—1954), the *German Grammar*, *German Legends*, *German Mythology*, *German Legal Antiquities*, *Aspects of German Wisdom*, the famous *Children's and Household Tales* etc.

[93] In 1837 seven Göttingen professors had protested against the abolition of the constitution by King Ernst August, whereupon they were dismissed: Wilhelm Eduard Albrecht, Friedrich Christoph Dahlmann, Georg Heinrich August Ewald, Georg Gottfried Gervinus, Jakob Grimm, Wilhelm Grimm, Wilhelm Eduard Weber.

[94] These were given in 1874 and 1875 and were published in two volumes, Berlin 1876.

[95] Herman Grimm, *Homers Iliad*, two vols., Berlin 1890/95.

[96] See Herman Grimm, *Fragmente*, vol. 2, Berlin and Stuttgart 1902, p. 175.

[97] Ernest Renan (1823—1892) left the Catholic seminary and after a journey to Palestine wrote his famous work *La vie de Jésus* (Paris 1863).

[98] Painted in 1504, Milan, Pinacoteca Breva.

[99] Herman Grimm, *Fragmente*, two vols., Berlin and Stuttgart 1900/02.

[100] Herman Grimm, *Das Leben Raphaels*, Berlin 1872, *Leben Michelangelos*, Berlin 1860/63.

[101] See 'Raphael als Weltmacht' ('Raphael as a World Power'), in *Fragmente*, vol. 2, Berlin and Stuttgart 1902, p. 153.

[102] Ibid., p. 171.

[103] Herman Grimm, Novellen 1862; third enlarged edition, Berlin 1897.

[104] 1867; third edition in two volumes, Berlin 1902.

[105] Ibid., vol.2, p. 399—401.

[106] See 'Heinrich von Treitschkes Politik', in *Fragmente*, vol. 2, Berlin and Stuttgart 1902, p. 269.

[107] Herman Grimm, *Das Leben Raphaels*; the first edition of 1872 was fully revised in 1886 and 1896. The quotations cited in this lecture are taken from the 4th edition, Stuttgart and Berlin 1903.

[108] In *Wilhelm Meisters Wanderjahre*, Part one, 10.

[109] The title of a philosophical book by Lessing which appeared in 1780.

[110] Rudolf Steiner demonstrated this in his 13 slide-lectures in Dornach, 8—29 October 1916. See *Kunstgeschichte als Abbild innerer geistiger Impulse* ('Art History as an Image of Inner Spiritual Impulses'), GA 292, comprising a volume with the lectures and one with 700 illustrations.

[111] Aurelius Augustine (354—430) wrote his *Confessions* around the year 400.

[112] *The Entombment*, 1507, Rome, Galleria Borghese,
Camera della Segnatura, Rome, Vatican, Stanze,
The Transfiguration (1519—20), Rome, Vatican, Pinacoteca.

[113] This has to do with the entry into Perugia in 1495 of Astorre Baglione (died 1500). See Francesco Matarazzo, *Cronache della città di Perugia*, edite da Ariodante Fabretti, 2 vols., Turin 1888, p. 113, 115, 118, 121. See also Jacob Burckhardt, *Die Kultur der Renaissance in Italien. Ein Versuch* ('The Culture of the Renaissance in Italy', London 1878), ninth German edition revised by Ludwig Geiger, 2 vols., Leipzig 1904, vol. 1 p. 31: 'At that time Raphael was as a twelve-year-old boy being taught by Pietro Perugino. Perhaps some impressions of these days were immortalized in the early little paintings of St. George and St. Michael'.

[114] Painted 1504—5, St Petersburg, Hermitage. A second picture of St George by Raphael is in the Louvre, Paris.

[115] Girolamo Savonarola (1452—1498), Dominican, Prior of the monastery of San Marco in Florence, radical repentance-preacher and moralist who made political and religious enemies (including the Borgia Pope Alexander VI) and was hanged and burnt as a heretic, schismatic and despiser of the Holy See.

[116] Fra Bartolomeo (1475—1517) withdrew to the monastery of San Marco after Savonarola's execution.

[117] Duke Karl August to his friend Karl Ludwig von Knebel on14 October 1783. See Herman Grimm, *Fragmente*, vol. 2, Berlin and Stuttgart 1902, p. 167f.

[118] See the cycle of frescoes consisting of 28 pictures on the legend of St Francis in the upper church of San Francesco (around 1295) by Giotto di Bondone.

[119] Painted around 1514/16, Florence, Palazzo Pitti.

[120] 'A mother with her child is always the noblest thing that the world offers. The poorest mother could sit there as the Madonna della Sedia': *Das Leben Raphaels*, Berlin 1872.

[121] In his poem 'Warum gabst du uns die tiefen Blicke' Goethe uses the expression 'former times' when he speaks of his and Frau von Stein's previous earthly lives:
Ah, you were in former times
My sister or my wife.

[122] 'Natura non fecit saltus' was first stated by Fournier, *Varietés historiques et litteraires*, 1613, IX, 247, then by Leibniz, *Nouveaux essays sur l'entendement humain*, 1756, Foreword and IV, ch. 16 and Linnaeus, *Philosophia botanica*, 1751, no. 77.

[123] 1509—10, Rome, Vatican, Stanza della Segnatura.

[124] 1510—11, Rome, Vatican, Stanza della Segnatura.

[125] 1509—11, Rome, Vatican, Stanza della Segnatura.

[126] *Das Leben Raphaels*, p. 4.

[127] Ibid., p. 333f.

[128] The reference has not been found in this form, but see *Homers Ilias*, Berlin 1895, p. 381f.

[129] *Das Leben Raphaels*, p. 1.

[130] Ibid., p. 334.

[131] Goethe's *Fairy Tale* appeared in 1795 in Schiller's journal *Die Horen*. See Rudolf Steiner, *Goethe's Standard of the Soul as illustrated in 'Faust' and in the Fairy Story 'The Green Snake and the Beautiful Lily'* (1918), GA 22 and *Goethe's Secret Revelation,* Rudolf Steiner Publishing Co., London 1932.

[132] Tübingen, 1795.

[133] See note 92.

[134] Wilhelm Wundt, *Völkerpsychologie. Eine Untersuchung der Entwicklunsgesetze von Sprache, Mythus und Sitte*, 10 vols., Leipzig 1900f.

[135] This has not been identified.

[136] This has also not been identified.

[137] This fairy tale is entitled 'A Hundred with one Stroke' and can be found in German in *Ungarische Volksmärchen*, translated by G. Stier from the original text published from Georg Gaal's literary estate, Pest 1857, p. 106—113.

[138] This may possibly have been Ludwig Laistner (1848—1896).

[139] 'Über Leonardo da Vincis Abendmahl', a review of Joseph Bossi's book (1810) in *Kunst und Altertum*, I, 3, 1817.

[140] Matthew 26:21, Mark 14:18, Luke 22:21—22, John 13:21.

[141] See, for example, Goethe's memorandum entitled 'Erster Entwurf einer allgemeinen Einleitung in die vergleichende Anatomie, ausgehend von Osteologie' ('A First Outline of a General Introduction to Comparative Anatomy from the standpoint of Osteology'), VII, B, in: *Naturwissenschaftliche Schriften*, vol. I, GA 1a, p. 262.

[142] Moritz Benedict (1835—1920), a medical doctor. See *Aus meinem Leben*, Vienna 1906, p. 121f.

[143] See Lecture 4 in this volume.

[144] Maurice Maeterlinck (1862—1949), *La Mort*, Paris 1911. English translation published by Methuen, London 1913 under the title *Death*.

[145] Ibid., ch. 8 entitled 'Reincarnation'.

[146] In the Foreword to the first edition of *Die Welt als Wille und Vorstellung* (August 1818): 'Destiny, ...which is always an integral part of truth, to which only a brief festival of victory is granted between the two long periods when it is condemned as a paradox and belittled as trivial'. *Arthur Schopenhauers sämtliche Werke, mit Einleitung von Dr. Rudolf Steiner*, Stuttgart and Berlin 1894, vol. 2, p. 13.

[147] See his *Politics (The State)*, 379 a—d.

[148] In 'Skizze einer Geschichte der Lehre vom Idealen und Realen', in 'Parerga und Paralipomena', I, *Arthur Schopenhauers sämtliche Werke*, vol. 8, p. 26.

[149] See note 22.

[150] This was Lord Byron (1778—1824), of whom Herman Grimm writes in his essay 'Lord Byron und Leigh Hunt'. See Herman Grimm, *Fünfzehn Essays*, first series, third revised edition, Gütersloh 1884, p. 319—336. The event cited by Rudolf Steiner is on pages 330 to 332.

[151] See Lecture 4 in the present volume.

[152] See Schopenhauer's prize-essay 'Über die Grundlage der Moral' ('Concerning the Foundation of Morality'), in: *Arthur Schopenhauers sämtliche Werke, mit Einleitung von Dr. Rudolf Steiner*, Stuttgart and Berlin, 1894, vol. 7, p. 234.

[153] Ibid., p. 260.

[154] Euripedes, *Helena*, Act IV, Scene 1 (free rendering of four lines of a speech of Theone's).

[155] In his book *De L'infinito universe et mondi* (1584) Bruno criticizes the idea derived from Aristotle of eight finite spheres of the cosmos and postulates the infinity of the universe.

[156] *Die Bestimmung des Menschen*, 1800.

[157] See Karl Vorländer, *Immanuel Kants Leben*, supplementary volume to Immanuel Kant, Sämtliche Werke (Collected Works), Leipzig 1911, p. 68: 'He knew all Rousseau's works, his picture alone... adorned the otherwise bare walls of his study; and when *Emile* appeared in 1762 the unusual event occurred that, on reading it, our philosopher was prevented for several days in succession from taking his regular walk'.

[158] *Was ist Aufklärung?* 'Enlightenment is man's exit from his self-inflicted dependence... Have the courage to avail *yourself* of your *own* powers of reason!'

[159] Descartes formulated this proposition in *Discours de la méthode* (1637), I, 7 and 10 and (not in the same words) in *Meditationes de prima philosophia* (1641), 2nd meditation.

[160] See, for example, *Soliloquia*, II, 1 and *De trinitate*, X, 10, 14.

[161] Karl Rosenkranz, *Georg Wilhelm Friedrich Hegels Leben*, Berlin 1844, p. xii.

[162] Two of the lectures that Ralph Waldo Emerson (1803—82) gave in England about *Representative Men* (1847/48) appeared in German in a translation by Herman Grimm under the title *Ralph Waldo Emerson über Goethe und Shakespeare*, Hanover 1857. See also Herman Grimm, *Fünfzehn Essays*, first series, third improved and enlarged edition Gütersloh 1884, p. 426—448 (Essay XV, 'Ralph Waldo Emerson').

[163] See note 104.

[164] Herman Grimm, *Homers Ilias*, 2 vols., Berlin 1895, p. 399 (the concluding chapter, 'Abschied').

[165] Goethe's actual words were: 'Microscopes and telescopes actually confuse the pure human senses'. From *Sprüche in Prosa* ('Prose Maxims'), p. 351. Also in Goethe, *Maximen und Reflexionen.*

[166] Rudolf Steiner is referring here to the title of Lessing's book *Die Erziehung des Menschengeschlechts* ('The Education of the Human Race'), 1780.

[167] See Johannes Kepler, *Harmonices mundi,* Book IV, ch. 7.

[168] The source of this has not been found.

[169] Conversation of 11 April 1827.

[170] See note 52.

[171] See note 5.

[172] Otto Liebmann, *Gedanken und Tatsachen, Philosophische Abhandlungen, Aphorismen und Studien*, 2 vols., Straßburg 1882—1904, vol. 2, p. 284: '...eines transmakroskopischen Riesengehirns...'

[173] See the conclusion of the 'Foreword spoken in Heidelberg on 28 October 1816' to the 'Lectures on the History of Philosophy' in *Georg Wilhelm Friedrich Hegels Werke*, vol. 13, Berlin 1833, p. 5f.

Rudolf Steiner's Collected Works

The German Edition of Rudolf Steiner's Collected Works (the *Gesamtausgabe* [GA] published by Rudolf Steiner Verlag, Dornach, Switzerland) presently runs to 354 titles, organized either by type of work (written or spoken), chronology, audience (public or other), or subject (education, art, etc.). For ease of comparison, the Collected Works in English [CW] follows the German organization exactly. A complete listing of the CWs follows with literal translations of the German titles. Other than in the case of the books published in his lifetime, titles were rarely given by Rudolf Steiner himself, and were often provided by the editors of the German editions. The titles in English are not necessarily the same as the German; and, indeed, over the past 75 years have frequently been different, with the same book sometimes appearing under different titles.

For ease of identification and to avoid confusion, we suggest that readers looking for a title should do so by CW number. Because the work of creating the Collected Works of Rudolf Steiner is an ongoing process, with new titles being published every year, we have not indicated in this listing which books are presently available. To find out what titles in the Collected Works are currently in print, please check our website at www.rudolfsteinerpress.com (or www.steinerbooks.org for US readers).

Written Work

CW 1 Goethe: Natural-Scientific Writings, Introduction, with Footnotes and Explanations in the text by Rudolf Steiner

CW 2 Outlines of an Epistemology of the Goethean World View, with Special Consideration of Schiller

CW 3 Truth and Science

CW 4 The Philosophy of Freedom

CW 4a Documents to 'The Philosophy of Freedom'

CW 5 Friedrich Nietzsche, A Fighter against His Time

CW 6 Goethe's Worldview
CW 6a Now in CW 30
CW 7 Mysticism at the Dawn of Modern Spiritual Life and Its Relationship with Modern Worldviews
CW 8 Christianity as Mystical Fact and the Mysteries of Antiquity
CW 9 Theosophy: An Introduction into Supersensible World Knowledge and Human Purpose
CW 10 How Does One Attain Knowledge of Higher Worlds?
CW 11 From the Akasha-Chronicle
CW 12 Levels of Higher Knowledge
CW 13 Occult Science in Outline
CW 14 Four Mystery Dramas
CW 15 The Spiritual Guidance of the Individual and Humanity
CW 16 A Way to Human Self-Knowledge: Eight Meditations
CW 17 The Threshold of the Spiritual World. Aphoristic Comments
CW 18 The Riddles of Philosophy in Their History, Presented as an Outline
CW 19 Contained in CW 24
CW 20 The Riddles of the Human Being: Articulated and Unarticulated in the Thinking, Views and Opinions of a Series of German and Austrian Personalities
CW 21 The Riddles of the Soul
CW 22 Goethe's Spiritual Nature and its Revelation in 'Faust' and through the 'Fairy Tale of the Snake and the Lily'
CW 23 The Central Points of the Social Question in the Necessities of Life in the Present and the Future
CW 24 Essays Concerning the Threefold Division of the Social Organism and the Period 1915-1921
CW 25 Cosmology, Religion and Philosophy
CW 26 Anthroposophical Leading Thoughts
CW 27 Fundamentals for Expansion of the Art of Healing according to Spiritual-Scientific Insights
CW28 The Course of My Life
CW 29 Collected Essays on Dramaturgy, 1889-1900
CW 30 Methodical Foundations of Anthroposophy: Collected Essays on Philosophy, Natural Science, Aesthetics and Psychology, 1884-1901
CW 31 Collected Essays on Culture and Current Events, 1887-1901
CW 32 Collected Essays on Literature, 1884-1902
CW 33 Biographies and Biographical Sketches, 1894-1905
CW 34 Lucifer-Gnosis: Foundational Essays on Anthroposophy and Reports from the Periodicals 'Lucifer' and 'Lucifer-Gnosis,' 1903-1908
CW 35 Philosophy and Anthroposophy: Collected Essays, 1904-1923
CW 36 The Goetheanum-Idea in the Middle of the Cultural Crisis of the Present: Collected Essays from the Periodical 'Das Goetheanum,' 1921-1925

CW 37 Now in CWs 260a and 251
CW 38 Letters, Vol. 1: 1881-1890
CW 39 Letters, Vol. 2: 1890-1925
CW 40 Truth-Wrought Words
CW 40a Sayings, Poems and Mantras; Supplementary Volume
CW 42 Now in CWs 264-266
CW 43 Stage Adaptations
CW 44 On the Four Mystery Dramas. Sketches, Fragments and Paralipomena on the Four Mystery Dramas
CW 45 Anthroposophy: A Fragment from the Year 1910

Public Lectures

CW 51 On Philosophy, History and Literature
CW 52 Spiritual Teachings Concerning the Soul and Observation of the World
CW 53 The Origin and Goal of the Human Being
CW 54 The Riddles of the World and Anthroposophy
CW 55 Knowledge of the Supersensible in Our Times and Its Meaning for Life Today
CW 56 Knowledge of the Soul and of the Spirit
CW 57 Where and How Does One Find the Spirit?
CW 58 The Metamorphoses of the Soul Life. Paths of Soul Experiences: Part One
CW 59 The Metamorphoses of the Soul Life. Paths of Soul Experiences: Part Two
CW 60 The Answers of Spiritual Science to the Biggest Questions of Existence
CW 61 Human History in the Light of Spiritual Research
CW 62 Results of Spiritual Research
CW 63 Spiritual Science as a Treasure for Life
CW 64 Out of Destiny-Burdened Times
CW 65 Out of Central European Spiritual Life
CW 66 Spirit and Matter, Life and Death
CW 67 The Eternal in the Human Soul. Immortality and Freedom
CW 68 Public lectures in various cities, 1906-1918
CW 69 Public lectures in various cities, 1906-1918
CW 70 Public lectures in various cities, 1906-1918
CW 71 Public lectures in various cities, 1906-1918
CW 72 Freedom—Immortality—Social Life
CW 73 The Supplementing of the Modern Sciences through Anthroposophy
CW 73a Specialized Fields of Knowledge and Anthroposophy
CW 74 The Philosophy of Thomas Aquinas
CW 75 Public lectures in various cities, 1906-1918
CW 76 The Fructifying Effect of Anthroposophy on Specialized Fields
CW 77a The Task of Anthroposophy in Relation to Science and Life: The Darmstadt College Course
CW 77b Art and Anthroposophy. The Goetheanum-Impulse

CW 78 Anthroposophy, Its Roots of Knowledge and Fruits for Life
CW 79 The Reality of the Higher Worlds
CW 80 Public lectures in various cities, 1922
CW 81 Renewal-Impulses for Culture and Science—Berlin College Course
CW 82 So that the Human Being Can Become a Complete Human Being
CW 83 Western and Eastern World-Contrast. Paths to Understanding It through Anthroposophy
CW 84 What Did the Goetheanum Intend and What Should Anthroposophy Do?

Lectures to the Members of the Anthroposophical Society

CW 88 Concerning the Astral World and Devachan
CW 89 Consciousness—Life—Form. Fundamental Principles of a Spiritual-Scientific Cosmology
CW 90 Participant Notes from the Lectures during the Years 1903-1905
CW 91 Participant Notes from the Lectures during the Years 1903-1905
CW 92 The Occult Truths of Ancient Myths and Sagas
CW 93 The Temple Legend and the Golden Legend
CW 93a Fundamentals of Esotericism
CW 94 Cosmogony. Popular Occultism. The Gospel of John. The Theosophy in the Gospel of John
CW 95 At the Gates of Theosophy
CW 96 Origin-Impulses of Spiritual Science. Christian Esotericism in the Light of New Spirit-Knowledge
CW 97 The Christian Mystery
CW 98 Nature Beings and Spirit Beings—Their Effects in Our Visible World
CW 99 The Theosophy of the Rosicrucians
CW 100 Human Development and Christ-Knowledge
CW 101 Myths and Legends. Occult Signs and Symbols
CW 102 The Working into Human Beings by Spiritual Beings
CW 103 The Gospel of John
CW 104 The Apocalypse of John
CW 104a From the Picture-Script of the Apocalypse of John
CW 105 Universe, Earth, the Human Being: Their Being and Development, as well as Their Reflection in the Connection between Egyptian Mythology and Modern Culture
CW 106 Egyptian Myths and Mysteries in Relation to the Active Spiritual Forces of the Present
CW 107 Spiritual-Scientific Knowledge of the Human Being
CW 108 Answering the Questions of Life and the World through Anthroposophy
CW 109 The Principle of Spiritual Economy in Connection with the Question of Reincarnation. An Aspect of the Spiritual Guidance of Humanity
CW 110 The Spiritual Hierarchies and Their Reflection in the Physical World. Zodiac, Planets and Cosmos

CW 111	Contained in CW 109
CW 112	The Gospel of John in Relation to the Three Other Gospels, Especially the Gospel of Luke
CW 113	The Orient in the Light of the Occident. The Children of Lucifer and the Brothers of Christ
CW 114	The Gospel of Luke
CW 115	Anthroposophy—Psychosophy—Pneumatosophy
CW 116	The Christ-Impulse and the Development of I-Consciousness
CW 117	The Deeper Secrets of the Development of Humanity in Light of the Gospels
CW 118	The Event of the Christ-Appearance in the Etheric World
CW 119	Macrocosm and Microcosm. The Large World and the Small World. Soul-Questions, Life-Questions, Spirit-Questions
CW 120	The Revelation of Karma
CW 121	The Mission of Individual Folk-Souls in Connection with Germanic-Nordic Mythology
CW 122	The Secrets of the Biblical Creation-Story. The Six-Day Work in the First Book of Moses
CW 123	The Gospel of Matthew
CW 124	Excursus in the Area of the Gospel of Mark
CW 125	Paths and Goals of the Spiritual Human Being. Life Questions in the Light of Spiritual Science
CW 126	Occult History. Esoteric Observations of the Karmic Relationships of Personalities and Events of World History
CW 127	The Mission of the New Spiritual Revelation. The Christ-Event as the Middle-Point of Earth Evolution
CW 128	An Occult Physiology
CW 129	Wonders of the World, Trials of the Soul, and Revelations of the Spirit
CW 130	Esoteric Christianity and the Spiritual Guidance of Humanity
CW 131	From Jesus to Christ
CW 132	Evolution from the View Point of the Truth
CW 133	The Earthly and the Cosmic Human Being
CW 134	The World of the Senses and the World of the Spirit
CW 135	Reincarnation and Karma and their Meaning for the Culture of the Present
CW 136	The Spiritual Beings in Celestial Bodies and the Realms of Nature
CW 137	The Human Being in the Light of Occultism, Theosophy and Philosophy
CW 138	On Initiation. On Eternity and the Passing Moment. On the Light of the Spirit and the Darkness of Life
CW 139	The Gospel of Mark
CW 140	Occult Investigation into the Life between Death and New Birth. The Living Interaction between Life and Death
CW 141	Life between Death and New Birth in Relationship to Cosmic Facts

CW 142	The Bhagavad Gita and the Letters of Paul
CW 143	Experiences of the Supersensible. Three Paths of the Soul to Christ
CW 144	The Mysteries of the East and of Christianity
CW 145	What Significance Does Occult Development of the Human Being Have for the Sheaths—Physical Body, Etheric Body, Astral Body, and Self?
CW 146	The Occult Foundations of the Bhagavad Gita
CW 147	The Secrets of the Threshold
CW 148	Out of Research in the Akasha: The Fifth Gospel
CW 149	Christ and the Spiritual World. Concerning the Search for the Holy Grail
CW 150	The World of the Spirit and Its Extension into Physical Existence; The Influence of the Dead in the World of the Living
CW 151	Human Thought and Cosmic Thought
CW 152	Preliminary Stages to the Mystery of Golgotha
CW 153	The Inner Being of the Human Being and Life Between Death and New Birth
CW 154	How Does One Gain an Understanding of the Spiritual World? The Flowing in of Spiritual Impulses from out of the World of the Deceased
CW 155	Christ and the Human Soul. Concerning the Meaning of Life. Theosophical Morality. Anthroposophy and Christianity
CW 156	Occult Reading and Occult Hearing
CW 157	Human Destinies and the Destiny of Peoples
CW 157a	The Formation of Destiny and the Life after Death
CW 158	The Connection Between the Human Being and the Elemental World. Kalevala—Olaf Åsteson—The Russian People—The World as the Result of the Influences of Equilibrium
CW 159	The Mystery of Death. The Nature and Significance of Middle Europe and the European Folk Spirits
CW 160	In CW 159
CW 161	Paths of Spiritual Knowledge and the Renewal of the Artistic Worldview
CW 162	Questions of Art and Life in Light of Spiritual Science
CW 163	Coincidence, Necessity and Providence. Imaginative Knowledge and the Processes after Death
CW 164	The Value of Thinking for a Knowledge That Satisfies the Human Being. The Relationship of Spiritual Science to Natural Science
CW 165	The Spiritual Unification of Humanity through the Christ-Impulse
CW 166	Necessity and Freedom in the Events of the World and in Human Action
CW 167	The Present and the Past in the Human Spirit
CW 168	The Connection between the Living and the Dead
CW 169	World-being and Selfhood
CW 170	The Riddle of the Human Being. The Spiritual Background of Human History. Cosmic and Human History, Vol. 1

CW 171 Inner Development-Impulses of Humanity. Goethe and the Crisis of the 19th Century. Cosmic and Human History, Vol. 2
CW 172 The Karma of the Vocation of the Human Being in Connection with Goethe's Life. Cosmic and Human History, Vol. 3
CW 173 Contemporary-Historical Considerations: The Karma of Untruthfulness, Part One. Cosmic and Human History, Vol. 4
CW 174 Contemporary-Historical Considerations: The Karma of Untruthfulness, Part Two. Cosmic and Human History, Vol. 5
CW 174a Middle Europe between East and West. Cosmic and Human History, Vol. 6
CW 174b The Spiritual Background of the First World War. Cosmic and Human History, Vol. 7
CW 175 Building Stones for an Understanding of the Mystery of Golgotha. Cosmic and Human Metamorphoses
CW 176 Truths of Evolution of the Individual and Humanity. The Karma of Materialism
CW 177 The Spiritual Background of the Outer World. The Fall of the Spirits of Darkness. Spiritual Beings and Their Effects, Vol. 1
CW 178 Individual Spiritual Beings and their Influence in the Soul of the Human Being. Spiritual Beings and their Effects, Vol. 2
CW 179 Spiritual Beings and Their Effects. Historical Necessity and Freedom. The Influences on Destiny from out of the World of the Dead. Spiritual Beings and Their Effects, Vol. 3
CW 180 Mystery Truths and Christmas Impulses. Ancient Myths and their Meaning. Spiritual Beings and Their Effects, Vol. 4
CW 181 Earthly Death and Cosmic Life. Anthroposophical Gifts for Life. Necessities of Consciousness for the Present and the Future.
CW 182 Death as Transformation of Life
CW 183 The Science of the Development of the Human Being
CW 184 The Polarity of Duration and Development in Human Life. The Cosmic Pre-History of Humanity
CW 185 Historical Symptomology
CW 185a Historical-Developmental Foundations for Forming a Social Judgement
CW 186 The Fundamental Social Demands of Our Time—In Changed Situations
CW 187 How Can Humanity Find the Christ Again? The Threefold Shadow-Existence of our Time and the New Christ-Light
CW 188 Goetheanism, a Transformation-Impulse and Resurrection-Thought. Science of the Human Being and Science of Sociology
CW 189 The Social Question as a Question of Consciousness. The Spiritual Background of the Social Question, Vol. 1
CW 190 Impulses of the Past and the Future in Social Occurrences. The Spiritual Background of the Social Question, Vol. 2

CW 191 Social Understanding from Spiritual-Scientific Cognition. The Spiritual Background of the Social Question, Vol. 3
CW 192 Spiritual-Scientific Treatment of Social and Pedagogical Questions
CW 193 The Inner Aspect of the Social Riddle. Luciferic Past and Ahrimanic Future
CW 194 The Mission of Michael. The Revelation of the Actual Mysteries of the Human Being
CW 195 Cosmic New Year and the New Year Idea
CW 196 Spiritual and Social Transformations in the Development of Humanity
CW 197 Polarities in the Development of Humanity: West and East Materialism and Mysticism Knowledge and Belief
CW 198 Healing Factors for the Social Organism
CW 199 Spiritual Science as Knowledge of the Foundational Impulses of Social Formation
CW 200 The New Spirituality and the Christ-Experience of the 20th Century
CW 201 The Correspondences Between Microcosm and Macrocosm. The Human Being—A Hieroglyph of the Universe. The Human Being in Relationship with the Cosmos: 1
CW 202 The Bridge between the World-Spirituality and the Physical Aspect of the Human Being. The Search for the New Isis, the Divine Sophia. The Human Being in Relationship with the Cosmos: 2
CW 203 The Responsibility of Human Beings for the Development of the World through their Spiritual Connection with the Planet Earth and the World of the Stars. The Human Being in Relationship with the Cosmos: 3
CW 204 Perspectives of the Development of Humanity. The Materialistic Knowledge-Impulse and the Task of Anthroposophy. The Human Being in Relationship with the Cosmos: 4
CW 205 Human Development, World-Soul, and World-Spirit. Part One: The Human Being as a Being of Body and Soul in Relationship to the World. The Human Being in Relationship with the Cosmos: 5
CW 206 Human Development, World-Soul, and World-Spirit. Part Two: The Human Being as a Spiritual Being in the Process of Historical Development. The Human Being in Relationship with the Cosmos: 6
CW 207 Anthroposophy as Cosmosophy. Part One: Characteristic Features of the Human Being in the Earthly and the Cosmic Realms. The Human Being in Relationship with the Cosmos: 7
CW 208 Anthroposophy as Cosmosophy. Part Two: The Forming of the Human Being as the Result of Cosmic Influence. The Human Being in Relationship with the Cosmos: 8
CW 209 Nordic and Central European Spiritual Impulses. The Festival of the Appearance of Christ. The Human Being in Relationship with the Cosmos: 9

CW 210	Old and New Methods of Initiation. Drama and Poetry in the Change of Consciousness in the Modern Age
CW 211	The Sun Mystery and the Mystery of Death and Resurrection. Exoteric and Esoteric Christianity
CW 212	Human Soul Life and Spiritual Striving in Connection with World and Earth Development
CW 213	Human Questions and World Answers
CW 214	The Mystery of the Trinity: The Human Being in Relationship with the Spiritual World in the Course of Time
CW 215	Philosophy, Cosmology, and Religion in Anthroposophy
CW 216	The Fundamental Impulses of the World-Historical Development of Humanity
CW 217	Spiritually Active Forces in the Coexistence of the Older and Younger Generations. Pedagogical Course for Youth
CW 217a	Youth's Cognitive Task
CW 218	Spiritual Connections in the Forming of the Human Organism
CW 219	The Relationship of the World of the Stars to the Human Being, and of the Human Being to the World of the Stars. The Spiritual Communion of Humanity
CW 220	Living Knowledge of Nature. Intellectual Fall and Spiritual Redemption
CW 221	Earth-Knowing and Heaven-Insight
CW 222	The Imparting of Impulses to World-Historical Events through Spiritual Powers
CW 223	The Cycle of the Year as Breathing Process of the Earth and the Four Great Festival-Seasons. Anthroposophy and the Human Heart (*Gemüt*)
CW 224	The Human Soul and its Connection with Divine-Spiritual Individualities. The Internalization of the Festivals of the Year
CW 225	Three Perspectives of Anthroposophy. Cultural Phenomena observed from a Spiritual-Scientific Perspective
CW 226	Human Being, Human Destiny, and World Development
CW 227	Initiation-Knowledge
CW 228	Science of Initiation and Knowledge of the Stars. The Human Being in the Past, the Present, and the Future from the Viewpoint of the Development of Consciousness
CW 229	The Experiencing of the Course of the Year in Four Cosmic Imaginations
CW 230	The Human Being as Harmony of the Creative, Building, and Formative World-Word
CW 231	The Supersensible Human Being, Understood Anthroposophically
CW 232	The Forming of the Mysteries
CW 233	World History Illuminated by Anthroposophy and as the Foundation for Knowledge of the Human Spirit

CW 233a Mystery Sites of the Middle Ages: Rosicrucianism and the Modern Initiation-Principle. The Festival of Easter as Part of the History of the Mysteries of Humanity

CW 234 Anthroposophy. A Summary after 21 Years

CW 235 Esoteric Observations of Karmic Relationships in 6 Volumes, Vol. 1

CW 236 Esoteric Observations of Karmic Relationships in 6 Volumes, Vol. 2

CW 237 Esoteric Observations of Karmic Relationships in 6 Volumes, Vol. 3: The Karmic Relationships of the Anthroposophical Movement

CW 238 Esoteric Observations of Karmic Relationships in 6 Volumes, Vol. 4: The Spiritual Life of the Present in Relationship to the Anthroposophical Movement

CW 239 Esoteric Observations of Karmic Relationships in 6 Volumes, Vol. 5

CW 240 Esoteric Observations of Karmic Relationships in 6 Volumes, Vol. 6

CW 243 The Consciousness of the Initiate

CW 245 Instructions for an Esoteric Schooling

CW 250 The Building-Up of the Anthroposophical Society. From the Beginning to the Outbreak of the First World War

CW 251 The History of the Goetheanum Building-Association

CW 252 Life in the Anthroposophical Society from the First World War to the Burning of the First Goetheanum

CW 253 The Problems of Living Together in the Anthroposophical Society. On the Dornach Crisis of 1915. With Highlights on Swedenborg's Clairvoyance, the Views of Freudian Psychoanalysts, and the Concept of Love in Relation to Mysticism

CW 254 The Occult Movement in the 19th Century and Its Relationship to World Culture. Significant Points from the Exoteric Cultural Life around the Middle of the 19th Century

CW 255 Rudolf Steiner during the First World War

CW 255a Anthroposophy and the Reformation of Society. On the History of the Threefold Movement

CW 255b Anthroposophy and Its Opponents, 1919–1921

CW 256 How Can the Anthroposophical Movement Be Financed?

CW 256a Futurum, Inc. / International Laboratories, Inc.

CW 256b The Coming Day, Inc.

CW 257 Anthroposophical Community-Building

CW 258 The History of and Conditions for the Anthroposophical Movement in Relationship to the Anthroposophical Society. A Stimulus to Self-Contemplation

CW 259 The Year of Destiny 1923 in the History of the Anthroposophical Society. From the Burning of the Goetheanum to the Christmas Conference

CW 260 The Christmas Conference for the Founding of the General Anthroposophical Society

CW 260a The Constitution of the General Anthroposophical Society and the School for Spiritual Science. The Rebuilding of the Goetheanum
CW 261 Our Dead. Addresses, Words of Remembrance, and Meditative Verses, 1906-1924
CW 262 Rudolf Steiner and Marie Steiner-von Sivers: Correspondence and Documents, 1901-1925
CW 263/1 Rudolf Steiner and Edith Maryon: Correspondence: Letters, Verses, Sketches, 1912-1924
CW 264 On the History and the Contents of the First Section of the Esoteric School from 1904 to 1914. Letters, Newsletters, Documents, Lectures
CW 265 On the History and from the Contents of the Ritual-Knowledge Section of the Esoteric School from 1904 to 1914. Documents, and Lectures from the Years 1906 to 1914, as well as on New Approaches to Ritual-Knowledge Work in the Years 1921–1924
CW 266/1 From the Contents of the Esoteric Lessons. Volume 1: 1904–1909. Notes from Memory of Participants. Meditation texts from the notes of Rudolf Steiner
CW 266/2 From the Contents of the Esoteric Lessons. Volume 2: 1910–1912. Notes from Memory of Participants
CW 266/3 From the Contents of the Esoteric Lessons. Volume 3: 1913, 1914 and 1920–1923. Notes from Memory of Participants. Meditation texts from the notes of Rudolf Steiner
CW 267 Soul-Exercises: Vol. 1: Exercises with Word and Image Meditations for the Methodological Development of Higher Powers of Knowledge, 1904–1924
CW 268 Soul-Exercises: Vol. 2: Mantric Verses, 1903–1925
CW 269 Ritual Texts for the Celebration of the Free Christian Religious Instruction. The Collected Verses for Teachers and Students of the Waldorf School
CW 270 Esoteric Instructions for the First Class of the School for Spiritual Science at the Goetheanum 1924, 4 Volumes
CW 271 Art and Knowledge of Art. Foundations of a New Aesthetic
CW 272 Spiritual-Scientific Commentary on Goethe's 'Faust' in Two Volumes. Vol. 1: Faust, the Striving Human Being
CW 273 Spiritual-Scientific Commentary on Goethe's 'Faust' in Two Volumes. Vol. 2: The Faust-Problem
CW 274 Addresses for the Christmas Plays from the Old Folk Traditions
CW 275 Art in the Light of Mystery-Wisdom
CW 276 The Artistic in Its Mission in the World. The Genius of Language. The World of Self-Revealing Radiant Appearances—Anthroposophy and Art. Anthroposophy and Poetry
CW 277 Eurythmy. The Revelation of the Speaking Soul
CW 277a The Origin and Development of Eurythmy

CW 278	Eurythmy as Visible Song
CW 279	Eurythmy as Visible Speech
CW 280	The Method and Nature of Speech Formation
CW 281	The Art of Recitation and Declamation
CW 282	Speech Formation and Dramatic Art
CW 283	The Nature of Things Musical and the Experience of Tone in the Human Being
CW 284/285	Images of Occult Seals and Pillars. The Munich Congress of Whitsun 1907 and Its Consequences
CW 286	Paths to a New Style of Architecture. 'And the Building Becomes Human'
CW 287	The Building at Dornach as a Symbol of Historical Becoming and an Artistic Transformation Impulse
CW 288	Style-Forms in the Living Organic
CW 289	The Building-Idea of the Goetheanum: Lectures with Slides from the Years 1920–1921
CW 290	The Building-Idea of the Goetheanum: Lectures with Slides from the Years 1920–1921
CW 291	The Nature of Colours
CW 291a	Knowledge of Colours. Supplementary Volume to 'The Nature of Colours'
CW 292	Art History as Image of Inner Spiritual Impulses
CW 293	General Knowledge of the Human Being as the Foundation of Pedagogy
CW 294	The Art of Education, Methodology and Didactics
CW 295	The Art of Education: Seminar Discussions and Lectures on Lesson Planning
CW 296	The Question of Education as a Social Question
CW 297	The Idea and Practice of the Waldorf School
CW 297a	Education for Life: Self-Education and the Practice of Pedagogy
CW 298	Rudolf Steiner in the Waldorf School
CW 299	Spiritual-Scientific Observations on Speech
CW 300a	Conferences with the Teachers of the Free Waldorf School in Stuttgart, 1919 to 1924, in 3 Volumes, Vol. 1
CW 300b	Conferences with the Teachers of the Free Waldorf School in Stuttgart, 1919 to 1924, in 3 Volumes, Vol. 2
CW 300c	Conferences with the Teachers of the Free Waldorf School in Stuttgart, 1919 to 1924, in 3 Volumes, Vol. 3
CW 301	The Renewal of Pedagogical-Didactical Art through Spiritual Science
CW 302	Knowledge of the Human Being and the Forming of Class Lessons
CW 302a	Education and Teaching from a Knowledge of the Human Being
CW 303	The Healthy Development of the Human Being
CW 304	Methods of Education and Teaching Based on Anthroposophy
CW 304a	Anthroposophical Knowledge of the Human Being and Pedagogy

CW 305 The Soul-Spiritual Foundational Forces of the Art of Education. Spiritual Values in Education and Social Life
CW 306 Pedagogical Praxis from the Viewpoint of a Spiritual-Scientific Knowledge of the Human Being. The Education of the Child and Young Human Beings
CW 307 The Spiritual Life of the Present and Education
CW 308 The Method of Teaching and the Life-Requirements for Teaching
CW 309 Anthroposophical Pedagogy and Its Prerequisites
CW 310 The Pedagogical Value of a Knowledge of the Human Being and the Cultural Value of Pedagogy
CW 311 The Art of Education from an Understanding of the Being of Humanity
CW 312 Spiritual Science and Medicine
CW 313 Spiritual-Scientific Viewpoints on Therapy
CW 314 Physiology and Therapy Based on Spiritual Science
CW 315 Curative Eurythmy
CW 316 Meditative Observations and Instructions for a Deepening of the Art of Healing
CW 317 The Curative Education Course
CW 318 The Working Together of Doctors and Pastors
CW 319 Anthroposophical Knowledge of the Human Being and Medicine
CW 320 Spiritual-Scientific Impulses for the Development of Physics 1: The First Natural-Scientific Course: Light, Colour, Tone, Mass, Electricity, Magnetism
CW 321 Spiritual-Scientific Impulses for the Development of Physics 2: The Second Natural-Scientific Course: Warmth at the Border of Positive and Negative Materiality
CW 322 The Borders of the Knowledge of Nature
CW 323 The Relationship of the various Natural-Scientific Fields to Astronomy
CW 324 Nature Observation, Mathematics, and Scientific Experimentation and Results from the Viewpoint of Anthroposophy
CW 324a The Fourth Dimension in Mathematics and Reality
CW 325 Natural Science and the World-Historical Development of Humanity since Ancient Times
CW 326 The Moment of the Coming Into Being of Natural Science in World History and Its Development Since Then
CW 327 Spiritual-Scientific Foundations for Success in Farming. The Agricultural Course
CW 328 The Social Question
CW 329 The Liberation of the Human Being as the Foundation for a New Social Form
CW 330 The Renewal of the Social Organism
CW 331 Work-Council and Socialization
CW 332 The Alliance for Threefolding and the Total Reform of Society. The Council on Culture and the Liberation of the Spiritual Life

CW 332a The Social Future
CW 333 Freedom of Thought and Social Forces
CW 334 From the Unified State to the Threefold Social Organism
CW 335 The Crisis of the Present and the Path to Healthy Thinking
CW 336 The Great Questions of the Times and Anthroposophical Spiritual Knowledge
CW 337a Social Ideas, Social Reality, Social Practice, Vol. 1: Question-and-Answer Evenings and Study Evenings of the Alliance for the Threefold Social Organism in Stuttgart, 1919-1920
CW 337b Social Ideas, Social Realities, Social Practice, Vol. 2: Discussion Evenings of the Swiss Alliance for the Threefold Social Organism
CW 338 How Does One Work on Behalf of the Impulse for the Threefold Social Organism?
CW 339 Anthroposophy, Threefold Social Organism, and the Art of Public Speaking
CW 340 The National-Economics Course. The Tasks of a New Science of Economics, Volume 1
CW 341 The National-Economics Seminar. The Tasks of a New Science of Economics, Volume 2
CW 342 Lectures and Courses on Christian Religious Work, Vol. 1: Anthroposophical Foundations for a Renewed Christian Religious Working
CW 343 Lectures and Courses on Christian Religious Work, Vol. 2: Spiritual Knowledge—Religious Feeling—Cultic Doing
CW 344 Lectures and Courses on Christian Religious Work, Vol. 3: Lectures at the Founding of the Christian Community
CW 345 Lectures and Courses on Christian Religious Work, Vol. 4: Concerning the Nature of the Working Word
CW 346 Lectures and Courses on Christian Religious Work, Vol. 5: The Apocalypse and the Work of the Priest
CW 347 The Knowledge of the Nature of the Human Being According to Body, Soul and Spirit. On Earlier Conditions of the Earth
CW 348 On Health and Illness. Foundations of a Spiritual-Scientific Doctrine of the Senses
CW 349 On the Life of the Human Being and of the Earth. On the Nature of Christianity
CW 350 Rhythms in the Cosmos and in the Human Being. How Does One Come To See the Spiritual World?
CW 351 The Human Being and the World. The Influence of the Spirit in Nature. On the Nature of Bees
CW 352 Nature and the Human Being Observed Spiritual-Scientifically
CW 353 The History of Humanity and the World-Views of the Folk Cultures
CW 354 The Creation of the World and the Human Being. Life on Earth and the Influence of the Stars

SIGNIFICANT EVENTS IN THE LIFE OF RUDOLF STEINER

1829: June 23: birth of Johann Steiner (1829–1910)—Rudolf Steiner's father—in Geras, Lower Austria.

1834: May 8: birth of Franciska Blie (1834–1918)—Rudolf Steiner's mother—in Horn, Lower Austria. 'My father and mother were both children of the glorious Lower Austrian forest district north of the Danube.'

1860: May 16: marriage of Johann Steiner and Franciska Blie.

1861: February 25: birth of *Rudolf Joseph Lorenz Steiner* in Kraljevec, Croatia, near the border with Hungary, where Johann Steiner works as a telegrapher for the South Austria Railroad. Rudolf Steiner is baptized two days later, February 27, the date usually given as his birthday.

1862: Summer: the family moves to Modling, Lower Austria.

1863: The family moves to Pottschach, Lower Austria, near the Styrian border, where Johann Steiner becomes station master. 'The view stretched to the mountains . . . majestic peaks in the distance and the sweet charm of nature in the immediate surroundings.'

1864: November 15: birth of Rudolf Steiner's sister, Leopoldine (d. November 1, 1927). She will become a seamstress and live with her parents for the rest of her life.

1866: July 28: birth of Rudolf Steiner's deaf-mute brother, Gustav (d. May 1, 1941).

1867: Rudolf Steiner enters the village school. Following a disagreement between his father and the schoolmaster, whose wife falsely accused the boy of causing a commotion, Rudolf Steiner is taken out of school and taught at home.

1868: A critical experience. Unknown to the family, an aunt dies in a distant town. Sitting in the station waiting room, Rudolf Steiner sees her 'form,' which speaks to him, asking for help. 'Beginning with this experience, a new soul life began in the boy, one in which not only the outer trees and mountains spoke to him, but also the worlds that lay behind them. From this moment on, the boy began to live with the spirits of nature . . .'

1869: The family moves to the peaceful, rural village of Neudorfl, near Wiener Neustadt in present-day Austria. Rudolf Steiner attends the village school. Because of the 'unorthodoxy' of his writing and spelling, he has to do 'extra lessons'.

1870: Through a book lent to him by his tutor, he discovers geometry: 'To grasp something purely in the spirit brought me inner happiness. I know that I first learned happiness through geometry.' The same tutor allows him to draw, while other students still struggle with their reading and writing. 'An artistic element' thus enters his education.

1871: Though his parents are not religious, Rudolf Steiner becomes a 'church child,' a favourite of the priest, who was 'an exceptional character.' 'Up to the age of ten or eleven, among those I came to know, he was far and away the most significant.' Among other things, he introduces Steiner to Copernican, heliocentric cosmology. As an altar boy, Rudolf Steiner serves at masses, funerals, and Corpus Christi processions. At year's end, after an incident in which he escapes a thrashing, his father forbids him to go to church.

1872: Rudolf Steiner transfers to grammar school in Wiener-Neustadt, a five-mile walk from home, which must be done in all weathers.

1873–75: Through his teachers and on his own, Rudolf Steiner has many wonderful experiences with science and mathematics. Outside school, he teaches himself analytic geometry, trigonometry, differential equations, and calculus.

1876: Rudolf Steiner begins tutoring other students. He learns bookbinding from his father. He also teaches himself stenography.

1877: Rudolf Steiner discovers Kant's *Critique of Pure Reason,* which he reads and rereads. He also discovers and reads von Rotteck's *World History.*

1878: He studies extensively in contemporary psychology and philosophy.

1879: Rudolf Steiner graduates from high school with honours. His father is transferred to Inzersdorf, near Vienna. He uses his first visit to Vienna 'to purchase a great number of philosophy books'—Kant, Fichte, Schelling, and Hegel, as well as numerous histories of philosophy. His aim: to find a path from the 'I' to nature.

October 1879–1883: Rudolf Steiner attends the Technical College in Vienna—to study mathematics, chemistry, physics, mineralogy, botany, zoology, biology, geology, and mechanics—with a scholarship. He also attends lectures in history and literature, while avidly reading philosophy on his own. His two favourite professors are Karl Julius Schröer (German language and literature) and Edmund Reitlinger (physics). He also audits lectures by Robert Zimmermann on aesthetics and Franz Brentano on philosophy. During this year he begins his friendship with Moritz Zitter (1861–1921), who will help support him financially when he is in Berlin.

1880: Rudolf Steiner attends lectures on Schiller and Goethe by Karl Julius Schröer, who becomes his mentor. Also 'through a remarkable combination of circumstances,' he meets Felix Koguzki, a 'herb gatherer' and healer, who could 'see deeply into the secrets of nature'. Rudolf Steiner will meet and study with this 'emissary of the Master' throughout his time in Vienna.

1881: January: '... I didn't sleep a wink. I was busy with philosophical problems until about 12:30 a.m. Then, finally, I threw myself down on my couch. All my striving during the previous year had been to research whether the following statement by Schelling was true or not: *Within everyone dwells a secret, marvellous capacity to draw back from the stream of time—out of the self clothed in all that comes to us from outside—into our innermost being and there, in the immutable form of the Eternal, to look into ourselves.* I believe, and I am still quite certain of it, that I discovered this capacity in myself; I had long had an inkling of it. Now the whole of idealist philosophy stood before me in modified form. What's a sleepless night compared to that!'

Rudolf Steiner begins communicating with leading thinkers of the day, who send him books in return, which he reads eagerly.

July: 'I am not one of those who dives into the day like an animal in human form. I pursue a quite specific goal, an idealistic aim—knowledge of the truth! This cannot be done offhandedly. It requires the greatest striving in the world, free of all egotism, and equally of all resignation.'

August: Steiner puts down on paper for the first time thoughts for a 'Philosophy of Freedom.' 'The striving for the absolute: this human yearning is freedom.' He also seeks to outline a 'peasant philosophy,' describing what the worldview of a 'peasant'—one who lives close to the earth and the old ways—really is.

1881–1882: Felix Koguzki, the herb gatherer, reveals himself to be the envoy of another, higher initiatory personality, who instructs Rudolf Steiner to penetrate Fichte's philosophy and to master modern scientific thinking as a preparation for right entry into the spirit. This 'Master' also teaches him the double (evolutionary and involutionary) nature of time.

1882: Through the offices of Karl Julius Schröer, Rudolf Steiner is asked by Joseph Kürschner to edit Goethe's scientific works for the *Deutschen National-Literatur* edition. He writes 'A Possible Critique of Atomistic Concepts' and sends it to Friedrich Theodor Vischer.

1883: Rudolf Steiner completes his college studies and begins work on the Goethe project.

1884: First volume of Goethe's *Scientific Writings* (CW 1) appears (March). He lectures on Goethe and Lessing, and Goethe's approach to science. In July, he enters the household of Ladislaus and Pauline Specht as tutor to the four Specht boys. He will live there until 1890. At this time, he meets Josef Breuer (1842–1925), the co-author with Sigmund Freud of *Studies in Hysteria,* who is the Specht family doctor.

1885: While continuing to edit Goethe's writings, Rudolf Steiner reads deeply in contemporary philosophy (Eduard von Hartmann, Johannes Volkelt, and Richard Wahle, among others).

1886: May: Rudolf Steiner sends Kürschner the manuscript of *Outlines of Goethe's Theory of Knowledge* (CW 2), which appears in October, and which he sends out widely. He also meets the poet Marie Eugenie Delle Grazie and writes 'Nature and Our Ideals' for her. He attends her salon, where he meets many priests, theologians, and philosophers, who will become his friends. Meanwhile, the director of the Goethe Archive in Weimar requests his collaboration with the *Sophien* edition of Goethe's works, particularly the writings on colour.

1887: At the beginning of the year, Rudolf Steiner is very sick. As the year progresses and his health improves, he becomes increasingly 'a man of letters,' lecturing, writing essays, and taking part in Austrian cultural life. In August–September, the second volume of Goethe's *Scientific Writings* appears.

1888: January–July: Rudolf Steiner assumes editorship of the 'German Weekly' *(Deutsche Wochenschrift)*. He begins lecturing more intensively, giving, for example, a lecture titled 'Goethe as Father of a New Aesthetics.' He meets and becomes soul friends with Friedrich Eckstein (1861–1939), a vegetarian, philosopher of symbolism, alchemist, and musician, who will introduce him to various spiritual currents (including Theosophy) and with whom he will meditate and interpret esoteric and alchemical texts.

1889: Rudolf Steiner first reads Nietzsche *(Beyond Good and Evil)*. He encounters Theosophy again and learns of Madame Blavatsky in the theosophical circle around Marie Lang (1858–1934). Here he also meets well-known figures of Austrian life, as well as esoteric figures like the occultist Franz Hartmann and Karl Leinigen-Billigen (translator of C.G. Harrison's *The Transcendental Universe).* During this period, Steiner first reads A.P. Sinnett's *Esoteric Buddhism* and Mabel Collins's *Light on the Path.* He also begins travelling, visiting Budapest, Weimar, and Berlin (where he meets philosopher Eduard von Hartmann).

1890: Rudolf Steiner finishes Volume 3 of Goethe's scientific writings. He begins his doctoral dissertation, which will become *Truth and Science* (CW 3). He also meets the poet and feminist Rosa Mayreder (1858–1938), with whom he can exchange his most intimate thoughts. In September, Rudolf Steiner moves to Weimar to work in the Goethe-Schiller Archive.

1891: Volume 3 of the Kürschner edition of Goethe appears. Meanwhile, Rudolf Steiner edits Goethe's studies in mineralogy and scientific writings for the *Sophien* edition. He meets Ludwig Laistner of the Cotta Publishing Company, who asks for a book on the basic question of metaphysics. From this will result, ultimately, *The Philosophy of Freedom* (CW 4), which will be published not by Cotta but by Emil Felber. In October, Rudolf Steiner takes the oral exam for a doctorate in philosophy, mathematics, and mechanics at Rostock University, receiving his doctorate on the twenty-sixth. In November, he gives his first lecture on Goethe's 'Fairy Tale' in Vienna.

1892: Rudolf Steiner continues work at the Goethe-Schiller Archive and on his *Philosophy of Freedom. Truth and Science,* his doctoral dissertation, is published. Steiner undertakes to write Introductions to books on Schopenhauer and Jean Paul for Cotta. At year's end, he finds lodging with Anna Eunike, née Schulz (1853–1911), a widow with four daughters and a son. He also develops a friendship with Otto Erich Hartleben (1864–1905) with whom he shares literary interests.

1893: Rudolf Steiner begins his habit of producing many reviews and articles. In March, he gives a lecture titled 'Hypnotism, with Reference to Spiritism.' In September, volume 4 of the Kürschner edition is completed. In November, *The Philosophy of Freedom* appears. This year, too, he meets John Henry Mackay (1864–1933), the anarchist, and Max Stirner, a scholar and biographer.

1894: Rudolf Steiner meets Elisabeth Fürster Nietzsche, the philosopher's sister, and begins to read Nietzsche in earnest, beginning with the as yet unpublished *Antichrist.* He also meets Ernst Haeckel (1834–1919). In the fall, he begins to write *Nietzsche, A Fighter against His Time* (CW 5).

1895: May, *Nietzsche, A Fighter against His Time* appears.

1896: January 22: Rudolf Steiner sees Friedrich Nietzsche for the first and only time. Moves between the Nietzsche and the Goethe-Schiller

Archives, where he completes his work before year's end. He falls out with Elisabeth Förster Nietzsche, thus ending his association with the Nietzsche Archive.

1897: Rudolf Steiner finishes the manuscript of *Goethe's Worldview* (CW 6). He moves to Berlin with Anna Eunike and begins editorship of the *Magazin für Literatur.* From now on, Steiner will write countless reviews, literary and philosophical articles, and so on. He begins lecturing at the 'Free Literary Society.' In September, he attends the Zionist Congress in Basel. He sides with Dreyfus in the Dreyfus affair.

1898: Rudolf Steiner is very active as an editor in the political, artistic, and theatrical life of Berlin. He becomes friendly with John Henry Mackay and poet Ludwig Jacobowski (1868–1900). He joins Jacobowski's circle of writers, artists, and scientists—'The Coming Ones' (*Die Kommenden)*—and contributes lectures to the group until 1903. He also lectures at the 'League for College Pedagogy.' He writes an article for Goethe's sesquicentennial, 'Goethe's Secret Revelation,' on the 'Fairy Tale of the Green Snake and the Beautiful Lily.'

1898–99: 'This was a trying time for my soul as I looked at Christianity. . . . I was able to progress only by contemplating, by means of spiritual perception, the evolution of Christianity. . . . Conscious knowledge of real Christianity began to dawn in me around the turn of the century. This seed continued to develop. My soul trial occurred shortly before the beginning of the twentieth century. It was decisive for my soul's development that I stood spiritually before the Mystery of Golgotha in a deep and solemn celebration of knowledge.'

1899: Rudolf Steiner begins teaching and giving lectures and lecture cycles at the Workers' College, founded by Wilhelm Liebknecht (1826–1900). He will continue to do so until 1904. Writes: *Literature and Spiritual Life in the Nineteenth Century; Individualism in Philosophy; Haeckel and His Opponents; Poetry in the Present;* and begins what will become (fifteen years later) *The Riddles of Philosophy* (CW 18). He also meets many artists and writers, including Kothe Kollwitz, Stefan Zweig, and Rainer Maria Rilke. On October 31, he marries Anna Eunike.

1900: 'I thought that the turn of the century must bring humanity a new light. It seemed to me that the separation of human thinking and willing from the spirit had peaked. A turn or reversal of direction in human evolution seemed to me a necessity.' Rudolf Steiner finishes *World and Life Views in the Nineteenth Century* (the second part of what will become *The Riddles of Philosophy)* and dedicates it to

Ernst Haeckel. It is published in March. He continues lecturing at *Die Kommenden,* whose leadership he assumes after the death of Jacobowski. Also, he gives the Gutenberg Jubilee lecture before 7,000 typesetters and printers. In September, Rudolf Steiner is invited by Count and Countess Brockdorff to lecture in the Theosophical Library. His first lecture is on Nietzsche. His second lecture is titled 'Goethe's Secret Revelation.' October 6, he begins a lecture cycle on the mystics that will become *Mystics after Modernism* (CW 7). November–December: 'Marie von Sivers appears in the audience. . . .' Also in November, Steiner gives his first lecture at the Giordano Bruno Bund (where he will continue to lecture until May, 1905). He speaks on Bruno and modern Rome, focusing on the importance of the philosophy of Thomas Aquinas as monism.

1901: In continual financial straits, Rudolf Steiner's early friends Moritz Zitter and Rosa Mayreder help support him. In October, he begins the lecture cycle *Christianity as Mystical Fact* (CW 8) at the Theosophical Library. In November, he gives his first 'theosophical lecture' on Goethe's 'Fairy Tale' in Hamburg at the invitation of Wilhelm Hubbe-Schleiden. He also attends a gathering to celebrate the founding of the Theosophical Society at Count and Countess Brockdorff's. He gives a lecture cycle, 'From Buddha to Christ,' for the circle of the *Kommenden.* November 17, Marie von Sivers asks Rudolf Steiner if Theosophy needs a Western–Christian spiritual movement (to complement Theosophy's Eastern emphasis). 'The question was posed. Now, following spiritual laws, I could begin to give an answer. . . .' In December, Rudolf Steiner writes his first article for a theosophical publication. At year's end, the Brockdorffs and possibly Wilhelm Hubbe-Schleiden ask Rudolf Steiner to join the Theosophical Society and undertake the leadership of the German section. Rudolf Steiner agrees, on the condition that Marie von Sivers (then in Italy) work with him.

1902: Beginning in January, Rudolf Steiner attends the opening of the Workers' School in Spandau with Rosa Luxemberg (1870–1919). January 17, Rudolf Steiner joins the Theosophical Society. In April, he is asked to become general secretary of the German Section of the theosophical Society, and works on preparations for its founding. In July, he visits London for a theosophical congress. He meets Bertram Keightly, G.R.S. Mead, A.P. Sinnett, and Annie Besant, among others. In September, *Christianity as Mystical Fact* appears. In October, Rudolf Steiner gives his first public lecture on Theosophy ('Monism and Theosophy') to about three hundred people at the Giordano Bruno Bund. On October 19–21, the

German Section of the Theosophical Society has its first meeting; Rudolf Steiner is the general secretary, and Annie Besant attends. Steiner lectures on practical karma studies. On October 23, Annie Besant inducts Rudolf Steiner into the Esoteric School of the Theosophical Society. On October 25, Steiner begins a weekly series of lectures: 'The Field of Theosophy.' During this year, Rudolf Steiner also first meets Ita Wegman (1876–1943), who will become his close collaborator in his final years.

1903: Rudolf Steiner holds about 300 lectures and seminars. In May, the first issue of the periodical *Luzifer* appears. In June, Rudolf Steiner visits London for the first meeting of the Federation of the European Sections of the Theosophical Society, where he meets Colonel Olcott. He begins to write *Theosophy* (CW 9).

1904: Rudolf Steiner continues lecturing at the Workers' College and elsewhere (about 90 lectures), while lecturing intensively all over Germany among theosophists (about 140 lectures). In February, he meets Carl Unger (1878–1929), who will become a member of the board of the Anthroposophical Society (1913). In March, he meets Michael Bauer (1871–1929), a Christian mystic, who will also be on the board. In May, *Theosophy* appears, with the dedication: 'To the spirit of Giordano Bruno.' Rudolf Steiner and Marie von Sivers visit London for meetings with Annie Besant. June: Rudolf Steiner and Marie von Sivers attend the meeting of the Federation of European Sections of the Theosophical Society in Amsterdam. In July, Steiner begins the articles in *Luzifer-Gnosis* that will become *How to Know Higher Worlds* (CW 10) and *Cosmic Memory* (CW 11). In September, Annie Besant visits Germany. In December, Steiner lectures on Freemasonry. He mentions the High Grade Masonry derived from John Yarker and represented by Theodore Reuss and Karl Kellner as a blank slate 'into which a good image could be placed'.

1905: This year, Steiner ends his non-theosophical lecturing activity. Supported by Marie von Sivers, his theosophical lecturing—both in public and in the Theosophical Society—increases significantly: 'The German Theosophical Movement is of exceptional importance.' Steiner recommends reading, among others, Fichte, Jacob Boehme, and Angelus Silesius. He begins to introduce Christian themes into Theosophy. He also begins to work with doctors (Felix Peipers and Ludwig Noll). In July, he is in London for the Federation of European Sections, where he attends a lecture by Annie Besant: 'I have seldom seen Mrs Besant speak in so inward and heartfelt a manner... Through Mrs Besant I have found the way to H.P. Blavatsky.' September to October, he gives a course of 31 lectures for a small group of esoteric students. In October, the annual meeting of the German Section of the Theosophical Society, which still remains very small, takes place. Rudolf Steiner reports membership has risen from 121 to 377 members. In November, seeking to establish esoteric 'continuity,' Rudolf Steiner and Marie von Sivers participate in a 'Memphis-Misraim' Masonic ceremony. They pay 45 marks for membership. 'Yesterday, you saw how little remains of former esoteric institutions.' 'We are dealing only with a "framework" . . for the present, nothing lies behind it. The occult powers have completely withdrawn.'

1906: Expansion of theosophical work. Rudolf Steiner gives about 245 lectures, only 44 of which take place in Berlin. Cycles are given in Paris, Leipzig, Stuttgart, and Munich. Esoteric work also intensifies. Rudolf Steiner begins writing *An Outline of Esoteric Science* (CW 13). In January, Rudolf Steiner receives permission (a patent) from the Great Orient of the Scottish A & A Thirty-Three Degree Rite of the Order of the Ancient Freemasons of the Memphis-Misraim Rite to direct a chapter under the name 'Mystica Aeterna.' This will become the 'Cognitive-Ritual Section' (also called 'Misraim Service') of the Esoteric School. (See: *Freemasonry and Ritual Work: The Misraim Service,* CW 265.) During this time, Steiner also meets Albert Schweitzer. In May, he is in Paris, where he visits Édouard Schuré. Many Russians attend his lectures (including Konstantin Balmont, Dimitri Mereszkovski, Zinaida Hippius, and Maximilian Woloshin). He attends the General Meeting of the European Federation of the Theosophical Society, at which Col. Olcott is present for the last time. He spends the year's end in Venice and Rome, where he writes and works on his translation of H.P. Blavatsky's *Key to Theosophy.*

1907: Further expansion of the German Theosophical Movement according to the Rosicrucian directive to 'introduce spirit into the world'—in education, in social questions, in art, and in science. In February, Col. Olcott dies in Adyar. Before he dies, Olcott indicates that 'the Masters' wish Annie Besant to succeed him: much politicking ensues. Rudolf Steiner supports Besant's candidacy. April–May: preparations for the Congress of the Federation of European Sections of the Theosophical Society—the great, watershed Whitsun 'Munich Congress,' attended by Annie Besant and others. Steiner decides to separate Eastern and Western (Christian–Rosicrucian) esoteric schools. He takes his esoteric school out of the Theosophical Society (Besant and Rudolf Steiner are 'in harmony' on this). Steiner makes his first lecture tours to Austria and Hungary. That summer, he is in Italy. In September, he visits Édouard Schuré, who will write the Introduction to the French edition of *Christianity as Mystical Fact* in Barr, Alsace. Rudolf Steiner writes the autobiographical statement known as the 'Barr Document.' In *Luzifer-Gnosis*, 'The Education of the Child' appears.

1908: The movement grows (membership: 1,150). Lecturing expands. Steiner makes his first extended lecture tour to Holland and Scandinavia, as well as visits to Naples and Sicily. Themes: St John's Gospel, the Apocalypse, Egypt, science, philosophy, and logic. *Luzifer-Gnosis* ceases publication. In Berlin, Marie von Sivers (with Johanna Mücke (1864–1949) forms the *Philosophisch-Theosophisch* (after 1915 *Philosophisch-Anthroposophisch) Verlag* to publish Steiner's work. Steiner gives lecture cycles titled *The Gospel of St John* (CW 103) and *The Apocalypse* (104).

1909: *An Outline of Esoteric Science* appears. Lecturing and travel continues. Rudolf Steiner's spiritual research expands to include the polarity of Lucifer and Ahriman; the work of great individualities in history; the Maitreya Buddha and the Bodhisattvas; spiritual economy (CW 109); the work of the spiritual hierarchies in heaven and on earth (CW 110). He also deepens and intensifies his research into the Gospels, giving lectures on the Gospel of St Luke (CW 114) with the first mention of two Jesus children. Meets and becomes friends with Christian Morgenstern (1871–1914). In April, he lays the foundation stone for the Malsch model—the building that will lead to the first Goetheanum. In May, the International Congress of the Federation of European Sections of the Theosophical Society takes place in Budapest. Rudolf Steiner receives the Subba Row medal for *How to Know Higher Worlds*. During this time, Charles W. Leadbeater discovers Jiddu Krishnamurti (1895–1986) and proclaims him the future 'world teacher,' the bearer of the Maitreya Buddha and the 'reappearing Christ.' In October, Steiner delivers seminal lectures on 'anthroposophy,' which he will try, unsuccessfully, to rework over the next years into the unfinished work, *Anthroposophy (A Fragment)* (CW 45).

1910: New themes: *The Reappearance of Christ in the Etheric* (CW 118); *The Fifth Gospel; The Mission of Folk Souls* (CW 121); *Occult History* (CW 126); the evolving development of etheric cognitive capacities. Rudolf Steiner continues his Gospel research with *The Gospel of St Matthew* (CW 123). In January, his father dies. In April, he takes a month-long trip to Italy, including Rome, Monte Cassino, and Sicily. He also visits Scandinavia again. July–August, he writes the first Mystery Drama, *The Portal of Initiation* (CW 14). In November, he gives 'psychosophy' lectures. In December, he submits 'On the

Psychological Foundations and Epistemological Framework of Theosophy' to the International Philosophical Congress in Bologna.

1911: The crisis in the Theosophical Society deepens. In January, 'The Order of the Rising Sun,' which will soon become 'The Order of the Star in the East,' is founded for the coming world teacher, Krishnamurti. At the same time, Marie von Sivers, Rudolf Steiner's co-worker, falls ill. Fewer lectures are given, but important new ground is broken. In Prague, in March, Steiner meets Franz Kafka (1883–1924) and Hugo Bergmann (1883–1975). In April, he delivers his paper to the Philosophical Congress. He writes the second Mystery Drama, *The Soul's Probation* (CW 14). Also, while Marie von Sivers is convalescing, Rudolf Steiner begins work on *Calendar 1912/1913*, which will contain the 'Calendar of the Soul' meditations. On March 19, Anna (Eunike) Steiner dies. In September, Rudolf Steiner visits Einsiedeln, birthplace of Paracelsus. In December, Friedrich Rittelmeyer, future founder of the Christian Community, meets Rudolf Steiner. The *Johannes-Bauverein,* the 'building committee,' which would lead to the first Goetheanum (first planned for Munich), is also founded, and a preliminary committee for the founding of an independent association is created that, in the following year, will become the Anthroposophical Society. Important lecture cycles include *Occult Physiology* (CW 128); *Wonders of the World* (CW 129); *From Jesus to Christ* (CW 131). Other themes: esoteric Christianity; Christian Rosenkreutz; the spiritual guidance of humanity; the sense world and the world of the spirit.

1912: Despite the ongoing, now increasing crisis in the Theosophical Society, much is accomplished: *Calendar 1912/1913* is published; eurythmy is created; both the third Mystery Drama, *The Guardian of the Threshold* (CW 14) and *A Way of Self-Knowledge* (CW 16) are written. New (or renewed) themes included life between death and rebirth and karma and reincarnation. Other lecture cycles: *Spiritual Beings in the Heavenly Bodies and in the Kingdoms of Nature* (CW 136); *The Human Being in the Light of Occultism, Theosophy, and Philosophy* (CW 137); *The Gospel of St Mark* (CW 139); and *The Bhagavad Gita and the Epistles of Paul* (CW 142). On May 8, Rudolf Steiner celebrates White Lotus Day, H.P. Blavatsky's death day, which he had faithfully observed for the past decade, for the last time. In August, Rudolf Steiner suggests the 'independent association' be called the 'Anthroposophical Society.' In September, the first eurythmy course takes place. In October, Rudolf Steiner declines recognition of a Theosophical Society lodge dedicated to the Star of the East and decides to expel all Theosophical Society members belonging to the order.

Also, with Marie von Sivers, he first visits Dornach, near Basel, Switzerland, and they stand on the hill where the Goetheanum will be built. In November, a Theosophical Society lodge is opened by direct mandate from Adyar (Annie Besant). In December, a meeting of the German section occurs at which it is decided that belonging to the Order of the Star of the East is incompatible with membership in the Theosophical Society. December 28: informal founding of the Anthroposophical Society in Berlin.

1913: Expulsion of the German section from the Theosophical Society. February 2–3: Foundation meeting of the Anthroposophical Society. Board members include: Marie von Sivers, Michael Bauer, and Carl Unger. September 20: Laying of the foundation stone for the *Johannes Bau* (Goetheanum) in Dornach. Building begins immediately. The fourth Mystery Drama, *The Soul's Awakening* (CW 14), is completed. Also: *The Threshold of the Spiritual World* (CW 147). Lecture cycles include: *The Bhagavad Gita and the Epistles of Paul* and *The Esoteric Meaning of the Bhagavad Gita* (CW 146), which the Russian philosopher Nikolai Berdyaev attends; *The Mysteries of the East and of Christianity* (CW 144); *The Effects of Esoteric Development* (CW 145); and *The Fifth Gospel* (CW 148). In May, Rudolf Steiner is in London and Paris, where anthroposophical work continues.

1914: Building continues on the *Johannes Bau* (Goetheanum) in Dornach, with artists and co-workers from seventeen nations. The general assembly of the Anthroposophical Society takes place. In May, Rudolf Steiner visits Paris, as well as Chartres Cathedral. June 28: assassination in Sarajevo ('Now the catastrophe has happened!'). August 1: War is declared. Rudolf Steiner returns to Germany from Dornach—he will travel back and forth. He writes the last chapter of *The Riddles of Philosophy*. Lecture cycles include: *Human and Cosmic Thought* (CW 151); *Inner Being of Humanity between Death and a New Birth* (CW 153); *Occult Reading and Occult Hearing* (CW 156). December 24: marriage of Rudolf Steiner and Marie von Sivers.

1915: Building continues. Life after death becomes a major theme, also art. Writes: *Thoughts during a Time of War* (CW 24). Lectures include: *The Secret of Death* (CW 159); *The Uniting of Humanity through the Christ Impulse* (CW 165).

1916: Rudolf Steiner begins work with Edith Maryon (1872–1924) on the sculpture 'The Representative of Humanity' ('The Group'—Christ, Lucifer, and Ahriman). He also works with the alchemist Alexander von Bernus on the quarterly *Das Reich*. He writes *The Riddle of Humanity* (CW 20). Lectures include: *Necessity and Freedom in World History and Human Action* (CW 166); *Past and Present in the*

Human Spirit (CW 167); *The Karma of Vocation* (CW 172); *The Karma of Untruthfulness* (CW 173).

1917: Russian Revolution. The U.S. enters the war. Building continues. Rudolf Steiner delineates the idea of the 'threefold nature of the human being' (in a public lecture March 15) and the 'threefold nature of the social organism' (hammered out in May–June with the help of Otto von Lerchenfeld and Ludwig Polzer-Hoditz in the form of two documents titled *Memoranda,* which were distributed in high places). August–September: Rudolf Steiner writes *The Riddles of the Soul* (CW 20). Also: commentary on 'The Chymical Wedding of Christian Rosenkreutz' for Alexander Bernus (Das *Reich*). Lectures include: *The Karma of Materialism* (CW 176); *The Spiritual Background of the Outer World: The Fall of the Spirits of Darkness* (CW 177).

1918: March 18: peace treaty of Brest-Litovsk—'Now everything will truly enter chaos! What is needed is cultural renewal.' June: Rudolf Steiner visits Karlstein (Grail) Castle outside Prague. Lecture cycle: *From Symptom to Reality in Modern History* (CW 185). In mid-November, Emil Molt, of the Waldorf-Astoria Cigarette Company, has the idea of founding a school for his workers' children.

1919: Focus on the threefold social organism: tireless travel, countless lectures, meetings, and publications. At the same time, a new public stage of Anthroposophy emerges as cultural renewal begins. The coming years will see initiatives in pedagogy, medicine, pharmacology, and agriculture. January 27: threefold meeting: 'We must first of all, with the money we have, found free schools that can bring people what they need.' February: first public eurythmy performance in Zurich. Also: 'Appeal to the German People' (CW 24), circulated March 6 as a newspaper insert. In April, *Towards Social Renewal* (CW 23) appears—'perhaps the most widely read of all books on politics appearing since the war'. Rudolf Steiner is asked to undertake the 'direction and leadership' of the school founded by the Waldorf-Astoria Company. Rudolf Steiner begins to talk about the 'renewal' of education. May 30: a building is selected and purchased for the future Waldorf School. August–September, Rudolf Steiner gives a lecture course for Waldorf teachers, *The Foundations of Human Experience (Study of Man)* (CW 293). September 7: Opening of the first Waldorf School. December (into January): first science course, the *Light Course* (CW 320).

1920: The Waldorf School flourishes. New threefold initiatives. Founding of limited companies *Der Kommende Tag* and *Futurum A.G.* to infuse spiritual values into the economic realm. Rudolf Steiner also focuses on the sciences. Lectures: *Introducing Anthroposophical*

Medicine (CW 312); *The Warmth Course* (CW 321); *The Boundaries of Natural Science* (CW 322); *The Redemption of Thinking* (CW 74). February: Johannes Werner Klein—later a co-founder of the Christian Community—asks Rudolf Steiner about the possibility of a 'religious renewal,' a 'Johannine church.' In March, Rudolf Steiner gives the first course for doctors and medical students. In April, a divinity student asks Rudolf Steiner a second time about the possibility of religious renewal. September 27–October 16: anthroposophical 'university course.' December: lectures titled *The Search for the New Isis* (CW 202).

1921: Rudolf Steiner continues his intensive work on cultural renewal, including the uphill battle for the threefold social order. 'University' arts, scientific, theological, and medical courses include: *The Astronomy Course* (CW 323); *Observation, Mathematics, and Scientific Experiment* (CW 324); the *Second Medical Course* (CW 313); *Colour.* In June and September–October, Rudolf Steiner also gives the first two 'priests' courses' (CW 342 and 343). The 'youth movement' gains momentum. Magazines are founded: *Die Drei* (January), and—under the editorship of Albert Steffen (1884–1963)—the weekly, *Das Goetheanum* (August). In February–March, Rudolf Steiner takes his first trip outside Germany since the war (Holland). On April 7, Steiner receives a letter regarding 'religious renewal,' and May 22–23, he agrees to address the question in a practical way. In June, the Klinical-Therapeutic Institute opens in Arlesheim under the direction of Dr Ita Wegman. In August, the Chemical-Pharmaceutical Laboratory opens in Arlesheim (Oskar Schmiedel and Ita Wegman are directors). The Clinical Therapeutic Institute is inaugurated in Stuttgart (Dr Ludwig Noll is director); also the Research Laboratory in Dornach (Ehrenfried Pfeiffer and Gunther Wachsmuth are directors). In November–December, Rudolf Steiner visits Norway.

1922: The first half of the year involves very active public lecturing (thousands attend); in the second half, Rudolf Steiner begins to withdraw and turn toward the Society—'The Society is asleep.' It is 'too weak' to do what is asked of it. The businesses—*Der Kommende Tag* and *Futurum A.G.*—fail. In January, with the help of an agent, Steiner undertakes a twelve-city German lecture tour, accompanied by eurythmy performances. In two weeks he speaks to more than 2,000 people. In April, he gives a 'university course' in The Hague. He also visits England. In June, he is in Vienna for the East–West Congress. In August–September, he is back in England for the Oxford Conference on Education. Returning to Dornach, he gives the lectures *Philosophy, Cosmology, and Religion*

(CW 215), and gives the third priests' course (CW 344). On September 16, The Christian Community is founded. In October–November, Steiner is in Holland and England. He also speaks to the youth: *The Youth Course* (CW 217). In December, Steiner gives lectures titled *The Origins of Natural Science* (CW 326), and *Humanity and the World of Stars: The Spiritual Communion of Humanity* (CW 219). December 31: Fire at the Goetheanum, which is destroyed.

1923: Despite the fire, Rudolf Steiner continues his work unabated. A very hard year. Internal dispersion, dissension, and apathy abound. There is conflict—between old and new visions—within the Society. A wake-up call is needed, and Rudolf Steiner responds with renewed lecturing vitality. His focus: the spiritual context of human life; initiation science; the course of the year; and community building. As a foundation for an artistic school, he creates a series of pastel sketches. Lecture cycles: *The Anthroposophical Movement; Initiation Science* (CW 227) (in Wales at the Penmaenmawr Summer School); *The Four Seasons and the Archangels* (CW 229); *Harmony of the Creative Word* (CW 230); *The Supersensible Human* (CW 231), given in Holland for the founding of the Dutch society. On November 10, in response to the failed Hitler-Ludendorff putsch in Munich, Steiner closes his Berlin residence and moves the *Philosophisch-Anthroposophisch Verlag* (Press) to Dornach. On December 9, Steiner begins the serialization of his *Autobiography: The Course of My Life* (CW 28) in *Das Goetheanum.* It will continue to appear weekly, without a break, until his death. Late December–early January: Rudolf Steiner re-founds the Anthroposophical Society (about 12,000 members internationally) and takes over its leadership. The new board members are: Marie Steiner, Ita Wegman, Albert Steffen, Elisabeth Vreede, and Gunther Wachsmuth. (See *The Christmas Meeting for the Founding of the General Anthroposophical Society,* CW 260.) Accompanying lectures: *Mystery Knowledge and Mystery Centres* (CW 232); *World History in the Light of Anthroposophy* (CW 233). December 25: the Foundation Stone is laid (in the hearts of members) in the form of the 'Foundation Stone Meditation.'

1924: January 1: having founded the Anthroposophical Society and taken over its leadership, Rudolf Steiner has the task of 'reforming' it. The process begins with a weekly newssheet ('What's Happening in the Anthroposophical Society') in which Rudolf Steiner's 'Letters to Members' and 'Anthroposophical Leading Thoughts' appear (CW 26). The next step is the creation of a new esoteric class, the 'first class' of the 'University of Spiritual Science' (which was to have been followed, had Rudolf Steiner lived longer, by two more advanced classes). Then comes a new language for

Anthroposophy—practical, phenomenological, and direct; and Rudolf Steiner creates the model for the second Goetheanum. He begins the series of extensive 'karma' lectures (CW 235–40); and finally, responding to needs, he creates two new initiatives: biodynamic agriculture and curative education. After the middle of the year, rumours begin to circulate regarding Steiner's health. Lectures: January–February, *Anthroposophy* (CW 234); February: *Tone Eurythmy* (CW 278); June: *The Agriculture Course* (CW 327); June–July: *Speech Eurythmy* (CW 279); *Curative Education* (CW 317); August: (England, 'Second International Summer School'), *Initiation Consciousness: True and False Paths in Spiritual Investigation* (CW 243); September: *Pastoral Medicine* (CW 318). On September 26, for the first time, Rudolf Steiner cancels a lecture. On September 28, he gives his last lecture. On September 29, he withdraws to his studio in the carpenter's shop; now he is definitively ill. Cared for by Ita Wegman, he continues working, however, and writing the weekly installments of his *Autobiography* and *Letters to the Members/Leading Thoughts* (CW 26).

1925: Rudolf Steiner, while continuing to work, continues to weaken. He finishes *Extending Practical Medicine* (CW 27) with Ita Wegman. On March 30, around ten in the morning, Rudolf Steiner dies.

Index